THE FORMATION OF SCIENCE IN JAPAN

THE FORMATION OF SCIENCE IN JAPAN

Building a Research Tradition

JAMES R. BARTHOLOMEW

Yale University Press

New Haven and London

The publication of this book was made possible through the generous support of The Japan Foundation and the Ohio State University College of Humanities Publications Award program.

Designed by Sonia L. Scanlon and set in Primer type by The Composing Room of Michigan, Inc. Printed in the United States of America by BookCrafters, Inc., Ann Arbor, Michigan.

Library of Congress Cataloging-in-Publication Data

Bartholomew, James R., 1941– .
  The formation of science in Japan / James R. Bartholomew.
    p.   cm.
  Includes index.
  ISBN 0–300–04261–2 (alk. paper)
  1. Science—Japan—History. 2. Research—Japan—History.
I. Title.
Q127.J3B37   1989
509.52—dc19   88–36817
                                                              CIP

The paper in this book meets the guidelines for permanence and durability of the Committee on Production Guidelines for Book Longevity of the Council on Library Resources.
10 9 8 7 6 5 4 3 2 1

For Maureen

CONTENTS

ILLUSTRATIONS

Illustrations follow page 124

TABLES

PREFACE

People have often asked how I came to be interested in Japanese science. There are many routes by which an American might develop this interest today, but my own goes back some years and probably had an unusual genesis. I think it began in 1952, when I was a naive fifth-grader in Rapid City, South Dakota. My school happened to show a documentary film on atomic energy that Bell Telephone Laboratories (as I later learned) had produced and distributed. For reasons I am wholly at a loss to explain, I remembered just one thing from the film that day—its brief discussion of Yukawa Hideki, the Japanese physicist and Nobel laureate! Because of this episode I grew up with an attitude about Japan which at that time was unusual, namely, that Japan was a country of great achievements in science. A few years later the Sputnik crisis came, and I promptly resolved to do my part by studying physics at Cal Tech or Princeton. What I actually did was enter Stanford, where I initially hoped to study mathematics. But I soon discovered that my talents lay elsewhere and completed a degree in history and Japanese.

Thomas C. Smith, who taught Japanese history at Stanford (and later at Berkeley), had a formative influence on me both at this stage and later. He first suggested that I study Japanese and subsequently steered me to a dissertation topic. It might be interesting, he intimated, to find out why some Japanese became scientists in the Meiji period. I wrote my thesis on Kitasato's career, but I continued to find Tom's idea intriguing, and my later research on it became chapter 3 of this book. I owe Tom Smith a special debt of thanks. He has always been a friend, a helpful critic, and an unfailing mentor. He read chapters 3 through 6 with particular care. Many of his suggestions I readily incorporated, and any remaining faults reflect on me and not on him.

The lengthy genesis of this book has caused me to incur a great many debts. One is to Itō Shuntarō, historian of science at Tokyo University, who sponsored my affiliation to his own institution and made me part of his research seminar. My long-time friend Kuramoto Hiroyuki of Kitasato University put me in touch with the late Ōtori Ranzaburō, historian of medicine at Keio University. Ōtori generously shared his knowledge of Japanese medical history with me and introduced me in turn to Dr. Aki Motō, clinical neurologist at Toranomon Hospital and a gifted historian of medicine. Dr. Aki's vast knowledge of Kitasato Shibasaburō was very helpful for my work on this subject. Sidney Alford, a visiting chemist at Tokyo University, provided intellectual stimulation and moral support. Bernard Krisher, Tokyo Bureau Chief for *Newsweek*, offered me the needed distraction of part-time reporting and patiently worked to improve my writing!

At Harvard University, Everett Mendelsohn helped especially by arranging funding for me and providing leadership to a group of avid researchers in the Department of the History and Philosophy of Science. Albert M. Craig gave me an office in the East Asian Research Center and offered valuable suggestions and interpretive comments on parts of the manuscript. My long and valued friendship with Nathan Sivin also dates from this period. Nathan's keen appraisal of an early version of chapter 6 caused me both to rethink some issues and add new material. For his assistance and support I am particularly grateful.

Numerous people have assisted me on my research trips to Japan. Two librarians at the National Diet Library helped me find certain materials I needed—Sakuma Nobuko, of the Reference Department, and Imagawa Koichi, Head of the Parliamentary Documents Room. Miura Yoshiaki, biochemistry professor at Chiba University, gave me extraordinary guidance in obtaining material from medical journals. Several other colleagues were also very helpful: Yoshida Mitsukuni, Fujino Tsunesaburō, Yagi Eri, Ōya Shin'ichi, Terasaki Masao, Amano Ikuo, and Itakura Kiyonobu. Dr. Itakura also arranged my affiliation with the National Institute for Education Research. My work has benefited over the years from discussions with Watanabe Masao, Yuasa Mitsutomo, and especially Nakayama Shigeru. I must offer Shigeru particular thanks for our long years of friendship and many discussions. The notes to his work throughout the present book are one indication of the respect I have for him.

Several months at the Institute for Advanced Study in Princeton in 1977 and a seminar presentation to the Shelby Cullom Davis Center for Historical Studies at Princeton in 1979 contributed positively to my research. For these opportunities I thank John Elliott, Marius Jansen, and Lawrence Stone. Other valuable exchanges took place at meetings of the Midwest Japan Seminar sponsored by the Social Sciences Research Council. I owe special thanks for bibliographical assistance and moral support to several colleagues and friends at The Ohio State University and the University of Michigan. These include, at Michigan, Naomi Fukuda and Masaei Saitō, and at Ohio State, Alan Beyerchen, John C. Burnham, Maureen H. Donovan, Barbara Reeves, William J. Studer, and June Z. Fullmer. Others for whose inspiration and encouragement I am grateful include James M. Kittelson, Laurence Schneider, Gerald Holton, Rolf Barth, Ronald Overmann, Fred Notehelfer, Alfred Donovan, Robert E. Cole, Michael Les Benedict, Richard Samuels, Merrit Roe Smith, Randolph A. Roth, Samuel Coleman, Harry

Harootunian, Bernard Silberman, Byron Marshall, and the late Joseph Ben-David.

Research projects always cost money, this one particularly so. My original dissertation project was supported by Stanford University, the Fulbright-Hays Fellowship Program of the U.S. Office of Education, and the Josiah Macy, Jr., Foundation. Research for this book was carried out with the aid of grants from Ohio State University, the National Endowment for the Humanities, and the Social Sciences Research Council. Writing was mostly funded by the National Science Foundation, while publication costs have been partly defrayed by the Japan Foundation and the College of Humanities of Ohio State University.

For help with various aspects of the publication process I am obliged to: the Japan Society for the History of Science (Nihon Kagakushi Gakkai) for permission to reprint from my previously published article "Why Was There No Scientific Revolution in Tokugawa Japan?" in chapter 2; Princeton University Press for permission to use part of my article "Science, Culture and Freedom in Meiji Japan" in chapter 5 (from Tetsuo Najita and J. Victor Koschmann, eds., *Conflict in Modern Japanese History: The Neglected Tradition.* Copyright © 1982 by Princeton University Press. Excerpts reprinted with permission of Princeton University Press); Nakagawa Toru (of the National Science Museum), Tokuda Hiroshi (of Mainichi Newspapers), and Nakano Minoru (of Tokyo University) for help in locating photographs; Alan Zanyk, Paul Shewmon, and Dwight Burford (all of Ohio State University) for photographic and technical assistance; Charles Grench, executive editor of the Yale University Press, and the Press's reviewer for their suggestions and encouragement at various stages.

A final expression of thanks goes to my wife, Maureen H. Donovan, to whom this book is dedicated. There must be few researchers, I think, who are fortunate enough to receive both emotional encouragement and professional help from the person to whom they are married. In any case, I am one—and am deeply grateful for it.

THE FORMATION OF SCIENCE IN JAPAN

CHAPTER ONE

THE SOCIAL FORMATION OF JAPANESE SCIENCE

In the years following Japan's defeat in World War II, Japanese scientists intensely criticized their own profession. Medical researcher Tamura Masao claimed that relatively little original work had been done in Japan because of the "apprenticeship system," which bound men to their seniors.[1] The physicist and historian of science Hiroshige Tetsu argued that the power of senior professors was a handicap to cooperative effort.[2] Two physicists and a biochemist lamented the general lack of democracy in science.[3] And the distinguished theoretical physicist Sakata Shōichi insisted that Japanese science had suffered from academic inbreeding, suppression of freedom, and a tendency to hoard resources.[4]

The same critics also took aim at society. Japanese allegedly regarded scientists as little more than "tools for the extraction of knowledge [from the West]." Though treated well enough from this point of view, they were rarely considered real "creators of knowledge."[5] In fact, scientists were usually excluded from official decisions even when the promotion of research was at stake,[6] and science had little support except from the Japanese government. One point of view held that this pattern developed in the nineteenth century from the paucity of connections with industry. In 1868, Japanese capitalism was so far behind capitalism in Europe that the state had to intervene on its behalf. Because of this technology and science became dependent upon the state, and their natural development was distorted.[7]

Had these various criticisms been an isolated phenomenon, we might link them to postwar despair. Military defeat had been hard on the country not only economically but spiritually and psychologically. The country was controlled by the Allied Occupation, and sweeping reforms had been launched. It is no coincidence that Sakata defined his target as science's "Führer system."[8] And American delegations of educators and scientists offered their views on Japanese science without asking whether they were welcome.[9]

These criticisms of society and science have a far broader context, for in the 1980s American and English-language media have repeated such claims as frequently as the Japanese of decades past. Japanese organization "tends to stifle initiative, especially youthful initiative," according to astronomer Robert Jastrow (1983).[10] The Japanese have a saying about the nail that sticks its head up getting hit, noted computer scientist Edward Feigenbaum in 1981, and "that tells the Japan[ese] researcher, 'Don't propose something novel.'"[11] *Time* criticized "rigidity in [Japanese] research laboratories" in 1983.[12] A study conducted by the Stanford Research Institute knocked academic "inbreeding" in *Science 85*.[13] The views of the émigré physicist Leo Esaki are especially worth noting.[14] Japan, he says, has failed to "shake free of its copying habit."[15] Its strength in technology is "not buttressed by a broad base of scientific research," and its "contribution to . . . learning is minimal." Why is this so? According to him, it is because Japan is a strongly group-oriented society. Now is the time, in Esaki's estimation, "to recognize that Japan's future does not lie in group solidarity, but in the cultivation of individuality."[16]

Esaki and others who articulate this theme of individualism stand in a line that can be traced back to 1881. American zoologist Charles Otis Whitman claimed in a report on the status of his field at Tokyo University that the "baneful influence of caste [factions]" had "survived the overthrow of [Japan's] feudal system" and still had "vitality enough to work immense mischief."[17] A few years later, in 1892, bacteriologist Sata Yoshihiko claimed that the influence of factions had impaired his job search.[18] Medical and other journals of opinion were lamenting factionalism in science by the turn of the century,[19] and a 1917 report on the scientific community went so far as to attribute scientific success to the right social system.[20] Between the wars intellectuals continued to denounce the negative effects of Japanese society on the progress of science.[21]

These complaints on behalf of individualism in science have a long tradition in Europe and America. Sociologists from Max Weber to Talcott Parsons, as well as numerous historians and scientists, have insisted for decades that science can develop only in societies that have thrown off all vestiges of feudalism. Sociologists and social historians have usually condemned feudalism for obstructing social mobility, impeding disclosure of technical information, and impairing development of personality.[22] Leading figures of the French Enlightenment even saw feudalism as contrary to nature.[23] Some scholars have begun to recognize the value for early modern science of medieval corporatism, political decentralization, and the church-state duality associated with feudalism, but the opposing views are far from extinct.[24]

Whatever the validity of the antifeudal opinions, they do call attention to three basic questions in the Japanese context, where feudalism had long been entrenched. How did Japan in the modern era—after about 1860—build a tradition of modern scientific research out of nothing? How did the Japanese—officials *and* scientists—make use of indigenous and some foreign traditions to construct their model of scientific research? And how was the operation of that model tempered or checked by the various realities of Japanese life—its society, economy, or political system?[25]

Such questions are more easily asked than answered. Despite (or because of) the ideological undercurrents of the various criticisms, the historical record is especially important. This book, for several reasons, focuses attention on the Meiji and early Taishō years (1868–1920). Meiji and early Taishō marked the period in which the Japanese people created their tradition of scientific research. Critics emphasize this time on the assumption that such "feudalistic" values as loyalty and solidarity were more vigorous closer to the Tokugawa period (1600–1867), when they enjoyed official sanction. The period also marks the era immediately before and after the formal abolition of feudalism, which mostly occurred in the 1870s.

This brings us to the question of what "science" is when seen through the lens of historical perspective. Scientific development anywhere in the world was once thought to result from "correct" research methodology (empiricism), "right" views about nature (the mechanical world view), or from something called the "scientific attitude." There is now a recognition (reflected in this book) that these historical features of early modern science cannot fully carry the burden of explanation, whatever their importance in some contexts or periods.[26]

There are other facts to note in discussing Japan. It has not historically been part of the Western tradition, and while this fact is obvious, some of its implications are not. Japan's dominant Confucian intellectual tradition was loosely structured and relatively tolerant of new ideas and perspectives. There was no legacy of revealed religion with an elaborate structure of natural philosophy intricately woven with a formal theology.[27] Controversial theories of modern Western science like heliocentrism or the origin of species aroused little opposition in the Japanese context and were readily espoused.[28] Japanese scientists did not consider it necessary to slay the dragons of traditional religion but adapted to popular beliefs and refrained from developing a "scientific" philosophy.[29] The physicist Yuasa Mitsutomo, who noted and disapproved of this fact, even wrote: "It was as though Japanese science had had the teeth of its spirit of [cultural] criticism removed."[30]

Another singular feature of the Japanese scene is the external origin of science. Science was imported from Europe at the instigation of the government as a commodity, mostly in the period after the Meiji Restoration (1868). The conceptual schemes of Western science at the time were taken as true because they came from the West,[31] and Meiji commentators gave little attention to differences between science and technology, regarding them as the same thing, and foreign.[32] Decision makers in the government eschewed debates on the properties of science. Recruiting men to science, building institutions for teaching and research, and putting in place the bureaucratic structures to manage the science establishment were more important.[33] It is particularly notable that Japanese *scientists* were inclined to support this agenda. "We should remember," wrote the historian of science Yoshida Mitsukuni, "that among the scientists [of Meiji Japan] was the desire to participate in building a new era."[34]

Japanese science after 1868 was not an amateur occupation. Professionalization was already under way in European science, particularly in Germany, which most inspired Japan. The German approach to science was important for how science was organized in Japan, though the Japanese drew on the experience of several countries. Such questions as whether science should be housed primarily in universities or in separate, specialized institutes were hot issues and occasioned much debate.

Japanese science represented a departure from the pattern of development in Europe. There the classical scientific revolution of the sixteenth and seventeenth centuries began with physics and then spread elsewhere. Compare with this how Japanese intellectuals first studied Western science: not through physics, but through medicine.[35] Medical endeavors were important in the Tokugawa period for other kinds of technical studies, and it was medicine that developed most fully between 1868 and 1920.[36] Even the concept of science was different in Japan. Some writers in the Tokugawa period used the term *kyūri* ("investigation of the basic principles of things") for the subject matter of physics and, less frequently, other disciplines. But by about 1871 a new term had been coined which had little to do with the philosophy of nature. The present term for science in Japanese, *kagaku*, refers less to content or method and more to the spectrum of specialized fields.[37]

Despite changes—in terminology and in other areas—Tokugawa developments left their mark on modern science. Meiji (1868–1912) scientists did not draw on Tokugawa ideas, for they were almost entirely abandoned after 1868, replaced by ideas from the West.[38] The Tokugawa contribution to modern science was not in the realm of the intellect but in recruitment: the kinds of people, in terms of family background and class origin, who had shown serious interest in science during Tokugawa times were the same kinds who came forward after 1868. And this same Tokugawa legacy had a substantial effect on the growth of particular disciplines. Medical research in Japan did relatively well after 1868 because medicine had flourished in the earlier period. Similarly, physics developed slowly in Meiji Japan, partly because of earlier restrictions.

Tokugawa developments also affected the growth of research institutions, not because modern institutions had Tokugawa predecessors, though a few important ones did, but by the continuity of political synergisms. Tokugawa Japan had 277 daimyo administrations that retained considerable powers despite the centralizing force of the shogunal government in Edo. In the decades following the Meiji Restoration, these local allegiances continued to operate and in some sense revived, inspiring competition which greatly helped science. Most criticism of Japanese science has passed by the issues of recruitment and the growth of institutions and focused instead on the behavior of individuals, whether scientists or government officials.

The Tokugawa legacy was certainly complex and highly problematic. Meiji Japan's bureaucracy as it came to maturity after 1890 tended to follow established Tokugawa patterns, and its ways of doing business were not always congenial to scientists. But the behavior of the scientists is quite another matter. Criticisms of scientists' behavior are suffused with the influence of ideology and are difficult to approach in a spirit of fairness. I would argue that Japanese scientists have historically tried to balance personal judgment and a scientific creativity that came, to a certain degree, from the West with deep-rooted norms of solidarity and loyalty inherent in Tokugawa (and modern) culture. Their success in this effort has been greater than generally recognized.[39]

This means that the critics are wrong. Japanese science *has* made important contributions, contrary to what its critics assert. Two contributions of the Meiji-Taishō years should almost certainly have received the Nobel Prize. In 1901 Emil von Behring of Germany received the prize in medicine and physiology for the discovery of natural immunity. But this work was actually done with Kitasato Shibasaburō, and his exclusion from the accolade has never been explained. In 1926 the same Nobel Prize in medicine and physiology was given to Johannes Fibiger of Denmark when it probably should have gone to a Japanese pathologist, Yamagiwa Katsusaburō of Tokyo University, who during the World War I years had discovered a technique for induction of tumors in laboratory animals which many consider basic to modern oncology.[40] (See chapter 6.)

The critics have certainly made some valid points. During the period before 1914, many Japanese officials *did* stress importation of Western technology and science in preference to supporting research at home.

This often expressed itself in spending money on overseas study instead of on domestic research. The error is to think that these priorities were unanimous, when they were usually debated rather vigorously. Not even among officials was there a consensus on the priority of "copying" foreign work over research at home. Scientists sometimes resisted the priorities that were set; and they managed to prevail on occasion.

But if the critics are wrong in most of their claims, how does one explain the persistence of their views? Are they simply ignorant of facts? Certainly this is a possibility. Physicists like Esaki and Sakata take little or no notice of contributions in medicine or at least seem oblivious to their historical importance, and they ignore important work which they themselves have done. Sakata, in partial collaboration with two other scientists, made a significant contribution to theoretical physics by predicting mathematically the existence of two particles. In 1973 Esaki received the Nobel Prize for discovering the tunnel diode effect. And both men—contrary to misleading impressions—achieved these results entirely in Japan.[41] Such covering up of facts suggests an ideology at work, in this case the individualism so deeply rooted in the history of science. Probably because it came from the West and therefore retains a certain prestige, individualism has appealed to Japanese who find themselves at odds with their society.

Another local factor linked to the past has strongly affected the research tradition. This was (and is) the relative isolation of Japan and its culture from other research centers. As every student of Japanese history knows, the Tokugawa regime maintained strict isolation from the outside world for over two hundred years (1639–1853). Travel abroad by Japanese and travel to Japan by foreigners (especially the former) were almost nonexistent; the flow of ideas was also, not surprisingly, limited. There was *some* traffic in ideas, and on occasion it had significant local consequences. But Japanese development of science and technology was much less than it might have been.

Of course, the isolation of Japanese science was not solely political. Japan is also geographically distant from most other countries, especially those active in science, and its language and culture are highly distinctive. Rapid communications with Japan were technically impossible before World War II. To a lesser extent such factors still matter, as many researchers are keenly aware.

This book takes up several themes in the formation of modern research in Japan. Recruitment, training, and socialization of scientists—community formation in science—is one. These themes, which are treated in chapter 3, are related both to Tokugawa experience (chapter 2) and the effects of foreign study. It is my conclusion that the social object of such efforts (what is usually called the "scientific role") was not fully established until about 1920 or so. In chapter 4 I treat research institutions as they developed in Japan before World War I. In addition to the Tokugawa background, I discuss the influence of different Western models and the politics of selection. Chapter 5 considers official decision making as it affected the availability of material resources, especially in the period before World War I. Who could decide what, and under what conditions, is a major theme, as are differences between various government ministries. Chapter 6 looks at behavioral patterns in the scientific community and their apparent meaning for Japanese research. It suggests that Japanese scientists usually *were* able to balance different values in the substance of their actions, if not in the forms.

Chapters 7 and 8 describe and analyze the impact of World War I on Japan's scientific establishment. The war marked a turning point in the organization, funding, and applications of science in Japan and many other countries. Medical research lost its preferred status as the physical sciences made significant gains. Funding increased substantially for virtually every field, and new institutions appeared on the scene. The Ministry of Education's Science Research Grants Program (1918) and the National Research Council (hereafter NRC; 1920) were especially important and are discussed at some length for their long-term implications.

World War I had an impact on science that transcended effects in particular countries. Shortly before the Armistice in November 1918, scientists from Allied nations held a meeting in London to decide how to punish their colleagues in Germany. Because the Central Powers were deemed guilty of monstrous crimes, many scientists (especially in France) opposed the renewal of technical cooperation with the Germans or even the Austrians. They organized the International Council of Scientific Unions (ICSU) partly to bolster their political ostracism. Because it was formally a leading Allied power, Japan was an organizer and a charter ICSU member. In fact, participation in this group was a matter of prestige for so new a scientific community.

It was also a source of considerable discomfort. Many of the older scientists had close ties to Germany, and some were afraid of direct retaliation. Would the Germans exclude Japanese from access to their laboratories out of spite for their role in founding the ICSU? Others taunted those who made this kind of argument because they believed that Japanese science had now proven itself to the world. Many scientists thus saw the issue as one of autonomy or continuing dependence—one theme of this book. Certainly the formation of a modern research tradition demands a complex blending of indigenous and foreign influences. I have emphasized indigenous factors in the Japanese case partly to compensate for the bias of others who attribute the process to cultural diffusion from the centers of science to non-Western countries.[42] Japan was not a center by 1921, but it had reached the point of self-sustaining growth and stood on the threshold of major contributions.[43]

CHAPTER TWO

SCIENCE AND SOCIETY IN THE TOKUGAWA PERIOD

The Tokugawa period was in some ways an unlikely time for science to flourish. Japan was formally isolated from the outside world, and political affairs were controlled by warriors who were not always keen on scholarship. These warrior officials consistently tried to shape intellectual affairs to serve their own interests. Relatively few institutions with permanent support existed for scholarly activities. Scientists themselves were often unable—or unwilling—to share their work, and the scholarly researcher had no social role.

Nevertheless, Tokugawa Japan was the scene of positive, unprecedented developments for scientific study. Numerous texts on technical subjects were imported from China and devoured by Japanese scholars, who in the seventeenth century based their indigenous mathematics partly on this Chinese-language literature. In the eighteenth century technical literature was imported from Europe and gradually absorbed by various groups. Ultimately, of course, these developments seem abortive, since Meiji Japan made a new beginning after 1868. But although European science and its leading practitioners did supply the paradigms and sometimes the precedents for Japanese efforts during the Meiji period, beneath these Western influences was a layer of attitudes and practices that had been formed in the Tokugawa period.

Which parts of the Tokugawa experience were decisive? The paradigms in effect in the Tokugawa period were all replaced by Western ones, and government policies restricting certain fields did not survive the demise of the shogunate. The Tokugawa era continued to shape science through a combination of attitudes and trends in society, for example, the patterns in recruitment of Japanese scientists, which survived the Meiji Restoration. Inherited institutional weaknesses, and strengths of particular disciplines, influenced the modern tradition. Some Tokugawa administrative practices lasted even beyond the end of the Meiji (1912), and some behavioral norms that had appeared among scientists in the Tokugawa period affected their successors as well. Finally, the effects on Japanese research of Japan's long-term isolation—cultural, linguistic, intellectual, and geographical—have yet to be calculated fully.

Recruitment to Science in Tokugawa Japan

There can be no science without scientists, but the use of the word *scientist* in the Tokugawa context can only be ambiguous. In recent times *scientist* has had the connotation *researcher,* but research was not well developed in Tokugawa times and was only haphazardly practiced. Some people did conduct careful experiments and even publish their findings, but there was neither an institutionalized research role nor anything like a modern scientific community. Journals did not exist—let alone grants awarded by peers. Even those customs of European science that developed in the early modern period—a dispassionate attitude and a stress on objectivity—were not always accepted in Japan. And many Tokugawa scientists had an "unprofessional" and certainly "unmodern" code of conduct. They might, for example, keep vital information from qualified colleagues or refuse to publish their findings.

Consequently, the term *scientist* applied to a person of Tokugawa Japan refers simply to one with an active interest in nature who made a reputation for that interest. Tokugawa society did not support the pursuit of knowledge for its own sake, nor did Japanese scientists think that they should contribute to universal knowledge.[1] Most commentators believed that the goal of knowledge was its application, which could be a search for better surgical procedures and medical therapies, correction of discrepancies in the calendar, more accurate maps of the Japanese coastline, or a variety of other uses. Nearly all the translation of European and Chinese technical works that engaged so many scientists had a practical motivation.

How science was defined affected recruitment of scientists, but one can rarely find out why a particular individual chose to become a scientist because the pertinent biographical information does not exist in most cases. Even if it did, the Tokugawa emphasis on heredity for allocating roles would usually make the information superfluous.[2] One needs to consider broader social forces. Scientists were recruited from several groups in Tokugawa society. One was the population of official translators based in the port of Nagasaki, where official foreign trade was conducted. These men knew Dutch and Chinese and took an early lead in bringing foreign scientific and technical materials to the attention of other Japanese. Another group was the medical community. Physicians often had not only the motivation but the intelligence and the money prerequisite to technical studies. Some abandoned routine medical practice and devoted themselves to science. Astronomers employed by the shogunate and occasionally by daimyo had (in varying degrees) the desire and qualifications to undertake scientific work, and by virtue of their official status, they often had access to resources not usually available to men working outside the government.

But other Japanese outside these groups also got interested in science on occasion.[3] A few came from merchant families, and some of those were among the leading scientists. Another source was the general samurai population. Samurai training was not designed to produce technical specialists, but the spread of formal education among the samurai in the eighteenth century, together with the desire to improve their positions, led some samurai into the sciences. And there were even recruits from the farm population. Beginning in the eighteenth century, Tokugawa society included a decent number of educated, affluent farmers who had some leisure time. Certainly, farmers rarely became active in experimental science, but a number of students of advanced mathematics emerged from their ranks after the middle of the century.

Samurai society in this period did not especially encourage interest in science or technology; scholarship of any sort had relatively low prestige among samurai when the Tokugawa period began. Before the seventeenth century and for decades thereafter, learning was a monopoly of Japan's Buddhist clergy. (To survive as a scholar, one needed support from a temple or at least some feudal lord.)[4] The clergy at that time were not well regarded, a condition ambiguous for learning.[5] The new Tokugawa regime eventually separated Confucianism from Buddhism by creating a separate hierarchy, but even this action did not wholly solve the problem, for Confucian scholars' status failed to match that of the learning they espoused.[6] For a time scholars became so dependent on government that they had relatively little standing of their own.[7]

Tokugawa scholars were chronically underpaid. Where high-ranking samurai retainers of the Shogun might receive 8,000 koku per year, no Confucian scholar ever received more than 3,500—and very few reached that level.[8] The head of the Hayashi family (which ran the shogunal academy in Edo) generally earned 3,500 koku but 300 was a more usual salary for scholars in official positions.[9] Compensation levels for technical specialists were not very different. For example, the shogunate paid its astronomers stipends "equivalent only to [those] of lower grade samurai."[10] But the salary range could be greater than that among Confucian *philosophers*. The affluent Higo domain in Kyushu was well known for its medical establishment, and compensation for physicians there varied from 150 to 5,000 koku.[11]

There were also nonpecuniary compensations for professional service. The professional opinions of official astronomers were highly regarded by the samurai elite,[12] and scholars were often treated deferentially. A daimyo might allow them to wear special clothing or even ride about in palanquins, and when attending a scholarly lecture might show his respect by taking an inferior seat.[13] Warriors, of course, did not always view technical specialists with a high degree of esteem. Even in 1869, a local newspaper for samurai readers declared that physicians were "not greatly respected" in spite of their "considerable technical knowledge."[14]

The opinions of other Japanese about scholarly professions also influenced recruitment. Commoners respected even ordinary medical practitioners without official positions. Prominent Tokugawa intellectuals like Motoori Norinaga and Ogyū Sorai came from families of physicians.[15] At least one samurai native of Satsuma was induced to take up medical studies by the high social standing of a village physician.[16] For the commoner population of Japan, scholarly activities—including technical ones—offered the prospect of upward mobility. The great surveyor Inō Tadataka, born in 1743 to a peasant family, rose to samurai status late in his life almost entirely on the basis of professional achievements, as did the astronomer Shibukawa Harumi.[17]

Scholarship could not have developed without support of this kind. Although status was supposed to be inherited in feudal society, scholarly posts, not being attractive to the warrior class, needed other recruits. Scholars were supposed to hold positions on the basis of competence; but what if their heirs were not competent? One answer was adoption, which became common and in some families normative. The Hayashi family of Confucian humanists maintained its position over many generations by a number of careful adoptions,[18] and the important physicist Shizuki Tadao was adopted from the Nakano merchant family by a Nagasaki family of official interpreters. For Shizuki his adoption was doubly fortunate since the professional position of his new family gave him access to the resources he needed.[19]

None of these features or strictures applied to one technical field— mathematics. After the earlier decades of Tokugawa rule, mathematics developed not only outside the formal status system but in many respects apart from the scholarly world. In part this was the nature of the discipline, because mathematics shared with astronomy the need for special abilities among its practitioners if they were to produce important achievements. Families wishing to specialize in mathematics might have solved the problem of lack of innate ability by adoption, but mathematics never became a specialty of particular families, because there was little demand for mathematical work and no prospect of economic gain.[20]

Conceivably this pattern was unique to mathematics and needs no special explanation. Even in the developed countries of nineteenth-century Europe, mathematics had difficulty creating occupational niches and lost recruits to other technical specialties.[21] But the Western situation was better in other ways. In Europe and North America, mathematics at least had a home in universities as a traditionally prestigious academic discipline. Tokugawa Japan offered nothing so substantial as a base of material support. Authors of elementary textbooks like Yoshida Mitsuyoshi, whose 1627 work on the abacus went through several editions, could live in comfort. But works of advanced mathematics, even when published, had a very small market and could not sustain their authors.[22] Most domain schools did not employ anyone to teach mathematics as a specialty even at the end of the Tokugawa period.[23] Consequently, the occupational base for Tokugawa mathematicians, with few exceptions, consisted of inadequate patronage by wealthy individuals.[24]

In spite of the practical problems, technical specialties attracted recruits and managed to expand their activities. The most important achievements took place in medicine and to a lesser degree in astronomy. Medicine, after all, was immediately useful, and a country so dependent on rice agriculture needed an accurate calendar. Except in mathematics, progress in most fields initially depended on the work of physicians, astronomers (*temmongata*), and the Nagasaki interpreters. Medical progress was able to build on the existing base of Chinese medicine, and physicians trained in the Chinese tradition later helped to introduce Western science.[25]

European medicine was first brought to Japan by Spanish and Portuguese missionaries and by Dutch traders in the sixteenth century. Prior to the accession of Tokugawa Ieyasu in 1600, interest in Western medicine naturally focused on surgery and materia medica. Sustained investigation of other disciplines began after seclusion was fully in place. In 1650 the shogunate ordered the Dutch trade mission at Nagasaki, thereafter Japan's only regular contact with Europe, to procure a European anatomy text for examination by certain officials, and four years later it directed a Nagasaki physician to study Western medicine, but major interest remained focused on surgery for a considerable period.[26]

During the eighteenth century there were two important developments in medicine, the diffusion after 1774 of Chinese-style vaccination techniques and the founding of European anatomical studies. The

Kyoto physician Yamawaki Tōyō published *Zōshi*, a book on internal organs, in 1759 after making some effort to verify the description given in a German anatomical text by dissection.[27] This stimulated considerable interest in experimental medicine and led directly to the epochal publication in 1774 of the *Kaitai shinsho* (New book on human dissection) by Sugita Gempaku and some Edo physicians. *Kaitai shinsho* was a translation with drawings of the Dutch edition of Johan Adam Kulmus' *Anatomische Tabellen*, first published in 1722.[28] Sugita's translation indicates the strongly empirical approach to nature increasingly typical of Tokugawa science; it helped undermine the prestige of Chinese medicine.

Progress came more rapidly after the turn of the nineteenth century. In 1805 Hanaoka Seishū became the world's first surgeon to excise a breast tumor under general anesthesia.[29] In 1807 smallpox vaccination was introduced to Hokkaido through contacts with the Russians.[30] During the 1820s medical studies benefited from the presence at Nagasaki of Philip Franz von Siebold, member of a prominent Würzburg family of professors of anatomy. Siebold opened a small medical academy and trained several Japanese.[31] In 1832 Takano Chōei published Japan's first translation of a European work on physiology, and in 1836 Homma Genchō employed stethoscopy in medical diagnosis.[32]

The strength of medicine's institutional base was a boon to other technical fields. By the end of the eighteenth century the medical profession was the "strongest voice raised in behalf of . . . natural science."[33] In fact, those who contributed most to natural sciences other than astronomy came "mainly from the medical group [of Edo physicians]."[34] Considerable evidence supports this conclusion. European botany was completely dependent on physicians, beginning with Noro Genjō, who published *Oranda honzō wage* in 1750. Noro was followed by Ono Ranzan (*Honzō sōmoku keimō*, 1803), whom a German physician called "Japan's Linnaeus"; Udagawa Yōan (*Botanika kyō*, 1822, and *Shokugaku keigen*, 1833); Itō Keisuke (*Taisei honzō meisō*, 1828); and the most important Linnaean pioneer, Iinuma Yokusai (*Sōmoku zusetsu*, 1855).[35] Scholarly activity by doctors was also important in physics: Aochi Rinsō contributed by publishing *Kikai kanran* (Overall view of the atmosphere) in 1827.[36] While Aochi was virtually the only physician to publish a major work of physics before the Restoration, only about a half-dozen such works were published altogether, so the medical contribution was not insubstantial.

There has been a tendency to accord major significance to Aochi's *Kikai kanran*, to publication of a longer version, *Kikai kanran kōgi*, by his son-in-law Kawamoto Kōmin in 1851, to Shizuki Tadao's un-

published *Rekishō shinsho* (1798; published after the Restoration) or to
Sakuma Shōzan's experiments with electrical phenomena in the 1850s.
Nevertheless, physical knowledge, except for Shizuki's work, remained
rather elementary, did not circulate widely, and rested on an extremely
narrow social base before 1868. The *Rekishō shinsho,* which introduced
Newtonian mechanics, suffered from the lack of suitable terms for
kinematics and attracted little attention.[37] Chemistry had a larger clientele, but here as well official impediments to the diffusion of knowledge
hindered advances.

Mathematics did make progress, and so did astronomy. Histories of
Tokugawa mathematics usually begin with the work of Mōri
Shigeyoshi, who reportedly first acquired significant portions of the
Chinese mathematical corpus in the 1590s. Mōri used the abacus to
teach arithmetic at Kyoto, and Yoshida Mitsuyoshi was his pupil.
Yoshida, the son of a Kyoto merchant (though raised to samurai status),
became famous as the author of the *Jinkōki,* a book that told merchants
how to perform simple calculations for commercial transactions.[38] At a
higher level, the principal early Tokugawa development was Seki Takakazu's work in geometry and algebra, which led him to devise a limited
form of calculus. Seki's calculus could not solve problems of motion; his
interest was limited to finding the areas of two-dimensional curved
geometric figures.[39] (Later mathematicians were able to calculate the
volumes of solid objects with considerable accuracy.) Through the
efforts of a pupil, Araki Son'ei, who inherited Seki's papers, Seki's great
work became institutionalized in the so-called Seki school, several of
whose members worked to extend the boundaries of mathematical
knowledge by importing, translating, and publishing such major Chinese works as Mei Wen-ting's eighteenth-century treatise *Li-suan
ch'uan-shu* (Comprehensive work on calendrical science and mathematics). Western trigonometry and logarithms reached Japan by the
end of the eighteenth century through the translation and publication
of other such treatises.[40]

Tokugawa astronomy focused almost exclusively on producing better calendars, and for much of the period depended mainly on the
acquisition (in some cases recovery) of information from China. However, earlier astronomical studies done in Japan by Jesuits also had an
effect. This was particularly true of a work known as the *Kenkon benset-
su* (Western cosmography, with critical commentaries). Compiled in
the 1640s by the apostate Jesuit Christovão Ferreira, it gave a detailed,
systematic account of Aristotelian and Ptolemaic views of nature and
the cosmos. Adding to its importance as a cultural artifact are commentaries by the Confucian scholar Mukai Genshō, who was ordered to
study it by Shogun Iemitsu. Specialists do not agree on how significant

the work was, but it did give Japanese readers a first description of Westerners' views of nature.[41]

With the introduction from China of the *Shou-shih* calendar (ca. 1670), Japanese astronomy began slowly to improve. Described as the "single most important influence on Japanese calendar-making" of the Tokugawa period, the *Shou-shih* calendar was noted for the sophistication of its mathematics and attracted attention from leading mathematicians like Seki Takakazu and Takebe Katahiro. It also formed the basis for Shibukawa Harumi's Jōkyō calendar of 1684, which the imperial court in Kyoto adopted after the failures of its own astronomers. Shibukawa's success won him the position of official astronomer to the shogunate and promotion to the status of samurai. His work was important scientifically because it was based on the "first systematic astronomical observations in Japan," but it is interesting to note his inability to resolve the difficult mathematical problem of reducing the ecliptic coordinates of the sun to equatorial coordinates. Shibukawa stated that he had merely copied relevant information from tables appended to the *Shou-shih* calendar in creating the Jōkyō calendar.[42]

Three important astronomical developments occurred in the eighteenth century: introduction of better instruments for observation, diffusion by stages of Copernican heliocentrism, and preservation, in truncated form, of Newton's mechanics. Importation and translation between 1726 and 1733 of three major Chinese texts led to the first of these advances. One was the *Li-suan ch'uan-shu*. The other two, *Ling-t'ai i hsiang chih* (1730) and the *Ch'ung-chen li-shu* (1733), compiled by Jesuits working in China, explained various European astronomical instruments, including accurate drawings and descriptions of their use. New instruments and information made creation of the Kansei calendar possible in 1798. This was the first time Japanese astronomers employed Western data officially.[43]

As for the Copernican heliocentric doctrine, the surprising thing is not its arrival in the late eighteenth century but its absence in the seventeenth. *De revolutionibus orbium coelestium* first appeared in 1543, but Japanese astronomers did not hear of it at all until 1769 and got a superficial description only in 1792. The indifference of seventeenth-century Jesuit astronomers in Japan and China, together with Chinese authorities' lack of interest in Western cosmology, meant that Japanese astronomers had to wait for the importation of texts from Europe. In 1769 Asada Gōryū, an influential astronomer outside the government, stated that many European astronomers believed the earth was not the center of the universe, and in 1772 Motoki Ryōei, an official translator for the shogunate at Nagasaki, first mentioned the name of Copernicus in a Japanese scientific treatise. Twenty years later

Motoki produced an extensive nonmathematical description of Copernican theory in a handwritten, seven-volume work. Of this work's intellectual content, an historian of astronomy wrote: "Elliptic orbits were introduced but were not associated with Kepler . . . Kepler's second and third laws were not given; the name of Newton was ignored. Dynamic theory did not appear, and mathematical formulation was consciously avoided. . . . Lack of accurate detail made this treatise of little practical value to Japanese calendar makers."[44] Inability to publish was a further limitation on the impact of Motoki's achievement. Manuscript copies circulated among a few intellectuals, but for most educated Japanese the details of Copernican theory remained under lock and key in a government warehouse, although Shiba Kōkan popularized the doctrine.[45]

Japanese astronomy did not change much before 1868. The most important developments were in instrumentation. By 1800 Japanese astronomers were regularly producing telescopes and even grinding lenses.[46] Using a telescope of his own devising, Kunitomo Tōbei observed sunspots in 1835 and published a drawing of the surface of the moon; other astronomers began to do systematic observations of the planets. However, the most important development was arrival (in 1803) of a book in Dutch by the French astronomer J. J. F. de Lalande. Lalande was a preeminent figure in eighteenth-century science, and his work was the first "advanced treatise on contemporary Western astronomy" to make its way to Japan. The shogun's official astronomer, Takahashi Yoshitoki, saw at once the importance of the work. He was determined to secure translation, with all the mathematics, but he was also aware that official translators were not up to the job. He therefore decided to begin learning Dutch in order to do it himself, but, unfortunately for the development of astronomy in Japan, died a year later. Takahashi did leave behind many unpublished notes (*Lalande rekishō kanken* [A personal view of Lalande's astronomy]), but no one took notice of them until many years later.[47]

That Tokugawa efforts did not lead to modern science directly can be linked to several conditions. One has to do with long-term trends in the recruitment of scientists, especially in mathematics and astronomy. Another relates to research institutions, schools and academies, and scientists' behavior. Government policy constitutes a third. What did Tokugawa officials tolerate or support? What did they proscribe or try to suppress? In examining these issues we look for connections. Did certain people enter one field or another on the basis of class? If so, did this make any difference for science as a whole? Did some fields have institutional support that others lacked? If so, why?

The kinds of people who became active in the scientific movement varied considerably over the years. In the seventeenth century most astronomers and students of the physical sciences were commoners. A substantial proportion came from the twenty or so families of Nagasaki interpreters.[48] Higuchi Gon'emon (1590–1640), Imamura Eisei (1671–1736), Kobayashi Kentei (1601–84), and Nishikawa Joken (1648–1724) were among the most prominent figures in the physical sciences, and all of them came from interpreter families.[49] But from about the beginning of the eighteenth century, more and more came from the samurai. The samurai Hiraga Gennai (1729–79), Koike Yūken (1683–1754), and Yamaji Shujū (1704–72) were active early in the century, although men of commoner origin like Aoki Kon'yō (1698–1769), Miura Baien (1723–89), Nakane Genkei (1662–1733), and Nishikawa Seikyū (1693–1756) continued to outnumber their samurai colleagues.

Samurai predominated in the physical sciences from about the middle of the eighteenth century. Honda Toshiaki (1744–1821), Mori Shikō (1750–1818), Ōtsuki Gentaku (1757–1827), and Takahashi Yoshitoki (1764–1804) were active at this time, and all were members of the warrior class. By the 1820s samurai were by far the majority. Takahashi Kageyasu (1785–1829), Aochi Rinsō (1784–1833), Nakanishi Fungaku (1763–1837), and Sakuma Shōzan (1811–64) were notable samurai scientific figures of the late Tokugawa. Of course there were other famous scientists who were not samurai. Hoashi Banri (1778–1852), the noted astronomer and Confucian scholar, was not of samurai origin, and neither were such men as Takeda Shingen (1785–1846) or, slightly earlier, Shizuki Tadao (1760–1806).

Mathematics showed quite a different trend. In the seventeenth century, most mathematicians came from the samurai population. Mōri Shigeyoshi (1580–1640), Furugoori Hikozaemon (1642–1720), Seki Takakazu (1642–1708), Araki Son'ei (1640–1718), and other early pupils of Seki were all from the warrior class.[50] Samurai were predominant in mathematics into the eighteenth century (examples are Tatebe Kenkō [1690–1760], Fujita Sadasuke [1734–1807], and Matsuoka Ryōsuke [1770–1830]), but their influence was decreasing; by 1800 commoners were more numerous. During the last decades of Tokugawa rule, *wasan* mathematics was largely controlled by men like Uchida Itsumi (1805–82), Kurita Nobutada (1800–70), and Akita Yūjirō (1811–70), who came from mercantile or agrarian families, although a few samurai—Baba Kotarō (1801–60), Abe Yūji (1825–1875), and Kanda Takahira (1832–90) were still active in mathematics.

Table 2.1 shows the evolution of these trends in the Tokugawa period. In 1650 samurai were only 22 percent of the astronomers and stu-

2.1. Samurai as a Percentage of All Tokugawa Scientists

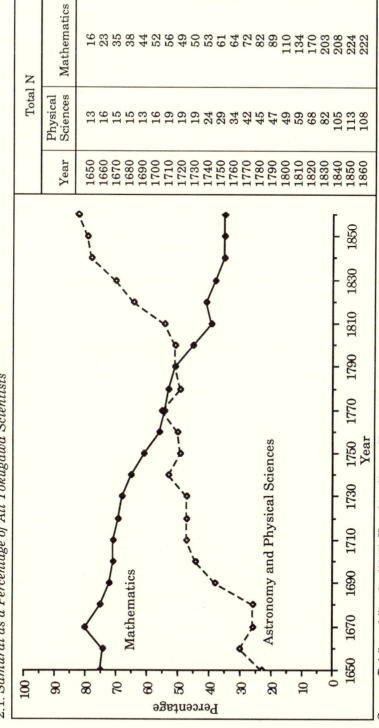

Year	Total N	
	Physical Sciences	Mathematics
1650	13	16
1660	16	23
1670	15	35
1680	15	38
1690	13	44
1700	16	52
1710	19	56
1720	19	49
1730	19	50
1740	24	53
1750	29	61
1760	34	64
1770	42	72
1780	45	82
1790	47	89
1800	49	110
1810	59	134
1820	68	170
1830	82	203
1840	105	208
1850	113	224
1860	108	222

Sources: Dai jimmei jiten 8 v.(1953); Kawakita Chōrin, *Honchō Sūgakka shōden* (1917); Hagino Kōgō, "Kyōdo no wasanka kenkyū shiryō," *Shūzankai* 103, 104, 106, 109, 110, 111 (1960–61); Ōya Shin'ichi, "Kyōdo no wasanka kenkyū shiryō hoi," *Shūzankai* 115 (1961).

dents of the physical sciences, but 75 percent of mathematicians. By 1700 the physical sciences had attracted more samurai: 45 percent of physical scientists and 70 percent of mathematicians were samurai. Samurai and commoners were about equally numerous in the physical sciences until almost the end of the eighteenth century; samurai specialization in mathematics declined slowly. But by 1820, nearly two-thirds of physical scientists were samurai, and a majority of mathematicians were of commoner origin. Time confirmed these trends. When the Tokugawa shogunate came to an end, 80 percent of physical scientists were samurai; two-thirds of mathematicians commoners.

Table 2.1 is based on many cases (263 astronomers and physical scientists and 515 mathematicians), but these are only a fraction of the total. As many as 8,000 mathematicians may have been active in the Tokugawa period, and there were certainly more students of physical science than the number represented in the graph.[51] But other evidence suggests that the pattern table 2.1 presents was real. Satō Shōsuke found that commoners were most active in the physical sciences during the early decades of the Tokugawa period.[52] The historian Takahashi Shin'ichi found that an Edo group active in Dutch studies in the 1850s was mostly samurai.[53] Katsu Kaishū in 1855 made a survey of "European"-style scholars in Edo for the Tokugawa shogunate and reported that two-thirds were samurai.[54] And Meiji publicist Fukuzawa Yukichi commented (ca. 1865), "During the ninety years that preceded the Hōreki and Meiwa periods [1751–72], most of the students of *Rangaku* [Western science] were physicians [mostly commoners]. However, since the Kōka and Kaei periods [1844–54], most of them have been samurai."[55]

What accounts for this bifurcation in the scientific movement? To answer this question we must first look at several others: Why in the seventeenth century did commoners dominate astronomy and the physical sciences? Why did samurai control mathematics? Why did both trends reverse in the eighteenth century? Why did samurai apparently lose interest in studying mathematics not long before they got interested in physical science? In the nineteenth century, why did more samurai not perceive the need for mathematics? To pose the question differently, why did more commoners who were active in mathematics not see the value of their work for the scientific movement?

Commoners became dominant in the scientific movement of the seventeenth century primarily because of differential opportunities. With the imposition of strict seclusion in 1639, it became almost impossible to import Western books, and contacts with foreigners sharply declined. But these effects hurt some groups more than others. Since the warrior class belonged to the chain of command, it was particularly hard hit by government restrictions. Some were motivated to remain active in science from an interest in defense and navigation, but they could not obtain any fresh stimulation and had little incentive to pass on their expertise. Nagasaki interpreters suffered as well, losing greatly in numbers and status, although they at least had access to information from Europe when it was almost impossible for others to get it. Commoners became most active in science because only they could become interpreters.[56]

The samurai's early interest in mathematics reflected the origins of the subject in Japan. Mōri Shigeyoshi had been a retainer of the famous general Toyotomi Hideyoshi and had studied in China with Hideyoshi's encouragement and endeavored to obtain Chinese works in mathematics.[57] Mōri's seventeenth-century successors like Seki Takakazu had also had access to foreign information and were further interested in applying mathematics. Seki studied European astronomy with a one-time Japanese resident of Macao and formally advised the new government about the calendar.[58] Samurai, as military experts, saw the value of mathematics for surveying, navigation, and calendar making.

While the imposition of seclusion disrupted these patterns, its partial relaxation by a subsequent Shogun gave them new vigor and a different direction. Samurai could have access to new kinds of knowledge once Shogun Yoshimune allowed Western technical literature into Japan (1720), but his action was not publicized and its effects were delayed.[59] Not until about 1750 did scientific learning change noticeably, and samurai importance in the scientific movement resulted primarily from formal education. The government put some effort into promoting education for samurai, and by 1760 forty-two domains and the shogunate had established their own schools, which local samurai were encouraged to attend.[60]

The preeminence of the samurai had other causes. To begin with, in the eighteenth century very little science was actually taught in any of the schools established by daimyo. Those interested in learning Dutch or a technical discipline had to enroll in a private academy, find a tutor, or work on their own. Commoners could certainly do any of these things; that samurai's tendency to do them was greater reflects differences in attitudes. Second, commoners' access to formal education was rising for a number of reasons. Certain fiefs established special schools for commoners beginning in the 1790s, and some domains (like Higo) even admitted them to the regular school. Commoners could always attend private academies, which operated in most larger cities.[61] By the late eighteenth century affluent commoners were tending to favor more formal education in emulation of samurai values. "The samurai virtues," Fukuzawa Yukichi wrote, "[by the late Tokugawa] were not confined to those who lived off rice stipends or wore swords [by virtue of their status]."[62]

Samurai still had better access to schooling than did commoners, and the education they got had special features because of their political position as the governing class. In that sense education for samurai was not suited to scientific studies but instead emphasized developing suitable moral character, gaining classical knowledge of the techniques of government, and meeting their responsibilities to society.[63] It included the military arts and Confucian humanism of a sometimes arid sort. But samurai education had other features which served science better, in that it tended to be somewhat philosophical and formal and was not tied too closely to occupational performance.[64] It also stressed comprehension of knowledge in general, not just mastery of particular specialties.[65]

Samurai had incentives to acquire education that were peculiar to their class, for their socialization seems to have produced a kind of "need achievement" of the sort that drives people to outdo and dominate others.[66] As their standing in the national economy deteriorated in the eighteenth century, this attitude combined with a new fervor. Because samurai youth were reared on stories of the privations endured by their ancestors, they had more courage to tolerate hardship in pursuing education than did commoners. For increasing numbers, at least toward the end of the century, education was seen as the best way to revive sagging family fortunes.[67]

Commoners' education also reflected needs and values, but their position in society was very different. Their education was heavily pragmatic: language instruction, moralistic aphorisms, and the subject matter required in their various occupations, including a substantial dose of arithmetic.[68] And though local regimes, including the shogunate, had some official interest in education for commoners, one should not overstate that interest. After all, only a small minority of fiefs provided special schools for commoners. Official steps were usually confined to employing itinerant lecturers who instructed villagers in the Confucian virtues of filial piety and obedience.[69] However, another factor influenced education for all. This was the sense of deprivation and the resentment samurai felt toward commoners whose incomes were tending to rise while theirs either remained constant or decreased.[70]

To explain the bifurcation in the social class basis of Tokugawa science one needs to consider the role of commoners in mathematics. Affluent commoners began to pursue mathematical interests when their position in society changed. Changes of position were linked to significant changes in the economy. The private commercial sector, where commoners were active, grew, and grew substantially. After 1700 especially, economic historians estimate that the Japanese economy grew significantly faster than total population, and such expansion demanded proficiency in arithmetic.[71] Tokugawa Japanese naturally distinguished between arithmetic and higher mathematics, but one could not pursue interests in higher mathematics without some acquaintance with arithmetic. Schooling for commoners was organized differently from that for samurai. Whereas samurai were schooled at public expense, most commoners were educated privately. Significantly, this was also the case with higher mathematics. By the mid-eighteenth century, Tokugawa Japan had nineteen schools of mathematics, each headed by a master practitioner who either pursued a separate occupation or subsisted on tuition payments.[72]

The private-school experience of commoners contrasts sharply with the experience of samurai, more and more of whom got their basic education in daimyo-supported schools where mathematics either was not taught at all or was limited to arithmetic. Seclusion had eliminated ocean navigation as a stimulus to interest in higher mathematics, and most samurai felt that mathematical studies had little or no value for society. The growing concern in the nineteenth century for practical studies at the daimyo schools made this sentiment, if anything, stronger.[73] Samurai could also see that commoners—especially merchants—were increasingly coopting mathematics. This made a difference in their fundamental attitudes because of their growing indebtedness to merchants.[74] They increasingly hated not only their creditors but anything associated with them. This point of view explicitly included higher mathematics. Ogyū Sorai condemned mathematicians as early as 1727.[75] The astronomer Nishimura Tosato wrote in 1761, "Mathematics is a childish subject in which only people wishing to seek fame by constructing impracticable theories . . . will indulge."[76] The biographer of the Meiji physicist Yamakawa Kenjirō, who received his early education in Tokugawa schools, noted that Yamakawa was unable to study mathematics at his domain school in Aizu because mathematics "was despised by samurai as something which only the merchants should study." According to the biographer, "The same situation existed in every other fief."[77]

The negative attitude toward mathematics also had an intellectual basis. Critics resented the increasingly trivial or esoteric character of later Tokugawa mathematics. By the time Nishimura was active, or even earlier, in the lifetime of Ogyū Sorai, *wasan* mathematics had developed the characteristics of an art form or a cult. A major preoccupation of later mathematicians was a type of problem called *yōjutsu* ("packing problems"), which consisted of efforts to inscribe the largest possible number of small circles of a certain size in a large circle or to circumscribe various polygons whose dimensions were given in the problem. Certainly *yōjutsu* did not represent the whole of Tokugawa mathematics. Seki Takakazu discovered—and his followers improved—the *enri* calculus for finding the areas of spaces bordered by curves. Wada Yasushi compiled tables of definite integrals and applied them to the mathematically infinite and infinitesimal. Other mathematicians developed calculus techniques which in some respects were better than Seki's.[78] But these achievements all came early and had no parallels in later mathematics.

Why should Tokugawa mathematics have been conceptually fertile in its earlier decades and increasingly sterile as the period went by? Some think that *wasan* mathematics' intellectual poverty is largely a product of the environing culture. Since many of Japan's basic cultural patterns were derived from overseas, specialists tended toward the artistic rather than toward the critical.[79] There may be some truth to this view, but a number of other factors were also at work.

Leaving aside the behavior of mathematicians themselves, the general direction of Tokugawa mathematics seems to have resulted from two different forces. One was surely class barriers to intellectual communication. For example, a samurai student of astronomy like Takahashi Yoshitoki, endeavoring in 1804 to translate Lalande, would never think of asking a merchant mathematician like Aida Yasuaki (1747–1817) for assistance, assuming Takahashi even knew of his existence.[80] The other was the shogunate's policy of national seclusion, which removed some powerful stimuli toward mathematics.

Instead, samurai after 1800 became increasingly interested in the physical sciences, a result in part of Western expansion. Shortly before and after the turn of the century, British and Russian ships appeared at Nagasaki; and the Americans were not far behind. These developments were alarming enough, but the Opium War (1839–42) was much more so. When Britain defeated China in this uneven conflict, the samurai were taken aback and began to reexamine their own defense needs. With coastal navigation and coastal defense suddenly brought sharply to the warriors' attention, ballistics, metallurgy, and naval engineering again seemed relevant to Japan's survival.

One might have expected that samurai and other nineteenth-century physical scientists would have included mathematics in their studies. Plotting trajectories or casting cannon is nearly impossible without it. Some of these men did see the connection, but *wasan* mathematics was incapable of responding to practical needs and was no longer controlled by the right kind of people. The first Japanese book on Western mathematics was published only in 1857, several years *after* the Perry expedition. Three factors may explain the tardiness of Tokugawa interest in Western mathematics. For one thing, the official Nagasaki translators did not translate Western works on mathematics and seem not to have known of local interest in the subject. Second, no important Western mathematician in this period ever visited Japan (unlike China) before or after seclusion was abolished.[81] Third, so many samurai had developed a hostility to *wasan* that it took time to change their minds about mathematics.

Curiously, most mathematical experts from the commoner population also failed to perceive the value of their subject for society, although there are exceptions. The Tsuwano school of *wasan* emphasized the practical value of mathematical work in the rules governing its students. And another commentator in 1816 declared mathematics a part of *gakumon*, a legitimate branch of higher Japanese learning.[82] But many did not much care whether it had any standing or not, let alone whether it could be applied. The eminent eighteenth-century mathematician Fujita Sadasuke spoke approvingly of what he called the "utility of the useless,"[83] and another mathematician insisted that his colleagues would take up problems from astronomy only if unable to find a topic from mathematics.[84] The forms of the discipline were set, and in the absence of new stimuli they were quite unlikely to change. The same lack of access to advanced information from Europe that affected science in general was also a powerful factor here. Hagiwara Teisuke (1828–1909), a talented practitioner of *wasan*, refused to convert to Western mathematics even after seclusion was lifted because a perusal of a British calculus text in translation convinced him that *wasan* was better.[85]

Tokugawa Educational and Scientific Institutions

Social class trends of the late Tokugawa may not have aided science in the early nineteenth century, but they had an effect later on. The modern research community was formed to a surprising degree by the extension of these trends (see chapter 3). Medicine had attracted a large share of the available talent in the Tokugawa period and continued to do so in the Meiji, and samurai predominance in the physical sciences persisted well beyond 1868. The marginality typical of Tokugawa mathematics exacted its price after 1868. Continuities in recruitment are striking, but they are much less obvious when we look at institutions. Relatively few scientific institutions of the Meiji era can trace their lineage to the Tokugawa period, and the Tokugawa institutions often had goals that set them apart from their modern successors.

Scientific institutions in the Tokugawa period developed under diverse conditions. Some constraints promoted competition and in that sense benefited learning. The system of Alternate Attendance established by the shogunate to control the daimyo by compulsory spending on travel, for example, brought many samurai retainers to Edo, where they acquired important new information and confronted "intellectual challenges . . . to their [traditional] way of thinking."[86] The political structure consisted not only of the central administration of the shogunate, but also of more than 270 local domains each headed by a daimyo. Sometimes local domains could be induced to compete in a way that was helpful to science. Institutions in the purely private sphere could—and did—challenge the position of those supported by government.

Other factors served to limit competition and constrain the scientific movement. The shogunate tried hard to dominate European studies (*Rangaku* or *Yōgaku*) and in some ways all forms of learning. Parochialism in a climate of seclusion certainly impeded some dissemination of knowledge. Fear of Christianity restricted the growth of the physical sciences. Some members of well-entrenched intellectual communities (for example, *kampō* physicians) even directly restrained competition to protect themselves. Many besides mathematicians had no wish for important new knowledge, and the private sector, in spite of its strengths, was in some respects weak and dependent. As for institutional functions, schools and even putative research facilities in Tokugawa Japan were not necessarily established for fully "modern" purposes. They *were* supposed to diffuse scientific knowledge and technical information, at least to those who created them, but they had little concept of adding to knowledge and never awarded degrees.

Tokugawa institutions were certainly valuable, however, for as R. P. Dore noted in a classic study, Tokugawa Japan saw a rebirth of learning. Peacetime conditions allowed for considerable curiosity. Official patronage of scholarship flourished. Subsidies for printing books, maintaining libraries, and hiring lecturers were on a scale without precedent, and a substantial recovery of knowledge from China took place. Also, while one would not wish to exaggerate its extent, there was some freedom for intellectual inquiry.[87] Political structures reinforced this remarkably favorable climate. Consider the effects of Alternate Attendance. Nagasaki, of course, had originally been the site of the Japanese scientific movement, while Kyoto and Osaka had their parts to play. But by bringing large numbers of samurai to Edo, the national system of political control eventually reshaped the learned establishment. Alternate Attendance indirectly promoted new ways of thinking among those who undertook to travel and eventually laid much of the groundwork for the capital's preeminence in science. Schools, academies, and other institutions sprang up out of all proportion to the wealth and population of Edo, and as a result, it came to dominate the scientific movement after about 1750. The capital's preeminence in scholarship became permanent in Japanese life.

But Alternate Attendance in and of itself did not bring about these results. Regional competition also stimulated scholarly activities. About fifteen daimyo domains built official academies in the seventeenth century, and by 1770 about thirty more schools had been built, followed by another sixty or so by the end of the century. School construction had several motivations. Confucianism held that formal education helped promote virtue and hence the governability of society, and troubling events could reinforce this notion. In the 1770s Tokugawa Japan faced a series of particularly severe famines, bad weather, daimyo financial crises, and peasant revolts. Some administrators thought that more education would help, at least with the last two. But building schools was also a way of keeping up with one's neighbors. In 1755 the Higo domain in Kyushu built a school at a time when they were still quite unusual, and this action by the Hosokawa family prompted other domains to do the same thing.[88]

Domains could also improve conditions for technical studies by adding programs to existing institutions. One domain added a mathematics course to its school in the 1760s. Four more did so in the next two decades, and an additional nine had added mathematics by 1803. Two domains introduced courses in astronomy—including calendrical science, geography, and surveying—during the 1790s. Two added medical courses in the 1780s, and seven more did so in the 1790s. In the nineteenth century this expansion continued, as nine domain schools added mathematics courses between 1804 and 1829, while one added medicine and two astronomy. From about the time of the Opium War, the pace accelerated, so that by the time Perry arrived in 1853, twenty-two additional domain schools had added mathematics, thirteen had added medicine, and four had created new courses in astronomy and related disciplines.[89]

These figures may suggest a preference for mathematics, but in fact, medicine was usually the discipline of choice and often had its own institutions. From the mid-eighteenth century on the more affluent domains began to establish separate academies for medical studies, Higo once again being the pacesetter. In 1757 the Higo daimyo, Hosokawa Shigekata, established the Saishunkan at Kumamoto as a specialized school for medical studies. His initiative was copied by Satsuma (1774), Kyoto (1782), Aizu (1801), and others.[90]

Disciplines considered more explicitly Western were also included in domain academies, though rarely before 1800. Higo's medical academy offered Dutch surgery from the start,[91] but the Chōshū and Sakura domain schools which did so only after the Opium War (from 1843) were by far the more typical cases. Often the military rather than the medical value of Dutch studies led to their adoption in domain academies.[92] Military studies based on Western texts were first conducted at Chōshū and Saga in 1840, and their popularity grew after Perry's arrival. The shogunate developed several new programs, but the domains were slower to act. A few forward-looking daimyo did send young samurai to Nagasaki, Osaka, or Edo for technical studies, but that was not until the mid-1840s.[93]

With the change of regime (1868) the daimyo began to catch up. In 1870, for example, a reformist administration in Higo closed the traditional Confucian academy (the Jishūkan, built in 1755) and replaced it with a Western-style school. Securing the services as instructor of a West Point graduate, the new Yōgakkō academy offered a broad program. Captain L. L. Janes devoted the entire first year to instruction in English. In the remaining three years he taught various subjects, including algebra, geometry, trigonometry, chemistry, physics, and geology.[94] Separately but simultaneously, the Higo administration created a new school for medical studies (the Igakkō) by reorganizing the existing Saishunkan. Although both schools were reform-minded, their sponsors viewed them quite differently. As an antidote to Westernization, Yōgakkō students had regular compulsory lectures on Confucian ethics and morality, but Igakkō students could attend the lectures or not as they liked. The Yōgakkō was housed in a Western-style building; the Igakkō used the Saishunkan's facilities and some of its equipment as well.[95]

Medicine's establishment in separate academies was a trend of particular importance. Domain academies taught a little science, but before the Opium War they were not very serious about it. Only elementary mathematics, botany, and medical subjects were usual, with astronomy less frequently offered. Partly for this reason the medical academies took on additional functions. Especially in the intermediate period of the scientific movement (1780–1840), the medical academy of a domain was the leader in accepting Western science. Many of their teachers of technical subjects were private physicians.[96]

The private-sector status of many physicians was a source of additional competition for daimyo-supported institutions. Private physicians were more likely to exploit new techniques like vaccination or Dutch surgery than their official counterparts. After all, private doctors received no fixed salary, and special expertise could justify a boost in their fees. Saga already possessed several private practitioners of Dutch-style medicine before it began to be taught in the daimyo's academy. In

Fukui, Dutch medicine was established in the domain academy only as a result of pressure from private physicians, and even then it was strongly opposed by conservative doctors on the academy staff.[97] But the attentions of private physicians were not confined entirely to medicine. An important development of the late eighteenth century was the cultivation of astronomy and other technical subjects by physicians. The noted Osaka physician Asada Gōryū (1734–99) became a highly successful astronomer. In the 1780s he discovered the secular diminution of tropical-year length, and two of his pupils in 1798 developed the Kansei calendar for the Tokugawa shogunate after Asada himself declined the assignment. This calendar was an important advance, and it used European measurements officially.[98]

The shogunate's founding of scientific institutions should certainly have enhanced the scientific movement. The number of these institutions was impressive. The Astronomical Bureau and Observatory (Temmongata) was the oldest of the group. Founded in 1684 as a result of Shibukawa Harumi's work on the Jōkyō calendar, the observatory got effective control over calendar making and made various contributions of note.[99] In the late eighteenth century it sponsored Inō Tadataka's survey of the Japanese coast, which used sophisticated mathematical techniques.[100] In the nineteenth century it became the base for many of the specialists in European astronomy.[101] Partly because of the observatory's successes, the shogunate began to expand its technical infrastructure, in 1791 adding an official academy of medicine, then an agency for the translation and diffusion of technical materials (1811), a full-fledged school for scientific studies (1856), a related bureau for mathematical studies (1863), and a number of other institutions. Not much was done, however, between 1811 and Perry's mission in 1853, and certain parts of the program, particularly in medicine, gained momentum not by competing with, but by coopting the accomplishments of private institutions. Government policy dictated that scholars attached to public institutions dominate and control the scientific movement rather than advance its mission.

The official policy of not competing is clear from the beginning, with the founding of the medical academy, which actually involved reconstituting an existing private facility. In 1765 the Taki family of shogunal physicians had established its own school, the Seijukan, for training Chinese-style doctors. The Seijukan was privately funded, but the shogunate publicized its existence among the daimyo and later required physicians living in shogunal territories to contribute to its maintenance. Though neither historically unprecedented nor programmatically innovative, the Seijukan was an important institutional development in the Tokugawa context, and for that reason it eventually became a public institution. [102] It would also initiate a longer-term pattern. The Seiyō Igakusho (Academy of Western Medicine) of 1861 was created in much the same way, and this same nationalizing of private institutions in the medical field continued beyond 1868.

The creation of the Office for Translating Dutch Books (Bansho Wage Goyō) in 1811 illustrates two of the shogunate's aims. One was to obtain useful knowledge through translation, the other to control its diffusion once the knowledge had been obtained. Before this, the Dutch studies movement had been in the hands of private physicians and curious samurai, who sometimes performed experiments while endeavoring to learn from European texts. But with the establishment of the translation office, official activities rose to the top, and interest in experiments waned. Baba Sajūrō, an able Nagasaki translator, and Ōtsuki Gentaku, a leading Edo Dutch scholar from the Sendai domain, were named to the staff of the translation office, but they and their staff were basically generalists with only occasional interests in science. While technical materials were included in their purview, much more of their work dealt with public administration. [103] Moreover, the translation office had duties ostensibly at odds with the scientific movement. Beginning in 1842 it had to censor all translations of European materials and oversee their circulation. Under these circumstances, it is hardly surprising that before 1856 the translation office made no more than a limited contribution to science in Japan. [104]

After Perry arrived, the government made changes. It expanded the work of the translation office and built a school in 1856. [105] This school initially taught only Dutch, but in 1862 English, French, and German were offered along with courses in mathematics, metallurgy, and industrial arts. Geography, physics, and history were added in the final years of Tokugawa rule. [106] In the Tokugawa context, the school was innovative. Students were admitted from all over Japan without regard to place of origin or status, and members of the faculty were not educated generalists but specialists in the subjects they taught. [107] Such specialists were hard to recruit. The shogunate could obtain just two of the teachers from among its own retainers and had to hire the other thirty-two from other domains. [108]

The school's program in physics shows its limitations. The eminently qualified Kawamoto Kōmin had charge of physics, but it is not at all clear what he did. Earlier Dutch studies specialists in physics had investigated topics in ballistics, electricity, friction, and celestial mechanics, but it is far from certain that any of this work continued in the Tokugawa academy. Kawamoto and his staff were forbidden to lecture and confined their efforts to translating documents. The only scientific work they are known to have accomplished is the installation and study of a telegraph system.[109]

Tokugawa institution building did not neglect medicine. Chinese medicine had had its own academy for decades. Fearing loss of their status, some of its members had opposed Western medicine, and in 1849 they persuaded the authorities to ban Western medicine except for surgery and ophthalmology, never specialties of Chinese medicine.[110] Ironically, the same year this ban was issued a German surgeon employed by the Dutch at Nagasaki managed through vaccination to achieve the desired prophylactic effect against smallpox, and opposition to Western medicine waned as the information spread.[111] Accordingly, a group of private physicians opened a vaccination office at Edo in 1857. In 1861 the shogunate took it over and made it a medical school. Initially known as the Academy of Western Medicine (Seiyō Igakusho), this academy later became part of Tokyo University.[112]

During the years of institutional expansion in Edo, similar events were occurring at Nagasaki. This is in some ways surprising, given the capital's rise as a center of scholarship, but throughout the period of national seclusion Nagasaki was the center of contacts with Europe, and it attracted several Westerners with scientific training. Philip Franz von Siebold, J. L. C. Pompe van Meerdervoort, A. F. Bauduin, and W. K. Gratama were especially influential toward the end of the period. Siebold was both the first to arrive and the most influential. Between 1823 and 1829 he lived in Nagasaki. Nagasaki officials gave him unprecedented social access. He attracted students to classes in medicine and biology where he promoted the Linnaean system and various current views in European medicine.[113] Siebold was particularly well prepared for his sojourn in Japan. He came from a prominent academic family and had taken his degree at the University of Würzburg. His interest in Japanese affairs had led the Dutch to appoint him physician at their Nagasaki trading post, and the same interests eventually got him in trouble. In 1829 he was expelled from the country because the shogunate believed him a threat to the nation's security.[114]

Partly because of this "Siebold Affair," Japanese scientists had few Western contacts in the years before Perry's arrival. However, Dr. Otto Mohnike resided at Nagasaki between 1848 and 1850, and he promoted vaccination and the use of the stethoscope. But a breakthrough came in 1857, when Matsumoto Ryōjun, aspiring student of European medicine, and the Dutch army physician Pompe van Meerdervoort arrived in Nagasaki and began a collaboration that stimulated the scientific movement. With formal approval from the Tokugawa authorities, the two opened a full-fledged academy of European medicine. Known as the

Nagasaki Igaku Denshū Jo, the academy offered a five-year program beginning with basic biology, chemistry, and physics and progressing to medical subjects.[115] The school was formally a companion subordinate to another facility located nearby. The simultaneous founding of this Nagasaki Kaigun Denshū Jo had been motivated by military concerns about coastal defense, and it was staffed by Dutch naval officers who taught physics, mathematics, chemistry, and engineering as well as various military subjects.[116]

The Nagasaki Igaku Denshū Jo grew in the 1860s. Pompe van Meerdervoort left Japan in 1862, but not before he had persuaded the shogunate to establish a teaching hospital and new facilities at the medical school.[117] A. F. Bauduin, who became his replacement, further recommended establishment of a separate academy for basic science, and this was done in 1864 by moving basic science out of the older institutions. Presiding over this Bunseki Kyūri Jo, as it came to be known, was another Dutch physician, W. K. Gratama, who reached Nagasaki in 1866. The political instability that preceded the demise of the Tokugawa shogunate led the authorities to remove the science school first to Edo in 1867 and finally to Osaka in 1869. There it became known as the Ōsaka Shamitsu Kyoku or Osaka School of Chemistry, and it continued to operate until 1881.[118]

The impact of these institutions outlasted their existence. Modern chemistry was taught at the Nagasaki institutions for the first time in Japan, and official restrictions on the teaching of physics that limited the work of the Edo academy (Bansho Shirabesho) had no effect in distant Nagasaki. The Bunseki Kyūri Jo never had many students after it moved to Osaka, but two that it did teach became highly influential. Takamine Jōkichi, perhaps the leading chemist of Meiji Japan, received his earliest training there, and so did Nagaoka Hantarō, its most prominent physicist.[119] Nor was the medical program without long-term results. Several prominent figures in the Meiji medical community were students of Pompe van Meerdervoort, including the five earliest recipients of the D.Sc. degree.[120]

Public institutions were certainly important for the scientific movement, but before the Perry expedition, *private* institutions had the edge. Private individuals dominated the movement from 1720 on, when Shogun Yoshimune had relaxed the ban on technical literature from Europe. Private physicians carried out the first anatomical dissections. Asada Gōryū, a late eighteenth-century astronomer with no official post, criticized the official calendar and instigated its successful revision.[121] Others had established various private academies, and these continued to proliferate well after Perry arrived. Although little information about their number exists, we know that by early Meiji there were nearly 1500 higher-level private academies, and some had a "Western" cast to them.[122] As always, medical institutions were especially numerous. During the last century or so of Tokugawa rule, twenty-three full-fledged medical academies opened their doors; the majority were private.[123]

Private academies made several contributions. They were the "basic communities in which the work of introducing and translating medical texts was sustained." They provided the most capable members of the shogunate's translation office in the Bureau of Astronomy and of many of the daimyo academies.[124] Ōtsuki Gentaku, founding member of the translation office, opened a private academy (the Shirandō) at Edo in 1786. This school was the most important Japanese center of Western studies in Ōtsuki's active years (he died in 1827). Of its ninety-four pupils, a number were quite influential. Udagawa Genshin and his heir, Udagawa Yōan, were prolific translators of technical materials. In fact, the younger, in translating Lavoisier's work in chemistry, coined many Japanese terms still used in that field.[125] Ōtsuki's initiative also started a trend. In 1801 two of his pupils established their own academies in Kyoto and Osaka. A pupil's pupil, Tsuboi Shindō, set up a school at Edo in 1829.[126] Other notable private foundations of the period included establishment of the Tekitekisaijuku of Ogata Kōan at Osaka in 1838. From Tsuboi's school came Tsuboi Shōgorō, subsequently professor of zoology at Tokyo University; and from Ogata's school came Fukuzawa Yukichi and Nagayo Sensai, leading figures in modern research policy.[127]

One should not, however, overrate the importance of private or public academies. They did contribute substantially to the later formation of the modern community of researchers. And the common responsibility of the public institutions to serve the state even at the expense of the learned community did not in itself make them peculiar.[128] But in other respects contributions were limited, and functions were not very modern. With the exception of those for mathematics or medicine, the academies were rarely very specialized in the courses they offered, but tended to present a general program that would appeal to young men of ambition. Even of a prominent institution like Ogata's Tekitekisaijuku, Nagayo Sensai could write: "[Ogata's academy] was originally described as a medical school. Actually it was a place for reading Dutch books. Thus among the pupils were not only physicians but men who came there for all kinds of Dutch learning, about military matters, botany, chemistry, or whatever."[129]

Apart from the character of the learning dispensed, each type of academy had its own limitations. The public institutions were late in incorporating Western forms of knowledge (except for some medicine and a little astronomy, few did much before the Opium War),[130] and they were supposed to restrict the diffusion of knowledge to their respective sponsors in government.[131] Private institutions did not have this problem, but they had others that were probably as serious. Daimyo or the shogunate tended to coopt their best talent, as the career of Ōtsuki Gentaku illustrates,[132] and most of these schools had limited funds. Scholars of Western studies could rarely make much money even when they ran their own schools. Students could not afford to pay high tuition unless they had scholarships from the shogun or a daimyo. Teaching at such an academy was more a hobby than a real occupation. Proprietors usually got most of their income from medical practice or, if they were samurai, from a daimyo's stipend.[133] The academies were not very numerous, and they developed too late, for by the time they began to proliferate, learning in the West was far better institutionalized. "[Modern science] now . . . required the creation of an institutional system around not self-taught amateurs, but professional scientists who had received a modern education."[134] As a result, Tokugawa institutions were not, for the most part, direct precursors of modern institutions.[135]

The degree of competition the academies generated was limited as well. Fukuzawa Yukichi argued that Tokugawa scholars were "confined to a cage called government" and therefore "spent their time in anguish within the small universe which this cage created."[136] Whether this judgment is true or not, the shogunate certainly wanted control over European studies at least, and in some sense *all* learning. Its skimming of leading scholars from the private sector was partly prompted by this aspiration, and so was a persisting tendency to link physical science with the supposed threat of Catholicism. Parochialism and seclusion impeded the dissemination of knowledge. "It is an old parochial tradition to seek exclusive profit for one's own fief and to keep secret any discoveries from others," wrote a "Dutch scholar" about 1800.[137] An 1864 incident illustrates this pattern. A Nihonmatsu samurai requested permission from his older brother to study applied physics and cannonry in Mito, but the brother refused on the grounds that pursuing such knowledge would upset society by diffusing very dangerous technology.[138] Such attitudes were probably common.[139]

Finally, entrenched opposition and a lack of demand for new knowledge could also impede competition. Mathematics gradually became more detached from society and separated from intellectual life. When mathematical works were actually published, they usually stated only problems, solutions, and sometimes rules. Among the reasons for this was a lack of "product" demand. Because there was such a limited market for any kind of book in advanced mathematics, production costs were high, and the authors themselves usually prepared the wood blocks for printing.[140]

Medicine's problems were entirely the opposite. There was a strong demand for medical "products" and some incentive to develop new therapies. Partly for this very reason, medicine was prestigious and offered specialists a living. Specialists who became successful then might resist innovations and novelties. It is misleading to say that Western science and medicine waged an "uphill battle against . . . [the older] Chinese-style science."[141] But the domain medical schools *were* controlled by relatively high-ranking samurai doctors who usually opposed innovation, and these doctors were able for a time to delay the introduction into their institutions of new forms of medicine from Europe.[142]

Tokugawa Science in Its Bureaucratic Setting

Tokugawa scholarship, asserted Fukuzawa Yukichi, was very little more than an "adjunct of government." Its practitioners mostly taught in schools and had little if any power and certainly no influence in formulating policies.[143] Scholars were also treated rather shabbily. "The samurai had a higher regard for Confucianism than [they did] for the professional Confucianist," so that scholars rarely became advisers to persons in power and even more rarely held secure official posts.[144] This was even more true of technical disciplines than of humanistic studies because of Tokugawa officials' no more than occasional interest in science and firm belief that general administrators should always hold sway over specialists. Technical experts had subordinate posts and could lose them at the whim of a shogun.[145]

Though well established, these patterns did vary as periods of outright proscription or repression alternated with periods of encouragement, and attitudes changed when new officials entered office. The seventeenth century, despite seclusion, offered better conditions for some kinds of research than any other era save the Bakumatsu years (1853–67). The official promotion of classroom instruction conspicuous of the late eighteenth century may actually have damaged the scientific movement by arousing suspicion of mathematics.

The incongruities between Tokugawa priorities and the needs of science are clear from the seclusion edicts of the 1630s, which frustrated navigational astronomy (so important to the work of Newton in England),[146] and in the same decade Shogun Iemitsu issued a ban on the use of Western mathematics in surveying activities, a proscription that lasted to the end of the century.[147] European astronomy got especially harsh treatment, probably because it was linked to the Jesuits, who had first introduced it to Japanese officials. Those who were interested in European astronomy were often suspected of professing Catholicism. The European-style astronomer Kobayashi Kentei was jailed in the 1640s, while a colleague, Hayashi Kichizaemon, was actually executed in 1646.[148] And these attitudes of suspicion persisted. In the eighteenth century only the shogunate and five other domains were allowed to compile a calendar.[149]

From the beginning, however, there was a different side to the shogunate's treatment of scholarship. Shogun Ieyasu thought that learning would contribute to peace and morality and began to support it once his power was secured. His policy was mostly confined to library contributions and publication subsidies, but successors went considerably further. His grandson Shogun Iemitsu hired Hayashi Razan to head an academy which received state support and official recognition. In 1690 Shogun Tsunayoshi authorized construction of new facilities for this Shōheikō Academy and exempted its faculty from Buddhist holy orders.[150] This patronage also extended to the sciences. In the 1680s Tsunayoshi appointed a talented mathematician of "lower-class" origin official astronomer and gave him a military rank. This astronomer's descendants included several mathematicians and prominent astronomers.[151] Daimyo governments, meanwhile, followed Edo's policies closely. A half-dozen had established schools by 1700, and several began subsidizing individual scholars, as, for example, when the daimyo of Mito created a mathematics post in 1661.[152]

These trends continued in the eighteenth century. More schools were built with official encouragement, and patronage of individual scholars increased somewhat: in 1730 another daimyo established a position to support mathematics.[153] Other initiatives were soon undertaken. In midcentury the Kumamoto domain launched reforms which included a medical academy and the mandatory certification by it of local physicians (1762).[154] Other domains were slower to act, but the action set a precedent. In the shogunal territories, a group of doctors got permission to publish a book on anatomy (*Kaitai shinsho*; 1774) that was largely based on a European text, and in 1793 its academy of medicine admitted Western surgery to the academic program.[155]

But limitations remained strict. Hiraga Gennai, a samurai student of both astronomy and medicine, was forbidden by his daimyo to employ his skills in any domain but his own.[156] Scientists could never be certain that government officials would tolerate their scholarly work. Which European technical and scientific works were officially translated was determined by government regulations,[157] and general circulation of the shogunate's translators' works was invariably forbidden. Private scholars were not so constrained, but even they could encounter many problems. In 1765 a work on botany by Goto Rishun was confiscated upon publication simply because it reproduced the Dutch alphabet,[158] even so long after Shogun Yoshimune in 1720 had authorized importation of nonreligious books.

Who was in power could make a big difference. Shogun Yoshimune's administration (1716–45), as often noted, was one of the best. He took several steps favorable to science besides admitting Western technical works. In 1730 he named the physician and mathematician Nakane Genkei to be the official shogunal astronomer strictly on the basis of Nakane's ability.[159] During his last year in office as Shogun, he authorized translation projects by two private physicians who were interested in European botany. This action was especially important in creating a precedent, for later officials could not easily oppose translation projects solely because of their Western subject matter.[160]

On the other side, the administration of Lord Matsudaira Sadanobu during the reign of Shogun Ienari was a low point for the scientific movement. Matsudaira was obsessed with political unity and despised all kinds of intellectual novelty. This led him to proscribe antimainstream schools of Confucian philosophy and to meddle systematically in the Shōheikō Academy. After proscribing heterodoxy in 1790, he took control of faculty appointments out of the hands of the Shōheikō's rector and named professors who agreed with his views. In 1791 he took it on himself to reshape the curriculum and issue new rules.[161] These actions were political and not aimed at science, but the scientific movement could not remain unscathed. In 1788 Matsudaira had authorized Honda Toshiaki to conduct geographical surveys in Hokkaido and Sakhalin, primarily to determine whether Sakhalin was an island. Investigations confirmed that it was an island, not a peninsula as many had claimed, but Matsudaira suppressed this by citing "state security."[162] His concept of security was wide-ranging. In 1793 he blocked publication of a work on heliocentrism by the shogunal astronomer Motoki Ryōei even though others had already publicized the theory.[163]

By the beginning of the nineteenth century, the scientific movement had developed to a point where major systemic changes might well have been expected. The first dictionary of the Dutch language had been published. Western anatomy was rapidly being assimilated. At least a small number of Japanese were studying Newtonian physics. Several botanical compilations had been launched which were based entirely or in part on the Linnaean classification. A survey of the entire

Japanese coastline using the most advanced mathematical techniques had begun. And the first fundamental revision of the national calendar using Western data had just been completed.[164] Nevertheless, these developments did not yield the sort of institutional breakthrough that occurred in European science, and the movement within which these advances took place did not even lead directly to modern Japanese science.

Government policy was one reason. The desire of shogunal officials to use scientists and their work for political goals restricted the diffusion of technical knowledge. In 1829 the shogunate sentenced its official astronomer, Takahashi Kageyasu, to prison and condemned him to death after the fact. In 1839 several intellectuals and scientists were imprisoned on a charge of opposing the regime. Nor were these acts the sole forms of oppression. In 1842 the Edo government ordered that translations of all Dutch books be censored before publication, and in 1850 it handed down an edict requiring that the title of every book imported from Europe be reported immediately to the governor of Nagasaki. In 1856, three years after the Perry expedition, the regime forced the Bansho Shirabesho to censor all translations of technical (and other) works from any European language.[165]

Most historians of these events justifiably emphasize Takahashi's persecution, the so-called Siebold Affair. The Tokugawa government had almost institutionalized suspicion and paranoia, and the effect of its policies on intellectual life could scarcely be supportive.[166] Takahashi got into trouble because he had shared Inō Tadataka's coastal survey maps of Japan with Philip Franz von Siebold in return for European-language materials dealing with the coast of Sakhalin Island. This exchange occurred in 1828 within the context of an official assignment to prepare a map of the Sakhalin area. Apparently Takahashi realized that his action broke the law, but he willingly assumed the risk of punishment because he was strongly committed to the task and because the information he got was not obtainable otherwise.[167] The consequences were severe. Takahashi was imprisoned and died four months later. His son was fired from a government post and sent to a place of internal exile. Several Nagasaki interpreters who had innocently carried messages between Takahashi in Edo and Siebold in Nagasaki were also sent to prison. And this was just the beginning. While living in Nagasaki (1823–29), Siebold had offered formal instruction in European medicine to Japanese pupils with the shogunate's approval. All but one of his twenty-four pupils were arrested and imprisoned because of this connection. (The exception, Takano Chōei, went into hiding. He was indicted ten years later in connection with the "Bansha Circle" persecution.) Siebold was detained for some months and then expelled from the country. The shogun's personal physician in Edo lost his position and samurai standing for having given Siebold a garment with the crest of the shogun in return for a medicine used to treat eye diseases.[168]

The "Siebold Affair" divided and demoralized the learned community. Most scholars kept silent, whatever their views, but others felt more threatened by official hostility. Aochi Rinsō, the first Japanese to publish a textbook of European physics, the noted botanist Udagawa Yōan, and several other scholars who resided in Edo felt compelled to deny they even knew Takahashi.[169] And effects were by no means confined to individuals. The "Siebold Affair" hastened Nagasaki's decline as a center of learning and laid the groundwork for another persecution.[170]

This "Bansha Circle Incident" of 1839 reflected the rising concerns about Western expansion and the scattered resentment of technical experts. In 1804, 1811, and 1837, foreign ships belonging to Russia, Britain, and the United States entered Japanese waters without permission and exposed the weakness of coastal defenses.[171] Fearing political criticism for dereliction of duty, the Tokugawa government ordered countermeasures. The "incident" began when the shogunate commissioned a conservative but incompetent official, Torii Yōzō, to conduct a survey of Edo Bay with a colleague named Egawa Hidetatsu. Torii was formally in charge of the project but lacked the necessary technical skills. Egawa was better equipped, because he belonged to a group of officials and scholars, the "Bansha Circle," who regularly discussed policy issues. The group, led by Watanabe Kazan, chief administrator of a daimyo domain, also included the noted mathematician Uchida Itsumi and Takano Chōei, the physician who had fled the Nagasaki dragnet the shogunate had launched in 1829.[172]

The Bansha group—especially Uchida—was able to help in completing the survey. But Torii Yōzō was deeply chagrined by the technical prowess of the Bansha intellectuals and his own incompetence. As an official censor (o-metsuke) for the Tokugawa shogunate, he also suspected their political motives and decided to take action against them. Egawa was too well connected and Uchida too apolitical, so he focused on Watanabe Kazan.

Police searches of Watanabe's house produced nothing directly incriminating, but they did turn up drafts of policy statements prepared for Egawa that could be construed as suspicious. One draft argued that scholars and others concerned with policy should investigate the actual causes of problems. Another called for an accurate appraisal of Japan's position in the world.[173] Torii claimed that these statements revealed the circle's opposition to seclusion and were basically treasonous.

His charges had the desired effect. Watanabe was arrested and sent to prison, where he committed suicide in 1841. Takano went into hiding and managed to survive for ten years on translation and consulting work for various daimyo. In 1850 he, too, was arrested and subsequently committed suicide in detention. Several other "Bansha Circle" members (though not Uchida) were arrested, while a number of lower-ranking shogunal retainers connected with the survey were indicted but escaped imprisonment. Meanwhile, public responses by unindicted associates followed the pattern of the "Siebold Affair." Egawa Hidetatsu remained aloof and assumed a posture of indifference. Officials in Watanabe's domain fell all over themselves in apologies to Edo. Apparently this response from his former associates prompted Watanabe to take his own life.[174]

Following the "revelations" of the "Bansha Circle Incident," scientific and Western studies were engulfed for some years in a cloud of official suspicion. Besides advance censorship of translations and reporting of titles of imported books, other measures were felt necessary. In 1849, physicians living in shogunal territories were forbidden to practice European-style medicine. In 1850 a ban on diffusion of the contents of any translation of a European book to the Japanese public went into effect.[175] Even mathematics suffered from the "Bansha Circle Incident." In 1839, Edo stopped publication of a book on tax calculations and practical measurements that was intended to help local Tokugawa officials![176]

In 1853–54 the American expedition of Matthew C. Perry visited Japan and ended seclusion. This event heightened the Japanese awareness of Western technology earlier aroused by the Opium War. But the Perry expedition did not lead at once to an unqualified embrace of science and technology. On the contrary, the shogunate displayed considerable ambivalence about how to deal with the American challenge. It did take some positive steps, in 1857 founding the Nagasaki Medical Academy (Igaku Denshū Jo) and a military college in the town of Numazu. The same year it undertook to upgrade the Bansho Shirabesho and gave it a more appropriate name, the Institute of Western Studies (Yōgaku Jo). A year later the Edo regime officially recognized the superiority of Western medicine over its Asian competitors. It also ordered shogunal retainers Matsumoto Ryōjun and Ono Tomogorō to study European medicine and mathematics in Nagasaki with the young Dutch surgeon Pompe van Meerdervoort.[177] In 1860 Edo sent official missions to Europe and North America, partly to collect Western technical information.[178]

But in other respects the shogunate's response was half-hearted. As late as March 1857, two high officials, Kawaji Toshiakira and Mizuno

Tadanori, could issue an edict against the teaching of physics at the Institute of Western Studies, saying:

> It is perfectly appropriate to deal with matters of a military nature in lectures at the [Western Studies] Institute. But whether works on science should also be presented is quite another matter. Those captivated by outlandish theories come inevitably to resemble the Europeans and Americans in the way they look at the world. Such things also lead to unorthodox views. There seems to be some element in physics [*kyūrigaku*] which inevitably gives rise to unorthodox views. We are concerned that the study of science . . . will destroy the relations—between lords and retainers or fathers and sons—which have existed in Japan for so long. Consequently, ordinary lectures [at the Institute of Western Studies] should deal only with military books.[179]

Whatever elicited these particular remarks, they probably drew on two distinct sources. Torii Yōzō was certainly one, because he was serving at the time as adviser to Mizuno. His wife belonged to the Hayashi family, which directed the Shōheikō Academy. And Torii's own views about European studies were clear cut and thoroughly hostile.[180] The other resource for the edict's point of view may well have been an official newsletter.[181] The *Oranda Fūsetsugaki* was regularly prepared for shogunal officials by Dutch representatives employed at Nagasaki to inform the Japanese about developments in Europe. There is no direct proof that it provoked Kawaji and Mizuno's statement, but the circumstances are suggestive. European thinkers had long contended that the atomistic concept of the physical universe developed by Newton should serve as a model for human society. Whatever the merits of this notion, it was highly obnoxious to traditional conservatives who opposed its espousal of individualism.[182] If European conservatives with a legacy of feudalism could find this offensive and a threat to society, it is hardly surprising that a feudal regime in Tokugawa Japan should draw a similar conclusion.

Only in the very last years of the Tokugawa shogunate was the government's policy toward European science unswervingly favorable. Eight shogunal delegations traveled abroad between 1860 and 1867, and they brought back two hundred books to Japan. In 1862 the first Japanese was sent to Europe for formal technical study. Akamatsu Daizaburō, an officer in the shogunate's new navy, enrolled at Leiden in mathematics and engineering. In 1864 Chōshū sent Inoue Masaru to the University of London, also for engineering studies.[183] But there were limits to change under Tokugawa feudalism: in 1863 several Chōshū samurai had to sneak out of the country for studies overseas,[184] while under the Restoration government of 1868, Inoue could help build the country's first railway.

Scholarly Conduct in Tokugawa Japan

The suspicion and paranoia reflected by Tokugawa policies had many ramifications in the scholarly world. With the shogunate's efforts to freeze society, occupational recruitment came to be based largely on inherited position. Although this may not have mattered so much for farmers, in technical professions like medicine or astronomy it posed problems. The oldest son of a particular family might not be suited to continue the specialty. Of course, adoption of a talented outsider was one solution. The Shibukawa family of shogunal astronomers followed this strategy, and so on occasion did others.[185] Even so, professional recruitment in Tokugawa Japan was hardly open in any modern sense. About 1770 the eminent samurai mathematician Fujita Sadasuke rejected the talented Aida Yasuaki as a pupil in his mathematics school in part because of his lower-class origins,[186] and such occurrences were probably common.[187]

Tokugawa policies caused other kinds of problems, too. By adopting Chu Hsi's intellectually imposing neo-Confucian synthesis of the twelfth century as the official ideology of state, the regime signaled its encouragement of ideas and attitudes that looked on the major questions of politics and nature as already answered and exempt from revision. "All that was worth inventing had been invented by the [Chinese] Sage Emperors; all that was worth knowing had been known by Confucius. The task of later generations was simply to absorb this body of knowledge."[188] Such a philosophy could not fail to affect definitions of scholarship and scholarly conduct as well. According to the ideology, scholars were "retailers of packaged knowledge," not innovative "participants in a developing branch of inquiry."[189] They worked with a finished product and were expected to transmit it to students unchanged.

Another policy intensified the effects of this conservative philosophy. The Tokugawa shogunate, in reaction to the conflicts that had preceded its accession, set the highest value on personal loyalties, and this emphasis affected the scholarly world no less than it did the rest of society. Students were admonished to be loyal to their teachers. In part this meant a high degree of formal deference, but at its most intense, it could include intellectual subservience.[190] "It was a basic principle of [Tokugawa] morality," according to the Meiji microbiologist Kitasato Shibasaburō, "that students always took their own status into account and did not oppose their teachers, whatever they did."[191] Formal practices exemplified this loyalty. Upon hearing a lecture or reading a text, students were supposed to be attentive and hold back their questions.[192] Students' curiosity and personal discoveries were of little importance. Consideration of different interpretations of particular texts was seldom allowed or expected. Bonds of loyalty between teacher and student were usually considered to be permanent and static, so much so that in some specialties, a student was not supposed to change teachers under any circumstances. Those who did so were severely condemned.[193]

These bonds of loyalty had important implications for the dynamics of particular groups. Certainly teachers were supposed to show benevolence toward pupils and offer their advice at critical moments, but they also insisted on receiving the deference that custom and ideology held to be theirs.[194] If anything, the political marginality and general poverty to which Tokugawa policies confined most scholars made them particularly insistent on respect from their students.[195] Personal ties in scholarly groups affected students' relations with men of learning by promoting extreme solidarity. Collective orientations and exclusivity in scholarship grew out of the "feudal tradition of . . . loyalty toward [the] master."[196]

One would like to suppose that the stultifying tendencies of Tokugawa social norms were confined to the mainstream system of Confucian studies or most of the various martial-arts fields, and such patterns were strongest in fields where feudal loyalties were most vigorously and consistently articulated. But they were prevalent in the scholarly world. R. P. Dore argues that the Confucian rejection of intellectual curiosity seriously stifled independent inquiry in anatomy before the mid-eighteenth century.[197] Mathematicians developed into sectarians, which greatly affected their discipline. "The members of the Saijo school [of mathematics]," wrote one historian, "had a strong group identification and looked upon [their mentor] Aida Yasuaki as more or less the founder of a religion."[198] The historian of Japanese culture and science Yoshida Mitsukuni stresses the influence of Confucianism on every field of scholarly endeavor.[199]

But the least "modern" aspect of Tokugawa science, which was its strong propensity toward secrecy, had only tenuous connections with Confucian aspirations and ideals. For one thing, secrecy antedated the seventeenth century, when Confucianism became a powerful influence. Much medical knowledge was being transmitted secretly in the sixteenth century, and so was information in astronomy.[200] Medical documents were still being "handed down privately from master to disciple" even in the seventeenth century.[201] Secrecy was so entrenched in mathematics that it persisted well into the nineteenth century. Knowledge—especially of ethics, ultimately of other things—in classical Confucianism was supposed to be objective and accessible to all.[202] Secrecy was probably connected with Confucianism because of the system's stress on personal loyalty. Considering the role of the teacher in transmitting knowledge and the attachment of pupils to their various teachers, it is not unlikely that the emphasis on loyalty had the effect of intensifying secrecy.

Secrecy was widespread in Tokugawa scholarship, including the technical fields. Shizuki Tadao's important late eighteenth-century work on Newtonian mechanics was never published, only privately circulated in manuscript.[203] There was no publication at all in the physical sciences until 1827, when the physician Aochi Rinsō published *Kikai kanran*.[204] Even in the 1830s, the astronomy student Koide Shūki could obtain access to information he needed only by enrolling in an academy and waiting eight years.[205] Nor were the physical sciences particularly unusual: the mathematician Yamazaki Yasunari was denied access to an important mathematical technique in the eighteenth century by the head of a school in Kanazawa.[206] Seki Takakazu's major discoveries were kept secret by a few disciples as long as their master was alive, and even after he died in 1708 publication was spotty and haphazard.[207]

By the mid-eighteenth century this extreme solidarity and its pattern of secrecy had only one exception: medicine. Beginning with the publication of *Zōshi* (On the viscera) by Yamawaki Tōyō in 1759 and the nearly simultaneous publication of *Idan* (Perspectives on medicine) by Yoshimasu Tōdō, medicine not only abandoned secrecy, it began openly to debate technical subjects in books. Yamawaki's work was a major contribution to Japanese anatomy based on a dissection in 1754 and aroused considerable interest from medical colleagues. It was also extremely controversial. Medical opinion had emphasized the functions of organs as the basis for treatment, viewing the observation of dead organs as entirely useless. Battle was joined when a professional rival developed this argument in a major refutation (Hi *Zōshi* [Against *Zōshi*]), published in 1760. Yoshimasu Tōdō's work was also controversial. Its central argument that all illness is due to a single toxic principle was not so well grounded in empirical research, and criticisms by his peers were intense. Hata Kōzan published a chapter-by-chapter refutation in 1762 called *Seki* Idan, (Against *Idan*), and other physicians had their say as well. Whatever the merits of either side in the matter, the debate clearly stimulated medical thought.[208]

Tokugawa medicine's pioneering role in abandoning secrecy and promoting publication requires some brief explanation. In the history of

European scholarship, after all, medicine, as the "elder sister of the sciences," has usually been seen as extremely conservative and strongly attached to "medieval traditions."[209] That Tokugawa medicine played a different role was due in some measure to the strength of competition. Doctors were not so close to the centers of power as mathematical astronomers or scholars of Confucianism. Because of their place in the private sector they were relatively free of official restraints on new ideas and procedures. They were also more numerous than other kinds of specialists. Nearly all samurai had access to doctors, and many villages, too, had some kind of physician. Other things being equal, this implied competition for preferment and professional recognition. Moreover, the medical world was geographically scattered and culturally diverse. The Taki family of shogunal physicians did try to centralize the medical community, but they ultimately failed. Doctors could and did move around; other "professionals" could not, at least not so easily. And unlike mathematics, medicine had no guilds to restrict competition or restrain new ideas.[210]

Another reason that medicine took the lead in developing new ideas and techniques of diffusion was its role in the history of Japanese printing. Printing began early (eighth century A.D.) in Japan, but for centuries it was confined almost entirely to Buddhist religious uses. Late in the period of unrestrained Western contacts (1542–1616), however, it began to be used for more secular purposes. As literacy spread through the influence of Confucianism, demand for materials to read increased (this was especially true in the seventeenth century). Publishing and printing became commercial operations, and many of the earliest printers were physicians. Ose Hoan (1564–1640), Isokawa Ryōan (1579–1666), and Manase Gensaku (1549–1631), three of the earliest Tokugawa printers, were all wealthy—and also physicians. Their publishing activities (and those of later printers) undoubtedly reflected their personal interests, but the printing of books was a way to make money, too. Given the relative independence of doctors in Tokugawa culture and their financial ability to carry on businesses, their role in early secular printing is not so surprising.[211]

The development in printing shows the society's capacity to generate trends congenial to science. Although secrecy was widespread, *some* information was shared. Among Confucian scholars, for example, it was considered bad manners to refuse to lend a book to a colleague.[212] Factional solidarity was not equally intense in every field of study. At least some circles tried objectively to assess the merits of students. And one should not overlook the increasing availability and variety of schooling. The influential Meiji chemist Sakurai Jōji, writing in 1910 of Tokugawa developments, argued that their most important contribution to modern Japanese science derived from education and its patronage by officials.[213]

The deeply rooted factionalism of Tokugawa society helped to generate competition. We have already considered medicine, where the works of Yamawaki Tōyō and Yoshimasu Tōdō inspired lively debate. Vigorous public discussion of professional issues, some of it clearly traceable to factional loyalties and cliques, existed in other fields, too. Mathematics, divided as it was into nineteen different "schools," is good evidence for this pattern. One competitive practice in Tokugawa mathematics was the posting in public of *idai*. These were problems that the challenger had solved and was challenging other mathematicians to solve. Though hardly akin to the best modern practice, the posting of *idai* stimulated mathematical thought and competition among various schools.[214]

A late eighteenth-century incident shows how intense mathematical competition could be. After the samurai mathematician Fujita Sadasuke rejected the commoner Aida Yasuaki as a pupil, Aida not only founded his own Saijo school but vigorously attacked Fujita and the parent Seki school. In 1784 Aida claimed that the Seki school had tried to monopolize mathematics and had done considerable harm by neglecting applications. His attacks were published and aroused great interest. In 1799 Fujita's pupil, Kamiya Sadaharu, lashed out at Aida in print for demeaning his teacher and harming mathematics. "[Aida] is bigoted, has little knowledge, and does not understand . . . the principles of mathematics." For emphasis he added that Aida was guilty of superstition and of "making a good technique into a bad one." Aida himself was wholly unrepentant when he finally replied in 1801. "As if in a war, they boasted of . . . killing my followers, but all they did was give us a nosebleed. I can boast of beheading their chief!"[215]

One does not find such open, public conflict in any of the physical sciences. On the contrary, the close relationship between Inō Tadataka and his teacher Takahashi Yoshitoki exemplified the dominant pattern. Takahashi taught Inō astronomy and advanced mathematics and continued to advise him throughout his career; his son was a member of Inō's survey party. Inō expressed the desire in his will to be buried by the side of his teacher.[216] But intellectual differences were by no means always suppressed. One can find cases like that of Koide Shūki (1797–1865) and Shibukawa Kagesuke (in astronomy), where strong commitments to use of empirical evidence stimulated competition between teacher and pupil and led to improvements in the shogunate's calendar. But it is true that their differences remained strictly confidential and never became known outside the government.[217] If anything, the physical sciences suffered less from suppression of differing views and more from lack of scrutiny by peers. The work of Shizuki Tadao on Newtonian mechanics, for example, "may have represented the early stages of an important new natural philosophy," but in the absence of a "mature support group," it did not become a new scholarly tradition.[218]

Assessment of merit in students or others is a critical factor in the progress of science, and here no clear trends existed. Some scholars tried to be fair in evaluating students. Many domain schools regularly seated students according to achievement, not status, and the number that did this increased over time.[219] Emphasis on merit was a well-established theme in the Confucian tradition. Still, Fujita Sadasuke apparently did reject the otherwise qualified Aida Yasuaki as a student of mathematics partly because of his lower-class origins, and this incident was probably far from unique. But the major problem with merit in professional recruitment was the society. Tokugawa Japan had a powerful inclination to allocate all roles by ascription, and those who controlled the highest positions were rarely inclined to disregard rank.[220] Thus when Asada Gōryū nominated his two best students for official posts in the Bureau of Astronomy (late 1790s), the outcome was wholly predictable. The shogunate would give an official position only to the one (Takahashi Yoshitoki) with samurai status. The equally qualified commoner, Hazama Shigetomi, had to settle for a lowly assistantship.[221]

Conditions affecting deployment of talent did improve over time, especially after Perry's visit. It became possible to buy samurai status, and there was some relaxation of distinctions by class.[222] Society in this era was very far from stable, and many forces were stimulating new attitudes and values. There were plenty of men committed to changes, "despite the efforts of . . . Tokugawa educators."[223] Certainly one sees this in the scientific community. Long-term loyalty to teachers began to wane, at least in medicine, where the striking publications of the mid-eighteenth century had already shaken the profession to the roots. Both lively debates on medical topics and a tendency to "shop around" for teachers became normal. Ōmura Masujirō moved around extensively in his medical studies, and so did Takano Chōei, dumping at least one teacher he considered inadequate.[224] And when one considers the case of Koide Shūki, who began studying astronomy with Tsuchimikado Yasukuni and later switched to Shibukawa Kagesuke, it is evident that attitudes were changing in other fields, too.[225]

Even group solidarity and the sharing of scholarly information began to change in the late Tokugawa. Mathematics had been the most factionalized of disciplines—and remained so—but even here efforts were made to change. In 1830 Hasegawa Kan published a readable textbook of *wasan* mathematics that thoroughly explained its techniques. He was, predictably, ostracized by other mathematicians, but their hostile response did not end such attempts. A mathematician named Akita Giichi wrote a textbook for local officials in 1837 which is notable for its stress on applications. The book emphasized such mainstays of political economy as the calculation of taxes, construction of buildings, and measurement of fields. The author apparently intended the book as a response to the Tempō famine that year, but colleagues attacked him for "disclosure of secrets," showing just how long a way mathematics had to go.[226]

CHAPTER THREE

FORMATION OF THE MEIJI
SCIENTIFIC COMMUNITY

"Japan," wrote J. M. Cattell and Dean Brimhall about 1920, "had no distinguished scientific men a generation ago . . . but it may be that in a few years its contributions to science will rival ours."[1] This remark by the compilers of *American Men of Science* is not an accurate assessment of Japanese science in the interwar period, but it does underscore the importance of recruitment into science. Technology, ideas, organization, and values all contribute to the scientific enterprise, but the scientific community is the engine of progress. For this reason the Marquis de Condorcet once cited the "number of men acquainted with science's leading and most important truths" as the essential indicator of national progress, while the sociologist of science Jean Dessau lists recruitment, training, and maintenance of scientists first among requirements for the "implantation of science" in countries, like Meiji Japan, that have no tradition of research.[2]

Specialists on the subject of recruitment disagree broadly on two basic points. Where were the scientists of Meiji Japan recruited? Did they come from traditional elites, long engaged in intellectual pursuits?[3] Were they products of a wholly new class?[4] Role formation is also fundamental to community building in science. "The social role of the scientist . . . and the organizational surroundings of his work in Japan," wrote Joseph Ben-David in 1970, "[were variations of] social forms originating in Western Europe. They were [not modifications of] the traditional pattern of intellectual work that existed there before the adoption of Western science."[5] Some Japanese who were active at the time would certainly have agreed with this view. According to education ministry official Koba Sadatake, speaking to a Diet committee in 1893: "The scientists Japan had at the time of the Restoration were capable only of transcribing foreign books and could not really perform like scholars in the truest sense."[6] Others, however, had a different opinion. "The scientific or scholarly progress that occurred in the time of the shogunate," stated the minister of education on this occasion, "has had a cumulative effect [on science's modern progress]."[7] In fact, the role of scientists in Meiji Japan was partly an extension of their Tokugawa role.

We have to consider the status of scientists in both periods, as well as any contributions to modern Meiji science made by Tokugawa scientific studies. We have seen that by 1800 medicine, dominated by commoners, held a moderately high-level status well surpassing mathematics but inferior to physical science, where samurai were predominant. To be sure, Fukuzawa Yukichi criticized one component of traditional science—*kampō* medicine—as "old moldy theories."[8] Historians of science like Sugimoto and Swain argue that *kampō* medicine imposed an "uphill struggle on modern Western medicine,"[9] and another historian thinks that neither Dutch studies nor the traditional Japanese sciences provided the basis for Meiji science's great successes.[10] But other scholars think otherwise. Nakayama Shigeru writes that Tokugawa doctors "brought modern . . . science to Japan."[11] Tominari Kimahei argues that the researches of the *Rangaku* (Dutch studies) scholars "justify their being recognized as the forerunners of Meiji science."[12]

Whether Tokugawa medicine should be described as "old moldy theories," or whether *Rangaku* laid the intellectual foundation for Meiji science is of little concern here, for neither Tokugawa medicine nor *Rangaku* was compatible with the Western scientific tradition. Neither was consistently—or at all—dedicated to the goals of Western science, nor did either anticipate full-scale efforts to expand human knowledge of nature. But the *latent* effect of Tokugawa traditions was substantial and positive. The kinds of people who went into science had been pinpointed, their choices of fields to some extent predetermined. And the Tokugawa legacy influenced the success of efforts to establish a Western-style researcher role.

Studies of recruitment to science in Meiji Japan face serious methodological problems. One study was neither comprehensive nor in any sense typical,[13] another restricted to academic scientists.[14] And there is very little point to a comprehensive study of everyone who received an undergraduate degree. (About 7,800 such degrees were awarded in technical fields between 1877 and 1921.) Such a study would identify the recruitment base for science but would not in itself be entirely germane, since few such graduates took jobs in research.[15] Even looking at everyone who contributed to the scientific literature would not be ideal. Such a search would be costly, difficult, and unpersuasive since many works were not reviewed by peers. We cannot impose a definition of "scientist" on a society where the role was unformed. Japanese society had not fully established the scientific role as that role had developed in Europe. Knowledgeable observers at the time commented on and commended central differences from Western practice as appropriate to the needs of society.

Hakushi, or holder of the doctor's degree, is the definition for scientist used in this book. The degree was invented by Mori Arinori, minister of education in the late 1880s.[16] It included most learned fields then recognized in continental Europe: law and letters (which I ignore), medicine, science, agriculture, engineering, forestry, and veterinary medicine.[17] But the system introduced by Mori lacked explicit precedent and cannot easily be linked to a single country's practice.[18] Thus, the meaning of some categories is probably self-evident, but others are ambiguous. "Science" (*rigaku*) included mathematics, physics, astronomy, botany, zoology, geology, chemistry, and physical anthropology. But exclusivity of labels was not a feature of the system, nor were boundaries sharply defined. Several different doctoral degrees were awarded to chemists, and physicists, among others, could qualify for two (science and engineering).

Degrees were supposed to be conferred for significant contributions certified by peers. The term *hakushi* approximates the concept of "scientist" operative among government officials and the public. There was increasing reliance on the doctorate in science as a criterion for appointments at the rank of full professor.[19] The German-style trend toward formal dissertations under academic auspices mitigates the problem of setting standards. But readers are cautioned that my definition has problems. Favoritism and clique affiliations were factors in some conferrals. One pathologist has suggested that degrees were sometimes awarded for work never done.[20] And my choice of definition excludes some people who published their papers before 1910 or held probationary posts in the imperial universities.

Medicine was the dominant element in Japanese scientific or technical studies. Among the 1,360 holders of the *hakushi* degree awarded between 1888 (when conferrals began) and 1920 (when the system was changed), 656 men (48 percent) did their work in medicine, 366 (27 percent) in engineering, 138 (10 percent) in agriculture or forestry, and 200 (15 percent) in all other fields (see table 3.1).[21] The small numbers awarded in physics (54) and mathematics (22) are particularly significant. In fact, the small number even of *undergraduate* degrees (about 452 in physics and 125 in mathematics for all of the imperial universities combined) further underscores the neglect of these fields.[22]

These numbers show the strength of the Tokugawa legacy. The testimony of Meiji and later commentators, as well as the body of literary evidence, not only singles out medicine as the principal field but

TABLE 3.1
Japanese Doctorates in Technical Fields, 1888–1920

SPECIALTY	NUMBER	SPECIALTY	NUMBER
Chemistry (D.Sc.)	27	Agriculture	108
Physics	54	Forestry	30
Biology	56	Engineering	366
Mathematics	22	Medicine	656
Geology	18	Veterinary medicine	23

Sources: Iseki Kurō, ed., *Dai Nihon hakushi roku,* 5 vols. (1921–30); *Jinji kōshin roku,* 1903–37 eds.; Tsunesaburō Kamesaka, ed., *Who's Who in Japan,* 1914–37 eds.

links its development to the Tokugawa past.[23] As we have seen, Tokugawa doctors had no guild structure to impose uniformity or suppress competition, were mobile geographically and socially, were usually free from official interference, and often had money to live in some comfort. Conversely, that small numbers entered the physical sciences was partly a function of historical obstacles—restrictions on information, poor job opportunities, few schools (and those latecomers), and suspicion of contamination by Christianity.

Whether the smallness of the number of Japanese who entered mathematics after 1868 was also the result of Tokugawa conditions is an interesting question. Certainly Tokugawa developments had not been favorable to the growth of modern mathematics. *Wasan* mathematicians were competitive, interested in publication, and even on occasion inventive, but the details of their work were usually concealed. Devotees tended to disdain applications. The subject was introduced late to the schools, and many of the samurai hated mathematics. However, even samurai interest in *Western* mathematics in the Bakumatsu (1853–67) years failed to yield major results before 1921, so factors other than tradition must have been at work. The principal difficulty was the narrow range of occupational choice available to Meiji mathematicians. They either taught their subject, worked in the government, or went into another field.[24]

Recruitment to Science in Meiji Japan

The predominance of samurai after 1868 was one of the ways Tokugawa developments affected mathematics and other technical fields. Though medicine and the physical sciences had been dominated by commoners in the seventeenth and early eighteenth centuries, the influx of samurai after 1775 set the stage for a new situation. More experiments were carried out. European books became more common. Domain and shogunal schools showed more interest in the sciences and after the Opium War taught them more often. Samurai remained dominant in the scientific movement throughout the Bakumatsu and Meiji eras. About 72 percent of D.Sc. recipients in basic chemistry between 1888 and 1921 came from samurai families. In physics they accounted for 66 percent, in engineering for 64 percent, in mathematics and geology for 50 percent, and even in medicine for 43 percent of doctorates. Overall, 53 percent of the scientists active before 1921 were samurai (see table 3.2).

Categorizing scientists by region shows that samurai status was not decisive for recruitment into science, though several regions with high proportions of them did compile good records. Tokyo, with somewhere between 3.4 (1869) and 2.8 (1889) percent of total population, produced 146 scientists or 11.4 percent. Four (4.0) percent came from Yamaguchi-Chōshū, with its 1.9 to 2.3 percent of total population, while Fukuoka prefecture (1.3 to 3.0 percent of total population) produced 3.2 percent of the scientists. These areas all had samurai populations above the average for 1889 (5.0 percent). In Tokyo, samurai were reported as 10.0 percent of population, in Yamaguchi as 7.6 percent, and in Fukuoka, 6.5 percent.[25]

But Osaka and Kagoshima-Satsuma do not fit this pattern. Though its samurai were just 1.4 percent of the population in 1889, the percentage of scientists from Osaka was exactly proportional to its percentage of the national (3.0 percent; 41 scientists) population. Kagoshima-Satsuma, with a 24 percent samurai population, was a conspicuous underproducer. Satsuma had 3.4 percent of total population in 1869 (2.5 percent in 1889) and produced just 19 scientists, which was 1.4 percent of the total.

Local education was as important for the recruitment of scientists in Meiji Japan as the number of samurai. The country's four largest cities yielded many scientists, undoubtedly because of their academies and schools. Tokyo and Osaka, of course, did well, and so did the city of Kyoto. With 1.7 (1869) to 2.2 (1889) percent of total population, it produced 3.3 percent of all scientists. And Aichi prefecture (Nagoya) with 2.9 to 3.6 percent of Japan's population, produced 4.6 percent of the scientists. Only the strength of local education could explain the record of Fukui. This region was one of the most remote in the country, had no large city or even a small one, and its samurai were only 4.0 percent of population. But in 1857 Fukui carried out a sweeping reform

TABLE 3.2
Class Origins of Doctorate Recipients, 1888–1920

SPECIALTY	SAMURAI N %	COMMONERS N %	SPECIALTY	SAMURAI N %	COMMONERS N %
Chemistry (D.Sc.)	19 72	8 28	Agriculture	60 55	48 45
Physics	36 66	18 34	Forestry	19 62	11 38
Biology	34 60	22 40	Engineering	232 64	134 36
Mathematics	11 50	11 50	Medicine	281 43	375 57
Geology	9 50	9 50	Veterinary medicine	15 65	8 35

Sources: Iseki Kurō, ed., *Dai Nihon hakushi roku*, 5 vols. (1921–30); *Jinji kōshin roku*, 1903–37 eds.; Tsunesaburō Kamesaka, ed., *Who's Who in Japan*, 1914–37 eds.

of its educational system that led to great changes. All Fukui officials were required to prove their attainments in formal education before assuming any office, and one of the first foreigners to teach science in Japan, W. E. Griffis, came to Fukui in 1870.[26] The results were impressive. With only 1.0 percent of total population in 1869 and 1.5 percent in 1889, Fukui between 1888 and 1920 produced 43 scientists, 3.2 percent of the total. Fukui had more scientists per capita than anywhere else in Japan—one scientist for every 6,784 residents. The rate for Osaka, an average region, was 1:18,750, and second-place Tokyo's was 1:6,849.

Kagoshima-Satsuma made a very poor showing, though several of its daimyo had an interest in science. Shimazu Nariakira, who ruled the area in the 1850s, was acquainted with Philip Franz von Siebold and Udagawa Yōan. Shimazu read scientific works in Japanese translations. He sponsored the translation of Pompe van Meerdervoort's treatise on vaccination and established a translation agency (1855). In 1856 he created a scholarship fund for Satsuma youth who wished to study outside their region, and in 1864 his successor established a full-fledged Western academy. But there was less to this than might appear. Satsuma suffered greatly from a rebellion against Tokyo (1876–77), industrial development mostly passed the region by, and it lagged behind in creating modern schools. Although 40 percent of Japanese adults had elementary literacy by 1868, most Satsuma adults could not read or write even in 1884. If this were not enough, formal education for samurai in Satsuma did not encourage science.

Consider the anti-intellectualism and controls on free time imposed by an institution called *gōjū*. *Gōjū* were neighborhood confraternities of samurai youth six years of age and above common throughout many parts of the country and usually dedicated to academic work and military training. But the *gōjū* of Satsuma had a different program. Formal education was not much emphasized. Unlike the rules of other domain *gōjū*, those of Satsuma ignored all book learning. They instead encouraged their members to excel in martial arts, morality, recreation, and obedience. Samurai youth could not escape the system by retreating to their homes because *gōjū* activities had penetrated the home.[27] Their freedom was restricted, and personal autonomy, including time for activities and interests apart from the peer group, is an important element in socializing youth who later enter science.[28] The Satsuma system did not provide this freedom—or many scientists. The pattern was noted at the time. As Takagi Kanehiro told another leading figure in the medical community, "Since the Restoration, we Satsuma men have been prominent in the Army and government. But our record has not matched that of other domains in the scholarly or learned professions."[29]

Tokugawa education's contribution to the modern research tradition can also be seen from the scientists' fathers' occupations. A large percentage (certainly over half) of Meiji scientists had fathers in traditional intellectual roles. *Kampō* physicians formed the largest single group (perhaps 46 percent) with Confucian scholars (*jusha*) in second place (7 percent). A few sons of *wasan* mathematicians and of *Rangaku* scholars became scientists. Most doctors' sons went, predictably, into medicine, but they also turned up in physics, chemistry, biology, forestry, and engineering. Confucian scholars' sons were most numerous in engineering but also studied medicine, geology, and forestry. *Rangaku* scholars' sons chose mathematics, zoology, and medicine in particular, while one son of a *wasan* mathematician became professor of mining and metallurgy at Tokyo University.

Sons of officials were numerically second to the sons of *kampō* physicians. About 21 percent of scientists came from the families of Tokugawa or Meiji bureaucrats. They were relatively scarce in the large medical community (about 9 percent) but in other categories ranged from 14 (agriculture) to 40 percent (engineering and basic science). Officials' sons entered every field, but they were especially active in physics. About 40 percent of the physicists had fathers in official positions; the rest came from doctors' families and various other backgrounds.

Tokugawa traditions aided formation of the entire modern scientific community, but they certainly did not affect every field equally. Medicine received considerable stimulus. There were important linkages in biology and chemistry. Mathematics received at least some benefits; physics derived rather few. Individual cases of recruitment to science help to shed light on the situation.

The first to consider are three recruits into medicine. Neither Kitasato Shibasaburō, Takagi Kanehiro, nor Noguchi Hideyo was the son of a *kampō* or Western-style doctor. Each came to the field through personal contacts. Three physicians influenced Kitasato: his great-uncle, Hashimoto Ryu'un, a teacher named Tanaka Shiba, and a Dutch navy doctor, C. G. von Mansveldt. Kitasato, who was born in 1852, lived with Hashimoto and studied with Tanaka. In 1871 he entered Lord Hosokawa's Kumamoto Medical Academy (Igakkō) where he spent about three years with Mansveldt. Mansveldt's influence was greatest, as Kitasato was not close to Hashimoto personally and ignored admonitions from Tanaka to study. Mansveldt made him an Igakkō assistant and took pains to teach him German. The Dutchman also taught him medicine and introduced him to studies of bacteria through microscopy. He told Kitasato to study at Tokyo University and then go to Germany.[30]

How Kitasato came to study with Mansveldt is not at all clear. His early interests were in soldiering and martial arts; he was initially uninterested in book learning, and his parents had hoped he would farm. Moreover, the young Kitasato could not be easily disciplined and was not very close to his parents.[31] His enrollment at the Igakkō was probably the result of contradictory conditions. A friend dissuaded him from a military career. His parents encouraged his ambitions, and he apparently came to view *Rangaku* as the "basis of European culture."[32] Local choices for formal education were limited to two schools, the Igakkō and the Yōgakkō, whose images differed greatly. Kumamoto residents considered the Yōgakkō avant-garde, even radical. Its curriculum—physics, history, English, and the rest—was quite out of the ordinary, whereas the Igakkō's was more familiar. The two student bodies also differed. Yōgakkō students were mostly young teenagers facing obligatory lectures on Confucian morality, an antidote to Westernization.[33] Igakkō students were older (from eighteen to twenty-four years of age) and had the choice of skipping these lectures.[34] One cannot know particular reasons for Kitasato's choice, but a number of factors were operating. He was already eighteen when the two schools opened. He had always disliked Confucianism, and he had already had exposure to medicine. The Igakkō offered more advanced training and an easier adjustment to the future.

Considerations of status, worldly ambitions, and *Rangaku* contacts were important to Takagi Kanehiro (1848–1920). Takagi was the son of a low-ranking Satsuma samurai who also worked as a carpenter. He reportedly decided on a medical career as early as the age of thirteen. A local physician aroused his interest in part because of his high status. Commoners, before the Restoration, could not wear white *tabi* (socks), but the doctor was among those who could. Takagi's parents were impressed by this fact and commended the man to their son. Another physician was also influential. Ishigami Ryōsaku had studied with Ogata Kōan in Osaka and became a mentor to Takagi. Ishigami taught him medicine, arranged his marriage to another doctor's daughter, and got him a job in a government bureau.[35]

Noguchi Hideyo's was a different sort of case. He came from the peasantry instead of the samurai, and his contacts were wholly with medicine from the West. Noguchi would certainly have gone into farming had a childhood accident not made this impossible. In 1878, at the age of two, he severely burned his left arm in the family's hearth. Several years later the principal of his school sent him for treatment to a doctor in Wakamatsu. The doctor had credentials that impressed young Noguchi. Watanabe Kanae had taken his M.D. at the University of California. He had also traveled extensively in Europe and owned many books on medicine and science. Noguchi spent two weeks at his house and decided to go into medicine.[36]

Modern Japanese biology was significantly influenced by Tokugawa developments. The largest single group of biologists came from the families of government officials, but about 40 percent came from *kampō* medical families. Moreover, 20 percent of the biologists (12 of 57) came from just one area—Aichi-Shizuoka, the former Owari province. The advances made by the men from Owari could have been predicted. The intellectually tolerant Asai family had dominated local medicine from the late eighteenth century. The local Shohyaku society encouraged scholarship in botany from the early 1820s. And Owari was one of the first areas in Japan to obtain the Linnaean system.

These advantages help to explain why Itō Keisuke became a biologist. Itō was born in 1803 to a prominent Nagoya medical family. His father, commended by the daimyo for his medical work, was a scholarly man with an interest in botany, and Keisuke's older brother, who later became head of the domain's medical academy, also dabbled in botany. Itō's exposure to medicine and botany was all-pervasive. From 1810 to 1815 he studied with his father. In 1815 he began Chinese and Western-style medical studies in earnest and later studied botany with Mizutani Toyobumi. Subsequent studies and research took him from one end of Japan to the other, including some months' study in Kyoto and Nagasaki (1827–28). The high point of his early education was his association with Siebold. Itō originally met the German physician at Nagoya in April 1826 with his father and brother. Two years later Siebold gave him a comprehensive explanation of Linnaeus' classification, and much later, in 1861, they resumed their discussions.[37]

Itō was far from typical, as contemporary evaluations show clearly. From 1828 to 1861 he practiced medicine and carried out and published botanical studies. In 1861 he became lecturer at the Bansho Shirabesho in Edo. In 1870 he was named consultant in biology to what became the Ministry of Education and in 1881 became professor of botany at Tokyo University. But Itō never attended a university or went abroad and became professor at 78 years of age! On the other hand he published many important works, helped found the Tokyo Academy of Sciences, and was awarded the Silver Medal of the Royal Swedish Academy. A career like Itō's, mixing traditional and modern roles, evoked varying evaluations from peers. An influential group of scientists, including the mathematician Kikuchi Dairoku and the chemist Nagai Nagayoshi, successfully blocked an important academic award to

Itō on the grounds that he was "not a real university man."[38] On the other hand, the minister of education Inoue Kowashi praised Itō publicly for his "contributions to knowledge."[39]

Itō's route into science was hardly unique, though his career was very unusual. The zoologist Ishikawa Chiyomatsu (1860–1935) came from Itō's area and was similarly encouraged by *his* father. The elder Ishikawa was an official in the Shizuoka domain with ongoing interests in science and was personally acquainted with the anatomist Sugita Gempaku (1733–1817), with Sugita Gentan, the student of electricity, and with Philip Franz von Siebold. He was an ardent bibliophile, and his hobby was natural history. The son was close to the father and shared his interests in science. From collecting and pressing leaves between the pages of books, Ishikawa Chiyomatsu progressed to butterfly collecting and to notable studies on crustaceans. After graduation from Tokyo University he studied at Berlin and Freiburg, where he worked with August Weismann.[40]

Other important biologists came to their work by much the same sort of pattern. Itō Tokutarō, who studied at Cambridge University, was the son of Itō Keisuke and became professor of biology at Tōhoku University. Mitsukuri Kakichi, founder of the Misaki Institute for Marine Biology, was the son of a doctor who taught European studies. The Tokyo University zoology professor Tsuboi Shōgorō had an even more impressive pedigree. His father was physician to the Fukui daimyo, and his grandfather was the renowned Tsuboi Shindō (1795–1848), physician, *Rangaku* scholar, and teacher of Ogata Kōan.

Generalizations about chemistry are much more difficult. The field did not have the high status in Japan that it had in Britain, France, Germany, or the United States, but the number of chemists (177) was still substantial.[41] Chemists were the third largest group of scientists, surpassed by only the medical and engineering communities, with which they overlapped. There were 54 chemists among the 366 Japanese holding engineering doctorates and 19 biochemists or medical chemists among the 656 with degrees in medicine. There were also 25 chemists from the basic science group, 48 pharmacological chemists, and 31 chemists among the 108 holders of the doctorate in agriculture (see table 3.3).

Many chemists were not from samurai or professional families, although the scarcity of data makes it difficult to tell. Samurai percentages varied from 72 percent among chemists with D.Sc. degrees to 32 percent of agricultural chemists and just over a quarter of biochemists. Physicians' sons were numerous among the basic chemists, pharmacological chemists, and biochemists. Chemists in engineering came from a cross-section of professional families—teachers, officials, military of-

TABLE 3.3
Class Origins of Chemists

CATEGORY	NUMBER	% SAMURAI	% COMMONERS
Basic chemistry	25	72	28
Pharmacology	48	42	58
Engineering	54	39	61
Agriculture	31	32	68
Medicine	19	26	74
Total	177	43	57

Sources: Iseki Kurō, ed., *Dai Nihon hakushi roku,* 5 vols. (1921–30); *Jinji koshin roku,* 1903–37 eds.; Tsunesaburō Kamesaka, ed., *Who's Who in Japan,* 1914–37 eds.

ficers, Confucian scholars—while the agricultural chemists contained a high proportion of men from farming families. Though fragmentary, the data indicate the range of recruitment motivations. Basic chemists came to the field *from* samurai families and *for* intellectual reasons. Recruits to chemistry through agriculture or engineering were probably concerned with practical problem solving in the interests of society.[42] An unspecifiable number must have been prompted by desires for higher social status.

As for individual cases, the decision of Takamine Jōkichi, discoverer of adrenalin (1900), to enter chemistry was primarily the result of encouragement from his father, a domain physician with an interest in science. The father studied Chinese and Dutch medicine with Koishi Genzui in Kyoto and later worked in Dutch studies with Tsuboi Shindō in Edo. After 1849 he carried out a number of scientific studies, manufacturing gunpowder for his domain, making nitric acid from silkworm cocoons—and gaining a reputation as a clever inventor. These activities had their impact on the son, as attested by his biographer, Takamine's involvement in the work of his father, and his later research.[43]

Paternal influence also figured in the recruitment of a number of chemists at Tokyo University. Majima Toshiyuki was the son of a samurai physician in Kyoto who had studied Dutch medicine with Ogata Kōan.[44] Shibata Yūji was the grandson of a *kampō* physician and the son of a chemist. His father served as professor of pharmacology and his brother as professor of botany, both at Tokyo University.[45] Nagai Nagayoshi's father was a Tosa domain physician who made a point of taking his son on nature walks in which he explained the medical uses of local plants. Nagai went into the subdiscipline of pharmacological chemistry, where he pursued these interests.[46] One can see still other patterns in the choices of Sakurai Jōji and Suzuki Umetarō. Sakurai became a theoretical chemist (Japan's first) only after entering the Daigaku Nankō, later part of Tokyo University. The pathology professor Miyake Shū, later dean of the medical faculty, had just returned from Europe and aroused the young man's interest in chemistry.[47] Suzuki Umetarō, who also became a professor at Tokyo, was a farmer's son who first came to study agriculture in 1893 and then chose agricultural chemistry out of a desire to "do something for agriculture."[48]

Physics had fewer ties with the cultural past than did chemistry or any other field. A number of physicists came into the discipline by accident, and relatively few had fathers in related occupations. But the field did have some links to the past. Samurai representation among chemists and medical men was only 43 percent of recruits, while among physicists it rose to 60 percent (among the earliest to well over 80). Tokyo natives were far more numerous among physicists than among chemists or other scientists. One-quarter of physicists were born in the capital, compared to 12 or 13 percent of chemists. Sons of officials made up nearly half the physicist community, compared to a quarter among chemists or scientists in general.

The gulf between physics and society could be put down to the earlier absence of a role for physicists, but the absence of a "modern" professional role was hardly confined to physics. A more plausible reason for the gap is the earlier suspicion of physics as an adjunct of Catholicism. Some Tokugawa officials linked the diffusion of physics to social unrest or political dissent and imposed restrictions on it. Access to books on physics had been limited to certain samurai officials, and information about physics could not be published or taught in schools. Predictably, since acquaintance with physics was restricted to bureaucrats, it was divorced from advanced mathematics, lacked any place in the schools or on the job, and had an exceedingly narrow base for recruitment. Most physicists came from the samurai because most Meiji officials belonged to that class. Physicists were heavily recruited from Tokyo because of its role in the political system and its high concentration of samurai families.

Yamakawa Kenjirō illustrates some of these patterns. He was born into a family of high-ranking officials and came into physics largely by accident. He received a standard Confucian education in Aizu's domain school between 1862 and 1868 and then studied privately while wandering around the country. He began studying Western subjects at the domain's academy in Tokyo and was sent abroad in 1871. (The government chose him to study abroad because he came from a very cold region and thus was thought capable of working where it wanted people, in Hokkaido.) His commitment to physics resulted from events on this trip. For example, witnessing a preannounced exchange of mail between two ships sparked his interest in geometry and physics, and he happened to read a magazine article by Herbert Spencer that stressed the importance of physics.[49]

Yamakawa found areas of agreement between his own way of thinking and Spencer's ideas. Confucianism explained the achievement of moral perfection as the result of education for particular individuals and society as a whole. Spencer argued that political improvements rest on social reforms, which depend on sociology, biology, and ultimately on physics. Yamakawa was attracted to physics because of its place among academic disciplines. As the field of learning basic to the rest, it clearly should serve as the basis of morality. By committing himself to a career in physics, Yamakawa felt he could contribute not only to science but to social morality as well.[50]

Tanakadate Aikitsu's decision to go into physics grew from a synthesis of influences. Early upbringing in the pro-Tokugawa domain of Morioka pushed him toward politics and government service, but the political alliances of the Meiji Restoration made it impossible to fulfill these ambitions. He considered engineering as a way to make a living but abandoned this plan under two teachers' influence. Tanakadate believed strongly in national service and looked for a way to combine his ideals with the prospects open to him. Physics was the solution because he thought it "basic" and "pure."[51]

From Tanakadate's earliest upbringing one could not have predicted this outcome. He was the grandson of a Shinto priest and the nephew of a Kokugaku (national learning) scholar. His father was a martial-arts teacher openly skeptical of book learning.[52] But in the large extended family where he grew up, others made a deeper impression on him, and he developed the usual samurai affection for scholarship *and* martial arts. The family's move to Tokyo in 1870 was a turning point in his life. There he read a Yamakawa essay repeating Spencer's arguments about physics, and he entered the Keio academy of the science enthusiast Fukuzawa Yukichi. Fukuzawa having taught him that education must begin with the most basic studies, and the taint of disloyalty having ruled out politics, he followed his interests in a scholarly direction. "Tanakadate," wrote one historian, "rationalized his isolation from politics and turned it in a creative direction."[53]

Nagaoka Hantarō and Honda Kōtarō came to physics by more conventional routes. They grew up in or adjacent to major urban centers (Nagasaki and Nagoya) and in their youth received Western-style training. Both attended Tokyo University and then went on to study at the University of Berlin. Beyond these similarities were a number of differences. Nagaoka's father was a well-connected official; Honda was the son of a commoner and a farmer. Nagaoka's upbringing led directly to physics; Honda's led, if anything, solely to farming. Nagaoka is best known abroad for theoretical work, Honda for experimental studies.[54]

Nagaoka was encouraged to study science at an early age by his father, who traveled to the West with the Iwakura mission (1871–72). When the father returned, he gave his son a book and an influential piece of advice. The book was the Eton and Harrow text by Balfour Stewart entitled *Physics*, and the recommendation was to study it thoroughly. Nagaoka Chisaburō explained that the early education his son had received would not be adequate in the Japan of the future and stressed the importance of scientific study. The father went on to become a leading science educator, eventually president of the Tokyo Prefectural Normal School, and wrote a well-known statement of science education policy for the Tokyo metropolitan government.[55] None of this spared Nagaoka Hantarō from a year of anxiety over physics. In 1884 he left Tokyo University for about half a year. He seems to have been troubled by the odd belief that Caucasians alone were creative in physics and only abandoned this belief after months of reading on the history of science in China.[56] His later work made him the leading physicist of the period.

Honda Kōtarō, the third son of a farmer, had a low self-image and was considered a dullard. The origin of his interest in science is unclear, but we do know that a samurai teacher encouraged his interest and gave him self-confidence. After elementary and middle school in the early 1880s, Honda followed one of his brothers to the First Higher School and Tokyo University with the declared plan of studying agriculture. But he changed his plans when he finished higher school. His brother convinced him his interests in agriculture were shallow, and his reading included an essay on physics that reflected Spencer.[57] These influences led Honda to physics and a lifetime career.

Foreign Teachers and University Training

Except for Yamakawa Kenjirō and Noguchi Hideyo, trained at Yale and Pennsylvania, respectively, the scientists discussed in the preceding section, like 70 percent of their peers, were trained at Tokyo University or one of its predecessors. This was not fortuitous, for Keio closed its medical school in 1882 and did not reopen it until 1917; the Harris School of Science at Dōshisha, opened in 1882, closed in 1892; Kyoto University produced no graduates until after 1900; and Waseda's Engineering College began only in 1907. Tokyo University's monopoly on science education was all but complete in the Meiji years. At the same time, the university had to hire foreigners since formation of an indigenous scientific community took time. Who were these foreigners, and what influence did they have?

Having foreign scientists in the universities was vital to Meiji reformism. In 1877–78 salaries paid to foreign professors were a third of the budget of Tokyo University, and during the 1880s they were usually even more.[58] Wide gaps appeared between Japanese salaries and foreigners'. Ernest Tiegel and Josef Disse, who taught physiology and pathology, were paid 350 and 380 yen per month in the early 1880s, while their successors, Ōzawa Kenji and Miura Moriharu, received just 120 and 100 yen.[59] Similarly, Edward Divers earned 650 yen per month teaching chemistry in the 1890s, while Haga Tamemasa received 105.

This did not commend instruction by foreigners to numerous perceptive critics. In July 1875 Nagayo Sensai, chief of the public health bureau, wrote the chemist Nagai Nagayoshi complaining that many people the government had hired to teach chemistry were "ignorant impostors" impeding the field.[60] Mori Rintarō, as a medical student at Berlin University, protested geologist Edmund Naumann's assertion that Japan was succeeding because of the foreigners, not by their own initiative.[61] Nakamura Yaroku, who had a degree in physics from the University of Munich, proposed in 1892 to dismiss the foreigners at Tokyo University on grounds of intellectual senescence, saying, "I have heard that the present scholarly competence of these men is about where the level of scholarship was in their own countries in 1883. Needless to say, today's science is much more advanced. So far indeed has scholarship progressed that none of these foreigners would be able to hold jobs if they should return to their homes."[62] Wakizaka Gyōzō told the Diet in 1897 that employment of foreign professors should be solely a last resort, since communities of scientific specialists were emerging in Japan.[63]

The foreigners teaching at Tokyo University were the elite of all foreign employees. The larger group of 8,000 or so foreigners employed by the government over time did include some incompetents and troublemakers, but this was not true of the university contingent. A few were cantankerous, but nearly all came from distinguished institutions and continued their careers after leaving Japan, a few to the summit. E. S. Morse, a zoologist from Bowdoin College, and T. C.

Mendenhall, a physicist from Ohio State University, both became members of the National Academy of Sciences. C. O. Whitman became professor of zoology at the University of Chicago. Josef Disse became professor of anatomy at the University of Marburg. W. E. Ayrton became professor of physics at Cambridge University. J. A. Ewing became professor of physics at the University of London. And John Milne essentially founded seismology. They were on the whole a highly competent group.[64]

Considering the haphazard methods of selection, the degree of competence was rather remarkable. By 1870 it was common for medical men to be chosen in Germany, whereas British subjects and to a lesser extent Americans reigned in physical science. Germany's Ambassador Maximilian von Brandt was an influential gatekeeper in the early 1870s, but Japanese officials stationed in Berlin took over the process in 1874. Ambassador Aoki Shūzō, a scholarly man married to a German and fluent in the language, began to consult various leading professors. In 1874 he recruited Wilhelm Schultze for anatomy and surgery, in 1876 Ernest Tiegel to teach physiology, and in 1880 Josef Disse for pathology. There were, of course, other procedures. The bureau chief Nagayo recruited F. W. Donitz in 1873 following his trip to Europe with the Iwakura mission. In 1875 Erwin von Baelz began teaching internal medicine and pathology at Tokyo University following a chance contact with a Japanese official who became his patient. And in 1876 Bernhard Gierke began lecturing in anatomy on the recommendation of Albrecht von Kolliker at Würzburg.[65]

Hiring of British and American experts worked somewhat differently. Since the 1856 Consular Act forbade U.S. diplomats to recommend Americans for jobs overseas, recruitment in the U.S. was especially chancy.[66] E. S. Morse was recruited for the zoology post at Tokyo because Toyama Shōichi, once a student at Michigan and a ranking education ministry official, had heard him lecture in Ann Arbor.[67] Mendenhall was recruited by Morse while Morse was passing through Columbus on his way to California and Japan.[68] Recruitment procedures in Britain were only slightly more structured. Hugh Matheson of the Jardine Matheson Company arranged Henry Dyer's appointment in mechanical engineering and John Milne's in geology at Itō Hirobumi's request and on the recommendation of W. J. M. Rankine at Glasgow. Chemists Edward Divers and R. W. Atkinson were recommended by Itō's friend Alexander W. Williamson, professor of chemistry at the University of London, where Itō had studied in the 1860s. And the Japanese Embassy found J. A. Ewing with the help of Williamson and his physicist friend Lord Kelvin of Glasgow University.[69]

Foreign instructors in engineering or physical science had more influence on students than medical colleagues had. Dyer, Milne, Ayrton, Mendenhall, Ewing, and Divers took pains to involve students in research projects. Mendenhall's students built their own equipment and used it to measure the sound emitted by a fired cannon, to detect and measure geomagnetic waves, and to study the forces of gravity over different latitudes and elevations.[70] Divers undertook twenty-seven different studies in organic chemistry with four different Japanese collaborators including Haga Tamemasa, Shimizu Tetsukichi, Ogawa Masataka, and Haneda Kiyohachi.[71] Ayrton was a leading student of electricity, an unabashed workaholic, an active publisher, and an inspiration to all of his students. In a practically minded academic setting he stressed theory, together with the cultivation of scientific attitudes, over memorization of facts, noting Japan's need for generalists able to solve many different problems.[72] Dyer's contribution was mostly institutional. As director of the Imperial College of Engineering (Kōbu Daigakkō), he built an innovative program modeled on that of Zurich's Polytechnic Institute. His college offered curricular depth and diversity along with three years' practical experience. Later merged with Tokyo University's engineering faculty, it graduated a number of important engineers and was imitated abroad.[73]

Milne, Morse, and Ewing were particularly influential. Milne spent almost twenty years in Japan (1876–95) and trained a substantial number of students. He stimulated their interest in earthquakes, invented several seismographs, and instigated construction of seismological stations. Morse stayed only three years, but his influence was long-lasting. He was the first active exponent of Darwin's theories in biology, and his research in Japanese anthropology gave that field a physicalist bias that it has only begun to transcend.[74] Ewing was a highly accomplished physicist and an inspiring mentor. He constructed a model based on Weber's theory of magnetism, wrote several papers on seismology, and received a medal from the Royal Society for his observation of magnetic hysteresis. His age (just twenty-five when he arrived in 1878) affected his relations with students, whom he treated like peers and strongly supported in their researches. These efforts clearly paid off. Ewing's pupils, instead of choosing careers in government or business, mainly became university professors.[75]

While physical science and engineering flourished, basic medicine faced problems. The government was primarily interested in producing medical clinicians, not basic researchers. Facilities for research were poor or nonexistent in the 1870s and early 1880s. Several of the German medical professors had difficult personalities, and most returned home as soon as they could. Theodor Hoffmann and Karl Mueller were the first to arrive and stayed only five years between them. F. W. Donitz left after two years because of a dispute with the Japanese authorities. Bernhard Gierke came to teach anatomy in 1876 but became seriously ill and died in a mental institution. Wilhelm Schultze, who taught anatomy and surgery, had come highly recommended but did little of importance. Despite his brilliant academic record and studies with Lister, his students disliked him, and he published no papers. Even the better-endowed clinical side was not exempt from such problems. A. L. Wernich, who taught internal medicine and obstetrics in 1874–76, published a number of scientific papers, but became hypercritical of the Japanese and left in a fit of pique.[76]

The negative effects on students, however, were less than one might have expected. Physiology had an excellent mentor figure in Ernest Tiegel, who stayed six years (1876–82). The paper he published with Ōzawa Kenji in 1877 on nervous systems in reptiles marked the first appearance of a Japanese investigator's work in a European medical journal.[77] Pathology had no real specialist before Josef Disse's arrival in 1880 but still developed a distinguished research tradition, and even anatomy was not much harmed by erratic leadership from the Germans. There were eight advanced anatomy students during the period of direct German tutelage; three won their doctorates and continued in research.[78]

Foreign professors' influence, then, had its limits. Foreigners often affected students' choice to study overseas but rarely the places they went. Von Baelz influenced Aoyama Tanemichi to study pathology (in Germany), and James A. Ewing induced Tanakadate Aikitsu to study physics (at Glasgow).[79] But usually the influence of foreigners was limited in this area. Japanese decisions to study medicine in Germany did not result from contacts with German professors; the German professors were invited to Japan because the government had selected German medicine as the model for Japanese medicine.[80] Students in other fields did not necessarily pursue advanced studies in the countries from which their professors had come. Mendenhall was an American, but only Yamakawa studied physics in the U.S., and that well before Mendenhall reached Japan. Shibata Yūji's chemistry professor in Tokyo was from England, but he chose to study in France and Switzerland.[81] Nagaoka Hantarō went to Vienna and Berlin to continue his research on magnetism even though the teacher who suggested this study to him and sponsored his publication on it in English had come to Japan from Great Britain.[82] In another area where influence might have occurred, there is little or no indication of it: few Japanese chose foreign scientists working in Japan for role models, nor did foreigners much influence Japanese commitments to particular lines of research.[83]

The Foreign Study Experience

Foreign study (*ryūgaku*), however, did inspire commitment to particular kinds of research. It gave Japanese scientists professional role models and values, and it affected establishment of research activities. Nevertheless, the research tradition was not merely a result of overseas study and scientists' views. The government and the public had opinions of their own, especially on the issue of overseas study. There was a compelling need to reduce Japan's backlog of knowledge. Professors were required to staff the universities. Experts were needed for factories, experiment stations, bureaus, and commissions. Technical skills were also essential for military and diplomatic reasons. There were limits to what could be done: research demanded a level of support that was not in all cases forthcoming, developmental priorities sometimes led scientists away from research, and complex, hybrid roles emerged in response to local demands. Past experience delimited how far Western values and norms were adopted. Foreign study certainly affected development of the researcher role, but so did other priorities and traditions.

Officials generally saw foreign study as a means of acquiring new knowledge. An 1872 document declared that only foreign study offered the prospect of gathering the technical expertise the country desperately needed. Inoue Kaoru, as public works minister, spoke in 1879 of foreign study as a means of "acquiring strength in various fields."[84] In 1897 Education Vice Minister Makino Nobuaki declared, "We will not go forward unless we send people to study in the advanced countries, observe things, and study the ideas of leading [foreign] scientists."[85] Putting knowledge to use was equally important. Officials put major emphasis in the 1870s and 1880s on training Japanese to replace costly foreigners, but this priority had shifted by the late 1890s. The establishment of Kyoto University in 1897 and its sister institutions at Sendai (1906), Fukuoka (1910), and Sapporo (1918) required major expansion of the university professoriat, and overseas study was the means to achieve it. In 1898 the vice minister of education cited need for professors as the main reason to increase spending on overseas study,[86] and in 1901 Education Minister Kikuchi Dairoku answered a hostile question about it by stating that almost every university professor or higher-school teacher had studied abroad.[87]

Administration of overseas study was designed to further the aim of training professors and technical experts. In 1869 the Meiji government resumed support for students sent abroad by the shogunate and quickly expanded their number. When an 1873 inspection tour by the Ministry of Education turned up widespread abuses and poorly prepared students, the students were ordered home and the rules rewritten. Even then, some compromises had to be made. For example, it was not initially possible to demand extensive precollegiate training of all students selected, and few had the language skills to enter a foreign university. Students were required to attach themselves to a government school in Japan and to pass a formal screening.[88] Beginning in 1885 the mandatory school affiliation was dropped, but all Japanese pursuing foreign studies still had to follow rigid rules: they had to register with the foreign ministry in Tokyo, send annual progress reports to the local ambassador, and, if using government money, pledge two years' public service for every year of support.[89]

Because growing numbers of critics thought spending on overseas study came at the expense of domestic research, it is a useful—though difficult—task to estimate the cost of *ryūgaku*. Unfortunately, records were kept haphazardly, several different ministries were involved, students sometimes switched their status from public to private or private to public, and estimates of numbers vary widely among sources.[90] But estimates of the minimum expenditure are possible if certain assumptions are made. By accepting my definition of scientist, together with the figures for time spent abroad and (average) levels of expenditure reported below (table 3.4), it is clear that Japan could not have spent less than 6,303,350 yen on overseas study in the fifty or so years being

TABLE 3.4
Foreign Study Expenditures (Doctorate Recipients)

	STUDENT YEARS ABROAD (#)	ANNUAL EXPENDITURE/ STUDENT (AVG.)	COST
1867–77	138	600 yen	82,800 yen
1878–82	163	1,650 yen	268,950 yen
1883–1914	2,842	1,800 yen	5,115,600 yen
1915–20	418	2,000 yen	836,000 yen
Totals:	3,561		6,303,350 yen

Sources: *NKGST* 8/1: 350–53; Uzaki Kumakichi, *Aoyama Tanemichi*, p. 54; Watanabe Minoru, "Japanese Students Abroad and the Acquisition of Scientific and Technical Knowledge," pp. 254–93.

discussed. Whether this estimate is reasonable or not, it is at least compatible with another. In the early 1960s, Satō Kenzō of the Ministry of Education conducted a study of this period that estimated 7,108,054 yen as the cost of supporting government-funded students (only) in all fields of study.[91]

Foreign study costs at first had simply to be borne, but later they caused serious disagreements. One Diet member attacked the government for excessive spending in 1898. Another that year said that the idea was good, but students should pay more.[92] And in 1901 a third representative quoted unnamed others as believing the program to be "of little [or no] value."[93] Criticisms intensified as expenditures rose 70 percent in the 1890s and very nearly doubled in the next decade. A 1914 editorial called foreign study spending "foolish," "unbeneficial," and "a drain on foreign exchange."[94] Others demanded outright termination of the program to improve academic morality. According to them, foreign education was so highly valued that potential nominees were bending the rules and "selling their friends for selection."[95]

These criticisms were not true in all cases. Selection procedures emphasized grades, good character, and faculty recommendations—in about that order. By 1879, when the program was fully developed, to be a *ryūgakusei* (foreign-study student) one usually had to have graduated first or second in one's class, and even that was no guarantee. In 1882 Aoyama Tanemichi, the number three man, was chosen for pathology and internal medicine along with the number two man because the number one man had a reputation for drinking to excess.[96] In 1884, Kitasato Shibasaburō, eighth in his graduating class, got to go because his employer, the Bureau of Public Health, introduced a tax plan to the government which yielded more revenues.[97] The stipends paid to the *ryūgakusei* did not assure opulent living. Nagayo Matarō, studying pathology at Freiburg in 1908, got additional money from his brother.[98] Nagaoka Hantarō, studying physics in Vienna in 1894, had to do his own cooking and lacked money for books.[99] Aoyama could barely live in Berlin on his stipend.[100] And Kitasato in his first year "saw nothing of the city but the street which ran between his boardinghouse and the University of Berlin."[101] Honda Kōtarō, studying physics at Göttingen in 1908, and Nagai Nagayoshi, in chemistry at Berlin in 1879, found they could live quite well, but each had an assistantship, a stipend, and a landlady who kept his rent low.[102]

Ryūgakusei problems were a matter of concern to the officials in charge. In 1897 Vice Minister Makino pointed out how inadequate were the stipends for Europe. "Students want to buy books and reference materials but often cannot. They always ask for more money."[103] Ōyama Kenzō, chief of the Bureau of Vocational Education, told the

Budget Committee of the House of Representatives in 1898 that the foreign students "really have to scrimp," explaining that many had formerly benefited from favorable exchange rates but no longer did so.[104] Toyama, the minister of education, had this to say:

> *Ryūgakusei* sponsored by the Ministry of Education are practically beggars. They have to live in shabby boardinghouses and cannot go out in society freely. I talked with Prime Minister Itō [Hirobumi] about this when I was president of [Tokyo] University. He had seen some of these places in Europe and said we have to do something. . . . The Ministry of Education's stipends for foreign students are much too meager. When I and others went to Europe during the time of the shogunate, we got £200 sterling a year, and even that amount was not adequate for living in Cambridge or Oxford. Our present foreign students do not even have stipends sufficient for them to live in the more remote areas of Germany.[105]

It was appropriate for Toyama to make reference to Germany, since so many of the *ryūgakusei* went there. In the 1870s Germany attracted only 27 percent of Japan's budding scientists, but the percentage climbed in the following decades. In the 1880s it reached 59 percent, in the 1890s 69 percent; and in the first decade of the twentieth century it topped out at just under 74 percent. Overall two-thirds of the man-years of study were spent in Germany during the period 1869–1914. Prior to the outbreak of war in 1914, no other country did nearly so well. Britain and the United States attracted between 20 and 35 percent each in the 1870s but rapidly lost ground after Germany became popular. France in its best year attracted only about 19 percent and was minor for the period as a whole. In the same forty-five-year period, France got just under 7 percent of the Japanese *ryūgakusei,* the United States and Britain got about 11 percent each, and the remainder were scattered in other countries—Italy, Belgium, Switzerland, the Netherlands, and Austria.

The pattern was the same for nearly every field. Among scientists who took agriculture degrees, 43 percent had previously gone to Germany. Two-thirds of all chemists went there, 69 percent of the physicists, and 90 percent of the medical men. Engineers were less overwhelmed by Germany, but even they made it first choice. While their pattern of movement makes calculation difficult, a reasonable estimate says that Germany got 30 percent of their time abroad, the U.S. about 28 percent, Britain 26 percent, and France 14 percent. Only a few engineers studied or worked abroad in other countries.[106]

The reasons for Germany's popularity may seem obvious, but this is deceptive. Certainly German science and engineering were outstanding in this period. Wilhelm Roentgen discovered X-rays in 1895. Max Planck founded quantum theory in the early twentieth century. Adolf von Baeyer did important work in the chemistry of organic dyes, and Rudolph Diesel invented the diesel engine. German medicine also attained a preeminence unequaled before or since. Robert Koch provided the first hard proof of the pathogenic specificity of a particular microorganism. Max von Pettenkofer founded modern public health studies. Emil von Behring helped establish immunology. And by some estimates, in the 1880s a majority of major medical discoveries worldwide were the work of German scientists.[107]

Nevertheless, the Japanese inclination to study in Germany could not have resulted just from intellectual factors. Other countries were doing good science. Spontaneous radioactivity was discovered first in France, and the theory of electrolytic dissociation was developed by a Swede. The chemistry of radioactive substances was most notably investigated by Lord Rutherford of Britain. The structure of the nervous system was elucidated by an Italian and a Spaniard. Besides, German preeminence, in medicine at least, was actually in decline. The putative majority of world medical discoveries in the 1880s dropped to 32 percent in the 1890s and to 20 percent between 1910 and 1919 because of diminishing opportunities for younger researchers.[108]

But Germany had its advantages. It was more willing than most other countries (especially Britain) to relax the special privileges accorded its nationals under the system of unequal treaties (1857–99).[109] German political philosophy had won considerable favor with the majority of Japanese officials. In particular, the German academic system made it easy to collect information. Unlike the French or British systems, where students studied at one institution, the German system encouraged migration. A student could attend lectures at Leipzig one term, at Munich the following term, and finish at Berlin in the term after that. Registration was easy, requiring just a letter, the array of courses impressive, and the number of German universities (almost two dozen) more than twice that of any other European country. Even so, we really know little about individuals' motives. Noguchi Hideyo studied with Simon Flexner at Pennsylvania because of the accident of their having met in Tokyo. Kitasato worked with Robert Koch in Berlin because of Koch's work with various microorganisms. Shibata Yūji moved successively from Leipzig (Arthur Hantzsch) to Zurich (Alfred Werner) and on to Paris (Georges Urbain) in pursuit of a single research theme: stereochemistry, initiated by Hantzsch and developed by the others.[110] But most of the time neither government records nor biographies report the reasons for these choices.

Widely held conceptions of the *ryūgakusei* role may be part of the reason we know so little. *Ryūgakusei* were supposed to go abroad when sent, study particular subjects, work with particular professors, come home when directed, and assume the positions the government gave them. For many things did work this way. Sakurai Jōji quietly complied with an order to return home from London in 1881 despite his exemplary record and the excellent work he was doing.[111] Similarly, Shibata returned to Tokyo in 1913 at Sakurai's insistence even though his research in Paris had hardly begun to bear fruit.[112] Considering how powerful the government was, it is remarkable that any scientists defied it. Nagai Nagayoshi, studying chemistry in Berlin in 1874, simply told his supervisors he would pay his own way when he was ordered to return home as a result of the 1873 survey by the education ministry.[113] Yamakawa Kenjirō wrote Ambassador Mori Arinori a flat rejection to the same request, partly because a wealthy New Haven widow had offered to pay his expenses at Yale.[114] But the most salient example of student noncompliance involved Kitasato Shibasaburō, who in 1887 shocked his superiors by refusing their order to transfer his studies from Berlin to Munich.

Kitasato's experience is important because it identifies knowledge gathering—not research training—as the primary purpose of foreign study for *officials*. In 1884 Kitasato graduated from Tokyo University and entered the Bureau of Public Health, which sent him to Germany. In keeping with the needs of the public health program, it was decided he should spend most of his time at Koch's laboratory in Berlin but be prepared to move if conditions required. In 1887, the bureau's other *ryūgakusei*, Nakahama Tōichirō, who had been studying public health with Pettenkofer in Munich, asked the bureau to study with Koch. The government ordered Kitasato to move to Munich to trade places with his colleague Nakahama.[115]

But Kitasato refused on professional grounds, telling a local official who relayed the order that the plan took no cognizance of medical research. Pettenkofer claimed that diseases resulted exclusively from poor sanitation; Koch defended the pathogenic significance of discrete microorganisms. Kitasato also insisted that he needed more time to learn the methods of bacteriological research. Fortunately, Mori Rintarō urged Tokyo to accept these arguments, and the order to transfer was canceled. Two years later Kitasato isolated the bacterium causing tetanus and then helped to found immunology by his discovery of natural immunity.[116] Because of Pettenkofer's bitter opposition to the germ theory of disease, these discoveries might not have occurred had Kitasato consented to study in Munich.

It must be stressed, however, that Japanese officials did sometimes recognize and support research as a legitimate component of *ryūgaku*. In 1891 the Ministry of Education sent three junior faculty members from Tokyo University to Koch's laboratory to investigate his claim that tuberculin could help to treat tuberculosis.[117] In 1894 it granted 1,000 yen to physicist Tanaka Shōhei in Germany for research in musical acoustics. The same year it underwrote Nagaoka Hantarō's studies of magnetic phenomena. But officials were inconsistent, and their responses to requests for research support could not be predicted. Tanaka's study was funded apparently because prominent German musicians endorsed it, Kitasato's work through the German instructional budget. Nagaoka's 1893 request for money to study magnetic distortion was rejected.[118] The Tokyo tuberculin mission proved abortive because Koch rejected the "students."[119] The education minister, Toyama, was asked directly in 1898 whether the ministry ever paid the expenses of Japanese invited abroad for research. Toyama stated that Itō Hirobumi and Ōkuma Shigenobu favored this policy, but he admitted it was practiced erratically. The pertinent conditions, he said, were that someone be officially invited, that Tokyo University professors not object, *and* that no *ryūgakusei* already abroad be affected adversely if a researcher were sent![120]

Toyama's remarks show how solicitous of *ryūgakusei* officials could be on occasion. Nagaoka's stipend was increased in 1894 after he complained of currency devaluations, hunger, and cold.[121] Kitasato was permitted to remain in Berlin even after his fellowship expired in 1888.[122] Tanakadate was given extra money for travel in 1886 despite his having gone to Britain for physics at his own expense.[123] Nagai Nagayoshi received personal loans and lucrative commissions in the 1870s and 1880s from a number of prominent officials. Nagai's case is particularly instructive. In June 1875 he was given 2,300 yen to buy books and equipment for the Tokyo Medical Academy (later the medical faculty of Tokyo University). A month later he was asked to help recruit professors in chemistry and physics. In 1878 the Bureau of Agriculture began paying him a consulting fee of 30 yen per month (which became 50 yen only two years later). In 1881 the Bureau of Public Health sent him money to cover travel costs, and in 1883 he got 100 yen in commissions for arranging the sale of pharmaceutical manufacturing equipment. Officials, of course, had excellent reasons to treat *ryūgakusei* well. There were not very many of them, in the early years especially, and the country was greatly in need of their services. Nagai noted that Ambassadors Shinagawa and Aoki in Berlin treated him very much like a personal friend and observed that his status as the only "full-fledged Japanese chemist" (1878) made him a "prominent person in Japan."[124]

The Meaning of Overseas Study

Initiation of specific traditions of research was among the important, if predictable, results of studying overseas. Physicist Honda Kōtarō created a major metallurgical research tradition at Tōhoku University following three years at Göttingen with the physical chemist Gustav Tammann, founder of modern metallurgy.[125] Ishikawa Chiyomatsu helped establish zoological research at Tokyo University after a close collaboration with the influential Darwinian August Weismann at Freiburg.[126] Ishihara Jun made notable contributions to theoretical physics at Tōhoku after studying with Albert Einstein (Zurich) and Arnold Sommerfeld (Munich).[127] Nagai Nagayoshi did significant work in pharmacological chemistry at Tokyo that followed closely from his studies with Hofmann.[128] Tanakadate Aikitsu's researches paralleled those of his teacher, Lord Kelvin, in ranging from geophysics to magnetism.[129] And Kitasato Shibasaburō discovered the plague bacillus and established a tradition of bacteriological research after having studied six years with Koch.[130]

Mentor-pupil relationships clearly contributed to many such research endeavors. Honda worked diligently under Tammann for three years at Göttingen, Nagai was Hofmann's assistant for four years in Berlin, Ishikawa did much of the actual research for the myopic, debilitated Weismann,[131] and Kitasato's closeness to the very reserved Koch exceeded that of any of Koch's German pupils.[132] The exceptions highlight the more typical pattern: bacteriologist Kitajima Ta'ichi took a strong dislike to Emil von Behring and considered his years at Marburg a waste;[133] Nagaoka Hantarō, critical of the aged Hermann von Helmholtz and the beginner Max Planck, moved from an early interest in theoretical physics to concentrate on experimental studies;[134] Ogata Masanori, professor of hygiene at Tokyo, ignored the antibacterial views of his teacher Pettenkofer to make his career in the field of bacteriology;[135] chemist Shibata Yūji found Georges Urbain at the Sorbonne more congenial than Alfred Werner at Zurich, and whether for that reason or some other, abandoned his work in stereochemistry to study, like Urbain, the various rare earths.[136]

Relations with European mentors also shaped the scientists' conceptions of their roles. Shibata's evolution as an exclusively academic chemist paralleled the careers of his European teachers.[137] Sakurai Jōji's career in theoretical chemistry was certainly influenced by the later interest of his teacher A. W. Williamson in theory.[138] Tanakadate's interest in research, teaching, and the nonacademic world approximates Kelvin's career pattern, except that the British physicist worked with commercial interests on telegraphic communications and his Japanese pupil with the military on air power.[139] Gustav Tammann and Honda Kōtarō were both interested in pure research and business applications.[140] Nagai Nagayoshi shared his teacher Hofmann's commitment to experimental results and their utility in industry.[141] Kitasato modeled his career directly on Koch's, founding a comparable institute where research was done, serums manufactured, and patients given treatment.[142]

At times, Japanese scientists even adopted the personality traits of their teachers in Europe. Nagai Nagayoshi, who spent fourteen years in Germany, took on Hofmann's cosmopolitan style and became Germanicized to the point of marrying a German woman, converting to Catholicism, and adding Wilhelm to his name.[143] "I [consciously] patterned myself after Einstein from the time I first came to Zurich," wrote the physicist Ishihara Jun.[144] Colleagues said Honda Kōtarō had the same blunt manner as his German mentor, Tammann.[145] Sakurai Jōji imitated the aristocratic, refined style of his British teacher, Williamson.[146] Students often called Tanakadate "Lord Kelvin" behind his back.[147] And Kitasato adopted the extreme neatness, punctuality, and fatherly manner typical of Robert Koch. "His actions and gestures are just like Koch's," according to the German scientist's wife. "They even hold a pointer the same way when they're lecturing!"[148]

Kitasato's emulation of Koch was particularly striking to associates. In 1908 Koch paid a six-week visit to Japan, and during that time Kitasato managed to obtain a lock of his hair from a barber. When Koch died in 1910, Kitasato, though not a believer in life after death, asked the Shinto priests of the Izumo Grand Shrine to pray for the soul of his teacher. The following year he built a small Shinto shrine on the grounds of the Institute of Infectious Diseases, the lock of hair and photograph of Koch indicating the scientist's presence at the site. On the anniversary of Koch's death (May 27), he always requested that prayers be offered at the shrine.[149] Nor was this his sole form of remembrance. Every year on Koch's birthday (December 11), Kitasato sponsored a conference to commemorate his mentor's contributions to medicine.[150] "Dr. Koch's soul may no longer exist," Kitasato declared. "But through our work he is still very much alive."[151]

Many of the German professors had strong authoritarian tendencies. Kitajima described Behring as "quick-tempered," "secretive," "stern," and "always the military man."[152] The pathologist Nagayo Matarō observed in 1907 that some German professors assumed a "haughty attitude" toward *ryūgakusei*.[153] Shibata Yūji said Alfred Werner could be "mean, explosive, and sarcastic" if he became angry with a student.[154] Koch was seen by many as cold and rather forbidding.[155] Paul Ehrlich was described by a Japanese student as supervising students so relentlessly that their work invariably reflected his way of thinking.[156]

Tanaka Minoru says students were reprimanded by their German professors if they failed to address them correctly.[157]

The French were seen differently. The mentor of astronomer Terao Hisashi, the Sorbonne professor François Tisserand, is described as "modest," "kind," and "very solicitous toward young astronomers."[158] Shibata recalled that his teacher, Georges Urbain, criticized the German professorial style. "He forbade us to address him by the French equivalent of 'Herr Professor.' He said, 'We do not use such German forms here. You are to call me 'Monsieur Urbain' like Louis, our laboratory custodian.' "[159] Britain probably resembled the French pattern more closely than the German. Williamson is described as the "natural choice" as a mentor for Japanese students.[160] James A. Ewing of Cambridge, formerly of Tokyo, spent a great deal of time with visiting Japanese students or colleagues.[161] Lord Kelvin treated anyone sent to his laboratory by Tanakadate, even for a short visit, as if he were the Scotsman's own student.[162]

Where authoritarian behavior was present (and it was not an unvarying feature of German academic culture), it did not always repress creativity. Koch's laboratory produced a succession of brilliant discoveries including his own isolation of the tubercle bacillus (1882), Friedrich Loeffler's discovery of the diphtheria bacillus (1884), Georg Gaffky's cultivation of the typhoid bacillus (1885), Kitasato's pure culture of the tetanus bacillus (1889), and the brilliant work on antitoxic immunity done by Kitasato and von Behring (1890).[163] Nor was the Franco-German group founded by Werner at Zurich wholly closed minded and authoritarian. G. Schwarzenbach speaks of the infectious enthusiasm of Werner's students, an excitement that transcended every difficulty.[164] Shibata says that Werner was "unstinting in his kindness toward and willingness to help dedicated, capable students." "He respected and praised those who had the courage to stand up to him."[165]

Authoritarianism in German science did not spring solely from inclinations inherent in German culture. Joseph Ben-David and Awraham Zloczower argue that the servility and dependency of junior scientists toward senior ones appeared in the last quarter of the nineteenth century as a result of systemic rigidity. Because the universities allowed only one chair per field, institutional expansion could occur only by dividing an existing field, by founding new universities, or by creating a hierarchy of institutions and laboratories. After a certain point only creation of institutions and laboratories remained viable for growth. Younger men found themselves increasingly dependent on the help of their seniors for advancement and were forced to assure their preferment by obsequious behavior.[166]

One should also remember that German science, like that of the

West as a whole, inherited the values and ideals of creative research. "First, completeness and thoroughness; second . . . community, and [last] cooperation" was the description of John Theodore Merz:

> The German man of science was . . . not an isolated thinker . . . He lived mostly at a university, surrounded by others, whose labours came in contact with his own, or who treated the same subject from a different point of view . . . His object could not be to produce simply a work of individual greatness or of finished artistic merit; his work was an integral portion of one great science . . . The German man of science was a teacher; he had to communicate his ideas to younger minds . . . not to teach *une science faite*, but to draw out original talent in others, to encourage cooperation in research, to portion out the common work to the talents which surround[ed] him.[167]

Merz went on to say that the German (or Western) man of science had "generally come under the influence of some . . . school, the teaching of which he desired either to uphold or to combat."[168]

Foreign study in this sense aroused behavioral commitments in Japanese scientists and affected the ways they conceived of research. Residence in Europe exposed them to the traditional values of European science in ways that working at home never could have. They learned directly what cooperation, community, and uninhibited criticism meant in the laboratory setting. They experienced first hand the criticisms of academic "inbreeding" or sociopolitical involvements which, however infrequently observed, were normative ideals in Europe. They internalized—or were at least exposed to—both respect for teachers and willingness to defend scientific truths whenever occasion demanded. And they learned to defend their ideas in a professional forum. Foreign study also inspired loyalties to certain conceptions of science. Medical study in Britain encouraged a clinical approach to disease; study in Germany placed greater stress on research. Mentors affected the growth of ideas *and* careers.

Takagi Kanehiro's work on beriberi shows the importance of *where* one studied in Europe. Takagi, a career physician in the navy, had gone to Britain in 1875 because he wanted an alternative to German-style training.[169] Following the advice of William Willis, an associate of government leaders, Takagi, a Satsuma native, enrolled in the St. Thomas Hospital Medical College of London and spent five years studying anatomy and clinical medicine. In November 1880 he returned to his work in the navy, becoming chief of the Bureau of Medical Affairs about a year later. He also began doing research on beriberi. His compilation of data on its occurrence in particular settings suggested that diet was a differentiating element. Takagi obtained funds and authorization for an enriched diet that produced striking results. The new diet focused on fresh vegetables, meat, fish, and barley in contrast to rice and pickled vegetables, greatly reducing the incidence of disease or even eliminating it. Internal opposition, inadequate reporting abroad, and the popularity of the germ theory of illness delayed recognition of his work, but Takagi was the first researcher anywhere to link beriberi convincingly to dietary factors.[170]

Takagi might have done this work had he studied in Germany or France, but his having studied in Britain encouraged such research more. His conception of beriberi was basically physiological. From actual trials he argued that 310 grams of carbon were required in the military ration for every 20 grams of nitrogen; that is, the ratio of nitrogen to carbon is 1:15.5.[171] Physiology was more highly developed in France and Germany than in Britain when Takagi was there, but its relation to clinical treatment was different in Britain, far more intimately linked to practice than on the Continent.[172] At the time he did his research, Takagi's approach was unusual. Researchers were sensitive to the clinical aspects of beriberi, but many looked exclusively for a bacterial explanation. This was as true of Japanese beriberi researchers trained in Germany as it was of Germans.[173] Takagi seems to have benefited from the particular combination of physiological research and clinical treatment then found only in Britain.

A quarrel between Nagai Nagayoshi and Sakurai Jōji shows that overseas study could also produce divergent conceptions in chemistry. From 1873 to 1884 Nagai worked with Hofmann in Berlin. Sakurai studied in London with Williamson (1876–81). Both attempted to follow in the footsteps of their European mentors. Hofmann and Nagai were basically organic chemists interested in experimental work and its industrial applications, whereas Williamson and Sakurai, despite earlier experience, shared an interest in chemical theory. In 1881 Sakurai returned to a professorship in theoretical chemistry at Tokyo University; Nagai stayed in Germany for three more years. When he did return, in October 1884, he received an appropriate joint appointment in the faculties of medicine and science. But Sakurai took offense at this, insisted on other arrangements, and in November 1885 secured Nagai's dismissal from the university on the grounds that his interest in pharmacological chemistry was not academic in nature.[174] Nagai was forced to resign and pursue a career elsewhere. From 1885 to 1888 he worked for the Ministry of Education, and from 1888 to 1891 he held a technical appointment in the Ministry of Agriculture and Commerce. His professorship at Tokyo University was restored in 1893, but Sakurai's control of the science faculty deanship relegated him to a position in medicine alone.[175]

In the case of Nagai and Sakurai, it seems that resentments between

Williamson and Hofmann (stemming from professional differences) were either transferred to their Japanese pupils, or else some nonprofessional jealousy led to Sakurai's actions. It is possible that nationalistic rivalries complicated relations between the two senior chemists. Williamson and Hofmann had pursued very similar careers for part of their professional lives, both studying with Justus von Liebig at Giessen (Hofmann from 1839 to 1843 and Williamson from 1844 to 1846). Both were active for a time in the same general area of chemistry. Williamson used Hofmann's work in his theory of etherification, and both performed experiments whose results were important to the theory of chemical types.[176] Both were also concerned with industrial applications of chemistry. Hofmann made a fortune from his work in the chemistry of dyes; Williamson made his students visit chemical factories and helped found a chair of practical chemistry at London. In London they were practically colleagues for a number of years, from 1849 to 1863.[177]

Their coincidental tenure in London and Williamson's medical problems helped fuel the conflict. Both laboratories—Hofmann's at the Royal College of Chemistry and Williamson's at Imperial College—were flourishing in the early 1850s, but in 1855 poor eyesight and a paralyzed arm forced Williamson to give up research, and students began flocking to Hofmann instead.[178] In 1863 Hofmann went to Berlin, and by 1870 Williamson was "devoting his time to high-flown theorizing while posing as a statesman of science."[179] Whether or not the two were rivals, their pupils imputed this to them. Sakurai was not only a brilliant student of chemistry; by the late 1870s he was just about Williamson's only student. Similarly, Nagai worked as Hofmann's assistant and even consulted with him in choosing a wife.[180] The facts suggest two explanations for the quarrel. Sakurai either transferred to Nagai a resentment that Williamson felt toward Hofmann or identified so closely with him that he imagined a rivalry that had never existed. In either event, the quarrel influenced how chemical research was established in Japan.

Kitasato's career in bacteriology provides an even more momentous example of the impact of study in Europe. In 1886, at Koch's instigation, he became involved in a controversy over beriberi that became an object lesson in the values of science, and in 1893 he repeated Koch's experience in founding a laboratory of his own for research. Both affairs conflicted with Japanese values and were resolved in striking ways. The beriberi dispute required Kitasato to criticize the work of a supposed professional superior directly. The laboratory affair was seen as a challenge to the preeminence of Tokyo University (see chapter 4). In neither case did the conflict result exclusively from conditions in Japan.

Foreign study provided both the occasion and the logic for how they turned out.

As we saw in the case of Takagi's career, beriberi research had generated controversy. Medical literature of the period offered five kinds of explanations, and the true cause—vitamin B deficiency—was not fully established until well after World War I.[181] Kitasato and others incorrectly favored a bacterial explanation but disagreed on major details. In 1886 Ogata Masanori claimed to have isolated a beriberi pathogen but failed to convince Friedrich Loeffler and Robert Koch, in whose laboratory Kitasato was working at the time. Koch asked Kitasato, as a Japanese national, to publish a rebuttal in Japanese, but Kitasato expressed reluctance: Ogata was considered Kitasato's senior because he had graduated from Tokyo University a year earlier, and Kitasato said that Japanese colleagues would reject open criticism from an ostensibly junior man. When Koch and Loeffler nonetheless insisted that scientific professionalism required frank discussion of scientific issues, Kitasato wrote two reviews for medical journals. The reviews were objective and moderate in tone, but they aroused exactly the reactions he had feared.[182] Katō Hiroyuki, the president of Tokyo University, declared him ignorant of how to behave toward superiors. Two medical faculty graduates employed in the Ministry of War privately circulated a pamphlet that accused him of jealousy. Mori Rintarō, chief of the army's Bureau of Medical Affairs, said that Kitasato was guilty of "exaggerating science and neglecting human feelings."[183]

Kitasato's understanding of research arrangements was also affected by his friendship with Koch. Koch was professor of hygiene at Berlin University during the years that Kitasato first knew him, but in 1891 he demanded—and got—a laboratory separated from the university. The immediate cause for the demand was a setback in his tuberculosis research that he thought academic colleagues had sabotaged, but for a more adequate explanation one must refer to his career as a whole. Koch was a maverick in the German profession. Most German medical scientists concentrated on research to the exclusion of outside involvements, but he was socially engaged and concerned with clinical treatment. He had only an M.D., and most of his peers held Ph.D.'s. He espoused the germ theory of disease, while many retained affection for Virchow's cellular theory. He stressed the need in bacteriology for intimate relations between clinical and basic medicine—in an era of growing separation between them.[184] Academic associates at Berlin were especially disturbed by his contacts outside the academy. Impractical research lines and a medical theory like cellular imbalance, which precluded effective treatment, were a means of assuring autonomy in an authoritarian political setting, so Koch's germ theory, which opened up possibilities for effective medical intervention, and the unwelcome attention the theory attracted, made professors apprehensive. Koch's connections outside the university explain his appointment to the directorship of the physiological laboratory of the Imperial Health Office (1880) and his hygiene professorship at the University of Berlin (1885).[185]

Ironically, external connections also led Koch to abandon his professorship. Trouble began with an announcement at the Tenth International Medical Congress in 1890 that he had discovered tuberculin, a substance elaborated by the tubercle bacillus. Such announcements were routine, but this one was not quite typical, because Prussia's Ministry of Education, which acted as host for the congress, wanted the propaganda value of a spectacular announcement. Tuberculosis and efforts to cure it were matters of intense concern to the public, and Koch's findings suggested a cure but were actually inconclusive. The situation began to unravel when tests raised serious questions. Tubercular patients and physicians specializing in treating them, who had come to Berlin with high expectations, were angered and greatly disappointed. The Prussian Ministry of Education was embarrassed. And Koch was publicly ridiculed.[186]

He responded by resigning as professor. Heretofore Koch had been a consultant to the Prussian Ministry of Education and as a professor subject to its authority. But academic string-pulling in the bureaucracy and university led him to seek another arrangement: the establishment of a new laboratory and a transferal of his consulting function in public health to his former employer, the Imperial Health Office. In this way he surmounted the characteristically German separation of basic research from clinical medicine that had long troubled him, for example, when as a professor of basic medicine, he had been required to surrender the testing of tuberculin to two colleagues in clinical medicine.[187] This was standard procedure in German academic medicine, but earlier experience made it unacceptable to Koch, who asked a compliant government to build an independent laboratory designed to his standards.[188] This laboratory, called the Prussian Institute of Infectious Diseases, provided the kind of inspiration for Kitasato's laboratory, just as Koch's example molded his career as a whole.

Creating the Role for Research in Japan

Japan in the Meiji and Taishō years created an establishment for scientific research without quite creating the researcher role. Universities were founded, laboratories built, and academic societies established;

but the researcher role remained vaguely defined, inchoate, and surrounded by hostile forces. Though a paradox from the view of Western experience, this circumstance was explicable historically, because no prior analogue existed for the researcher role. While research had been done, it had followed no pattern. The country also had a tradition of self-conscious borrowing and a need to overcome the effects of seclusion. Officials deemed foreign study a means to that end, and scientists generally concurred, seeing *their* ends well served.

But demands for expertise also impeded the establishment of a role for the researcher. Government needed consultants; business, technicians; the public, medical treatment and various other services. Universities provided support for research, but their commitment was ambiguous. Economic factors caused delays in establishing the researcher role. Deprivation (real or imagined) and a commitment to maintaining status led professors to take on extraneous work, while officials cited shortfalls of income as an excuse to delay founding laboratories. Scientists found it difficult to organize professional societies. Mathematicians had to deal with the legacy of *wasan*. Chemists and physicists were divided for a time by different languages of instruction, and medical men were sometimes distracted by factional infighting.

Some saw overseas study as a threat to the researcher role. Bacteriologist Sata Yoshihiko contended shortly before World War I that foreign study was undercutting "a genuine respect for research." There was "no clear reward" for those who did research, nor "any real penalty" for those who did not. Another writer said *ryūgaku* mostly encouraged the ability to expound Western scientists' theories. A third charged foreign study with making Japanese scientists lazy and professionally complacent. As a result of the ease with which one could gain the "sinecure" of a professorship and a doctorate by publishing "one or two small papers abroad," many scientists were living "half asleep and [no more than] half awake."[189] Foreign study was superfluous in the opinion of such critics, because the technique of how to copy had already been learned, and Japanese scientists had finally surpassed the achievements of the foreigners who had taught them at home.[190]

Debate naturally produced suggestions for change. One was that *ryūgaku* be drastically reduced in all fields and eliminated entirely in medicine. Any who did go abroad should spend one year at most in Europe or America and meet stringent selection criteria. They should be under thirty-five, fluent in German, French, or English, scientifically competent, and avoid too much deference to foreigners. The government should reform *its* priorities for science, too. Students sent abroad should receive larger stipends and be permitted after returning to choose their place of employment.[191] Physicist Yamakawa Kenjirō took another approach. As president of Tokyo University, he recommended in June 1914 that the three-year program be cut down to one, with the savings to go toward research.[192] While Yamakawa planned to spend savings on facilities, Sata Yoshihiko was thinking of research grants.[193] Even some officials favored changes in priorities. In 1899 Kabayama Sukenori, then education minister, had proposed some reallocation of funds from *ryūgaku*. Prime ministers Itō Hirobumi and Katsura Tarō later advocated reexamining the matter, and Aoki Shūzō as foreign minister had actually drawn up a plan for reform. But none of these proposals went into effect until World War I forced a change. As *Ikai jihō* noted ruefully in October 1914: "[Foreign study] is less an educational concern [for science] than an administrative and political problem."[194]

Consulting work and other side jobs (*naishoku*) were also a threat to research. Noting the large number of professors working in government ministries part time, a former vice minister of education, Kubota Yuzuru, in 1899 lashed out at the practice in a speech to the Peers. "What research have these professors done? What discoveries have they made? What have they written?"[195] "A large number of university professors," wrote a commentator in 1914, "are in effect social liaison officers who [just] teach society how to apply imported knowledge."[196] A physician member of the House of Representatives even argued that if professors did not do more research, they should be forced to retire to make room for those who would.[197] Moonlighting was definitely widespread. The vice minister of education Makino Nobuaki admitted in 1897 that most professors of physics and chemistry were holding down extra jobs,[198] and *Ikai jihō* reported that 26 of 30 professors in the faculty of agriculture were doing so in 1898.[199] Strong demands for engineering talent were said to have "corrupted" most professors in the faculty of engineering, whereas most professors of clinical medicine were giving the bulk of their time to treating private patients.[200]

Discussion of the problem focused on salaries and incentives for research. Many thought that salaries were at fault. The minister of education Toyama Shōichi described salaries as "very meager" in 1898,[201] and in 1900 the former vice minister Kubota said professors needed "two or three jobs" to make a decent living.[202] But salaries were in fact not all that bad. The range for assistant professors at Tokyo University in 1893 was 500 to 1,100 yen per annum (42 to 92 yen monthly), which compared very favorably with the starting minimum for management trainees at the Mitsui Bank (45 yen per month) or Shibusawa Eiichi's Dai-Ichi Bank (35 yen per month).[203] And full professors got much more—1,300 to 1,900 yen annually in 1893, and about the same in 1898.[204]

But although professors were reasonably well positioned in 1893 and even in 1898, their progress slowed later on. Subtracting incentive payments for research achievements, which ranged from 500 to 700 yen, the base salaries were from 800 to 1,200 yen for full professors in 1893 and in 1907 ranged from 800 to 2,000 yen. The range for assistant professors increased from a maximum of 600 yen to 1,000 yen in that period.[205] But these sums were just not enough—that is, to alter behavior. *Naishoku* continued because incentives were strong and obstacles weak. One has only to look at professorial incomes in the faculty of medicine to see what was really at stake. In 1909, when the average medical professor's salary was a mere 1,800 yen, the actual total incomes of selected individuals were: 35,400 yen for a professor of dermatology; 41,000 yen for a professor of otorhinolaryngology; more than 30,000 yen for one of the professors of internal medicine and 16,850 for another; more than 35,000 for a professor of ophthalmology; and 11,050 yen for a professor of pediatric medicine.[206] Professors of basic medicine were forbidden to treat patients and so earned far less than their clinical colleagues. The total income for one professor of hygiene was 3,400 yen, and a professor of biochemistry earned 2,500 yen. Significantly, the leading researcher in the faculty of medicine, the pathology professor Yamagiwa Katsusaburō, who nearly won a Nobel Prize (see chapter 6), had an income that year of just 2,350 yen—the lowest in the faculty of medicine.[207]

Nevertheless, prior to the war in 1914 little or nothing was done. Hamao Arata, the president of the university, did try to terminate outside employment in the 1890s, and Yamakawa Kenjirō tried once again in 1913,[208] but the professors fought back. Toyama Shōichi tried to buy them off in 1898 with promises of higher salaries, but few of his colleagues at the Ministry of Education shared his concern. Kikuchi Dairoku, president of the university in 1900, said it was "not necessary to make Tokyo University a major research center."[209] Ichiki Kitokurō, the education minister, in 1914 conceded that professors "should not fall behind in the progress of scholarship," but flatly refused to take any action.[210]

Besides the better pay, why else did *naishoku* continue? After all, the practice was never explicitly authorized, only tolerated,[211] and it obviously clashed with official views of the professor's role in society. "The professor," wrote Inoue Kowashi in 1893, "will deliver lectures, instruct students, and carry on research in his [particular] field."[212] Three factors explain the persistence of *naishoku*. Men came into academic life not only because of their talents but because of the prestige, and in the earlier years they were paid well directly and made part of the elite. Demand for their services was great. The number of providers was small. In thirty-eight years (1877–1914) Tokyo University had produced just 14,192 graduates in all fields of study, and none had to face unemployment.[213] As late as 1920, the vice minister of education declared that professorial side jobs might be desirable, "considering the [need for services] in Japan."[214]

Professional societies also contributed to the researcher role, though their impact had its limits. The Tokyo Mathematical and Physical Society, founded 1877, was the oldest of its kind and the most unusual. A majority of early members (83 of 117) were *wasan* practitioners, and the earliest leadership was extremely diverse, including military officers, *wasan* mathematicians, university professors, and undergraduate mathematics majors. Apart from the prospects of cultural enhancement, the society wished to "communicate with the public." This issue of utility led to reform. In 1882 a navy mathematics instructor challenged the society's role in its journal. Pointing to the continuing popularity of the traditional *wasan*-style problem, he described such topics as the number of circles of X diameter inscribable in a certain sized polygon as irrational, and their devotees as "small-minded and petty." He emphasized the need for technological application and greater practicality, predicting major gains once these changes occurred.[215] The instructor's essay had a potent effect. Most *wasan* mathematicians left the society. Several adopted the new notation and sense of problematic of Western mathematics. The society's journal abruptly changed content, and university professors took control of the leadership. In this way, the Tokyo Mathematical and Physical Society became a typical Western-style learned academy.

Westernism thus appeared to triumph completely, but the society's achievement award was designated the Seki Prize after the founder of *wasan,* an open-minded *wasan* mathematician donated space in his home for the society's first headquarters, and the *wasan* community gave the society its critical early momentum. Unlike most Meiji scientific societies, this one was founded by Japanese practitioners. *Wasan* was not simply replaced by Western mathematics; it faded into it and was largely absorbed.[216]

Societies for physics and chemistry conformed more closely to Western models. The Tokyo (later Japan) Chemical Society was founded in 1878 by foreign professors and Tokyo University students; the Physical Society branched off from it just after World War II, in 1946.[217] Each society published a Western-style journal. The Physical Society's journal appeared quarterly from 1903; the journal of the Tokyo Chemical Society commenced publication in 1880, expanding in 1887 from four to ten issues yearly.[218] Founders of both societies had Western-style training. Nearly all had studied in Europe at the doctoral level. Practitioners in all subspecialties joined one of the groups, and virtually all members published papers.

The societies' growth and development were not just a product of Western conceptions. Many founding figures in both were the sons of *Rangaku* scholars and *kampō* physicians, and local conditions helped to shape institutions.[219] The key local factor was the need for instruction. Because no single country held the palm in physics and chemistry as of 1868, the Japanese for some years carried on instruction in three European languages. Physics had a French-language course (1875), an English-language course (1873), and a German-language course (1877), and there was no overarching structure until Tokyo University opened. This situation naturally led to overseas study in each of the three language areas. Yamakawa Kenjirō, Tanakadate Aikitsu, and Sekiya Seikei studied in Britain or the United States in English. Kitao Jirō, Muraoka Han'ichi, and Shiga Taizan studied in Austria or Germany in German. Terao Hisashi, Nakamura Kiyoo, and Miwa Kan'ichirō studied physics in France or Belgium in French.[220] Returned foreign students with lecture notes in English found it easiest to lecture in English. Those with notes on their subject in French could most efficiently teach in French, and those with German-language notes preferred to teach physics in German.

Tokyo University's founding initiated a sorting-out process. Tanakadate was appointed to its faculty of science because instruction in that unit was in English. Muraoka was appointed in medicine because German was dominant there. Terao joined the astronomical observatory because its work was conducted in French.[221] Publication of Japanese-language technical dictionaries finally overcame these divisions. In 1883 the *Butsurigaku jutsugo jisho* (Dictionary of physical terms) appeared, and in 1891 the *Kagaku yakugo shū* (Compilation of chemical terms) was published. These events made lecturing in Japanese possible and marked the beginning of professional traditions.[222]

Medicine developed a number of practices that differed from German ideals. After the middle of the nineteenth century, it was common for researchers and clinicians in Germany to have separate professional societies,[223] and Japanese medical men also formed specialized societies, for example, for anatomy, pathology, and internal medicine, but directed much energy elsewhere. Many preferred to take part in one of the two comprehensive associations whose organizing principles were strictly political. The Meiji Medical Association (MMA), founded in 1893, included virtually all the clinicians *and* basic researchers who had graduated from Tokyo University or one of the two military medical academies.[224] The Great Japan Medical Society, created at the same

time but often known by other names (for example, Japan Federation of
Medical Societies), included ordinary practitioners trained by private
and provincial medical colleges and researchers with ties to Kitasato.[225]

Japanese medicine rejected Germany's exclusion of clinicians from
access to research facilities.[226] In Japan, ordinary practitioners *could*
use academic research facilities, at least when they had the right political connections. Clinicians with degrees from an imperial university
could do research at Tokyo University, Kyoto University, Kyushu University, or one of their affiliated hospitals; those who had trained at
private or public medical colleges used the facilities of these and related
institutions.[227]

But German influence on the formation of medical roles in Japan was
not wholly absent. Following a system pioneered by the Germans and
later adopted by others, the Japanese Ministry of Education did sharply
segregate basic and clinical medicine within the academic setting.
Clinical professors (as we have seen) were allowed to treat private patients, while those in basic medicine were forbidden to do so.[228] Practice in Japan, however, did not conform strictly to practice in Germany.
Professors of basic medicine, while barred from clinical practice, were
not excluded from organizations like the MMA that were seemingly
limited to clinicians. Several professors at Tokyo University served as
presidents of the MMA, and the first president of the Great Japan Medical Society was a professor of anatomy at Tokyo.[229] None of this implied
separation between the roles of practitioner and clinical researcher.
German professors of clinical medicine, while treating private patients,
nevertheless honored the academic ideal.[230] Clinical professors at Japanese universities gave most of their time to treating private patients.[231]

CHAPTER FOUR

LAYING THE INSTITUTIONAL
FOUNDATIONS OF SCIENCE

Japan took its time creating institutions for research. The research conducted in the Tokugawa period had followed no discernible pattern. By 1868 some technical studies were stronger than others, but none were established securely. So wide was the gap between Japan and the West that just catching up would consume vast resources. But catching up began once the new regime was in place, and Japan in due time built its own institutions. Many difficult questions arose in the process. Should research be linked to industrial development? What purpose could it serve in manpower training? Should it be concentrated in higher education? Was original research necessary? If it were true, as many believed, that everything could be copied, perhaps Japanese needed only to absorb what the scientists of Europe had discovered.[1]

Debate focused at the time on policy essentials. Could one build on Tokugawa achievements? Who should initiate and carry out policies? After all, traditionally the government had controlled scholarly activity. Private resources were arguably so weak in Meiji Japan that the government had to be active.[2] But even assuming government sponsorship, the question was how it should act. What Western models could Japanese adopt? What should inform specific application? Should academic growth be based entirely on enrollments? Should other factors also be taken into account?

Japanese debate about research institutions was very sophisticated, all things considered. Decision makers followed European developments, but they never adopted Western models unchanged. They never proposed to build laboratories solely because foreigners had done so. Nor did they introduce features of foreign universities—privatdozenten, the one-chair rule—simply because they worked well (or were thought to work well) in their country of origin.[3] One is constantly impressed by the quality of discussion on how these features would work in Japan and whether they were needed at all. Officials sometimes realized that science had needs separate from society's. They did not base decisions about academic institutions solely on enrollments or what business wanted.

The salient issue in institution building was the country's need for original research, and the history of this issue was mixed. Alternate Attendance had diffused information. Daimyo domains had competed with each other. Tokugawa physicians had had some autonomy and occasional incentive to promote innovations. But private institutions had often been weak, deficient in funding, and coopted by government. Tokugawa scholarly institutions all had significant defects: unspecific programs, inefficient operations, and restraints on real competition. Nevertheless, the motivations and views of *Meiji* decision makers were varied and wide-ranging. A mainstream view minimized research, but its premises were frequently challenged. Scientists who had worked abroad for some years insisted that Japan must conduct its own research. Commercial organizations that were challenged in the marketplace decided that research must be part of their strategy. Physician politicians with scientific training promoted the cause of research while in office. The role of these groups in building institutions was important at the time but transcends their own era. With the outbreak of war in 1914, the proresearch movement became the new mainstream.

Early Post-Restoration Developments

Institutional developments in the earliest Meiji years (1868–73) were ad hoc and poorly coordinated. Political confusion impeded most changes in 1868, but some initiatives were launched in the next two years. At Numazu, site of the first Western-style military academy, Japan's first program for science education was established early in 1869. The Osaka Medical Academy opened its doors in December, while the former Bunseki Kyūri Jo of Nagasaki was reorganized in Osaka as the Osaka School of Chemistry. In December 1870 a comparable institution started up in Kyoto with the aim of fostering scientific techniques in the ceramics and lacquerware industries of that city. Dutch instructors staffed the two schools and attracted several pupils later active in research.[4]

Poor coordination and ad hoc efforts had their historical cause in the relatively decentralized scientific activities of the Tokugawa shogunate. Individual domains controlled their own schools, diffusion of knowledge in some fields was restricted, there were no national organizations of scientists or physicians, and the fields of mathematics and physical science, related in Europe, in Japan belonged to different classes.[5] The society valued each technical discipline differently. Medicine enjoyed broad social support, widespread official encouragement, a network of supporting institutions, and the beginnings of Western-style professionalism.[6] Chemistry, biology, and botany were modestly prosperous because of their links to medicine but were not yet recognized as distinct fields. Mathematics, despite remarkable progress before the mid-eighteenth century, had consigned itself to cultural irrelevance. Physics was subject to suspicion.[7]

Meiji officials confronting this legacy soon adopted an activist posture. They terminated the system of traditional statuses and began to create scientific institutions. Especially active were Ōkubo Toshimichi, grandson of a distinguished Tokugawa physician, and Itō Hirobumi, sometime pupil of A. W. Williamson. Ōkubo concentrated primarily on medicine, Itō on engineering and much of basic science. Using the control of public health afforded him as home affairs minister, Ōkubo in 1877 developed Japan's first program for attacking contagious disease, together with a campaign to counter beriberi.[8] Itō helped develop the Imperial College of Engineering (Kōbu Daigakkō) and later exerted his influence on Tokyo University.[9]

Ōkubo's initiative was not routine, since bacteriology was still in its infancy. "Much controversy existed as to whether contagious diseases were even caused by bacteria."[10] Itō also was very forward-looking. On the recommendation of Williamson's friend Lord Kelvin, he invited the young British engineer Henry Dyer to Japan in 1871 and gave him a free hand and sufficient funds to develop one of the world's first comprehensive institutions for basic science and engineering. Dyer's four-year program included physics and chemistry, mechanical, civil, and mining engineering, and courses in the strength of materials. It relied almost entirely on a British teaching staff.[11] No one graduated from it until 1879, but its founding was still remarkable. Only France and Switzerland had comparable institutions. There was nothing like the college in Dyer's own country nor even in Germany before the Franco-Prussian War (1870–71).[12]

The most important innovation was Japan's first university. In April 1877 Tokyo University emerged from a combination of Tokugawa schools, and it gradually expanded.[13] In 1886 it acquired the Imperial College of Engineering, a school of graduate studies, and the formal appellation "imperial university." Widely referred to as *saikō gakufu*, or "supreme institution of learning," Tokyo University became Japan's leading "window for the importation of Western knowledge" and gradually a center for research as well. This was not smooth transition, since many wished to restrict the university to educating undergraduate students, while others had a broader conception.

Establishing a comprehensive university was far from simple. Meiji leaders had inherited three institutions from the Tokugawa state—the Kaisei Gakkō, Igakkō, and Shōheikō—but did not agree on their futures. The Kaisei Gakkō had been created under the name Bansho Shirabesho after the Perry expedition (1853) but actually traced its lineage to the Office of Astronomy (Temmongata, founded 1684). It primarily taught foreign languages and natural science.[14] The Igakkō had existed under various names from the middle of the eighteenth century and had taught *kampō* medicine. But the seventeenth-century Shōheikō, with its Confucian curriculum, was seen as the most basic unit. The prior history of these institutions implied a role for the university different from Western conceptions. In 1868–70, the government envisioned a university that would censor newspapers and books; investigate (*kōkyū*) and teach languages, mathematics, geography, science, history, medicine, and *kokugaku* and Confucian studies as guarantors of social harmony and national power; and administer state-owned educational facilities in Tokyo, Osaka, and Nagasaki.[15] This scheme proved totally unworkable. Confucian scholars hated its Westernizing aspects, the censorship functions were reassigned elsewhere, and the plan was finally abandoned.[16]

Mindful of the need for Western-style experts, some officials favored higher professional schools (*semmon gakkō*). But others, including the Kaisei Gakkō director Katō Hiroyuki and the vice minister of education Tanaka Fujimaro, championed the idea of the comprehensive university. In 1875, Tanaka proposed—and the government nearly approved—establishing a comprehensive university in rural Chiba prefecture, on the grounds that Western universities were generally built in "elegant, secluded places far from the commotion of urban environments." In February 1877, Katō asked the Ministry of Education to change "Kaisei Gakkō" to "Tōkyō Daigaku," or Tokyo University, to convey the school's function more accurately. "It is misleading to use a name for our institution so [fundamentally] different from those in the West."[17]

Katō's letter raised an issue of importance. In the early years, the university was clearly regarded by many as a "training school for officials," somewhere between a middle school and a German *Universität*. The *Gakusei* edict of 1872, which envisioned a network of eight universities, mentioned only teaching as the purpose. Research is hardly ever mentioned in the earliest official documents, but interest in it gradually developed.[18] In 1880 Katō, citing the absence of a graduate school, was able to establish a special research course at Tokyo University for university graduates who wanted further study. Returning *ryūgakusei* brought research interest with them. And prominent officials like Itō Hirobumi began to see that research activities could divert professors from involvement in politics.[19]

Policies toward particular disciplines continued to differ during the early Meiji period. The Kaisei Gakkō from which the faculties of letters, science, and law derived represented a basic, new concept in Japanese education; but the Igakkō and its modern successor, the faculty of medicine, were seen to some extent as a single tradition. The post-Restoration medical school continued for some years to use facilities that were built by the shogunate. Some of its Japanese instructors were the same as before. By 1869 experimentation (*jikken*), if not research, was described as its function. In contrast, the instructors of the Kaisei Gakkō were all dismissed by the new Meiji government, new facilities were built in a wholly Western style, and any conception of genuine research was subsumed under the tepid "inquiry" (*ri o kiwame*).[20] None of this mattered in the early Meiji years, but it did make a difference later on, when research conditions, poor in most fields, were not quite so bad in medicine.

Tokyo University was institutionally innovative in more than a Japanese context. Its inclusion of engineering (1886) and agriculture (1890) in the curriculum indicates a forward-looking policy rarely encountered in Europe. Engineering acquired prestige in Japan because of its connection with the Japanese government and origin in advanced Western countries,[21] but its formal position in the academic system was higher than in Europe. When the university was founded in 1877, its college of science had departments of chemistry, mathematics, physics and astronomy, biology, geology, and engineering all together on a basis of equality.[22]

The government gave considerable support to other institutions, as it did to Tokyo University. The first nonacademic technical agency established (in 1871) was the navy's Hydrographic Department, charged with coastal and ocean surveying. Creation in 1884 of a similar land survey department affiliated with the army may suggest that military considerations were of primary concern, but most officials were more interested in the resource base for civilians. The Tokyo Meteorological Station and Central Meteorological Observatory were established in 1875; the home ministry's Geological Survey materialized in 1878, and the Geological Survey Institute in 1882. Agriculture programs were especially well supported. The Naitō Shinjuku Testing Station opened in 1872, the Mita Plant Nursery in 1877, the Forestry Experiment Station in 1878, and the Tokyo Agricultural Experiment Station in 1882. Rounding out the list were the Drug Control Station (later Tokyo Hygiene Institute [1874]) and the Komaba and Sapporo agricultural colleges (1876).[23]

Anxiety about manpower skills was a potent incentive to activism. Foreign experts could be hired to carry out vital tasks, but nationalism and finances made their long-term use unpalatable, so additional strategies were devised. One early effort relied on feudal coercion. In 1870 the government ordered all daimyo territories according to size and wealth to dispatch students to the Kaisei Gakkō, only to discover that insufficient student motivation—and less preparation—made this strategy ineffectual.[24] More realistic policies followed this so-called tribute (kōshin) system. In 1873 the government began granting scholarships to students in technical fields. Many, sometimes a majority, of students at the Imperial College of Engineering, Komaba Agricultural college, Sapporo Agricultural College, and the College of Science at Tokyo University in the 1870s and 1880s received not only tuition and fees but access to the refectory, free lodging, and a clothing allowance.[25]

Other new programs were also created. Within the new engineering faculty special departments of arms technology and explosives were established in 1887. These initiatives were taken to secure engineers for military arsenals and were unprecedented in Western countries.[26] The government, of course, was intent on results. Until 1897 students in technical programs had no electives in their academic major, and the level of performance demanded was high. At Tokyo's science department failure on a single examination meant cancellation of the scholarship; failure on a second, dismissal.[27]

The poor state of research facilities was one reflection of the bias toward training. It has even been argued that Japanese universities and schools were established in this period only to import foreign science, not to create knowledge.[28] In 1878 the physicist Tanakadate Aikitsu was unimpressed with the physics laboratory at Tokyo University, whose equipment comprised a professor's desk, three small tables, three instrument cabinets, a heliostat for light experiments, and a curtain to make a darkroom.[29] In 1879 T. C. Mendenhall and his four students "built everything with their own hands" because there was "no experimental equipment at all."[30] In 1880 the physicist Yamakawa Kenjirō was only slightly more hopeful. "Unfortunately we are dependent on foreign supplies. . . . While poorly equipped for work in electricity and magnetism, we do have equipment for optics, acoustics, and heat studies."[31]

Other laboratory facilities were also inadequate. German professors in Tokyo's medical school constantly complained of the lack of equipment in the late 1870s.[32] The zoologist Charles O. Whitman lamented the deficiencies in marine biology, in 1881 calling Tokyo University "inferior in every particular" to European institutions, upbraiding his colleagues for their lack of research, and castigating the government for indifference.

Will any Japanese admit that Dai Nippon, with its 34,000,000 inhabitants, is not able to support *one* first-class university? . . . Any science that offers small opportunities for pilfering 'squeezers,' makes no promise to improve the rice crop or the flavor of the sake, serves none of the wants of sensual pleasure, jingles no bells, and refuses to make use of the sop of flattery, may be suffered to exist for the sake of appearances, but it is certain to be stigmatized as unprofitable.[33]

The inglorious fate of the Tokyo Academy appears to support Whitman's view. Toward the end of 1878 education ministry adviser David Murray had called the attention of Vice Minister Tanaka Fujimaro to the contributions of foreign science academies to the development of their respective national states and formally proposed that Japan join their ranks by creating its own academy of science. Seven members of the former Meirokusha society learned of Murray's suggestion and added their endorsement. Tanaka and these seven met together and agreed on a number of points: academicians were to choose their own members, beginning with the nucleus of seven, up to a total of forty; all the arts and sciences were to be represented; the minister of education was to "approve" all appointments; members would meet periodically to discuss various topics, including current policies of the Ministry of Education; a ministry representative would attend each meeting; members would receive annual stipends of three hundred yen; and the government would recognize the academy officially.[34]

Nothing went as the sponsors had hoped. The academy lost its most committed supporter when Tanaka fell from power late in 1879, and few other officials wanted a science academy purely for national prestige.[35] Instead, they were concerned with useful results, which were not always quickly forthcoming. Observers like the chemist Sakurai Jōji hinted that this might be due to the small number of natural scientists who belonged to the academy—only one in 1879, two in 1885, and seven in 1898.[36] Katō Hiroyuki said it was because the government thought the members were "physical decrepits with no ability."[37] Hasegawa Tai claimed it resulted from the members' "excessive deference to officialdom," elicited by the overbearing presence of their former Meirokusha colleague Mori Arinori in the office of minister of education.[38] A present-day historian attributes the stagnation to cuts in support accompanying the Matsukata Deflation (1880–82).[39] Katō summarized the feelings of contemporary intellectuals when he claimed that the failure of the Tokyo academy was a major disgrace to the nation.[40]

But Katō's judgment lacked perspective. Meiji Japan had plenty of other problems: a civil insurrection to put down (1876–77), samurai indebtedness to resolve, children to educate, technicians to be trained, factories to be built. It needed to construct railroads and set up modern communications. Military reform demanded attention, as did medical care and modern public health. Moreover, Katō's and Whitman's charges are based on invidious comparisons, which historical facts do not justify. Conditions in Europe's best universities were better than those at Tokyo University, but they had reached that level quite recently. Prior to 1800 all European universities were supposed to pass on received information, not create knowledge.[41] Only in 1827 did Justus von Liebig build the first research laboratory in a German university (Giessen); Britain had nothing comparable until 1845. There was some expansion of facilities in the 1850s and 1860s, but research laboratories came to be considered an indispensable feature of the modern university only after the Franco-Prussian War.[42]

Nor was the desirability of a science academy clear for Japan at that time. Men like Galileo, Sprat, and Colbert had promoted them in the seventeenth century because the universities of their day were hostile to science, and they spread because the conditions that spawned them persisted.[43] Even in the eighteenth century science remained a modest component of European culture, despite its growing reputation. Scientists were either wealthy or practiced another occupation, and patrons belonged to the aristocracy or the affluent, rising middle class. Universities continued to reflect the conservative views of the landed elite, and governments that supported science academies, like that of Russia, did so for reasons of national prestige.[44] None of this changed before the French Revolution; the functions of academies changed first. Rather than performing contract research at official (or private) instigation, their primary mission was now to honor scientists. To the founders' dismay, the American National Academy of Sciences, created in 1863, served only this honorific function.[45] The St. Petersburg Academy of mid-nineteenth century Russia lost some of its research to the reformed universities.[46]

The late 1880s brought changes in conditions for Japanese research. During Tokyo University's first eight years the college of science had functioned with makeshift quarters, but in September 1885 new facilities were completed at the main Hongo campus. The two new buildings were described by one physicist as elegant. Modeled on the buildings at Berlin University, they had red brick facing and slate-tiled roofs. Chemistry laboratories and classrooms filled the second floor of one of the buildings, while physics and mathematics occupied the first.[47] The following year was equally momentous, with three major changes on the Tokyo campus. The Imperial College of Engineering was moved to Hongo and merged with the engineering component of the college of science to form a new faculty of engineering. The science and medical colleges also became faculties, and the graduate school was established. Creation of several nonacademic laboratories further expanded Japanese capacities for research. The Nishigahara Silk Experiment Station was built in 1886, the Experiment Station of the Bureau of Forestry and the Misaki Institute for Marine Life Studies requested by Whitman in 1887, and the Tokyo University Observatory in 1888.

These developments were part of a quest for useful knowledge. The prominent statesman Ōkuma Shigenobu declared in 1884 that technical research would help Japanese industry, and the Imperial University Ordinance (1886) made the same point.[48] For this reason a number of facilities for applied technical research were established. In 1891 the Electrotechnical Laboratory appeared, followed by the Central Institute for Weights and Measures (1903), the Fermentation Laboratory (also 1903), and the Railways Research Institute (1907). Their direction and the timing of their creation were affected by several different factors.

For one thing, German achievements with scientific institutions were arousing some interest in Japan. The German *technische Hochschulen* (higher technical schools) were teaching engineering in a systematic, straightforward manner. British-style hands-on experience was valuable, and Japanese did work in Britain to acquire it, but the schoolroom approach was faster and generally more efficient. Second, Germany had more industry-oriented laboratories, with higher levels of funding, than any other country. Because of this, W. H. Perkin, founder of the modern dye industry, left Britain for Germany in 1856. Germany's chemical industry surpassed Britain's.[49] Third, the German universities had established the world's first advanced training programs in medicine and basic science, attracting students from many other countries and eliciting fulsome praise from foreign academic reformers.

Nevertheless, officials in Japan were unwilling to adopt the German system wholesale. The Germans gave insufficient recognition to disciplines that they valued highly. Applied technical fields like engineering and agriculture were established in German academic institutions, but they were not accepted in German universities.[50] They were taught instead in the higher technical schools and had an implied lack of prestige. Japanese complained also about German organization. By the last quarter of the nineteenth century there were some twenty-eight German-speaking universities adhering more or less to a common set of traditions. Each field of knowledge at each university was represented by a single full professor, and professors had almost total control over the internal affairs of their institutions. Auxiliary, subordinate faculty members were appointed as needed. Private lecturers were allowed to offer courses as a means of stimulating academic competition, and they, together with the students, moved almost at will from university to university. Japanese officials were ambivalent about this system. Some praised its freedom of movement. Others thought it revealed a commitment to learning. But most just considered it far too expensive for Japan to adopt.

University relations with the German imperial government were also a source of objections. Although Germany by the last quarter of the century was a unified nation, the states still retained extensive authority, including much power in the area of education. The Universities of Berlin, Munich, and Heidelberg were state institutions, but the provinces controlled them, not the central government. Because the Meiji leaders wanted a highly centralized state, they investigated other models and were attracted to the French. French education had two major virtues from their point of view. It was highly centralized, with the University of Paris and the Ministry of Public Instruction at the top of a bureaucratic hierarchy, and the makeup of each component allowed professorships to be created as needed.

Meiji leaders' efforts to centralize also had their centripetal effects. Many wealthy farmers, now freed of the daimyo, preferred to be free of Tokyo as well. Christians and certain intellectuals often aspired to a higher moral end than the Meiji state and its all-pervasive cult of Shinto and the emperor. Some physicians cherished the freewheeling traditions of a loosely regulated profession. Samurai from formerly pro-Tokugawa domains resented the Satsuma-Chōshū leadership for blocking their political advancement. Such attitudes matter here because they impinged on research: groups with otherwise disparate interests would conspire in the areas of research and academic policy.

Diet Politics and Science in the 1890s

The 1890s was a watershed period for Japanese science in the years before World War I. Professors from Europe and North America had returned to their homes by 1900. Gaps in basic knowledge, which had previously loomed so large, were in most cases bridged by the end of this decade.[51] The university chair system was created in 1893, Kyoto University was founded in 1897, and the government began making commitments to basic research. Government initiatives—replacing foreigners with Japanese professors or founding new chairs—were particularly conspicuous. But by no means did officials take every forward step. Private individuals and groups were also active.

The Imperial Diet, founded in 1890, was the principal instrument they used. Given the parliament's character and subsequent history, this is rather surprising, but circumstances made using the Diet effective in this period. The creation of a representative assembly as a counterpoise to the leadership and the imperial bureaucracy had been a central demand of the popular rights movement in the 1870s and 1880s. After the general election of 1890, the first under the new constitution, many rich farmers, businessmen, and professionals (including several physicians) became members of the Diet and began to oppose the leadership. In 1890 the new parliament cut the budget by about 10 percent. In 1891 it filibustered legislation. In 1892 it almost impeached the cabinet, and in 1893 it sent a letter to the emperor which sought dismissal of Prime Minister Itō.[52] Some of this behavior was motivated by a desire to establish its place in the constitutional system of an autocratic state, but some of it also reflected commitments to particular policies.

Advancing research in Japanese agriculture was one of the goals of the Diet. Reflecting the size of the agricultural economy and the American Morrill Act precedent (1862) that established agricultural colleges, the Meiji government had awarded small subsidies for testing and research in 1886 and in 1890 had expanded the Agricultural Experiment Station at Komaba in Tokyo. In 1895 it established a seven-facility network, but this failed to satisfy the need or demand for a much greater effort in agricultural research. Further expansion was limited by financial commitments and allegedly by staff shortages, and the way was open for private individuals to launch their own proposals. A group of Shizuoka tea growers began agitating for a tea industry experiment station in 1895. The same year saw legislation introduced to provide modest subsidies to eighteen local and prefectural facilities. And Naha Kiyoshi, who had founded an entomological laboratory in 1896, requested a subvention in 1899.

Private proposals for research in agriculture were all rejected at first. In part this was because of costs. Naha's backers requested only 3,000 yen over a five-year period, but the tea growers' proposal and that for the additional experiment stations called for much larger sums—10,000 and 150,000 yen each year, respectively. As the chief of the Bureau of Agriculture declared during the Sino-Japanese War: "The government recognizes the need for these experiment stations but cannot grant subsidies because of heavy military spending."[53] But cost was just one of the problems. Did the country have enough agricultural researchers to manage an expanded program? The Bureau of Agriculture chief claimed in apparent good faith (but contrary to fact) that research workers were not sufficiently numerous.[54] Could they work with farmers and officials? Representative Nakamura Yaroku, who had a B.S. degree in physics, a D.Sc. in forestry, yet was an opponent of subsidies, said the researchers who were already working talked over farmers' heads, while a colleague who favored expansion noted accusations of researchers' condescension toward officials.[55]

The major obstacle in the 1890s was fear of the national government. Most officials approved of subsidies and considered them desirable in principle; the private sector wanted them desperately but was divided on the probable effects. Some farmers and their representatives put economic interests ahead of political concerns; others did just the reverse. Throughout the 1890s members of the Diet who had either taken part in the popular rights movement or were actively sympathetic depicted agricultural research subsidies as a means of intervention by Tokyo. As Representative Komatsu Sanshō declared in 1896: "When the government exerts itself to help in such matters, it almost always creates unendurable interference. . . . If we want to promote popular rights at all, if we truly wish to defend local autonomy, I am firmly convinced that we cannot ask for state support and at the same time avoid the interference by government that [usually] accompanies such proposals."[56] Government finances eased by 1900, and these scruples were partially overcome. Local experiment stations' first subsidies were awarded that year; and the Naha Laboratory got support two years later. But the tea growers had to wait until 1919.

Medical research was also of concern to both private and public sectors. In the latter seventeenth century government sponsorship had launched Western studies of anatomy, and in the eighteenth century, studies of smallpox vaccination. But subsequent breakthroughs in dissection and anesthesia were made by private physicians, creating a mixed history that set the stage in Meiji Japan for a complex set of relationships. The predominant tendency was for the private sector to be the innovator, while government agencies provided the research infrastructure and financed important separate projects. But some new research projects were launched by government agencies, and some private agencies wanted their own infrastructure. These political trends led to bitter conflicts between those who wished to keep public and private separate and those who wanted to merge them.

The establishment of the Institute of Infectious Diseases in 1893 illustrates these crosscurrents. The institute was the most important research facility built in Japan before World War I, and its legal sponsorship and initial funding came from the private sector, but the Diet provided a subsidy, approved only after a plan for full state funding had been rejected. Executive direction of the laboratory was vested in Kitasato Shibasaburō, a scientist and low-ranking official at that time.

The leading parliamentary sponsor of the subsidy was an irascible physician who had moved freely between the public and private sectors; the subsidy plan's leading opponent had previously been president of Tokyo University. All this begins to show the complexity of the forces at work, but to explain the outcome one must consider the social position of Tokyo University, the effects of the popular rights movement, and the impact of German precedents in organizing medical research.

The Institute of Infectious Diseases resulted from spectacular achievements by bacteriologists in the 1870s and 1880s, but its immediate inception traces to the discovery of tuberculin by Koch (1890). As noted earlier, his description of the substance as a cure for tuberculosis proved highly controversial and inspired further efforts to clarify the issues. The bureaucratic structure of medicine in Japan strongly influenced these efforts. One program to study tuberculin was initiated by physicians in the Ministry of Home Affairs, where public health programs were housed, and a second was directed by several university professors—subject to control by the Ministry of Education. The two agencies then developed plans for follow-up research as the testing proceeded. Inevitably, each ministry submitted plans to the cabinet for a research facility of its own.[57]

Kitasato's role in the subsequent conflict was a major and enduring complication. Adamantly opposed to any affiliation with the Ministry of Education, he had rejected Tokyo University's invitation to join its faculty upon returning to Japan late in 1891 and instead sought private support for his work. With the backing of Fukuzawa Yukichi, industrialist Morimura Ichizaemon, and a private medical foundation called the Great Japan Hygiene Society (Dai Nihon Shiritsu Eisei Kai), he managed to open a small laboratory for bacteriological studies in September 1892. It soon proved too small. Lacking the money for expansion, the society persuaded one of its members, Hasegawa Tai, also a member of the Diet, to request a subsidy from the national government. In the meantime, the cabinet of Prime Minister Itō Hirobumi had decided to seek approval of the education ministry's proposal, which would have created a bacteriological laboratory in conjunction with Tokyo University.[58] This line-up of forces set the stage for a long-term struggle.

Sponsorship and control were the issues. Both proposals called for Kitasato to be named research director, but with varying definitions of authority. Hasegawa's bill assigned him control over budget and staff appointments and made him a consultant to the Bureau of Public Health. The proposal of the Ministry of Education made no mention of consultancy and denied him executive independence.[59] Particularly intense debate focused on the role of Tokyo University. Hasegawa wanted to exclude it completely. According to him, the university did not need an infectious diseases laboratory because it already had a small laboratory for hygiene directed by Ogata Masanori. Moreover, the separation between basic and clinical medicine in the faculty was likely to obstruct Kitasato's work just as the same structure at Berlin had done with Koch's. Finally, he argued, the Ministry of Education would probably interfere with Kitasato's work, given the history of conflict between them.[60]

Opponents, however—especially the former university president Watanabe Kōki—insisted that the university's role should be large and argued that private sponsorship was wrong. According to Watanabe, Tokyo University was Japan's pacesetter for all advanced learning. Government sponsorship was necessary because of Kitasato's background of employment in public health and support from a government scholarship. Koch's laboratory in Germany was government-funded, so Kitasato's should be as well. Private sponsorship of such an important facility might give foreign countries the idea that Japan did not value research too highly, and supporting someone whose ties with the Ministry of Education were so strained seemed inherently undesirable.[61]

The government lost the debate. At the conclusion of formal argument the Diet rejected the education ministry's request for 34,659 yen and instead awarded the Kitasato group 20,000 yen for construction and 45,000 yen for three years' operations. This decision did not end the conflict. Watanabe was so bitterly opposed to what he called the "private" development of science that he led a campaign to block construction of the new institute. He became a leading spokesman for residents of Tokyo's Shiba Park district, where the facility was to be built. They objected to its presence in their neighborhood for a variety of aesthetic, financial, and hygienic grounds and tried to block implementation of the enabling legislation. Their opposition failed for a number of reasons. Kitasato was indispensable—Japan really had no other bacteriologists at that time—and his supporters proved politically adept. Hasegawa and other backers explained the work of the similarly constituted Koch and Pasteur institutes in lectures for the general public, they gained the active support of several Tokyo newspapers, and Kitasato himself held a series of meetings with delegations of Shiba Park residents. Their success was assured when the press called Watanabe's movement irrational and subjected his actions to "indiscriminate ridicule."[62]

The legacy of ties between government and various fields of learning gave Watanabe's views greater currency than his failure suggests. Attempts to control certain disciplines were by no means eliminated by the collapse of the Tokugawa shogunate in 1868. Public discussion in the Meiji period regularly featured conflict between the so-called *shigaku* (private learning) and *kangaku* (state learning) perspectives, focusing on the extent or incidence of private-sector initiative to be permitted in technical studies.[63] Meiji leaders frequently inclined toward *kangaku* but had to accept alternatives. Fukuzawa Yukichi thus created a medical school at Keio (1874), Ōkuma Shigenobu an engineering program at Waseda (1882) and Niijima Jō a full-fledged science and engineering college, the Harris School of Science, at Dōshisha (1889). But these actions were only grudgingly tolerated, and all three programs foundered. The Keio medical program closed down in 1876, Ōkuma's engineering course terminated in 1884, and the Harris School shut its doors in 1897.[64] While their circumstances differed, government refusal to grant these institutions legal equality with Tokyo University was a common factor.[65]

Other aspirations and views also contributed to the conflict. Activists in the popular rights movement, which had directed public anger against the leadership's power monopoly, took a strong position in favor of private education and consistently opposed efforts by the education ministry to restrict freedom of action. Shimada Saburō, Kōno Hironaka, and Hasegawa Tai, who had helped to found the Liberal and Progressive parties (Jiyūtō and Kaishintō), all sponsored the subsidy legislation for Kitasato's laboratory, criticizing the views of the Ministry of Education. Hasegawa ran a private medical academy, the Zaisei Gakusha, which the ministry repeatedly tried to close.[66]

Confronting them were the government's constitutional advisers from Germany and their like-thinking Japanese followers. Lorenz von Stein in 1882 and Herman Roesler in 1890 warned Japanese officials about what they considered to be the political dangers of private education. Roesler prepared a memorandum for the education ministry proffering this advice: "Ideas and opinions based on *science* [emphasis added] determine the nature and the scope of people's knowledge and exert great influence on their ideas about . . . law, politics, religion, the state, and society . . . [For this reason] higher education should never be . . . private."[67] To their credit, however, many Japanese officials rejected this basic philosophy. In a celebrated riposte to an 1879 memorandum on the same subject by Emperor Meiji's Confucian lecturer, Itō Hirobumi had dismissed the notion of ineluctable "spillover" from science to society, arguing that it was actually the politicizing tendency of Confucianism rather than the rationalism of science that encouraged seditious or subversive activities.[68]

Decisions about infrastructure, however, continued to generate controversy. Was the level of spending correct? How many universities should there be? How should they be organized? Was an upgraded science academy desirable? If so, what should it do? Could the German private-lecturer system invigorate the learned establishment? How should professorships be allocated by fields? The cleavages created by these issues were sharp, and they differed from their common portrayals. They did not center on which models to adopt, but on how to combine elements of a number of models. Nor was the conflict between officials—allegedly advocating German models—and spokesmen for the private sector favoring models from Britain or France. Instead German experience set parameters for debate over a "mixed Continental" system.[69]

These debates were also ironic in view of the apparent firmness of policy. A broad array of well-funded programs was supposed to exist, with access dependent on and proportional to the number of high school graduates. Professors were supposed to carry on research and teaching together. And the Ministry of Education was supposed to supervise a network of seven or eight institutions.[70] But serious problems existed in each of these areas and others. There were comprehensive programs, but funding was precarious. Many more students qualified for university admission than one institution could possibly accommodate. Faculty members were regularly accused of indolence or lethargy in research, and only one university—Tokyo—was actually operating. These difficulties, however understandable, gave critics more room for maneuvering. Representative Kamino Ryō attacked the concentration in Tokyo of educational resources.[71] The education journal *Kokka kyōiku* deplored the lack of competition among both professors and students.[72] Hasegawa Tai, criticizing the relatively high ratio of professors to students, labeled Tokyo a "caricature of a foreign university."[73] Such attacks were more than rhetoric. In 1890 the Diet tried to cut the university's budget by 17 percent—and did reduce it 6 percent in 1892.[74]

In 1893 the Ministry of Education took steps to respond to outside pressure. Acting on a proposal from the former university president Katō Hiroyuki, Minister Inoue Kowashi decided on a change in the university's structure. His reform called for establishment of a faculty chair system. Before this time, Tokyo University had operated under a department structure that many had attacked for inefficiency. Professors in a given academic unit—law, medicine, engineering—had been responsible for teaching any of its courses. This encouraged intellectual flexibility, but it impeded specialization and was thought to raise costs. Inoue wanted a sharper demarcation of professorial responsibility so he could replace costly foreigners and reduce expenses. After studying university organization in Germany and France, he created a chair system suited to Japan. Each professor was responsible for a specialty. Multiple chairs were established in certain high-demand fields. Occupants of chairs exercised formal academic and financial control over younger faculty and graduate students in their areas, and a two-part compensation system awarded extra funds to the more productive professors and laboratories.[75]

Short-term results from these changes were mixed. Some money was saved. The initial scheme presumed creation of 152 chairs for the university. Inoue reduced this to 125, but even this number allowed for expansion of the teaching staff and a 12 percent cost reduction.[76] The provision (after the French model) for multiple chairs in high-demand fields offered the possibility of greater competition in science. But most critics of higher education remained unimpressed. Some attacked the un-German use of full-time university administrators. Why should deans hold office full time? Could the university president not hold down two jobs? "At the University of Berlin, the president changes office every year."[77] Others said competition was still insufficient. Professors would improve their lectures if, as in Germany, students paid them fees to attend. The same result might follow from appointing privatdozenten to the faculty.[78] Better still would be to create more imperial universities. As things stood, professors were too often neglecting their main duties to attend sessions of the House of Peers in the Diet, do private consulting, or otherwise pursue side employment. "Those engaged in scientific research [and teaching], whether medicine or physical science, cannot finish anything by working only one hour a day or three days a week" was the contention of Hasegawa Tai.[79]

Education officials in the 1890s showed a flexible response to these charges. In some cases they maintained that solutions were in place. Professors' salaries, for example, were said to be docked if three weeks of classes were missed.[80] In other cases they repeated earlier arguments. Throughout the 1890s—and beyond—officials rejected such German practices as lecture fees, frequent rotation of administrators, and appointment of unsalaried lecturers on the legitimate grounds that the necessary conditions were lacking in Japan. Referring to the absence of a large corps of academics or of a national university network, Vice Minister Kubota Yuzuru remarked that Tokyo University's organizational framework was created "step by step," that officials had tried to develop organizational forms that were "suitable to Japan," and that the "foreign devices" suggested by critics would be "difficult to implement."[81] But in other situations these same officials were strongly inclined to equivocate. Asked late in 1893 whether the government planned to establish a second imperial university anytime soon, Makino Nobuaki, Kubota's successor, declared to the House of Representatives Budget Committee: "We do have to consider whether or not we should establish another university, whether the government or students would have a need for it. On that basis we might build another one. But I am not going to promise we will build one this year. There is no real obstacle if the need exists. If the question is what would be best in absolute terms, then of course a multiplicity is better."[82]

Establishment of a second imperial university was, in fact, a major event. Kyoto University began with faculties of science, engineering, and medicine which greatly enlarged infrastructure. In 1896 Japan had 85 university chairs in technical fields: 18 in basic science, 24 in engineering, 23 in medicine and pharmacology, and 20 in agriculture, forestry, and veterinary medicine. By 1898 basic science had 25 chairs, engineering 41, medicine 23, agriculture and the rest 20, for a total of 109. Expansion of this sort was probably inevitable, but its execution and timing were not. Cost was always one deterrent. In 1898 it cost the government 3,074 yen to maintain a chair at Tokyo but 4,445 yen for the same chair at Kyoto, and operating costs per student differed by a ratio of 28 : 73.[83] Moreover, educational philosophy was another deterrent for some in positions of influence. Academic administrators like Kikuchi Dairoku and Katō Hiroyuki saw university education as a route to power and for a time opposed expansion in order to maintain elitism.[84]

But the forces in favor of expansion were irresistible. Political demands for educational opportunities naturally had an effect. Tokyo University reached its mandated capacity of 460 students per graduating class as the chair system came into being. But the five higher schools were annually graduating about three times that number, and most wished to go on.[85] Furthermore, industry, which grew rapidly with the Sino-Japanese War, consistently demanded more engineers and technical specialists. Engineering enrollments mushroomed at all levels, and the educational system was hard pressed to respond. As early as 1894 Minister Inoue referred to the problem in a speech to the Diet. Vice Minister Makino in 1897 stressed the difficulties both of finding and of keeping engineering professors in his testimony before the House Budget Committee, and Representative Shiba Sankurō noted complaints from Tokyo students about academic engineers' neglect of their duties.[86] Such criticisms were justified. Prior to World War I, academic engineers rarely held one post for long. Universities competed for their services with government and business and were fortunate to keep them five years.[87]

But the principal reasons for founding Kyoto University were much more strictly academic. For example, many believed that Tokyo University had stagnated. Suzuki Manjirō, a physician, based his case to the Diet for a second university on the need to eliminate the "academic evils that derive from the monopolies of a single institution."[88] Toyama Shōichi, later minister of education, said a second imperial university would shake Tokyo University out of the "torpor into which it has tended to drift."[89] Hasegawa Tai in 1891 called the establishment of a second university in the Kansai region "indispensable to the development of education in Japan," adding: "Attentive observation shows that because of the lack of competition, [Tokyo University] professors have ceased to try to discover new scientific theories, and the students have ceased to pursue their . . . objectives."[90] Many, if not most, in authority agreed. Inoue in 1894 spoke favorably of Hasegawa's views in a letter to Itō Hirobumi.[91] Others commented approvingly on the rivalries between Cambridge and Oxford in Britain and between Yale and Harvard in the United States.[92] Vice Minister Makino underscored this theme at the time that Kyoto was founded, saying: "[Kyoto University] was created out of practical necessity. We [in the Ministry of Education] hope competition between the two institutions will yield many benefits. . . . Our hopes for progress had diminished with only the single university in Tokyo . . . [However], both institutions will have chairs in matching fields. So if one of the professors invents something, he will become widely known and trusted, and the students will greatly respect him."[93]

The university chair system Inoue had instituted also elicited concern. Hasegawa was a vigorous defender of the one-chair rule and was in principle opposed to large faculties. In December 1891 he had compared Tokyo with its 316 professors and 2,590 students unfavorably with Berlin (324 and 6,626) and Munich (172 and 3,646), citing the case of physics as a subject taught in two different colleges. "If first-year engineering students are weak in physics, they should enter the science college and study it for a year with a specialist."[94] After the chair system came into existence, he continued to insist on this view. It was "ridiculous" to have three chairs in pharmacology.[95] There should be no duplication of programs for applied chemistry.[96] Multiple chairs in physiology were not needed.[97] The Ministry of Education and it allies, of course, had their own views. Not only was it cheaper to expand by adding chairs as opposed to whole universities, one had always to consider objectives. "Our need for knowledge," said Representative Nakamura Yaroku in reference to mathematics, "is one of the reasons for the large number of university professors." Vice Minister Tsuji Shinji declared, "Scientific knowledge in Japan lags far behind that of other countries. For that reason we have to do a great deal of research. It is completely erroneous to say that there are too many professors for the number of students . . . The professors must first investigate the theories of the leading foreign scientists . . . Our scientists study their work and are making it known here."[98] The result—Kyoto University—was a compromise that allowed the country to develop a university network while avoiding fixed limits on chairs.

Founding a second university was difficult; making it function was more so. By imperial ordinance universities were supposed to be comprehensive and had to have at least two faculties. Because of the intense demand for more engineers and physicians, having faculties in those areas was a foregone conclusion, but little else was certain. Some members of the Diet favored faculties of agriculture and commerce; some officials were partial to letters and law.[99] The education ministry's basic plan called for a university two-thirds the size of Tokyo with space for 1,250 students: 400 in science and engineering, 400 in medicine, 300 in law, and 150 in letters. But the cost of this plan was too great for the limited resources. President-designate Kinoshita Hiroji estimated that a four-faculty institution of this size should cost 10 million yen, at a time when the government's entire budget for postsecondary education was only 1.5 million yen.[100] As a result, the decision was made to begin with engineering, science, and medicine and shortly thereafter add law.

Lack of funds caused other adjustments, too. Basic science and engineering were combined in a single faculty that excluded geology and the biological sciences. Maximum use was made of existing academic facilities. Because higher school programs paralleled those at the university level, for only 300,000 yen facilities for applied chemistry, metallurgy, and mining engineering were added to the physical plant of the Third Higher School, located in Kyoto, and the whole transferred to Kyoto University.[101] The government also got outside support. After lengthy negotiations, the Kyoto prefectural authorities donated 16.2 acres of land to the new university and 31,000 yen for construction.[102] Similar plans for the faculty of medicine, however, could not be fulfilled. One called for locating the faculty in Osaka and using the physical plant of the Osaka Prefectural Medical College. This had partisans in the Diet, the Ministry of Education, and the office of Osaka's prefectural governor, but the prefectural assembly balked, and the Kyoto authorities opposed it.[103] A second plan was to build the faculty in Kyoto and use the facilities of its prefectural medical college, but this ran afoul of the college's dean, Inoko Shikanosuke, who argued that the 51,000 yen budgeted was wholly inadequate. The upshot was an additional land purchase and the establishment of new facilities in Kyoto.[104]

Another difficulty in founding the university was a serious shortage of professors. One solution was to send more *ryūgakusei* abroad to qualify themselves for professorships. Vice Minister Makino estimated in March 1897 that a hundred professors should be hired just to open the first two faculties. Only about half that number were available, so the government requested 39,166 yen to support foreign study for 25 more.[105] Another solution was to appoint some foreigners. According to proponents, foreigners would not just compensate for a shortage of

Japanese, but their employment would shorten the time needed to "raise Japan to the level of [advanced] foreign countries." The foreigners would stimulate their Japanese colleagues. "There is a chance for renewal with the foreigners here since they bring new ideas . . . and present them to students."[106] Other solutions—to delay the commencement of programs or to hire private school graduates—were also proposed, but not with any enthusiasm.

Although none of these solutions got wholehearted support, some were less offensive than others. Increasing the number of students abroad was described as unnecessary, too expensive, and embarrassing to the academic community. Japanese universities were probably "not very good" if so many new professors were needed. Hiring the graduates of Dōshisha or Keio would "weaken private education." Delay in starting up academic programs would be "highly unfair to the students."[107] People particularly resisted hiring foreigners, saying that it would cause "friction with less educated [Japanese] professors,"[108] that linguistic problems would impede intellectual exchange, and that Japanese surely could cope with the complexities of "newfangled sciences."[109] After much debate, the government decided to postpone academic programs scheduled to begin in September 1899 to January 1900 for science and engineering and March for medicine and law. The proposal for expansion of overseas study was approved when the vice minister of education testified: "There is nothing more important for our country than implanting these advancing fields of science. We will regret it a hundred years from now if this effort is frustrated . . . It is quite impossible to push scientific research ahead by merely relying on foreigners."[110]

The university's problems raised serious issues of quality. Diet members worried that inordinate haste in appointing professors might produce an inadequate faculty. An education ministry spokesman said the library was much too small. Two years after the formal opening the university president complained that Kyoto had "no books, no equipment, no specimens, nothing." The greatest problems by every account existed in physical science. The physics section needed gas purification machines to break down water. The physical chemistry laboratory had no generators. The research facilities in general could not stand foreign comparison, and returned *ryūgakusei* had few colleagues. Officials thought that the reasons for this were largely historical. "Quite a number of people have carried on scientific research in the thirty years since the Restoration took place," the vice minister of education noted. "But we Japanese have little experience with any of the physical sciences."[111]

Public debates on the science academy were even more forceful and pointed. The academy had originally been conceived of as an adviser to government. Ministers of education were supposed to seek members' counsel on a wide range of issues, especially those important to policy. But after Mori Arinori's tenure in office (1885–89), the academy was pushed aside, and its influence declined. Instead of advising government officials, members devoted their energies to private consulting, translation activity, and editorial work for one journal. Each received an annual stipend of 300 yen for these tasks. Diet members once active in the popular rights movement deeply resented the changes, arguing that the academy had lost its guiding inspiration and had nothing substantive to say. They charged that some academy members were "senile," that only "sycophants" could become members, and that what little the academy did do was "inconsequential" and a waste of money. Rather than spend money on this kind of "almshouse," the government should give it to Tokyo University or direct it to some other purpose.[112]

Education officials rejected these charges and developed a defense claiming that the actual cost of the academy was rather small, that it was producing "good results for a backward country," that other countries with academies of science were receiving "significant benefits," that the Tokyo Academy of Sciences was "not really an academy in the foreign sense," and that one should never forget how far Japan had come in the years since the shogunate ended.[113]

Ministry officials also came up with an argument of greater importance: the Academy of Sciences was desperately needed for scholars who were academic misfits.[114] Their case in point was Itō Keisuke (1803–1901), the noted physician and botanist. As mentioned earlier, Itō did botanical research before the Restoration and remained quite active after it. He helped to found a group dedicated to scientific studies (the Yōyōsha), became director of Tokyo University's botanical garden, helped found the Tokyo Botanical Society, and joined the Tokyo Academy of Sciences as one of its earliest members. Between 1881 and 1886, Itō also served as professor of botany at Tokyo University. In 1888 he received the first doctoral degree.[115]

Nevertheless, Itō was not fully a part of the academic mainstream and was rejected by some (see chapter 3). This implied a need for other support, and options were not very numerous. A sinecure with the Tokyo Museum paid him 480 yen per year, while the botanical garden post and university professorship brought in 600 more yen.[116] The 300 yen Itō got from the academy was essential for a middle-class life. Minister Inoue Kowashi explained the situation this way: "There are still people [from Tokugawa times] with considerable experience who have made valuable contributions to the progress of knowledge. One such person, Itō Keisuke . . . would be reduced nearly to poverty if the

300 yen we give him were taken away. It would not be right to treat this eminent scholar in such a [cavalier] way."[117] The Diet was only partly convinced. It authorized payments of money to Itō but dismissed all plans to expand the academy.

The Struggle to Define a Research Posture

By the end of the nineteenth century the Japanese scientific and technical community had entered a new steady state, with support guaranteed but at minimal levels. Facilities were inadequate, budgets insecure, and expectations low except in medicine, where infrastructure and research activity occasionally reached the levels of the West. The fifteen years preceding World War I saw several major efforts to improve the situation. The imperial university system expanded with new foundations in Kyushu (at Fukuoka) and the Tōhoku region (at Sendai). The government decided after all to expand the Tokyo Academy of Sciences and restate its objectives. Several commercial organizations became actively interested in research. A slow but significant trend in government laboratories away from testing and toward genuine research showed itself. Various elements of society besides the research community sought to build up the physical sciences.

Some groups wanted more imperial universities, since such institutions could help to raise local levels of development. In 1901 Representative Noma Itsuzō, from the Tōhoku region, claimed that economic development in the Japanese islands was deformed and stressed that universities were "important for inducing civilization locally."[118] Establishing additional universities would also make education more accessible to Japanese youths outside Tokyo. In 1900 Representative Sugawara Den called the contrast between a vigorous Japanese military buildup and the neglect of higher education a "shameful circumstance," noting that Japan had only two universities for forty million people, whereas Germany had over twenty, and even Britain had at least five.[119] In 1902 Representative Ozaki Yukio, proponent of an imperial university in Tōhoku, compared the small number of Japanese university students unfavorably with far larger numbers in Europe and insisted that students were the wealth of the nation.[120]

Other proponents of university expansion were concerned for academic well-being. In 1902 Tokyo law professor Takane Yoshito published an influential book claiming that five years with two universities—Tokyo and Kyoto—had done little to promote competition. Since academic researchers become "lethargic and slack off," he argued, unless stimulated by external forces, it was imperative to found more chairs and universities and to involve graduate students in their professors' research.[121] His view was both popular and justified. In 1901 Representative Hiraoka Manjirō embarrassed the Ministry of Education by charging that Tokyo University was full of professors who "took ten hours to do two hours' work."[122] In 1911 the *Kawakita shimpō* newspaper in Sendai published a major editorial declaring that universities had a duty to compete with each other and deserved to be criticized severely if they "catered slavishly to society" or neglected research.[123]

For the government, universities were expensive to start up, and more so to maintain. On the other hand, the founding of Kyoto in 1897 had broken the ice for expansion, and basic public policy would never again restrict access to universities on principle. Both Yamagata Aritomo's second cabinet and the first cabinet of Ōkuma Shigenobu developed plans for serious expansion in 1898, and in 1900 Itō Hirobumi's new Seiyūkai party made a similar declaration of intent.[124] The government had promised university admission to every student with a higher-school diploma, and it had to make good on its promise. In 1894 there were only about 1,400 university students, but by 1898 the number of higher-school graduates had reached 2,400, and it was expected to grow fivefold in a decade.[125]

Fortunately outside support for added facilities was available. Almost before planning had begun, Yamagata's minister of education, Kabayama Sukenori, demanded and received commitments of 500,000 and 350,000 yen, respectively, from Fukuoka and Miyagi prefectures, where the new institutions would be. Tōhoku University became possible only in 1906 through support from a wealthy industrialist. One other factor also deserves to be stressed. Certain ministry officials were concerned about the obstacles faced by university researchers and were determined to improve conditions. Referring in 1897 to the difficulties faced by Japanese scientists who had come back from Europe, Vice Minister Makino Nobuaki noted that in Japan their "level of performance falls behind because of their lack of opportunity to debate issues with prominent scientists and the [poor] facilities they have for research."[126]

Even so, the government could not take up these problems simultaneously and was obliged to set priorities. On the basis of purely objective need, the case for engineering was most compelling. Makino noted in 1897 that the worst situation of neglect of students by professors was in engineering, that there were "not nearly enough facilities for engineering research in Japan," and that in some engineering fields there were scarcely any professors.[127] Conversely, the facilities in anatomy at Tokyo University were described at the time as "comparable to those in

European and American universities," whereas two years later (1899) hygiene, physiology, and pharmacology at that institution were said to have "the kind of equipment needed for research, in fact, the best available today."[128] And engineering facilities were cheaper to build. Startup costs, excluding land purchases, were estimated at 350,000 yen for engineering and 604,000 yen for medicine in 1901; annual maintenance costs for an engineering faculty were a fraction of those for a faculty of medicine.[129] But medicine still got priority in this phase of expansion. To the dismay of Diet members from the Tōhoku region, Itō's cabinet in 1901 decided to build a faculty of medicine in Kyushu while shelving indefinitely a faculty of engineering proposal for Sendai.[130]

Decisions in favor of medicine were common. The cause of medical research benefited from the prominent role in the imperial Diet of physicians—Suzuki Manjirō, Wakasugi Kisaburō, Yagi Itsurō, Tsuchiya Seizaburō, and especially Hasegawa Tai. Hasegawa was the era's leading parliamentary expert on educational and technical matters, and while he sought to promote all technical fields, he definitely favored some over others.[131] In 1893 he criticized the vice minister of education Kubota Yuzuru for his apparent lack of interest in the needs of engineering even as he himself proposed eliminating funds for an applied chemistry laboratory in Tokyo's engineering faculty and building instead a biochemistry laboratory in the Tokyo faculty of medicine.[132] Second, the favorable publicity that Kitasato and other medical researchers received aided the cause of medicine. Such achievements as the discovery of the plague bacillus in 1894 and the dysentery bacillus in 1897 captured widespread attention and made support of medicine attractive to government and public alike. Engineers and physical scientists had less to boast of in the pre–World War I era and could not arouse this kind of interest. Third, the government always tried to use existing facilities as a way of cutting the costs of university expansion. When Kyoto was built in the 1890s, the engineering and science faculty initially used the facilities of the Third Higher School, and major (though abortive) efforts were made to use those of a prefectural college for the faculty of medicine. In the second wave of expansion, the government proposed to convert the Sapporo Agricultural College into a university-level faculty of agriculture for Tōhoku University and to turn an existing prefectural medical college in Kyushu into a university-level faculty of medicine.[133]

This short-term practice of preempting facilities for imperial universities' use points to a more permanent one. Medicine expanded with particular rapidity in the Meiji period because it began from a position of strength. When the Yamagata cabinet decided to build the Kyushu faculty of medicine in 1901, it was able to expand facilities for medical education that had been in Fukuoka from the end of the Tokugawa period.[134] Few thought that using such facilities was unusual. (By contrast, the building of engineering and science facilities had earlier been seen as a radical, though necessary, move.)[135] The bias toward medicine and the desire to use existing facilities were so deeply entrenched that the minister of education Kikuchi Dairoku, trained in mathematics and physics, not only endorsed them but at political cost to himself intervened with cabinet and Diet in their favor.[136]

After 1901 the cause of expansion entered a period of stasis. Continuing military buildup prevented any budget increases for science or higher education in 1902 and 1903. In 1904 and 1905 government and public concentrated their attention on the Russo-Japanese War. Financial dislocations at the end of the war brought retrenchment in all ministries, and in 1906 the Saionji government was mostly concerned with the nationalization of the country's trunk railways. But at what seemed an unfavorable moment, interest in expansion revived. Saionji's finance minister, Hara Kei, a Furukawa Corporation director and native of the Tōhoku region, asked a wealthy friend and industrialist to help build a university in Tōhoku. Hara reminded Furukawa Toranosuke of the public's bitterness against his corporation for polluting agricultural waterways in the Ashio copper mine scandal and suggested that contributing to the cause of an imperial university might help to reduce the ill will. Furukawa assented to Hara's proposal and donated 1,060,000 yen. As a result, the Saionji cabinet decided to build an imperial university in Sendai.[137]

Tōhoku University's internal constitution may seem as unlikely as the factors which led to its founding. Despite public demands for more engineers and better trained doctors, and earlier planning by the Ministry of Education, Tōhoku did not begin with faculties of engineering or medicine but with a faculty of science and a faculty of agriculture. Behind the founding of a faculty of science was a desire to achieve regional balance in facilities. The existence of applied science faculties in Kyushu (medicine from 1903, engineering projected for 1911), Kyoto (engineering and medicine from 1897), Hokkaido (the Sapporo Agricultural College, now transferred in jurisdiction to Tōhoku), and Tokyo made these programs initially less essential for Tōhoku. Another factor was vagueness. Unlike university proponents in Kyushu, neither Ozaki Yukio, the Miyagi prefectural government, nor anyone else from the region was ever specific about what they wanted in a university. Seemingly most important were the views of the minister. Giving credence to the criticism that "policy changed when the minister changed," Makino Nobuaki, upon assuming office in 1906, decided to proceed with a faculty of science. Makino considered mathematics, physics, and chemistry the proper basis for all applied sciences and decided to organize the university accordingly.[138]

Makino's decision may appear remarkable for the time. According to many observers, the Japanese public and government viewed basic science with indifference. A 1907 editorial in a professional journal complained that basic researchers were considered "eccentrics whose work is a form of dissipation."[139] But Makino's decision was not so peculiar as such evidence would suggest. Certainly there was a connection between industry and the academy favoring applied science. Ministry officials or their constituents frequently requested government funds on the basis of enrollment or social demand.

Motives behind decisions about infrastructure, however, were never so simple. They were sometimes dictated by notions of how science functioned or where it was heading. In February 1901 a ministry councillor, Terada Yūkichi, told the Budget Committee of the Diet's lower house that biochemistry at Tokyo University had not been accorded a separate laboratory in 1896 because it was then a mere "part of physiology" but must now be so established because it had become mature. In December 1901 Okada Ryōhei, later minister of education, denied that growth in the number of students was the only criterion for expanding research facilities and insisted that electrical engineering must have additional space at Tokyo University because of "scientific progress [which has occurred] in that field."[140]

The role of notions about scientific progress is especially clear when we compare the number of chairs with changes in student preferences. Imperial university faculties of science produced only 5.2 percent of the graduates in 1900 yet contained 14.1 percent of the chairs, whereas the faculties of engineering held 23.8 percent of the chairs while turning out 32.7 percent of the graduates. Faculties of medicine had 17.8 percent of the chairs and produced just 8.3 percent of the graduates, whereas faculties of law held 21.6 percent of the chairs while turning out 31.7 percent of the graduates. Nor were the figures for 1900 atypical. Table 4.1 indicates that "overrepresentation" of basic science (and in part, medicine) was common before World War I. High student enrollment in some fields paid the costs of low enrollment in others.

Early developments in the new universities show the strengths and limitations of this policy. Kyushu University began in 1911 with the medical faculty transferred from Kyoto and, following the request of local industrialists, with a faculty of engineering as well. Both faculties were popular and reasonably well funded. Some 1,300,000 yen was spent on the faculty of medicine, and about a third of Furukawa's 1,060,000 yen went to the faculty of engineering.[141] Kyushu's first

TABLE 4.1
Imperial University Chairs and Graduates (% of Totals)

	1895	1900	1905	1910	1915
LAW					
–Chairs	17.7	21.6	22.3	19.8	18.0
–Graduates	37.5	31.7	34.5	33.4	41.7
SCIENCE					
–Chairs	14.5	14.1	12.6	10.8	12.8
–Graduates	7.8	5.2	3.7	4.2	4.1
ENGINEERING					
–Chairs	16.9	23.8	20.2	16.4	21.9
–Graduates	21.6	32.7	31.3	22.9	19.2
LETTERS					
–Chairs	16.1	10.8	9.2	14.5	12.1
–Graduates	11.2	18.9	11.4	12.3	7.0
MEDICINE					
–Chairs	18.6	17.8	25.6	22.9	20.7
–Graduates	10.8	8.3	14.9	18.3	16.9
AGRICULTURE					
–Chairs	16.1	11.9	10.1	15.5	14.5
–Graduates	11.2	3.2	4.1	9.0	11.1

Sources: *Tōkyō Teikoku Daigaku gojū nen shi*, 2 vols. (Tōkyō Teikoku Diagaku, 1932); *Kyōto Teikoku Daigaku shi* (Kyōto Teikoku Daigaku, 1943); *Kyōto Daigaku nanajū nen shi* (Kyōto Daigaku, 1967); *Tōhoku Daigaku gojū nen shi*, 2 vols. (Tōhoku Daigaku, 1960); *Kyūshū Daigaku gojū nen shi*, 3 vols. (Kyūshū Daigaku, 1967).

president, Yamakawa Kenjirō, a physicist serving concurrently as president at Tokyo, was effective politically, securing two new chairs from the ministry. The first group of 55 engineering students completed their studies in 1914, and in the same year some 83 finished in medicine.[142] Conditions at Tōhoku were not quite so good. No money came to it from the national treasury in its first year, and only 361,262 yen of Furukawa's money was available to the faculty of science, since the rest was devoted to agriculture. Money for equipment was scarce, and at first there was concern among the basic science professors whether students would actually appear for instruction.[143]

Nevertheless, professors at Tōhoku University were happier than their colleagues at Kyushu. Tōhoku had an excellent first president in Sawayanagi Masatarō. Though trained in humanities, Sawayanagi was fully trusted by the scientists because he deliberately took over their administrative burdens and paid for their research-related travel. Tōhoku students showed an interest in mathematics, physics, chemistry, and geology, and twenty-four graduated in 1914. The Ministry of Education managed to allocate another 60,000 yen for equipment in the faculty of science after the mandated funds were exhausted.[144] And a vigorous climate for basic research developed in most fields (see chapter 6).

Kyushu University, by contrast, had no basic science program at all. Its engineering faculty (apart from the engineering chairs) contained one chair in mathematics and mechanics, to which Yamakawa in 1912 added a chair for chemistry and another for physics. Program building efforts all failed in this period, and this structural weakness dismayed the Kyushu professors. Mano Bunji, a mechanical engineer, considered the inability to solve it his biggest failure as dean. Upon hearing that the ministry had decided to build a faculty of science at Tōhoku and an engineering faculty at Kyushu, pharmacology professor Hayashi Haruo accused the authorities of giving Tōhoku the "brains" and Kyushu the "remains." Similarly, the Kyushu anatomy professor and medical faculty dean Gotō Motonosuke said it was wrong to give engineering priority over basic science because applied sciences like his were so dependent upon it.[145]

Ambivalent government actions can also be seen in the movement to reform the Tokyo Academy of Sciences. Although reform had failed in 1898 conditions had changed by 1905. The Russo-Japanese War may have aroused deeper appreciation for science in some quarters, but a desire to achieve national prestige as reflected in science was clearly the proximate cause.[146] Prior to becoming minister of education and establishing the faculty of science at Tōhoku, Makino Nobuaki had served as ambassador to Austria when its government invited Japan to a conference (1906). The Austrians proposed a meeting in Vienna of the world's science academies and hoped that Japan could attend. This, of course, created a problem, because Japan did not have a real academy. Makino saw the invitation as an important opportunity and proposed to establish such a body. The government responded by deciding to upgrade what it had, and the Tokyo academy was officially renamed the Imperial Academy of Sciences.[147]

The reforms that followed had a twofold result. They first served to enhance the prestige of scientific studies. Academy membership had been fixed at forty, with the majority of the members from law and the humanities. Membership in the new institution was expanded to sixty, with the sciences to constitute half. In keeping with what was then the dominant view, the term *sciences* was broadly defined. Thus imperial academy members represented medicine, engineering, and agriculture as well as mathematics, biology, chemistry, and physics.[148] Reform had another at least equally important result: it helped the academy attract outside support for research and other activities. Fulfilling expectations that were voiced from the start, the heads of two business conglomerates (*zaibatsu*) and the imperial family in 1911 donated modest sums that were used to fund prizes for *published* research.

What was the meaning of all these reforms? Beginning in 1912, the academy launched five new journals as it had money to pay their expenses. It provided a more substantial way to give scientists recognition than anything previous. After a member of the Diet contrasted the substantial recognition accorded in Germany to Paul Ehrlich for work on syphilis with the modest recognition in Japan of his research partner Hata Sahachirō, the government proposed to award the Blue Cordon to prominent scientists and to recognize their achievements more publicly.[149] A development with great potential took place in 1913. Using small sums donated by Furukawa Toranosuke, Sumitomo Kichizaemon, the wealthy expatriate chemist Takamine Jōkichi, and a handful of others, the academy was able to announce its support for scholarly research *in progress*.[150]

But these developments meant less than one might imagine. The academy's operating budget was only 10,000 yen a year. Supporting research in progress was important as a precedent but could be done only very modestly. Until 1919 members alone could apply for the funds. The amount of money spent was small—2,460 yen in 1914— and the funds were divided among six projects that year, only three of them being in natural science.[151] Lack of funds forced termination of the journals after only a handful of issues.[152] Such disappointments disturbed the academy. Theoretical chemist Sakurai Jōji observed plaintively that science academies in Europe usually had budgets of more than a million yen.[153] Even the academy's more optimistic president, mathematician and former minister of education Kikuchi Dairoku, conceded that economic factors had prevented the academy from fully achieving its objectives.[154]

But economic factors relating to overseas competition were already producing new support for research related to Japanese industry. "When people, especially university professors, leave Japan on industrial inspection tours nowadays, [the foreigners] are said to be secretive and afraid to show them anything," Kikuchi Dairoku told the House of Peers in February 1900. "Because of this secrecy, the benefits to be obtained have been greatly reduced . . . and national needs can no longer be met merely by relying on foreign information."[155] At least some in the Diet agreed. In February 1899 several members representing banking and other business interests had criticized both the private and public sectors for their neglect of commercially applicable research, demanding that attitudes change. They contrasted European manufacturing and export success with Japan's stagnant exports and outmoded techniques and insisted that only greater commitment to technical research could repair this growing imbalance.[156]

Establishment of the Industrial Experiment Laboratory (Kōgyō Shiken Jo) in June 1900 was an immediate result of these pressures. This new Tokyo facility was charged with general "testing, analyses, and industrial appraisals"; but it specialized from the start. The Industrial Experiment Laboratory was basically a facility set up to do applied chemical research for private industry on a contract basis. The government's commitment was constrained by cost, so the laboratory began in a small way with two divisions, chemical analysis and industrial chemistry, and a research staff of eleven (four technical experts or *gishi* and seven technicians or *gishu*).[157] Institutional growth was slow for its first five years, but the war with Russia proved a turning point. As one member of the Diet later declared: "The Russo-Japanese War provided a solemn warning to us from the Western powers. After it, our citizens were refused entry to their factories and [laboratories] because of the alleged relationship between these tours and the commercial practices [of Japan]. They said we would just turn around and copy [their designs] if they showed their facilities to us."[158]

For this reason, the government was obliged to increase support for the Industrial Experiment Laboratory. In 1906 the research staff jumped to twenty-nine positions from the earlier ceiling of twelve. In 1911 two more positions were added and new divisions established for ceramics, dyeing, and electrochemistry. A drawback was that laboratory staff members were not so well trained as their colleagues in imperial universities. Only two had doctorates, and most were technicians (nineteen of thirty-two in 1912). Nevertheless, the work they did was of value and was publicly praised by professors. In 1910 Ōsaka Yūkichi, professor of chemistry at Kyoto University, declared that investigators at the Industrial Experiment Laboratory were doing "systematic research" and had achieved some "useful results."[159] And in 1912 Kamoi Takeshi, professor of chemical engineering at Tokyo University, noted that the laboratory was conducting some of the research needed to reduce Japan's unfavorable trade balance in chemical products.[160]

It was all a matter of perspective. Conditions in Japan for industrial research in chemistry had improved somewhat from the late 1880s, when Takamine Jōkichi had to emigrate to the U.S. for his work, but they were far from meeting Western standards.[161] Most Japanese industrial chemists had too many extraneous duties to devote themselves to research. Even when assigned to research tasks, they rarely had the equipment they needed.[162] And the Industrial Experiment Laboratory did not nearly fill the gap. In 1911 it was visited by a member of the Diet who said it appeared to be doing "important, valuable work" despite a number of problems: its staff was too small; its capacity was limited; the work it did took too long to complete; and few in business even knew it existed.[163]

Government officials acknowledged these deficiencies and promised to remedy them. The vice minister of agriculture and commerce, who supervised the laboratory, declared a need to expand the industrial chemistry and dyeing sections, and in early 1914 his ministry requested 200,000 yen in new funding for research in dyeing, electrochemistry, and the testing of iron and steel. Some of this money was earmarked for work on color fastness in silk textiles where, according to Minister Yamamoto Tatsuo, long-term deficiencies had produced major export losses to French and Italian producers. The situation had become so bad that only the Mitsui Bank would even finance sales overseas of finished Japanese silk textiles.[164]

Despite these increases in funding for research, the old inclination to copy died hard. In 1913 the Ministry of Agriculture and Commerce requested 20,000 yen to expand a facility called the Commercial Exhibitions Hall located near the Industrial Experiment Laboratory. Influential members of the Diet attacked (but could not defeat) this request on the grounds that exhibiting Western designs and prototypes in the hall would overshadow the work of the laboratory and encourage copying by Japanese producers, which was certain to embarrass the country.[165]

The Meiji record of research in agriculture shows many of the same ambiguities. By 1900 Japan had the nationally sponsored Agricultural Experiment Station at Nishigahara, Tokyo (with nine local branches), and nineteen stations supported by prefectures. The national facilities officially—and the prefectural stations unofficially—were assigned three major functions: "testing related to the improvement and expansion of agricultural production; itinerant lecturing [to farmers]; and the analysis and appraisal of soil, fertilizer, seed, and all other substances relating to agriculture."[166] But this does not fully explain what was occurring on a day-to-day basis. The chief of the Bureau of Agriculture thought the national stations should carry on "high-level research" and entrust applications to the prefectural facilities.[167] But ambiguities prevented execution of such ideas as conceived by officials. Representative Suzuki Kizaemon complained in February 1900 that the Agricultural Experiment Station was "too small and its budget wholly inadequate."[168] In fact, the station in 1900 had a total budget of only 39,000 yen for 10 facilities—less than the average annual expenditure of 4,509 yen of the prefectural stations.[169] The salaries paid to the technical experts (*gishi*) were very low even by Japanese standards. In 1900 its forty technical experts—including those who had graduated from Tokyo University—were receiving just 400 yen per year, which was a technician's salary at the Infectious Diseases Institute.[170] The system of experiment stations as a whole was substantially cut back later on. Though there had been some expansion of formal capacity in the 1900–05 period, in 1906 Nishigahara's nine branches were cut to three, while in 1910 the technical staff decreased from eighty-six to seventy-two.[171]

Japanese spending on agricultural research was low by European standards. In 1899 France reportedly spent 2,760,000 yen for this purpose, and Germany even more (4,270,000 yen). Japan had fewer resources, but that does not explain everything. If one considers total agricultural income a measure of capacity to pay, it seems significant that even in this sense, Japan's efforts were small. France's effort was sustained by an agricultural income exceeding 4.6 billion yen, that of Germany by an income of 4.2 billion. Japan, with a reported income of 700 million yen from agriculture, was spending at most 250,000 yen on research and diffusion—and even this figure is probably too high.[172] The Germans were investing in agricultural research as a function of ability to pay at a rate three times that of the Japanese, and the French at about a 160 percent greater rate.[173]

Nevertheless, one should not assume that the Japanese did nothing of importance. To do so would obscure *informal* redefinitions of *formal* authority by scientists with political sensibilities. Serving as director of the Agricultural Experiment Station for the period from 1903 to 1920 was the agricultural chemist Kozai Yoshinao, concurrently professor at Tokyo University. Kozai was both a skilled researcher and a good politician—in the early 1920s he served as Tokyo University's president—

quite capable of exploiting opportunities. In 1903 he proclaimed scientific research to be the principal duty of the Agricultural Experiment Station, which was not what its official description had stipulated.[174] And despite the budgetary retrenchment of 1906, Kozai also established a horticulture division at the Kinai (Osaka) station and had its staff investigate seed varieties of rice.[175] From work at Nishigahara he published a book in 1906 on the chemistry of fermentation, while Daikubara Gintarō did research on the relationships between soil acidity and seed varieties later used to improve yields in Hokkaido, Taiwan, and Korea.[176]

Informal redefinitions of formal authority were unnecessary at the Institute of Infectious Diseases, where "research into the treatment, causes, and prevention of infectious diseases" was set forth as the principal mission.[177] This facility prospered greatly in the 1890s and obtained full government support in 1899. From a budget that year of 56,036 yen, the institute's authorized spending rose to 60,540 yen in 1902 and continued to increase thereafter.[178] In 1905 the Institute for Infectious Diseases acquired an entirely new physical plant, together with full legal control of the home ministry's Vaccine Station and Serological Institute; by 1912 its regularly budgeted spending exceeded 210,000 yen.[179] It is clear enough from the staff's small size that salaries were not the main item. Despite the institute's possession of research facilities, animal barns for serum and vaccine production, and a hospital ward for human patients, there were only thirteen technical experts or technicians in 1900, seventeen in 1902, and twenty in 1912. Only eight of that number were *gishi*, but some of the others earned doctorates and managed to upgrade their positions.[180]

It is symbolic of medicine's position in the research community that the institute was a world-class laboratory. It had superior facilities, an excellent staff, and a director of the highest reputation. Japanese and foreign contemporaries compared it to the Pasteur Institute in Paris and the Koch Institute in Berlin, and the comparison was by no means farfetched.[181] The Institute of Infectious Diseases achieved major advances in medicine (see chapter 6), as its clinical work so clearly reflects. Kitasato had helped to create serology and serum therapy. As a result, Japan became the first country in the world to use serum therapy against cholera, tetanus, and diphtheria.[182] Kitasato called the diphtheria serum his colleagues manufactured the "best in the world" and, in fact, exported it to Europe and America.[183]

The physical sciences, however, had achieved nothing of comparable importance. As a result, university administrator and physicist Yamakawa Kenjirō from 1897 on began urging the establishment of major research facilities in physics and chemistry.[184] In 1908 his university physicist colleague Nakamura Seiji called public attention to such laboratories in Europe as the Physicalische Technische Reichsanstalt (PTR) in Germany, the National Laboratory in Britain, and the Institut Centrale des Arts et Manufactures in France and urged that Japan follow suit by constructing its own facilities.[185] In 1910 Ōkuma Shigenobu, who became prime minister in 1913, wrote an article stressing the importance of "first-class facilities for research" in all fields, with special emphasis on chemistry.[186] But it took the return to Japan of the expatriate chemist Takamine Jōkichi in 1913 to bring these movements together. In addition to promoting research facilities in meetings with industrialists, scientists, and government officials, Takamine delivered several speeches on the subject. He declared that Japan had gone as far as it could in imitating the West and would now have to reach a higher stage in science.[187] Several years later, all of these men became key players in a major new venture, the Institute for Physics and Chemistry.

Research Capacities on the Eve of the War

As we have seen, Japanese research capacities grew considerably between the founding of Kyoto University and the outbreak of World War I. Nevertheless, most of these developments were seriously limited in purpose, in scale, or in both. Total spending on the imperial universities did grow in this period, and Kyoto University did overcome its financial and other early problems. But the budget for Tokyo University, which had the only comprehensive facilities for research, was cut in 1905 and 1913 and grew scarcely at all in other years before the war,[188] and the university itself was far from ideal. *Ikai jihō* complained that in all the imperial universities teaching came first and research second.[189] Chemistry professor Sakurai Jōji noted that faculty research was nearly always funded surreptitiously as part of the instructional budget.[190] Other observers suggested that the standard for university professors was their ability to "name the [prominent] foreign scientists and explain their particular theories."[191] The Imperial Academy of Sciences offered small compensation, since its budget was tiny and its research stipends few.

Despite these significant institutional weaknesses, some areas of research fared better than others. Medicine and to a lesser extent engineering were well endowed by Japanese standards. Counting the medical preparatory program of Tōhoku University, which was established in 1912 and achieved faculty status in 1915, each imperial university had faculties of medicine and of engineering, whereas agriculture existed at just two schools and basic science at three. Basic science was also represented differently. Mathematics, physics, and chemistry were each represented by chairs at all four universities, though at Kyushu they were stuck in the engineering faculty. Geology was established at Tokyo and Tōhoku, but biology as established in a faculty of science could be found only at Tokyo.[192]

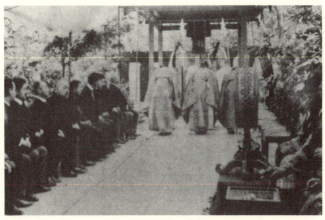

1. Shinto memorial service for Robert Koch, held annually at the Kitasato Institute on the anniversary of his birth (May 27)

2. Kitasato's lieutenants at the Kitasato Institute
Back row, left to right: Ōtani Morisuke, Umeno Shinkichi, Kusama Shigeru, Koga Gensaburō.
Front row, left to right: Terauchi Yutaka, Miyajima Mikinosuke, Kitajima Ta'ichi, Shiga Kiyoshi, Hata Sahachirō.

3. Aoyama Tanemichi's class in diagnostics

4. Tokyo University investigators of tsutsugamushi disease
(August 1915)
Left to right: Mitamura Makujirō, Nagayo Matarō, Imamura
Yoshio, Miyagawa Yoneji.

5. The Kitasato Institute (ca. 1921)

6. The Institute of Infectious Diseases, Japan's leading research laboratory in the Meiji period (ca. 1906)

7. Aoyama Tanemichi   8. Ichiki Kitokurō

9. Tokyo University physicists and graduate students (1903)
Front row, far right: Nagaoka Hantarō; *second from right:*
Tanakadate Aikitsu. *Back row, second from right:* Honda Kōtarō

10. Yamagiwa Katsusaburō

11. Nagayo Matarō

12. Microscopy training at the Institute of Pathology, Tokyo University

13. Ogata Masanori

14. Faculty of Science, Tokyo University (ca. 1905)

15. Kitasato Shibasaburō (ca. 1920)

16. Robert Koch in Japanese kimono (Tokyo, 1908)

17. Takagi Kanehiro

18. Nagaoka Hantarō (ca. 1934)

19. Nagai Nagayoshi 20. Yamakawa Kenjirō

21. Kozai Yoshinao 22. Sakurai Jōji

23. Kikuchi Dairoku

24. Yasui Kono, Japan's first woman scientist

25. Nakamura Yaroku

26. Hasegawa Tai

27. Makino Nobuaki

28. Okada Ryōhei

29. Ōkuma Shigenobu

30. Katsura Tarō

CHAPTER FIVE

SCIENCE AND THE BUREAUCRACY

It is both intuitively obvious and a matter of record that the establishment and prosecution of scientific research demand procedures for mobilizing resources. Without a means of expressing their views or making their desires known to the pertinent authorities, scientists would be as restricted in their work as if they had no facilities at all.[1] Yet many critics have both faulted the Japanese bureaucracy for failing to understand the scientific enterprise and called into question the government's philosophy of management.[2] Scientists supposedly found it hard to gain access to officials and had communication problems when they did. Sakurai Jōji, whose career spanned Meiji and Taishō, believed that scientists could rarely influence the government's policy even when they all joined forces together.[3] In such a case, the result was totally predictable: decisions inappropriate for science and for society.

One finds four explanations for the pathology of decision that has been imputed. First, the Meiji government was reluctant to accept autonomy or equality for science. It tried to coopt almost every private interest and to make science the servant of the state.[4] Then, traditions of policy management were highly autocratic. The political culture of Tokugawa Japan had been typified by a "preponderance of power," according to the Meiji educator Fukuzawa Yukichi.[5] Third, the technically trained came to be excluded from the supervisory ranks of the higher civil service. Scientists and engineers "could not hold high government office in areas of the bureaucracy concerned with science," wrote W. H. Leonard and H. C. Kelly in a 1948 report for the U.S. Occupation. "These posts were reserved for those with legal training [who had graduated] from the imperial universities."[6] Last, scientists failed to protest because of the way they had been socialized. They were "citizens first and servants of truth . . . second," wrote Bertrand Russell in 1931.[7] The "medieval spirit of servile solidarity" lay heavy upon them, argued Thorstein Veblen.[8] Worst of all, insisted Nakane Chie, scientists' own loyalty to particular factions disrupted the unity needed to check the state's power.[9]

One hears echoes in these views of technocratic thought and the Enlightenment from which it derives. Diderot, Condorcet, Saint Simon, and others thought the rationality of science would eliminate ignorance and political authoritarianism and usher in an era of leadership by scientists.[10] The disillusionment caused by two world wars and the unwillingness of most scientists to resist modern oppressions have diminished such views in Western democracies, but they remain influential in Japan.[11]

Meiji Japan's legacy from the Tokugawa period is one reason. Tokugawa society had repressed scholars and experts, rarely granting them a voice in determining public policy. The shogunate and its imitators in the ranks of the daimyo had sought to control political thought generally and technical knowledge selectively. These same regimes had usually given priority to lineage or personality over "merit" or expertise in recruiting officials.[12] The Meiji regime abandoned this stance but imposed its own priorities. The new leaders were obsessed with power and the issue of legitimacy and adopted a strategy of political cooptation to impose their control on society.[13] They did not at first accept foreign ideas of academic freedom and were obliged by circumstances to place burdens on scientists that limited their time for research. Partly to satisfy the Western great powers in respect to the Unequal Treaties, the leadership carried out its legal reforms in ways that affected scientists adversely.

In fact, the Unequal Treaties were a powerful incentive to change in the government of Meiji Japan. Foisted on the country in 1857 and remaining in force until 1899, they took away Japan's right to control its own tariffs and usurped jurisdiction over foreigners charged with crimes occurring on Japanese soil. Termination of the treaties was a cardinal aim of the Japanese government, but the United States and Europe imposed a high price. Japan must change its whole legal system to look like that of the West. This was no easy task, and it took a long time. The civil service reforms that were part of this process were, however, mostly in place by 1887.

Japan's civil service was ostensibly based on systems in continental Europe. One took an examination to secure appointment, but successful performance required formal training in what the Germans called *Cameralismus* (public administration). Frequently referred to by the English word *law*, cameralismus actually included what today would be called economics, statistics, law, and police administration.[14] As in Europe, the training and examinations excluded science, mathematics, engineering, agriculture, and medicine. But since no modern state could function without them, the Japanese adopted the European practice of recruiting the needed experts in these fields by screening— and assigning them to inferior posts.[15] In one particular the Japanese departed from European precedents in their civil service system. The Germans and some other Continental nations imposed the requirement of multiyear, probational unpaid service on men who had passed the civil service examinations before they could receive a salaried appointment. This was done to assure some level of experience in the hope of improving performance in office. But Japan rejected unsalaried probation as inherently unfair and prejudicial to the cause of recruitment based on merit.[16]

The form of Japan's modern civil service posed significant problems for the country's efforts in research. Meiji leaders like Yamagata Aritomo, Itō Hirobumi, and Inoue Kaoru were determined to create an authoritarian state, and in Europe this was linked to legal training.[17] But they failed to consider all the pertinent ramifications. Japan was not Europe. It lacked the array of broadly educated talent found in the most developed Western countries. And there was no proof that legal training was uniquely relevant to administrative performance. In fact, contemporary observers argued that the legalistic bias of the central bureaucracy and its correlate, neglect of technical expertise, produced inefficient management, low morale among the technically trained, duplication of effort, and bad decisions.[18]

Some qualifications are clearly in order here. Most scientists (over 80 percent) were employed in the prestigious public sector, not at the bottom civil service rung, but usually somewhere in the middle. Tenured university professors always held the second of the three major ranks (sōnin, within the classification system hannin, sōnin, and chokunin). University presidents held chokunin status, the same as bureau chiefs, who usually made policy; and a few nonacademic scientists like Kitasato, the director of a major state laboratory, also came to hold chokunin rank.[19] Conditions in some ministries were better than in others. The Ministry of Agriculture and Commerce was quite uncongenial, and the Ministry of Home Affairs had particular defects. But 79 percent of the scientists employed in government worked under the aegis of the Ministry of Education, and its managerial supervision was rather better.[20]

Scientists were respected in society. They tended, for example, to marry well. Kitasato, from a humble family and before becoming famous, married the daughter of Baron Matsuo Shinzen, later governor of the Bank of Japan.[21] They were recognized in other ways by the central government. Several were appointed to the House of Peers, and two named to the Privy Council.[22] Some fields coped better within the rigid system. Medicine was naturally ensconced in the imperial universities, but it was also well established in lesser institutions. It was also uniquely well positioned in the private sector. This gave medicine a political advantage, and medical researchers could fulfill ambitions beyond those of colleagues in any other field. These patterns were old and deeply rooted, but they were reinforced by contemporary priorities and persisted through 1914.

The Period of Early Decisions (1868–89)

In the earliest years of the Restoration government, a few leaders took major initiatives and had few constraints on their power. There was no parliamentary assembly. The bureaucracy was immature, and the Council of State (Dajōkan) had executive authority. Itō Hirobumi and Ōkubo Toshimichi were the most influential in science policy matters, but they were not alone in their activism. Between 1876 and 1880 Matsukata Masayoshi came to share Ōkubo's interest in animal breeding techniques, and through their control over both the Ministry of Home Affairs and the Ministry of Finance they were able to force substantial investment in animal husbandry.[23] These efforts at first relied on technical supervision by foreigners. In 1878, however, Ōkubo launched a medical project conducted by Japanese doctors. Pursuant to his interest in contagious diseases, he acted on the then common supposition that beriberi was such a malady and ordered several university physicians to study it.[24] This project had little success, but it did indicate an official interest in the subject that scientists could use to advantage.

Another characteristic of the earliest years was the use of Western consultants. The American Medical missionary Guido Verbeck guided the leadership away from British medicine and toward that of Germany. Henry Dyer had some influence in engineering and physical science because of his work at the Imperial College of Engineering. The British envoy in Japan, Sir Harry Parkes, helped in recruiting Western technical experts. But the direction of policy was in Japanese hands, and the foreigners were clearly subordinate.[25] The government was eager to use Japanese experts whenever they could be had. Men like Nagayo Sensai and Kanda Takahira, trained under the shogunate, served the new regime, which extended equal favor to Western-trained arrivals.[26]

While bureaucracy existed in the earliest years (1868–80), its structure was quite immature. From 1868 to 1885 there existed an agency known as the Ministry of Public Works (Kōbushō) which controlled the Imperial College of Engineering as well as the operations of government-owned factories. The Ministry of Education had formal control over most government schools from 1871. The Ministry of Home Affairs (originally the Ministry of Civil Affairs or Minbushō) held jurisdiction in most other technical matters. At the top were the Ministry of Finance, with control over revenues, and the Council of State, which set policy.

Lines of authority were naturally subject to change. For example, the Ministry of Education controlled all medical affairs from February 1872 through May 1875, but in 1875 the Council of State gave health administration to the Ministry of Home Affairs, leaving medical education with the Ministry of Education.[27] With its jurisdiction over transportation, telecommunications, industrial promotion, police, agriculture, and public health, the Ministry of Home Affairs was a powerful agency. Because its authority was also diffuse, it was a target of bureaucratic reformers. Following the phasing out of the Ministry of Public Works in the late 1870s, the leadership created the Ministry of Agriculture and Commerce in November 1880. Because this agency was assigned some functions of the Ministry of Home Affairs, disputes between ministries were inevitable.[28]

A second major feature of the early bureaucracy was the role played by technically trained men. In the early and middle years of Meiji, the government frequently assigned senior line positions in technical areas to men with technical training. Yoshikawa Akimasa, who had studied at the Imperial College of Engineering, became chief of the Bureau of Telegraphy in 1874. Nagayo Sensai, a physician, was named chief of the Bureau of Public Health in the next year. Tanaka Yoshio, a student of botany under Itō Keisuke at the former Bansho Shirabesho, in 1881 became chief of the Bureau of Agriculture.[29] Nor were these exceptional cases. The appointment of such men at the bureau chief level was common before the legal reforms were completed (see table 5.1).

During the 1870s scientific research was not well defined for the leadership. The Naito Shinjuku Testing Station for agriculture, the Central Meteorological Observatory, and other institutions of that decade were seen by officials as instruments for exploiting foreign knowledge; the Imperial College of Engineering and other government schools were supposed to produce educated manpower. Tanaka Fujimaro in the Ministry of Education, however, did promote the establishment of the Tokyo Academy of Sciences and also of Tokyo University. The Ministry of Home Affairs encouraged some work in medicine. In 1874 it established the Tokyo Hygiene Laboratory, in 1875 the Bureau of Public Health, and in 1879 the Central Hygiene Commission. Only the Hygiene Laboratory did research, but all three were important for Kitasato's career.[30]

The reluctance of many officials notwithstanding, one *could* get support for research. As noted in chapter 3, Takagi Kanehiro, a career navy officer and a physician trained at St. Thomas Hospital in London, conceived the idea of a link between diet and the incidence of beriberi in late 1880 and sought funding to prove his hypothesis. A number of barriers stood in his way (apart from the commitment of medical col-

5.1 *Educational Backgrounds of Bureau Chiefs (1872–1919)*

Source: Ijiri Tsunekichi, ed., *Rekidai kenkan roku* (Tokyo: Hara Shobō, 1967).

leagues to bacteriology). One was cost: the process of upgrading the diets of numerous sailors and comparing the results was very expensive. Another was resentment from colleagues in the military. A third was the tepid interest of superiors in the navy. Takagi's handling of these various problems throws light on the making of decisions at the time. In essence, he exploited the scarcity of well-trained physicians and contacts with three top officials.

Takagi succeeded because the leadership saw his educational achievements as a way to impress Europeans—and because his Satsuma origins gave him entree to the minister of finance, Matsukata. When Takagi returned from London in 1880, Inoue Kaoru sent a letter to the Tokyo diplomatic community recommending Takagi's services as a doctor and reminding them of Japanese progress. When Takagi decided to pursue the beriberi research, he used this goodwill effectively. In November 1882, Prince Arisugawa got him an audience with the Emperor. In October 1883 he became chief of the navy's Bureau of Medical Affairs. In late 1884 Matsukata and Itō got him invited to a meeting of the Council of State. These connections were essential because of the costs—about 50,000 yen for dietary protocols—and because of the authority he needed to function. Army officials like Yamamoto Gombei and Dr. Ishiguro Tadanori opposed his program, and even the minister of the navy, Kawamura Sumiyoshi, a Satsuma native, was at best lukewarm toward the project.[31]

Takagi's success in the 1880s undoubtedly aided the cause of research, as did an event of the previous year. The Emperor's Confucian lecturer Motoda Eifu charged in an 1879 letter that emphasis on "science" was politicizing society and endangering traditional morality. Itō Hirobumi, in rebutting these arguments, laid the blame for sociopolitical disputation in the lap of Confucianism and developed the notion of research as a weapon. Building on an argument of Otto von Bismarck, the Chancellor of Germany, Itō concluded that the most effective way to control intellectuals was to encourage them in academic research. Then they would quickly abandon politics and concentrate on specialized topics.[32]

But Itō's view of research was not popular everywhere. In the early 1880s the Ministry of Agriculture and Commerce saw very little need for significant new research, reflecting the views of their business constituency.[33] The sericulture research program of the 1870s based at the Naitō Shinjuku Testing Station contracted sharply after the ministry got control of it, and manufacturing research was completely neglected.[34] What did get attention was animal husbandry. The ministry imported Shropshire and Southdown sheep and placed them in special breeding pastures designed for their needs. The sheep did poorly, but the ministry persisted, spending hundreds of thousands of yen uselessly.[35]

The most important development in the Ministry of Agriculture and Commerce was the creation of the modern patent system. In the 1870s patent applications had been handled by the Ministry of Home Affairs on an ad hoc basis, but pressure from foreign and local business alike soon led to a different procedure. The problem was how to balance interests potentially opposed to each other. Japanese business wanted to import as much technology as desired. Foreign interests wanted protection for their own technology and future inventions. The Japanese government tried to satisfy both interests. Without new technology the economy would stagnate; but only legal reforms would end the Unequal Treaties, which limited Japan's sovereignty.[36] The ministry reached a solution in the 1880s. Following the suggestions of Takahashi Korekiyo, the chief of the Bureau of Patents, and his technical adviser, the chemist Takamine Jōkichi, the patent system of France was initially chosen as the basis for Japan's system.[37] But in 1888 three bureau chiefs criticized its protection of foreign inventions as an impediment to imports of technology. And the result was Japan's adoption of Spain's patent system as Western but not too restrictive.[38]

By the end of the decade Agriculture and Commerce was rapidly taking the lead in other ways, too. It became the first ministry with significant interests in science, technology, or medicine to witness the takeover of bureaucratic decision making by graduates of the university faculties of law. Nakamura Yaroku, who had a B.S. in physics and subsequently acquired a D.Sc. in forestry, joined the ministry in 1883 when he finished his studies at Munich. In 1887 he noted that the ministry had "initially needed men with new [technical] knowledge" but was now being taken over by those who "lacked the ability to understand this new knowledge." For him the exclusion of technically educated men from major posts was not just shocking but dangerous. In 1889 he was fired from the ministry, entered private business, and (in 1890) got elected to the Diet.[39] Nakamura was not alone in his views, but there were some countertrends in the ministry. The first minister of agriculture and commerce, Kōno Togama, in 1881 created an intraministerial committee that later helped to found the Industrial Experiment Laboratory.[40] His prescient vice minister, Shinagawa Yajirō, in 1884 gave private assistance to the chemist Takamine when he left government to work in American private industry.[41]

The Ministry of Education in the 1880s had a more nuanced posture toward research. Motoda's fears about "science" were not dead despite Itō's intervention, because influences from Germany reinforced them. In 1882 Councillor Kawashima Atsushi prepared a paper on the subject inspired by Lorenz von Stein of Vienna and quickly found his misgivings being echoed by the incumbent minister, Fukuoka Takachika (1881–83), and even by Mori Arinori (minister 1885–89).[42] But these two men were quick to take action. Fukuoka advocated Germany as Japan's academic model because of the affinity in law and basic outlook.[43] Mori, who shared Itō's views, developed a program for averting any problems.

Active promotion of "practical research" was one of Mori's principal strategies. He constantly invoked the applied-science argument, and during the years he held office as minister took steps to realize his views. Establishment of the faculties of engineering and agriculture at Tokyo University (in 1886 and 1890, respectively) can both be attributed to this.[44] Even prominent members of the university community joined in support of his views. President Watanabe Kōki declared in 1886 that the level of learning in Japan would be raised not only by producing men "learned in the principles of science" but equally by those with practical abilities.[45] And in 1888 Watanabe insisted that the most important part of the research done in Tokyo's college of science that year was an eminently practical "magnetic field survey of the [Japanese] countryside."[46] Some scientists opposed this trend. The mathematician Kikuchi Dairoku claimed that science's search for truth "produces infinitely more benefits than do the enterprises of the practical man."[47] And theoretical chemist Sakurai Jōji praised the scientist's role as "architect of the castle of knowledge."[48] But the applied-science movement was sufficiently powerful to win support even here. In 1889 Terao Hisashi, professor of astronomy and director of the university observatory, gave a lecture to a group of young mathematics students in which he declared that it was wrong to study mathematics "solely because of one's personal interests." One had to use it in service to society.[49]

Autocratic management was another component of Mori's approach as minister of education. Three weeks after he took office, he and Itō forced Katō Hiroyuki out as university president and installed their ally Watanabe Kōki.[50] Then the Imperial University Ordinance (1886) made their intentions even clearer. This declaration omitted any reference to an advisory role for the university president in the making of policy, authorized the minister of education to appoint faculty members to the university senate, and required the president to inform the minister about the discussions of the senate in detail.[51] Of course, there were carrots attached to the stick. Mori tried to flatter individual professors by inviting them to the ministry for private conversations. And he sought to impress the university as a whole by giving speeches at academic functions. Some observers correctly see a more intimate relationship between ministry and university during Mori's time in office than at others, but the relationship was at best a mixed blessing for professors.[52]

The management style of the minister of education finally produced a reaction. During the 1880s the routine interests of the scientific community were well represented in the ministry. Hamao Arata, who held the position of chief of the Bureau of Professional Education, while not trained in science, was sympathetic. In 1881 President Katō had proposed a necessary division of the undergraduate physical sciences program into separate majors for physics, mathematics, and astronomy. Hamao had actively supported this initiative and managed to persuade a reluctant minister, Fukuoka Takachika, to allow it.[53] Hamao also steered several able students into the natural sciences when he was university president (1893–97) and later helped found the Tokyo Institute of Technology.[54] But the managerial style instituted by Mori did not encourage officials to act like Hamao or professors to be involved in policy making, and demands that the university be granted autonomy began while Mori was still in office.

Three aspects of the professors' earliest campaign for university autonomy are worthy of notice. One is the lack of timely agreement on how to achieve autonomy. Two major proposals were put forward in 1888–89, but they differed in important details. One proposal was developed by the deans. It called for permanent faculty tenure but envisioned appointment of professors and allocation of funds entirely by the deans, with the professors to have a mere "right to assent." The other was developed by assistant professors who had recently returned from Germany. They requested financial autonomy and election of the president and faculty council, with nearly all powers to reside in the council.[55] The second noteworthy aspect is the scientists' role. The impression is that most were conformists (the appointment of scientists to sensitive posts in the 1930s, at a time of rising military influence, illustrates this well).[56] But the 1880s were quite another matter. Three of five deans active in the movement were scientific professionals at that time. So were most (63 percent) of the assistant professors.[57]

Less surprising but equally important was society's reaction to the autonomy campaign. In early 1889 a small group of professors called on the senior statesman Matsukata Masayoshi to argue on behalf of their cause. But a meeting of minds did not take place, and their appeal was clearly a failure. Matsukata called their request "unthinkable," and one young professor described the conversation as "wind in the ear of a horse."[58] Nor were other commentators much more responsive. Several newspapers accused professors of ignoring their place in Japanese society, and Fukuzawa Yukichi's *Jiji shimpō* sanctimoniously declared that a "university that must rely on public support ought not to be opposing the will of the public."[59]

In truth some of the concern of the young professors and part of the reaction against them derived not from the actions of the ministry but from the role expected of the Diet. In 1889 the entire country was awaiting parliamentary government with a mixture of hope and anxiety. Liberal young professors wanting support for their mission feared the Diet would cut back their funding. But liberal intellectuals like Fukuzawa Yukichi expected it to check the power of the leadership and resented what seemed like a threat to its power. These reactions show the importance of the Diet, and in fact, the emergence of the Diet in 1890 fundamentally changed how decisions were made.

Decision Making about Science in the 1890s

Several new trends came to the fore in the 1890s. The Imperial Diet asserted itself vigorously in matters of science and higher education. The Ministry of Education maintained a highly intimate—some would have said incestuous—relationship with Tokyo University that gave professors some voice in policy but occasionally cost them in scholarly research. Under the auspices of competent officials in the Ministry of Home Affairs, Kitasato's leadership produced a flourishing tradition of scientific research defended by allies and political maneuvering. The Ministry of Agriculture and Commerce came under the control of law faculty graduates whose actions were a scandal to some of the scientists. There were, of course, some negative trends in all of the ministries involved with science, but they were strongest in the Ministry of Agriculture and Commerce.

The Diet was a partial corrective to such trends in the various ministries. As in any system of parliamentary government, it had to approve the spending of money, but this was by no means the extent of its power. The Diet had the authority to summon officials to explain recommendations and justify their policies. It could invoke the authority of technical experts by inviting scientists and others to testify. It could organize special commissions of inquiry. And it could offer its own legislative proposals. The Imperial Diet did all of these things, sometimes with stunning results. Since few of the members knew much about science, one would not have predicted this behavior.[60] Nevertheless, it is important to stress that a handful of members were well informed. Elected in the first general election of 1890 and continuing to serve for a number of years were the physician Hasegawa Tai and the former official Nakamura Yaroku, with his degree in physics from Munich. These two men were very well informed and invariably raised major policy issues.[61]

Especially typical of the 1890s Diet was a tendency to originate legislation. Later proposals with a chance of success came from one of the ministries, but in the Diet's first years it was active on a number of fronts in the hope of making its mark. Policy toward science was one such arena. The Diet overrode the Itō cabinet's proposal for a medical laboratory at Tokyo University and instead voted to favor a Kitasato-backed bill (see chapter 4, above). In 1892 the Diet funded the Ministry of Education's modest proposal for the Seismological Research Commission by cutting the budget for the army.[62] These were quite spectacular interventions, but they were not historically unique. During its first decade the Diet took up seven privately sponsored proposals for science. Three were approved and implemented.[63]

While the Diet routinely summoned officials to discuss their policies, it called on scientists rather sparingly. But in May 1892 it did invite Noro Kageyoshi, professor of metallurgical engineering, to explain the technical details of a steel mill proposal the government wished to see funded.[64] And in December 1893 it heard testimony from Koganei Yoshikiyo, professor of anatomy, about subsidizing charity patients at Tokyo University Hospital as a way to gain the necessary research material.[65] On no occasion during this decade did it summon a member of the faculty of science, although the mathematician and physicist Kikuchi Dairoku when education minister gave expert testimony in 1901 on the work of the Seismological Research Commission.[66]

Other than supporting Kitasato and needling officials, the greatest contribution of the Imperial Diet was its appointment of a number of special commissions. The most important such body established in the period was the Committee to Investigate the Academic System (Gakusei Chōsa Kai). Originally created in the House of Peers by the former education vice minister Kubota Yuzuru in 1894, the committee did little in its first three years because most Diet members trusted the educational leadership of the government. In 1897 and 1898, however, the cabinets of Matsukata Masayoshi and Ōkuma Shigenobu showed some inclinations toward educational reform, and a lively debate ensued. This debate focused on a number of issues, among them the role of research.[67]

Stress on research is surprising despite the support that Itō Hirobumi and Mori Arinori gave it. Certainly the ministers of education of the 1890s gave consistent backing to the research ideal. In 1890 Yoshikawa Akimasa declared that the "flourishing or decline of a country has much to do with the flourishing or decline of its science."[68] In 1891 Ōki

Takatō maintained that the "investigation of basic theoretical principles and the advancement of high-level knowledge in all disciplines are the factors that bring about progress."[69] In 1897 Hachisuka Mochiaki praised Tokyo University as a "place for investigating basic principles."[70] But the gap between rhetoric and action made research support a big issue. The Ministry of Finance was extremely parsimonious in its funding of higher education.[71] University scientists were under pressure from the Ministry of Education to help build professional institutions.[72] The Diet itself was committed to reducing the level of public expenditure. It was symptomatic of the general situation that one of the strongest proponents of scientific research, Hasegawa Tai, was also a leading budget cutter.[73]

The combination of such contradictory stances made the education ministry both defensive and aggressive. For example, in 1890 Kitasato Shibasaburō requested support for an additional year of research in Germany. Because of his accomplishments and general reputation his request should have been routine. But Kitasato had previously (in 1886) criticized the work of a university professor. Sensitive as ever to the university's reputation, Katō Hiroyuki apparently retaliated. Using his authority as university president, he decided to oppose Kitasato's request, and the ministry withheld its approval.[74] This was to prove a momentous decision. When Kitasato returned to Japan fifteen months later, he refused to cooperate with the Ministry of Education, and their hostility was fixed for life. The ministry relentlessly pursued control over Kitasato's laboratory and launched a campaign to gain control over nonacademic laboratories in general.[75] In 1890 it took the Forestry Experiment Station over from the Ministry of Agriculture and Commerce, in 1896 the Central Meteorological Observatory from the Ministry of Home Affairs, and also in 1896, the Tokyo Astronomical Observatory came under its aegis. While the Ministry of Education controlled just five percent of nonacademic laboratories in 1893 (see table 5.2), by the end of the decade it had nearly a quarter.

The Ministry of Education's administrative imperialism aroused more than a little resentment. Hasegawa Tai in 1893 described the ministry as "feudalistic" and "good at holding its [political] ground" and attacked it for treating Kitasato as an "irreconcilable enemy" and for "constantly plundering the resources of others."[76] The education journal *Kyōiku jiron* in 1897 criticized it for employing "too many [Tokyo] professors as administrators."[77] And Representative Ichijima Kenkichi in 1899 deplored the university's "inordinate influence" in the ministry, claiming that relations between the two were "self-serving."[78]

A demand for general reform arose. In 1897 the ministry took the lead by creating the Higher Education Council (Kōtō Kyōiku Kaigi).

TABLE 5.2
Bureaucratic Affiliations of Nonacademic Scientific Laboratories

MINISTRY	1885 N	1885 %	1893 N	1893 %	1900 N	1900 %
Home Affairs	7	47	8	42	7	23
Agriculture and Commerce	5	33	7	37	11	35
Public Works and Communications	1	7	1	5	2	7
Navy	1	7	1	5	3	10
War	1	7	1	5	1	3
Education	0	0	1	5	7	22
Totals[a]	15	101	19	100	31	100

Sources: Yuasa Mitsutomo, *Gendai kagaku gijutsu shi* (Tokyo, 1962); *TGSIG*, various numbers.
[a]Percentage totals may be slightly higher or lower than 100 due to rounding.

This body had members (including ten scientists) from a broad professional spectrum, but its accomplishments were few. It had no guidelines.[79] Its members were named by the minister of education.[80] And it could only give advice on request.[81] In fact, the president of the House of Peers, who opposed reform, described it approvingly as an in-house committee.[82]

For just this reason the Diet insisted that there must be an outside commission. It was not acceptable for a commission to report to the Ministry of Education; it must have access to the prime minister directly. But this did not have to mean confrontation. "The Diet's Committee to Investigate the Academic System will try to assist the ministry and encourage its work." Since Tokyo University was a source of the problem, the minister and the Imperial Diet might want to form an alliance against it. Putative reformers had differing views. Some wanted to shorten the total course of study. Others wanted encouragement for private education. Still others favored diversion of resources to the various higher professional schools.[83] There was little consensus on what should be done, but on one point ten were agreed. "The imperial universities should become institutions where research . . . is the *principal* function."[84]

Actually the ministry was committed to promoting research by enlarging the size of the faculty. Between 1893, when the chair system was established, and mid-1901, when new efforts were launched, eighteen chairs in science were added at Tokyo University. But progress in building research infrastructure was never uniform over time. During the presidency of Hamao Arata six chairs were added, while one more was established during Toyama Shōichi's eighteen months in office. But the most rapid growth came under Kikuchi Dairoku. During the thirty-eight months between April 1898 and June 1901, eleven chairs were founded in the sciences, and all the faculties were represented.[85] No comparable growth took place again on the Tokyo campus until long after World War I.

Chairs were not established by one man's fiat. Article 14 of the Imperial University Ordinance had given faculty appointment powers to the minister of education. But exercising these powers required much consultation, and the president's role was important. It was, after all, President Katō Hiroyuki who in 1890 had actually proposed the system of chairs. Minister Inoue consulted fully with Katō's successor (Hamao Arata) on which chairs to establish.[86] The presidents themselves did not have free rein. While legally they could proceed as they wished (since their authority had not yet been challenged), they could not ignore the professors' advice.[87] When Inoue requested Hamao's views on chairs in 1893, Hamao immediately sought opinions from the faculty.[88] The Ministry of Education made a point of underscoring professors' involvement. In March 1897 Vice Minister Makino Nobuaki told the Budget Committee of the House of Representatives: "We [in the ministry] hold meetings with faculty members at the university to determine which fields are most urgently needed. I cannot tell you what they will be in advance because this is decided periodically."[89]

Nevertheless, the skill of the president was very important in determining the pace of expansion. Presidents Hamao and Kikuchi had both served extensively in the Ministry of Education before becoming president at Tokyo University, while Toyama moved, conversely, from university to ministry. All had extensive high-level connections and knew how to play the administrative game well. Hamao's accomplishments were limited by the financial pressures of the war with China; Kikuchi had the advantage of serving in peacetime. Even so, one has only to compare Kikuchi's accomplishments at Tokyo with those of his counterpart at Kyoto to appreciate the importance of the president's role. Kyoto had been created on a wave of enthusiasm. Its first president, Kinoshita Hiroji, had been chief of the Bureau of Professional Education (1893–97). But Kinoshita complained bitterly of financial neglect and managed to add only eight chairs in technical fields between 1898 and 1901. Kikuchi had excellent support and was able to found eleven. One cannot know all the pertinent factors, but their backgrounds were probably important. Kinoshita was a lawyer with no technical training, while Kikuchi was a scientist.[90]

In the 1890s scientific progress at the imperial universities benefited from sympathy at the Ministry of Education. Each of the chiefs of Professional Education was overtly sympathetic, and several were particularly helpful.[91] Professors had access to most top officials and were closely involved in the bureau.[92] Individual professors or academic units could propose a chair or laboratory, obtain support from the higher authorities, and hope to find it established in due time. However, an important point to note in comparative context is the formal nature of these ties. The Bureau of Professional Education was officially charged with promoting "all of the sciences and the arts" as well as with supervising the imperial universities.[93]

Ostensibly, the Ministry of Home Affairs and the Bureau of Public Health had a similar relationship with the Institute of Infectious Diseases. Under the terms of an 1893 letter to Kitasato from Minister Inoue Kaoru, all regulations of the institute, together with any revision or diversion of budgeted items, had to be approved by the minister of home affairs. The laboratory's activities were supposed to be supervised by the public health bureau's chief. The minister of home affairs had to be informed about activities in writing annually. The Board of Audit was empowered to inspect the institute's accounts whenever it wished.[94] But in some respects the relationship was rather anomalous. Before nationalization (March 1899), the Institute of Infectious Diseases was legally private, and Kitasato just a consultant. No restrictions or audits were ever in fact imposed, because Kitasato had the power to prevent interference. Shortly after nationalization, *Ikai jihō* declared: "Mr. Kitasato is the dominant force in the Bureau of Public Health. Everything it does is based on his views."[95]

Kitasato's friendships with successive bureau chiefs bolstered his status. Nagayo Sensai, in office until August 1891, was Kitasato's first major patron. In 1884 he gave Kitasato his first job (bureau technician and Hygiene Laboratory researcher) and in 1890 got additional funding for the now famous scientist after the Ministry of Education refused its support.[96] Kitasato was even friendlier with two of Nagayo's successors. He and Gotō Shimpei met in 1883 when both were working in the bureau and became close friends in Berlin about 1887 while studying bacteriology together. In 1892 Gotō became chief, and in 1893 he helped Kitasato found the institute.[97] Gotō left office in 1898 and was succeeded as chief by Hasegawa Tai. Hasegawa had served as legislative architect of the institute subsidies in 1893 and remained throughout his life Kitasato's ardent ally. Neither man was trusted by university professors. They called Hasegawa "Kitasato's puppet," and Gotō an "oppressor."[98]

These epithets symbolize the reality of factions in Japanese medicine. Sources disagree on their number and structure. One common depiction put graduates of the Tokyo University medical faculty in the "university faction," while Kitasato's associates were said to form another faction.[99] Whatever the validity of particular descriptions, polarization between factions was real. The Ministry of Home Affairs even respected these hostilities when it decided to sponsor a venture in research. In spring 1894 the Japanese consulate in Hong Kong informed Tokyo by cable of a plague epidemic afflicting the city. A brief consultation between a section chief in the Bureau of Public Health and one of Kitasato's research associates established that plague was not extinct, as had been thought, and that prestige would accrue to any country whose scientists succeeded in discovering the cause. Accordingly, the bureau recommended a medical expedition to Hong Kong. After due deliberation, the minister chose the university's Aoyama Tanemichi for the clinical work and Kitasato for the basic research.[100]

The scientific outcome of the Hong Kong expedition was important in at least two ways. Kitasato managed to isolate the bacillus and announced his success in *The Lancet*.[101] This, of course, was very big news, and when the expedition returned to Tokyo, a welcoming reception was held—ironically at Tokyo University. Prominent public figures heaped praise on the mission, and the Emperor's cousin captured the mood. According to Prince Konoe Tokumaro, the discovery by Kitasato of the plague bacillus "reflects credit on Japanese medical science and makes our civilization shine to the heavens . . . Such achievements can only raise the level of our nation and bring it [universal] acclaim."[102]

Prince Konoe's words had policy implications. In 1894 Kitasato began accepting short-term special students (*denshūsei*) at the Institute of Infectious Diseases. Because most were public health officials, the home minister in 1895 requested—and the Diet authorized—prefectural governors to recommend candidates with the government to pay for their training. These state-supported students, and others who paid their own way, studied bacteriology, epidemiology, toxic prevention, microscopy, culture making, and methods of clinical treatment.[103] By nationalization, this public program at a private institution had produced 450 graduates who had their own organization and were political allies of Kitasato.[104]

Kitasato's objectives were simple enough: maintenance of his autonomy and political independence, bolstering of funding, and above all protection of the Institute of Infectious Diseases from formal annexation by the Ministry of Education. He used service functions to protect his research, taking advantage of the institute's structure and ostensible mission—research, clinical treatment, and public health consultation. The *denshūsei* program meshed well with this mission, as did most of his other activities. Kitasato and his staff gave lectures for physicians, traveled to epidemic-infested areas at the home minister's request, and took every opportunity to publicize their work.[105] The results were impressive. Not surprisingly, a long-time associate was able to write: "Ordinary people considered Dr. Kitasato a [typical] *oyabun* [boss] or a common politician."[106]

If scientists' influence was greatest in the Ministry of Home Affairs, it was lowest in the Ministry of Agriculture and Commerce. This ministry had responsibilities in forestry and industry as well as agriculture, and in virtually every bureau the "lawyers" were powerful. After Maeda Masana retired as chief of the Bureau of Agriculture in July 1890, nonexperts controlled the office for thirteen years. In the Bureau of Forestry, one expert had three months' control in 1897; in the Bureau of Industry no technical man was ever bureau chief after October 1889.[107] Of course, control was not wholly definitive, for all three bureaus employed technical experts, and some of them made a significant difference. Some of the laboratories under the ministry had more autonomy. But technical projects were hard to advance, given the bureaucratic climate.

Consider the Bureau of Agriculture. With chiefs who were lawyers or even politicians, and technical men who were sometimes professors, there was a serious possibility of failure to communicate. Some members of the Diet criticized the Ministry of Agriculture and Commerce's concept of agricultural research, its deployment of resources, and its application of results. "The ministry's development plan was inadequate." "We need more research!" (Imai Isoichirō). The ministry was "sacrificing export profits by failing to stress agricultural research" (Nakamura Yaroku). The ministry was wasting money at the Agricultural Experiment Station by putting up Western-style buildings; traditional styles would be much more appropriate (Nakamura Yaroku). Technical experts were not used effectively because so many were at work in the ministry's headquarters (Fujita Magohei). Experiment station experts talked over the heads of the farmers; their extension programs were totally "haphazard" (Nakamura Yaroku). Ministry officials could not explain the technical work of the station even to the members of the Imperial Diet (Fujita Magohei).[108]

Responses to these charges from the chief of the bureau were par for the course. Since money was insufficient, the bureau had to rely on the cooperation of various private groups which "often do not follow through." It was difficult to obtain foreign seeds and plant species. The extension program needed "time to evolve." One had to proceed "slowly and cautiously." The research programs of the experiment station were "just a beginning."[109] But the bureau chief was willing to concede that many of the charges were valid. The number of technical experts at ministry headquarters was quite large but at the same time essential for "administrative purposes." The number of truly well-rounded agriculture experts was admittedly "not very large." The chief confessed that he was a "novice" in scientific agriculture, did "not understand much of farmers' conversations," and "did not know the scope of the [experiment station's] work in any real scientific sense"![110]

In the 1890s the bureau's performance at the topmost level showed marginal improvement at best. Technical experts, for example, were never deployed in a manner suitable for research. In 1896 the bureau had thirty-one technicians and technical experts at its administrative headquarters, but only thirteen at the experiment station at Nishiga-hara. In 1899 twenty experts worked at central headquarters and eleven at Nishigahara, both located in the city of Tokyo.[111] The chief of the bureau for most of this period (March 1893–May 1898), Fujita Shirō, was the first "lawyer" to hold the position and was undoubtedly appointed for reasons unrelated to agriculture. In 1896 he tried to meet the tea industry's demand for a research program by simply transferring 1,372 yen from the already modest budget for sericulture.[112] In February 1899, while serving as vice minister, he brushed aside requests for more research support saying it was "wrong to spend money . . . just to encourage agriculture."[113] This came at a time when Japan's spending on agriculture research was embarrassingly small.

In the Bureau of Forestry in the 1890s the problems were about the same. Technical and nontechnical men had to communicate, and barriers between them were real. Worse, the technical men were divided among themselves. In 1891 Shiga Taizan, who was both professor of forestry at Tokyo University and an expert employed in the Bureau of Forestry, recommended forestry conservation policies based on research, but these had to obtain the ministry's approval before the Diet could debate them, and that gave rise to two big problems. One was the composition of the ministry's review committee, the other the status of the technical men. Making up the committee were seventeen "lawyers" and two technical men. Other technicians were wholly subordinate.

The "lawyers" reacted with incomprehension, and the other technician challenged Shiga's findings. When Shiga protested at this reception, he was "warned directly by the minister himself."[114]

Indications are that the Bureau of Forestry had serious morale problems. Many well-trained experts worked there, but they never had any real authority. No matter how many years of commendable service they had or how much the administrative system was supposed to be based on scientific knowledge, they could never rise beyond section chief. Later this became a big issue (see chapter 8).[115]

Then there was the Bureau of Industry. The same kinds of people who served as bureau chiefs in agriculture or forestry were present here, too, and the men with technical degrees who did the major work were, like everywhere else, subordinate. Yet in other respects the Bureau of Industry was an exception. Its staff was small. In 1897 the Bureaus of Agriculture and Forestry had fifty-nine and forty-eight men on their staffs, respectively, while the Bureau of Industry had a mere twenty-three.[116] Other things being equal, an engineer or scientist employed in this bureau stood a somewhat better chance of obtaining a hearing. Moreover, the private-sector clients of the Bureau of Industry were more powerful than those of its rivals. Most forested land was government owned, so there were relatively few clients for the Bureau of Forestry, and the wealthy farmer clients of the Bureau of Agriculture were no political match for industry's wealthy businesses.

The real problem for science in the Bureau of Industry was the complacency of most clients. Before 1895, most private firms were uninterested in research and made relatively few demands for it on the government.[117] But once they saw the need to take action, they were powerful enough to get things done. After Japan's victory in the Sino-Japanese War, European facilities for industrial research and sophisticated manufacturing became less accessible to Japanese visitors.[118] In 1897 a bureau expert made a systematic effort to dispel business complacency. Takayama Jintarō, a chemical engineer, began publicizing the need for industrial research after officially touring facilities in Germany. The Japanese private sector responded to his efforts by organizing a group to carry on lobbying.[119]

The aim of this group, the Association for the Chemical Industry—and the major scientific project of the Bureau of Industry—was to establish what became the Industrial Experiment Laboratory. In October 1898 the bureau recommended the plan to the intraministerial committee of the Ministry of Agriculture and Commerce. This body consisted of the ministry's eight bureau chiefs and had been created in 1881 by Minister Kōno Togama. Committee approval was necessary before any official proposal could be reviewed by the Ministry of Finance or the Diet. Given the different backgrounds of the bureau chiefs, this procedure could easily have posed a problem, but in 1898 the committee contained an influential and atypical member, Watanabe Wataru, who had a B.S. degree in chemistry, was professor of metallurgical engineering, and had for some months been chief of the Bureau of Mining.[120] His presence may have made the difference. The committee decided to back the proposal.[121] Private business also tried to lobby the ministry. When the matter went to the Diet in February 1899, it was under private sponsorship, with the ministry's assent.[122] Of course, European precedents were critical in persuading the government to found the Industrial Experiment Laboratory.[123]

Decision Making for Science in the Prewar Years

Decision-making trends in the years before the war did not simply replicate earlier patterns, although changes may have been more apparent than real. The Imperial Diet was still influential, and the influence of the "lawyers" became more pervasive. In the Ministry of Education in the 1890s and in the opening years of the twentieth century, a few professors held major offices and could make decisions themselves, but they were succeeded mostly by "lawyers," who tended to delegate significant decision-making powers. Changes of this kind could also be latent, not perceptible to contemporary observers. Kitasato had as much power in the Ministry of Home Affairs after as before 1902, when "lawyers" replaced doctors in the Bureau of Public Health. But his position did change, and changes were partly due to the actions of "lawyers." But "lawyers" had not completely overrun the bureaus. In the Ministry of Agriculture and Commerce, where they were most entrenched, an agricultural chemist became agriculture bureau chief in 1903 and another vice minister in 1908.

The year 1900 saw intensified concern over higher education and science, with the Ministry of Education again under attack from politicians and educators. Representative Shimada Saburō accused the ministry of having a "closed-country mentality" and of lacking interest in reform.[124] Kyōiku jiron claimed the ministry's approach to management was "shallow and prejudiced" and attacked it for carrying on administration in secret.[125] Even Katō Hiroyuki saw the ministry as a place where accomplishments were few because officials were "preoccupied."[126] But the sharpest criticisms in these early years had more to do with research by professors. On the floor of the House of Peers, the former vice minister of education Kubota Yuzuru charged that university professors had done too much consulting and not enough research. After denouncing their neglect of research, he laid the blame on the ministry itself, saying it was largely "indifferent to higher education."[127]

Responses to Kubota's charges varied. The incumbent minister, Kabayama Sukenori, who agreed, criticized what he considered an excessive emphasis on overseas study, with its implied drain on funds and consequent diminution of faculty research, and proposed a program to turn this around.[128] His successor, Matsuda Masahisa, backed a number of ad hoc projects for scholarly research.[129] But some professors at Tokyo University took a far less favorable view of the charges. The former university president Toyama Shōichi had his own reform ideas and reportedly used "vituperative language" in his response.[130] Physics professor Yamakawa Kenjirō thought Kubota's statements only made it more difficult for scientists to function professionally.[131] The definitive reply came from mathematician Kikuchi Dairoku. Using the House of Peers as a forum, he stated that faculty were actually doing plenty of research (see chapter 6). Kubota had just failed to grasp its meaning. Foreign scientists had cited university publications for their research results, and faculty consulting was another form of research.[132]

Over the next five years these views were tested by four different ministers. The first was Kikuchi himself. Appointed to office in June 1901, he served two years and was then forced to resign. After an interim successor who served just two months, the office of minister was filled by Kubota. Kubota served two years and was also forced to leave office (in December 1905), after which the prime minister filled out the term. In the modern administrative history of Japanese science, nothing else resembles these five turbulent years. Continuity was supplied by the prime minister, who held office for the entire period, and his views gave some coherence and unity.

This man, Katsura Tarō, was atypical among Meiji prime ministers. He was a career military man who had also lived seven years in Berlin. He had an "extraordinary understanding of science" and was determined to promote it effectively.[133] Katsura saw two major problems in higher education and science. One was what he identified as the "common evils of the academic community."[134] The other was what he considered an excessive reliance on Europe for technical and scientific information.[135] But science and higher education were not his only interests. He was even more dedicated to strengthening Japan's international position, and for this reason he signed the Anglo-Japanese Alliance (1902), launched a major military buildup (1903), and went to war with Russia (1904–05). Unfortunately the domestic and foreign objectives of the Katsura cabinet were in basic conflict. The Diet would not allow higher taxes to pay for the military buildup and war,[136] and this led inevitably to major retrenchment, the issuance of bonds, and the deferment of new spending.

The prime minister aggravated his problems by his choices for minister of education. Kikuchi and Kubota appeared to be qualified, but they offended their major constituencies. Kikuchi's tenure was troubled from the start. In June 1901 he announced a plan to promote competition by instituting lecture fees, pooling the funds, and redistributing them to professors with large class enrollments. This lacked appeal for most scientists since their enrollments were usually small.[137] In September he proposed a two-track preprofessional education system that academic colleagues managed to defeat at a regular meeting of the Higher Education Council.[138] In November he denied any need for an imperial university in Kyushu, even though he had previously endorsed it.[139]

Of course, Kikuchi did some things his colleagues liked. In December 1901 he gave a masterful defense of the Seismological Research Commission, which some Diet members had opposed because the work it had done had not yet led to long-term *prevention* of earthquakes![140] In 1902 and 1903 he did propose and help to secure significant budget increases for the imperial universities. But in March 1903 he tried to prevent Waseda from acquiring the title *university,* saying it was in most ways inferior to Tokyo University.[141] Kikuchi favored research, but his policy views were unusual. Unlike most concerned Japanese, he wanted to stress education in the imperial universities and concentrate research in the Tokyo academy.[142]

Considering his past record and the prime minister's expectations, Kikuchi's term was a failure. *Kyōiku jiron* had criticized his administrative abilities in 1897 when he was serving as chief of the Bureau of Professional Education, but his overall record had belied it.[143] He was the only scientist ever to serve at this highest level of the government. He had served not only as professor of mathematics and dean of the science faculty but as university president and vice minister of education. Unfortunately his training and views made him politically unqualified to serve in the post of minister. Kikuchi had done university work in mathematics and science at St. John's College, Cambridge, from 1873 to 1877, and he came under the influence of Isaac Todhunter, a capable mathematician of reactionary views.[144] Cambridge was peculiar even in Britain, and Todhunter peculiar in Cambridge. While most British universities were institutionalizing science, the classical legacy was very strong at Cambridge. This implied vigorous opposition to experimental science and strict adherence to aristocratic values. Todhunter saw Cambridge as training members of the elite. He rejected aspirations for upward mobility and especially aspirations for changing society.[145] Kikuchi's views were not wholly Todhunter's, but they were closer to them than expediency dictated. In July 1903 the House of Representatives voted no confidence in Kikuchi, partly over the issue of university expansion.[146] The prime minister then appointed the home minister, Kodama Gentarō, as acting minister of education. Kodama proposed, and Katsura even supported, a scheme to abolish the Ministry of Education.[147] Kikuchi had gravely offended the Diet and the cabinet. When the Privy Council blocked this radical scheme, Kikuchi's long-time enemy Kubota Yuzuru became minister of education.

Ultimately, Kubota fared little better. A graduate of Keio, he had few connections at Tokyo University. Because of the military buildup and the war, he could not promise to allocate more money. In fact, funding for the two universities was frozen in 1903, and Tokyo took cuts in 1905.[148] Professors and scientists hated Kubota because he demanded so much and delivered so little. In 1905 they were given their chance. Seven Tokyo professors criticized the modest gains that came to Japan in the settlement with Russia, and Kubota imprudently sought their dismissal. This "Tomizu Affair" brought massive opposition from the university community, which was seeking to achieve institutional autonomy.[149] Many scientists joined the movement ostensibly in support of their colleagues but soon made their true feelings known: the issue was not upholding a principle but eliminating a foe. Once Kubota had been forced to leave office, their interest in politics faded.[150]

This turbulent era eventually gave way to greater stability. Makino Nobuaki became minister of education in March 1906 and set out to accomplish what his predecessors could not. Both imperial universities got significant funding increases for 1906 (13 percent for Tokyo, 14 percent for Kyoto) and decent ones for 1907 (5 and 10 percent, respectively).[151] The number of chairs in technical fields grew more rapidly than it had in some years.[152] The Tokyo academy was radically reorganized, and the decision was made to launch Tōhoku University.

Formal establishment of the Tōhoku science faculty offers a salient example of the "new" decision making. Under the rules of the higher civil service, scientists were not to hold policy positions, but they were allowed to contribute their views when officials considered them essential. Since Makino's administration embodied both views, he dispatched his subordinate to the Tokyo campus.[153] In early 1907 the vice minister Fukuhara Ryōjirō, who was also chief of the Bureau of Professional Education, conferred with the physicist Nagaoka Hantarō about internal details of the proposed new faculty. This all-day meeting yielded two principal results. Nagaoka proposed names for academic appointments, and the two men agreed on an organizing committee.[154]

As proposed, this committee would monitor developments, and for that reason it was made up of prominent scientists.[155] In fact, once it was known who would be the new professors, it was they who did most of the actual work. Their most important task was to allocate money for facilities and equipment. Four programs were to be funded—in geology, mathematics, physics and chemistry—and the government imposed a limit on spending (150,000 yen). Unfortunately, the efforts of the young professors yielded a budget twice that size, but over some months the problems were solved. The professors reached a formula for allocating their funds. The geology program was postponed for a year. The ministry decided to reward them with additional funds for equipment.[156]

Of course, Makino and his successors could make such commitments because military spending was dropping. But the success he achieved while holding this office cannot fully be explained in this way. Makino Nobuaki had a profound understanding of what one would now call the sociology of science and higher education. During his four years as vice minister of education in the 1890s he had pointed out Japan's special lack of experience with the physical sciences, expressed sympathy for the difficulties of Japanese research scientists after they returned home from Europe, defended the hiring of foreign academics as a stimulus for Japanese professors, supported university expansion as "best for the progress of learning," and stressed the importance of competition between chairs as beneficial to scientific research.[157] Makino had other qualities few colleagues could match. He was the son of Ōkubo Toshimichi, one of the Meiji state's founders, he had spent much time abroad in his formative years (primarily in the United States), and he had more than a modicum of political judgment. In 1908, when the Beriberi Research Commission was established with money from the Ministry of War, he refused to support professorial demands that the Ministry of Education be granted control on the grounds that this was not a fight he could win.[158] Makino's efforts were greatly appreciated by the scientific community. Tokyo University's president, the physicist Yamakawa Kenjirō, said in 1911 that Makino Nobuaki was "among the ministers of education who accomplished the most."[159]

Certainly no one said this of the three who succeeded. Komatsubara Eitarō (1908–11) was described as a "used-up official with neither the capacity nor the inclination for administration." His successor, Haseba Sumitaka (1911–12), was called "deficient in the ability to understand anything about education." And the third, Shibata Kamon (1912–13), was said to represent the "quintessential bureaucratic style."[160] The evidence supports such remarks. None of these men had served in the Ministry of Education before becoming its head. Haseba had never been to college, and Komatsubara had spent just one year at Keio. None of the three had taught in a school, and none was known for intellectual interests.[161]

Other trends in the higher bureaucracy made the situation, if anything, worse. Komatsubara's appointment (he was concurrently minister of agriculture and commerce) epitomized a tendency to assign someone to the Ministry of Education as a kind of secondary duty.[162] Shibata's appointment marked the definitive takeover of the ministry by university graduates of the faculties of law. So conspicuous was this trend that Kyōiku jiron, which in 1897 had editorialized against the appointment of technical men to administrative offices, in 1913 reversed its judgment to argue that men with legal training were "not necessarily qualified to serve as bureau chiefs, [at least] in the Ministry of Education."[163]

But it was in the area of policy decisions that the effects were most glaring. The period 1908–14 was a period of lost opportunities, although substantial institutional growth did occur at the two new regional campuses. Tōhoku's science faculty with its twelve chairs was inaugurated in 1911, and the faculty of engineering at Kyushu University commenced the same year. Partly this expansion was based on policy. Yamakawa Kenjirō, serving as president at Kyushu in 1911, got Haseba to agree that the two new universities must be made equal to their peers in Tokyo and Kyoto,[164] but education ministers in this period were otherwise not much involved. Makino had committed the government to the Tōhoku project before leaving office, and Kyushu's expansion was owing to decisions under Kikuchi and to the political intervention of industrialists. The price that was paid for this regional expansion could be, and certainly was, challenged. Between 1908 and 1914 Kyoto University managed to add only one chair in a technical field (internal medicine in 1909) while Tokyo added just four (mineralogy, 1909; geography, 1911; agricultural engineering, 1911; mining engineering, 1912). How they did it at all is not clear, since their budgets were virtually frozen.[165] Not surprisingly, Chūō kōron in 1913 called the Ministry of Education a "place long lacking in accomplishment"; while Kyōiku jiron in 1914 considered it the "principal victim of the government's cuts in spending."[166]

The pattern of government spending justified this criticism. Meiji Japan had never spent lavishly on higher education. In 1900 Kubota Yuzuru reminded the House of Peers that France and Germany were spending about 8 percent of their budgets on public education, as compared to 5 percent in Japan.[167] Kikuchi Dairoku testified in 1901 to education's status as a lower-ranking item on the financial agenda of the country.[168] The reasons for this are both comprehensible and incomprehensible. Historically, the samurai class had linked education not only with morality but also with frugality. The Meiji leadership was inevitably committed to a high level of spending on the Japanese armed forces. The tax base was narrow for a good many years, and much of the Diet was vigorously dedicated to a relatively low level of public expenditure.

But one should not overlook the Ministry of Finance and its role in the budget process. This ministry was a conservative agency whose officials invariably chopped budgets. It was also an agency of considerable prestige, where many university graduates of the faculties of law first got their footholds.[169] Ministers and vice ministers were not law graduates until after the Russo-Japanese War, but several had been bureau chiefs before the turn of the century. The predilection for appointing law graduates worked against science. In 1911 Yamakawa Kenjirō lamented the small number of competent generalists among university graduates and especially deplored the "ignorance of science" that typified the modern legal man.[170] The ministry had in fact blundered badly in 1906 when it blocked a plan by electrical engineers in the Ministry of Communications to standardize frequencies of electrical transmission.[171] Coincidentally Yamakawa had lashed out at the basic posture of the Ministry of Finance. The ministry's worst feature, according to him, was a tendency to support proposals from the military uncritically while inclining to "meddle in educational [and technical] matters where they wrongly think they are competent."[172]

Predictably the last man to serve as minister of education before World War I was a person who fit the legal mold closely. Not that Okuda Yoshindo lacked pertinent expertise, for in 1899–1900 he had served as vice minister of education, and he had some understanding of higher education. He was a staunch promoter of Tokyo University and had graduated from its law faculty in 1884. In 1913, as minister of education, he rejected proposals for privatdozenten and lecture fees because the conditions needed to support them were lacking in Japan.[173]

But Okuda Yoshindo was above all else an expert in law and finance. He never served in the Ministry of Finance, but he had held a comparable job in 1900–02, when he was chief of the cabinet Bureau for Legal Affairs. There he developed the plan for cutbacks that Katsura had endeavored to follow. But Okuda was largely unaware of technical issues. He claimed that Tokyo University "set the standard for scientific research in Japan" and recommended transfer of Kitasato's institute to the university.[174] Despite major opposition he proposed this again (unsuccessfully) in 1911 and in 1913.

But in 1914 Kitasato's laboratory was transferred, though many contemporary observers attributed the transfer to Dean Aoyama's machinations. Professor of internal medicine from 1887 and dean of Tokyo's faculty for sixteen years (1901–17), Aoyama Tanemichi was a Kitasato rival who was powerful, well-connected, and politically informed. He helped add six new chairs during the years of his deanship and avoided budget cuts during the years of no-growth funding.[175] In 1908 he managed to get a member of the medical faculty on the war ministry's Beriberi Research Commission.[176] He was also a close friend of Ōkuma Shigenobu, one of the country's most powerful politicians.[177] Many thought this connection led to the transfer. Since Ōkuma was prime minister at the time (see chapter 7), and since the two men dined together nearly every Friday evening, it was plausible that the dean had persuaded the prime minister to carry out this action.

In fact, Aoyama was neither responsible for the transfer nor capable of achieving it by those means.[178] Before he authorized the transfer, Ōkuma had supported Kitasato, and in any case Aoyama had other priorities. Certainly he did medical research, but his principal interests were treatment of patients and finding positions for academic clients. To that end he tried to influence the selection of students for overseas study, involved himself intimately in faculty appointments, and convinced the people holding the pursestrings to create new positions for university-trained doctors.[179] Aoyama was more adroit than other deans and held office longer, but his career was typical. Sakurai Jōji as dean of science, Watanabe Wataru as dean of engineering, and Kozai Yoshinao as dean of agriculture all used this same strategy.

Institution building on behalf of research required more than these sorts of talents, for one had to have support from laypeople and control of resources simultaneously. In 1914, before the war began, members of the faculty of science had neither. An effort to engender support by delivering lectures at the Tokyo School of Physics, a very poorly funded private institution, yielded no lasting results.[180] The faculty of science produced a relatively small number of fully trained graduates. The private money received to support basic science was not used entirely by that faculty. Private business had limited interest, and no basic scientist's name was a household word.[181]

Agriculture's situation was, in principle, different, because it was a traditionally strong field that had some support for nonacademic research and a capable leader in Dean Kozai Yoshinao. Kozai had access to the powerful. In 1913 he was invited by the cabinet to discuss a proposal for agricultural research at one of its regular meetings. Interestingly enough, this proposal—for an animal husbandry institute—was never adopted despite a favorable reaction.[182] But the Yamamoto cabinet whose initiative it was soon fell from power, and the proposal could be faulted on the merits. Did Japan really need an animal husbandry institute when it had so many other needs? It is likely that the principal difficulty was lack of external support. Such a facility would have benefited only a few wealthy farmers, a clientele not organized politically. Agriculture generally had few academic support groups, and those that it did have were formed late.[183]

Academic engineering faced similar obstacles. Professional and other support groups existed, but their influence was small,[184] and Japanese business's bias toward foreign technology made it disinclined to give money. About 1909 the metallurgical physicist Honda Kōtarō—who did raise private money after 1914—described the relationship between private business and academic research as "like that of partners in a very late marriage."[185] Aoyagi Eiji, professor of electrical engineering at Kyoto University, in 1912 complained in print that academic engineers had "very few contacts in the business community."[186] Even having such contacts was not always enough. In 1911 the Ministry of Finance managed to block a proposed mining research laboratory despite support from academic engineers, their business allies, and the Diet.[187]

Kitasato's career in the Ministry of Home Affairs showed quite a different pattern. In 1899 he secured the dismissal of a section chief in the Public Health Bureau, apparently on personal grounds.[188] In 1903 and 1912 he defeated proposals from the Ministry of Finance to reduce the budget of the Institute of Infectious Diseases.[189] In 1914 he instigated the founding of a national network of sanatoria and hospitals for victims of tuberculosis.[190] The size of his "empire" grew steadily. In 1905 the government built new facilities for the laboratory and hospital and added new agencies to them. Attaching the Vaccine Station and Serological Institute for vaccine and serum production to the Institute of Infectious Diseases significantly increased Kitasato's power, because such production was a government monopoly.[191] Not surprisingly, the Bureau of Public Health was then said to be little more than an "extension of the Institute of Infectious Diseases," and the bureau chief "could never take action without consulting Kitasato in advance."[192]

Kitasato took steps to hold on to his power. In about 1901 he got control of the Central Hygiene Commission, whose function was medical consulting. He exploited friendships with Tanaka Giichi (later prime minister) and Fukuzawa Yukichi to gain regular access to their two publications. He made extensive use of the Japan Federation of Medical Societies and later served as its president. And he threw lavish parties for the federation's members on the grounds of his private estate.[193] Kitasato could do this because of his wealth. Beginning in 1893 he had established a private sanatorium for tubercular patients, and it proved exceedingly lucrative.[194]

The major bureau chiefs were also Kitasato's friends. Kubota Seitarō, who served as chief of the Bureau of Public Health for about seven years, was the first of many lawyers to hold this position. After graduating from Tokyo University's faculty of law, he worked as an attorney in the Ministry of Agriculture and Commerce and as a councillor with the Court of Administrative Appeals. In 1903 he was named chief of the bureau, where he consistently supported Kitasato's proposals.[195] His immediate successor was a lawyer-politician who was Kitasato's childhood friend. Kobashi Ichita (1910–13) went from Kumamoto to Tokyo University, then to the Bureau of Public Health, the Bureau of Civil Engineering, and the vice ministership of home affairs. In 1929 he became minister of education. Some considered Kobashi an effective bureau chief because in 1912 he got significant new funding for the Institute of Infectious Diseases when the Ministry of Finance was demanding cuts everywhere,[196] but others were less happy with him. These critics stressed his lack of influence in 1911, when Saionji's cabinet proposed to transfer the institute to the Ministry of Education, and his seeming ineffectiveness in 1913, when Okuda Yoshindo wanted to abolish the bureau.[197]

The most interesting aspect of Kobashi's performance is how his background in law contributed. Since he was Kitasato's friend and tried to support him, it is tempting to conclude that it made little difference. But the editor of the medical journal *Ikai jihō* was not convinced this was true. This man, Uchigasaki Tōjirō, himself a graduate of the Tokyo law faculty, made two criticisms of his fellow alumnus. According to him, Kobashi had fallen short because he lacked institutional loyalty and because he was insufficiently familiar with the matters he controlled. "The chief of the Bureau of Public Health should be a physician," he wrote. "But since the changes were made in the higher civil service, they are no longer being appointed."[198] Interestingly enough, Uchigasaki was not the only lawyer who considered the system too rigid. Bureau Chief Kubota once noted that Kitasato had never held a post with much formal power and attributed this record to "bureaucratic defects."[199]

A bureaucratic lawyer eventually caused Kitasato to lose his position. The laboratory transfer of 1914 was primarily the work of Ichiki Kitokurō, from 1894 to 1905 professor in the Tokyo law faculty and for several years thereafter a career civil servant. Ichiki came to dislike Kitasato after having been in posts where he could observe the scientist's maneuvering. In 1899, as a member ex officio of the Central Hygiene Commission, he watched Kitasato use the commission to fire an obnoxious civil servant. In 1903 and 1911 he had to tolerate Kitasato's destruction of the bureaucratic reform plans drafted by Okuda Yoshindo, who preceded him as cabinet bureau chief for legal affairs. During the period from 1908 to 1911, while serving as home affairs vice minister, Ichiki became particularly incensed by the growing national power of the "Kitasato faction" and their consistent ability to disrupt administration he thought appropriate and reasonable.[200]

But Ichiki could act only after Kitasato was weakened (see chapter 7), which happened for at least three different reasons. One was the diminished role of the Ministry of Home Affairs in supervising scientific laboratories (see table 5.3).

TABLE 5.3
Post-1900 Affiliations of Nonacademic Scientific Laboratories

	1900		1909		1915	
MINISTRY	N	%	N	%	N	%
Home Affairs	7	23	7	17	6	13
Agriculture and Commerce	11	35	15	37	15	33
Public Works and Communications	2	7	2	5	2	4
Navy	3	10	4	10	4	11
War	1	3	3	7	3	7
Education	7	22	8	20	13	28
Railways	0	0	1	2	1	2
Finance	0	0	1	2	1	2
Totals	31	100	41	100	45	100

Sources: Yuasa Mitsutomo, *Gendai kagaku gijutsu shi* (Tokyo, 1962); *TGSIG*, various numbers.

One year after Kitasato's institute was nationalized, the Ministry of Agriculture and Commerce had a 35 percent share of all nonacademic laboratories controlled by the government, with Education running 22 percent and Home Affairs 23. This in itself was alarming enough; the longer-term trend was much worse. By 1909 the Ministry of Home Affairs controlled only 17 percent and the Ministry of Education about 20, and by 1915 Home Affairs had dropped to 13 percent, while Education's share had risen to 28. A trend so momentous did not pass unnoticed. As early as 1901 a member of the House of Representatives remarked that the decline of the home affairs ministry had "created difficulties for various projects" and demanded to know why. In response, the chief of the Bureau of Civil Engineering testified that the Ministry of Home Affairs indeed "lacked backbone" and had no "special plan for carrying out [its] programs."[201]

The growing numbers of bacteriologists also eroded Kitasato's position. There were only seven bacteriologists in Japan when the Institute of Infectious Diseases was founded. Within a year of nationalization, the number had increased to twenty-four, and there were thirty-one Japanese bacteriologists when Okuda first recommended the institute's transfer. By 1910 there were forty-two, and another crucial one was added by 1914.[202] The percentage of bacteriologists working for organizations controlled by admirers of Kitasato was declining (see table 5.4). In 1893, four of Japan's seven bacteriologists worked with Kitasato, and three worked in the hostile environments of Tokyo University and the

TABLE 5.4
Employment of Bacteriologists

	IN PRO-KITASATO ORGANIZATIONS		IN OTHER ORGANIZATIONS	
YEAR	N	%	N	%
1893	4	57	3	43
1900	13	54	11	46
1910	18	43	24	57
1914	18	42	25	58

Sources: Iseki Kurō, ed., *Dai Nihon hakushi roku*, vols. 2, 3 (Tokyo: Hattensha, 1930), and various biographies.

Tokyo Hygiene Institute.[203] In 1900, 54 percent of the bacteriologists in Japan still worked in institutions or for organizations controlled by his allies, but by 1910 this figure had dropped to 43 percent, and by the eve of the war to 42.

Erosion of skill monopoly and loss of political leverage made the decline in Kitasato's bacteriologists an important development. Most Japanese bacteriologists before 1900 were both loyal to Kitasato and employed in organizations where they were free of conflicting loyalties, but their movement into organizations controlled by hostile elements changed this pattern substantially. In 1898 Yokote Chiyonosuke became an assistant professor of bacteriology at Tokyo University, in 1908 Ishihara Kikutarō left the Tokyo Higher Normal School to assume the same position, and in 1909 Futaki Kenzō accepted a junior faculty post at Tokyo.[204] But the move that damaged Kitasato most was that of Saizawa Kōzō in 1913 to the faculty of the Army Medical College, where he was subject to the authority of a long-time critic, Mori Rintarō, chief of the Bureau of Medical Affairs in the Ministry of War. Saizawa's move was particularly damaging because of his special combination of skills. Yokote, Ishihara, and Futaki were competent researchers, but none had a prior Kitasato connection or the range of qualifications required to replace him. Saizawa, who had worked two years with Kitasato (1907–09) and two more at Koch's laboratory (1910–12) was not only trained in research and clinical treatment but was formally qualified to supervise production of serums and smallpox vaccine.[205] Because Ishihara, Futaki, Yokote, and Saizawa were reasonably well trained, and because Saizawa held a politically vulnerable post, the Ministry of Education in Ōkuma's government, by allying itself with the Ministry of War, was able to assemble a pool of talent that could formally replace the Kitasato staff in October 1914 when they resigned to protest the institute's transfer. None of this was apparent beforehand. According to *Ikai jihō,* Kitasato until that moment continued to occupy a "very special position in the Ministry of Home Affairs."[206]

No scientist had any such position in the Ministry of Agriculture and Commerce, but there were two or three with more than average influence. Sakō Jōmei studied in Germany and taught in the faculty of agriculture at Tokyo University before joining the ministry in 1892. During the next ten years he established himself as a leading agricultural chemist, received his doctorate, and held two section chief posts in the Bureau of Agriculture. In a highly unusual move, Katsura's government in May 1903 elevated Sakō to the post of bureau chief, which he occupied for three and a half years. The reasons for his appointment are not completely clear, but a number of factors were at work. For example, Katsura was more interested in science than most prime ministers, Sakō had impressive credentials, and a friend of Sakō, Hirata Tōsuke, who had more formal education than most of his peers, had become minister of agriculture and commerce. Hirata was the first Japanese to obtain a Ph.D. from the University of Heidelberg; and while his degree was in political economy, he had also translated medical works into Japanese *and* was a friend of Shinagawa Yajirō, a prominent lay promoter of the chemical industry.[207]

If Katsura and Hirata wanted radically new leadership, Sakō did not disappoint them. He built on his own research in setting directions. In the 1890s he developed, and as bureau chief promoted, the "dry rice field thesis," which called for leaving at least some paddy land fallow when cultivating rice. He drafted legislation for agriculture. Under Sakō, laws governing fertilizer use, regulating agricultural societies, and attempting to minimize damage from insects were all approved by the Diet. He also took initiatives in several other areas, giving new emphasis to livestock breeding, agricultural research, and taxation of imported grain.[208]

Sakō Jōmei's striking contribution was to make the best use of resources. Critics had attacked the wasteful policy that appointed law graduates as chiefs of bureaus with technical duties and then hired experts to act in their place.[209] Earlier chiefs of the Bureau of Agriculture had clearly been guilty of this. In 1896 there had been only thirteen experts in agricultural research and thirty-one pushing papers at headquarters. But this ratio changed after Sakō took office, and by the end of his tenure it had been reversed. Unfortunately for the bureau, the change was not permanent. Sakō could evaluate technical matters, but his successors, trained in law, had to rely on subordinate experts, so that the number of experts working at headquarters once again exceeded those in research (see table 5.5). Sakō's leadership was quite successful. Contemporaries called him the "famous bureau chief," and Katsura in 1909 offered him the post of vice minister.[210]

After Sakō, the bureau again came under the control of lawyers and other nonexperts. Maki Naomasa (1906–07), Oda Hajime (1907–08), and Shimo'oka Chūji (1908–12) were all from the Tokyo law faculty, while Dōke Hitoshi (1912–20) was a liberal arts graduate. Certainly these men had good intentions. They proclaimed the need for Japan to increase food production, sought to reduce dependence on imports of cotton and wool, and tried to boost exports of silk. But their policy priorities did not always build on comparative economic advantage. Sericulture was seriously neglected, while animal husbandry research was stressed. There was no serious interest in a silk research laboratory until 1909, and even then it developed quite slowly. (Because of sharp price declines in the two prior years, private producers were the ones

TABLE 5.5
Agriculture Bureau—Deployment of Experts

YEAR	BUREAU HEADQUARTERS	NISHIGAHARA EXPERIMENT STATION
1896	31	13
1899	20	11
1904[a]	50	46
1906[a]	51	52
1910	52	54
1913	52	46

Source: Naikaku Insatsukyoku, ed., *Shokuinroku*.
[a]Years that Sakō Jōmei (D.Sc.Agr.) was chief of the Bureau of Agriculture.

wanting research; the ministry was not in the vanguard of action, and legislative progress was slow.) Only in 1911 did the Diet get a bill proposing the Silk Research Laboratory, and the actual foundation was delayed two more years.[211] Complacency figured largely here. When scientists employed in the ministry recommended in 1909 immediate research on synthetic fibers, their superiors did not respond well. Ignorant of foreign progress, they considered the challenge to silk insignificant.[212] In 1912 such attitudes prompted a member of the Diet to contend that the ministry was behind current needs.[213]

But the lawyers did not make every decision. Interest in animal husbandry was longstanding, beginning with Matsukata and Ōkubo in the 1870s, and annual imports of wool exceeded thirty million yen.[214] In the late Meiji years Kozai Yoshinao exercised great influence in favor of animal husbandry. When he spoke before the cabinet, an agriculture expert who attended the meeting said that just "two or three members" understood all the issues, but that Kozai's "sincerity and reputation" had been decisive.[215] Moreover, this use of Kozai was by no means unique. The ministry also tried to promote the use of new strains of rice by featuring him at a conference.[216]

This raises the issue of the role of experts in determining sound public policy. There were serious arguments against a domestic sheep industry. Foreign sheep adapted poorly to the humid Japanese climate and did well only in Hokkaido. Much of their food was imported from

Europe. Dense rural population made traditional grazing impossible. Costs of production typically exceeded the resources of individual farmers. The financial salience of these arguments was especially apparent. As we have seen, the immediate prewar years were difficult, and many programs were cut in funding. For 1914 the ministry proposed to reduce sericulture research by 35,000 yen.[217] Tokyo University had to accept a modest cut from the Ministry of Education, and even Kitasato's funding was seriously threatened in the Ministry of Home Affairs. In this situation the Ministry of Agriculture and Commerce designated animal husbandry research a target for major *new* funding (50,000 yen).

Certain members of the Diet were greatly displeased by the ministry's action. One got Vice Minister Hashimoto Keizaburō to acknowledge the successes of the sericulture program. Hashimoto noted that a university zoologist had returned from Europe with the news that Japan's progress had eliminated the need to ape foreign models. But the chief of the Bureau of Agriculture took a different position when asked about the breeding of sheep. He admitted a lack of progress in the ministry's program but attributed it to ignorance of animal diseases, the difficulties of animal raising in a crowded environment, and neglect of systematic crossbreeding. He also insisted that progress was occurring, citing modest successes in the Hokkaido region as a reason to increase support.[218]

Technical experts' views were only one factor in generating sound public policy. As dean of Tokyo's faculty of agriculture, Kozai Yoshinao could hardly be expected to oppose his own field's interest. Animal husbandry was an integral part of the agriculture program and had intrinsic interest for agricultural scientists. In the Ministry of Home Affairs money was even allocated for medical research that turned out to be based on error. Kitasato, in the last twenty years of his research career, spent a large but undetermined sum of the ministry's money on an unsuccessful effort to cure tuberculosis.[219] The real problem with the Bureau of Agriculture was its structural imbalance. It kept its technical experts totally subordinate and relied on academic authorities with self-interested motives.

The Bureaus of Forestry and Industry did not even do this. Forestry after 1900 used "lawyers" to supervise experts, making use of their work but denying them recognition.[220] Industry promoted only lawyers and assigned them the task of advocating research. Oka Makoto, chief of the bureau for a decade, was considered a competent official by scientists, but he actually knew nothing of scientific matters. One of his duties was to present his budget to the Budget Committee of the Diet. Because he had control over the Industrial Experiment Laboratory, Oka had to meet its director on occasion. These conversations were a challenge to them both. On one occasion Oka grilled Director Takayama Jintarō about minute details without being able to understand the answers he was getting. Takayama believed the questions were ridiculous, and the discussion became an emotional struggle.[221]

The worst manifestations of the bureaucratic system were not yet fully apparent. In early 1914 technical experts continued to work in the ministries, and there was some expansion and greater autonomy in the imperial universities. Kitasato's network of influential friends seemed intact. A major proponent of scientific research became head of the government in April. Prime Minister Ōkuma Shigenobu was at least as knowledgeable about science as Katsura Tarō, and some of his actions in office (1914–16) proved it. Ōkuma increased spending for science and higher education, helped found a major new laboratory, encouraged research in private institutions, and proclaimed the need for involvement in government by prominent members of the scientific community. Ironically, his government also transferred the Institute of Infectious Diseases to the Ministry of Education, damaging significantly in just a few weeks what it had taken Kitasato many years to create (see chapter 7).

The fate of Kitasato is an instance of government's coopting science. By awarding subsidies for appointments or research, and monopoly status for production of serums, officials had hoped to control his activities, and by moving his laboratory to the Ministry of Education, this control could surely be strengthened.[222] Of course, these policies had a much broader context. As part of its plan for maintaining legitimacy, the government tried to deflect competition by emphasizing rules, impartiality, expertise, and bureaucracy as crucial to the making of proper decisions.[223] Not that these strategies were simple to execute; scientists resisted in various ways, the academics demanding autonomy and Kitasato constructing a political support group. The bureaucracy could rarely act as a unit. More than one ministry was often involved (or aspired to involvement) in projects for science, and scientists could make them compete with each other. The results were beneficial for research.[224]

CHAPTER SIX

SCIENTIFIC RESEARCH IN ITS SOCIAL SETTING

Among the problems Japanese research had to surmount in its formative years, few aroused greater interest than the values of the research community. Could Japanese scientists be equally faithful to the Western scientific norm of impersonal criticism and to Japanese society's expectations of loyalty to mentors? Would Japanese academics willingly ignore clique affiliations to choose the man who was best for the job? Could they respect the public nature of science by sharing information and other resources? While scientists everywhere confront these issues, they were particularly salient for Japan because the formal structures of Japanese feudalism, samurai privileges, had disappeared so recently and because the experience of studying abroad had exposed Japanese scientists to the ethos and values of the Western scientific tradition. In July 1898 the journal *Kōshū iji* (Public health) noted that professors in the faculty of medicine at Tokyo University were being accused of giving more thought to who should marry their daughters than to what they might contribute to knowledge.[1] In August *Ikai jihō* declared that many Tokyo professors "fear and try to resist the development of new forces, respond to those who flatter them, suppress people with vitality who antagonize them, ignore morality and scholarship, and only seek influence for their cliques."[2]

One of the principal issues was favoritism in recruiting professors. Becoming a professor was said to require an undergraduate degree from the institution where one wished to work, a relative on its faculty, or a powerful patron who would execute "underhanded, crafty maneuvers." According to a leading daily newspaper: "Professorial posts . . . are acquired by inheritance. A professor with a daughter will choose a son-in-law from among his students. He will then send that student abroad even if another to whom the opportunity has been promised must be kept at home. Upon the student's return, the father-in-law will appoint the son-in-law to succeed him, even if he has to remove some inconveniently placed assistant professor."[3] Other observers showed greater interest in the allegation that the imperial universities recruited faculty solely from the ranks of alumni. In a 1905 essay, *Ikai jihō* praised the appointment of Sudō Kenzō as assistant professor of biochemistry at Tokyo University on the grounds that his undergraduate association with Hasegawa Tai's Zaisei Gakusha medical academy presaged a trend toward "merit" appointments.[4]

Another contention was that scientists had created self-sufficient, isolated enclaves that blocked most cooperation across factional lines. Critics thought researchers should compete to discover new knowledge yet willingly share facilities and information with rivals. In 1902 Nakahama Tōichirō asserted that "nothing could be further from the behavior of a scientist" than what he saw as an effort by Kitasato to extend his "private fiefdom" to Tokyo University.[5] In 1914 an anonymous writer in *Ikai jihō* claimed that the university itself was no more than an "accumulation of individual cells" where every research group was demanding a separate laboratory, specimen room, library, and other facilities.[6] In the same year Yagi Itsurō persuaded the Diet to reject a special university appropriations bill on the grounds that professors who "refuse to cooperate and confine themselves to small domains" were really not scientists at all.[7] The problem with such behavior, according to critics, was really intellectual in nature. It harmed science by inhibiting the synthesis of knowledge and experience,[8] and it could keep vital information from those who most needed it. In 1913 physicist Nishikawa Masaharu investigated hemp and asbestos fibers that would have interested a number of chemists, but university restrictions on cross enrollments kept them in ignorance for seven more years.[9]

Critics remarked less frequently on behavior *within* groups. Tokutomi Sohō in 1902 did say that the atmosphere at Tokyo University was "suffocating" and warned that "disputes between the authorities and learned circles opposed to feudalism" would continue if nothing were done about it.[10] Similarly, Wakasugi Kisaburō in 1914 referred in the House of Representatives to "decrepit professors" whose presence at the university was discouraging younger scientists from doing more research. Another Diet member said much the same thing in 1918.[11] The issue of free discussion was very important to Japanese scientists. During the controversy over beriberi, Kitasato wrote in a medical journal: "If a theory is deemed false, it must be publicly criticized whether the scientists involved are father and son, brothers, teacher and student, or friends. This is a great responsibility for scientists . . . [To do otherwise] would reveal a spirit of servility counter to the spirit of scientific journals."[12]

Kitasato was the most influential critic of Japanese science in this period. A prodigious investigator with a broad reputation, he himself professed strong commitment to open recruitment, free discussion, and cooperation with other professionals. In 1910 he denounced scientists who "accept the theories of others uncritically" and declared that it was in the nature of science to cause conflict between teachers and students.[13] From the founding of his laboratory in 1893, he recruited his staff from many institutions and criticized the university for lack of professionalism. In 1892 he cited these alleged misbehaviors as his reason for declining an appointment and even said they negated the attempts of the Tokyo faculty to carry on research.[14] For twenty years he resisted the Ministry of Education's attempt to tie his laboratory to Tokyo University, and in 1914 he left government service rather than accede to the change.

The institutional focus of this conflict over values reflected the state of science in this period (1870–1914; see table 6.1). On the eve of World War I, Tokyo University employed 38 percent of the country's research scientists. The Institute of Infectious Diseases ranked first among non-university facilities. Kyoto University was second among the four universities, with Kyushu University in a distant third place. Tōhoku University ranked last in professors with doctorates but was actually second in chemistry and physics.

Medicine dominated Japanese research in numbers and quality. By early 1914 there were 147 medical researchers working in four universities, thirteen government colleges, two government laboratories, and one private academy. Medical men had received 300 of the 652 doctorates in technical fields conferred before 1914 and obtained seven of the twenty-six prizes of the Imperial Academy conferred before 1921.[15] Physicists also received seven of the prizes awarded in this period (1911–20), but neither physics nor any other field matched medicine's overall record. By January 1914 Japan had produced only 30 physicists with doctor's degrees, of whom 27 were employed in three universities, four government laboratories, and one normal school. Research chemists of all kinds numbered 96 at the time; they worked mostly in applied fields. Of the 16 with degrees in basic chemistry, 12 were employed in universities, two at the Tokyo Higher Normal School, one at the Tokyo Higher Technical School, and one at the Sixth Higher School.[16] The state of chemical research in Japan is to some extent indicated also by the small number of Imperial Academy prizes it received—just three in the prizes' first decade.[17]

These figures help in evaluating the criticisms referred to above. Information on whom university professors married and where they studied makes it possible to discuss academic recruitment with some precision. But reliance on literary sources requires selectivity in discussing concrete cases. Among the independent laboratories, the In-

TABLE 1

Institutional Affiliations of Research Scientists (1913)

	TOKYO UNIVERSITY		KYOTO UNIVERSITY		KYUSHU UNIVERSITY		TŌHOKU UNIVERSITY		INSTITUTE OF INFECTIOUS DISEASES		OTHER GOVERNMENT LABORATORIES		MEDICAL COLLEGE		HIGHER TECHNICAL SCHOOLS		OTHERS	
	N	%	N	%	N	%	N	%	N	%	N	%	N	%	N	%	N	%
Pharmacology	4	21	0	0	0	0	0	0	0	0	4	21	7	37	0	0	4	21
Forestry	4	57	0	0	0	0	2	29	0	0	1	14	0	0	0	0	0	0
Veterinary medicine	6	60	0	0	0	0	0	0	1	10	0	0	0	0	0	0	3	30
Medicine	38	24	35	22	9	6	1	1	8	5	1	1	63	40	1	1	0	0
Engineering	36	43	24	29	14	17	1	1	0	0	4	5	0	0	4	5	0	0
Science	47	55	10	12	0	0	11	13	0	0	8	9	0	0	10	12	0	0
Agriculture	12	46	0	0	0	0	6	23	0	0	3	12	0	0	0	0	5	19
Totals	147	38	69	18	23	6	21	5	9	2	21	5	70	18	15	4	12	3

Sources: *Dai jinmei jiten*, 10 vols. (1957), *Dai Nihon hakushi roku*, 5 vols. (1921–30). *Jinji kōshin roku*, 1st ed. (1903); 2d ed. (1908); 4th ed. (1915); 7th ed. (1925); 8th ed. (1928); 9th ed. (1931); 11th ed. (1937). *Who's Who in Japan*, 2d ed. (1913); 17th ed. (1936). *The Japan Biographical Encyclopedia and Who's Who*, 1st ed. (1958).

stitute of Infectious Diseases is a compelling place to begin. Tokyo University is represented by four laboratories because it employed 38 percent—and trained 70 percent—of the Japanese scientists active in the period. Within the university, I discuss laboratories in physics and chemistry because of their importance for a developing tradition, those in pathology and internal medicine to represent varying accomplishments in medicine. I also analyze conditions at Tōhoku because of their meaning for Japan's basic science and to illustrate transmission of values from Tokyo University to sister institutions.[18]

Kitasato and the Institute of Infectious Diseases

Kitasato Shibasaburō was impartial in recruiting his staff when he is judged by the usual standards. The permanent members of his researcher corps came from several different schools and rarely, if ever, had "connections." His first appointment (Umeno Shinkichi) was a graduate of the Tokyo School of Veterinary Medicine, while the second (Asakawa Norihiko) came from the undistinguished Zaisei Gakusha owned by Hasegawa Tai. Kitajima Ta'ichi was the first graduate of Tokyo University to be hired and Shiga Kiyoshi the second. After the Institute's first few years, about half the researchers came from Tokyo University and the rest from other institutions. For example, Shibayama Gorosaku's appointment (Tokyo) was balanced by that of Hata Sahachirō (Okayama Medical College) in 1898; in 1900 Terauchi Yutaka (Tokyo) and Toda Toranobu (Morioka College of Agriculture and Forestry) were hired. Between 1901 and 1914 Kitasato added six men from Tokyo University, two from Okayama Medical College, and one each from Kyoto University, Nagasaki Medical College, and the Zaisei Gakusha. None of these appointments was nepotistic. Asakawa married one of Kitasato's daughters, and Shibayama married Kitasato's wife's sister, but this was after, not before, they entered the institute. Kitajima married the daughter of a prominent physician, but only one staff member had a father in medicine.[19]

Kitasato was as careful in developing his talent as he was in recruiting it. He encouraged the diligent, reprimanded the lazy, stimulated the curious, and challenged the skeptical. His objective was always to encourage independence. Hata Sahachirō says he told them to work hard and accept only the research results they had replicated themselves.[20] "Dr. Kitasato wanted us to develop strong personalities," wrote Miyajima Mikinosuke.[21] Shiga Kiyoshi states: "Kitasato never gave us detailed instructions. Instead, he followed Koch's method. That is, we were supposed to compile our own bibliographies and perform our own experiments as a way of learning responsibility and advancing by ourselves."[22]

At the same time, Kitasato was a disciplined man and demanded the same of his colleagues. He was a stickler for punctuality, order, and routine. He arrived at the laboratory by eight in the morning and worked energetically until five in the afternoon.[23] "He took a very strict attitude toward research students," according to Shiga, "and showed no mercy if anyone slacked off." Students and staff members secretly dubbed him "kaminari oyaji" (Papa Thunder) for the way he bawled out lack-adaisical colleagues, and Shiga says he could sometimes be heard several doors away venting his anger on a hapless researcher.[24] Asakawa, when approaching Kitasato's office, would look at the floor as a way of deflecting criticism if he thought the director was angry with him.[25] Miyajima tells of a photographer visiting the institute who became so rattled by Kitasato's angry voice that he snapped his picture of the incubating room with the lens cap still on the camera![26]

But it seems unlikely that Kitasato's explosive character damaged staff morale. Evidence suggests that colleagues used the nickname "kaminari oyaji" more to imply affection than to express discontent. Kitasato was the quintessential *oyabun* (boss), and Kitajima said a conversation with him was often like "talking to my father."[27] The director had a deep personal affection for the people working under him and was highly adept at getting the response that he wanted. He secretly lent students money to finance their studies, entertained members of the staff and their families at an annual picnic, and constantly used his influence to advance their careers in research. He never actually criticized members of the staff publicly even though his voice was sometimes overheard, and, according to Miyajima, he constantly praised to outsiders even those he privately criticized.[28]

The institute's contributions to science under Kitasato show that his leadership helped creativity. As we have seen, he himself discovered the causative agent of plague at Hong Kong in 1894. In 1897 Shiga Kiyoshi isolated the pathogen of dysentery (Shiga bacillus) in Tokyo. In 1901 Umeno Shinkichi proved that a species of streptococcus bacteria causes lymph gland disease in horses. After 1900 the group divided its attention about equally between clinical and basic research. Hida Otoichi in 1902 produced a diphtheria serum much superior to its predecessors by adding sugar and peptone to a burdock culture base. In 1905 Umeno developed an improved inoculation technique for smallpox that diluted the antitoxin by passing it through animal bodies before it was administered to humans. After 1905 Kitasato himself worked primarily on a never-found cure for tuberculosis, while Miyajima, Asakawa, and Kitajima, among other things, clarified the relationship between field mice, chiggers, and tsutsugamushi disease.[29]

Recruitment to Professorships in Japan's Universities

Notwithstanding the claims of some critics, marriage to the daughter of a professor was not particularly common in the Meiji and early Taishō periods. Of the fifty-one men who by 1920 had served or would serve as full professors in Tokyo's faculty of medicine, only five had done so, and three of these were cited by *Tōkyō Asahi Shimbun* in a 1914 exposé. The assistant professor Kakiuchi Saburō in biochemistry was said to have secured his appointment by marrying the daughter of Koganei Yoshikiyo, professor of anatomy. Mitamura Makujirō reportedly became assistant professor of pathology by marrying the daughter of the ophthalmology professor, Kōmoto Jūjirō; while Manabe Kaiichirō was said to be in line for a post in internal medicine by virtue of being the son-in-law of Hirota Tsukasa, the professor of pediatrics.[30]

But family connections were numerous in medicine and could certainly help a career. Koganei Yoshikiyo became assistant professor in anatomy after marrying the sister of the army's medical affairs bureau chief (Mori Rintarō), and Ogata Masanori got an appointment in hygiene after he married the sister of a professor of psychiatry (Sakaki Hajime). Not all connections were established through marriage. Nagayo Matarō (pathology) was the son of Nagayo Sensai, one-time chief of the Bureau of Public Health. Ōzawa Gakutarō (anatomy) was the adopted son of Ōzawa Kenji, physiology professor and at one time dean of the faculty. Miyake Kōichi (psychiatry) was the son of Miyake Shū, professor of pathology and dean of the faculty in the 1880s.[31] *Asahi Shimbun* singled out Miyake, since his maternal grandfather (Satō Susumu) had also been physician to the Emperor, and two of his brothers-in-law were active in medicine.[32] If true kinship relations are added to relations by marriage, thirteen of the fifty-one doctorate holders who served on the faculty of medicine in this period had significant family connections.[33]

Tokyo University was hardly unique in this sense among its sister imperial universities. At Kyoto, five professors (out of seventy-one) in the faculty of medicine had married the daughters of professors, three in medicine at Kyoto, one in medicine at Tokyo, and one in engineering at Kyoto. Of the five, however, only one was adopted by the father-in-law—Asayama Chūai (internal medicine), who married the daughter of Asayama Ikujirō (ophthalmology). Besides these five, one professor was the son of a professor in medicine at Tokyo, and one had a brother on the engineering faculty there. Two of the Kyoto medical faculty, Ozaki Yoshitane (orthopedic surgery) and Ozaki Yoshizumi (pharmacology), were brothers. In addition, two had married sisters of a Kyoto medical professor, and two other professors' sisters.

Professors of medicine at the newer institutions had more connections than those at the older ones. At Kyushu University, relationships established through marriage undoubtedly influenced the appointments of Ishizaka Tomotarō in pharmacology and Sakurai Tsunejirō in anatomy. Each one's father-in-law was both a Tokyo professor and in the same field. The professors Mochizuki Daiji and Takayama Masao married the daughters of Tada Gakusaburō and Nakahama Tōichirō, both doctors of science in medicine. Kure Ken (internal medicine) was a nephew of Kure Shūzō, professor of psychiatry at Tokyo. Ogawa Masanaga (bacteriology) married Itō Keiko, daughter of the Tōhoku zoologist Itō Tokutarō and granddaughter of the Tokyo botanist Itō Keisuke. Sakaki Yasusaburō married the sister of Katō Terumaro, D.Sc.Med. and physician to the Meiji emperor.

At Tōhoku University Kimura Onari (pathology) apparently benefited from his marriage to the daughter of Kure Shūzō, as did Satō Akira (pediatrics) from marrying the sister of Tokyo's professor of otorhinolaryngology, Okada Waichirō. Two other Tōhoku professors, Yamakawa Shōtarō and Inoue Tatsuichi, had close relatives with doctorates in medicine. Ōhara Hachirō (surgery) married the niece of Kumagawa Muneo, professor of biochemistry at Tokyo. Three more of the Tōhoku faculty had brothers who were professors in technical fields at Tokyo. But the professor whose family connections evoked greatest comment was Kumagai Taizō (internal medicine) whose appointment allegedly resulted from the fact that his *brother* (Kumagai—now Aoyama—Tetsuzō) had become *yōshi* (adopted son) to Tokyo's powerful dean Aoyama.[35]

The real issues are not the pattern per se but its typicality and implications for academic quality. Consider the scientists with engineering (*kōgaku*) degrees. In Japan, *kōgaku* included not only such standard fields as civil, mechanical, mining, or electrical engineering, but also applied chemistry, applied physics, and applied mathematics. Although basic physics, geology, mathematics, or theoretical chemistry were generally excluded, it was common enough for men in those fields to have begun their studies in an engineering subspecialty or to have done basic research under the engineering label. This fact gives us some understanding of intermarriage among scientists with basic science (*rigaku*) or agriculture (*nōgaku*) degrees, even where the 1923 loss of Iseki Kurō's data on the subject in the Kantō earthquake and fire precludes more precise estimations.

Certainly "engineers" married into academic families. While only one man at Tokyo University (Kamo Masao in mechanical engineering) married the daughter of a Tokyo engineering professor (becoming the son-in-law of Watanabe Wataru [mining and metallurgy]), three married daughters of Tokyo law professors, one the daughter of a professor of physics, and another the daughter of a professor of medicine. Because the fathers-in-law of three of these men became university presidents, the career benefits of their marriages should be obvious (Terano Kanji [applied chemistry] married the daughter of Yamakawa Kenjirō, who was president at Tokyo from 1901 to 1905 and 1913 to 1920; Tawara Kuniichi [metallurgy] and Kondō Toragorō [civil engineering] each married a daughter of Katō Hiroyuki, president from 1877 to 1886 and 1890 to 1893). Other engineering professors were equally fortunate. Inoue Jinkichi (applied chemistry) married the sister of Araki Torasaburō, D.Sc.Med., who became president of Kyoto University in 1914. And Ishii Keikichi (architecture) became brother-in-law to Mano Bunji, D.Sc.Engr. and president at Kyushu from 1913. Several others had useful connections. Sakurai Seizō (naval architecture) was the brother of the chemist Sakurai Jōji, dean of Tokyo's science faculty. Suehiro Kyōji and Terano Seiichi, both also naval architects, had brothers in the faculty of law at Kyoto and in applied chemistry at Tokyo.

Marrying into an academic family from Tokyo aided several men in their careers in engineering at Kyoto. Takeda Goichi, in architecture—an engineering discipline in Japan—married the daughter of Sakata Teiichi in mechanical engineering. Matsumura Tsuruzō (also architecture) married the sister of Kinoshita Seichū (obstetrics and gynecology). Ogura Kōhei (electrical engineering) and Ōtsuki Chiri (chemistry) both married daughters of Kikuchi Takeo (Tokyo faculty of law), while Yokobori Jisaburō (mining and metallurgy) married the daughter of Watanabe Wataru, a prominent figure in his field. Two of the Kyoto men had relatives on the Kyoto faculty. One was Nakazawa Yoshio in chemistry, whose father, Nakazawa Iwata, was also professor of chemistry; the other was Tomonaga Shōzō (mechanical engineering), whose brother, Tomonaga Sanjurō, was professor of philosophy. His nephew, Tomonaga Shin'ichirō, later won a Nobel Prize (physics, 1965).

At Kyushu and Tōhoku universities, professors of engineering more commonly had relatives on the Kyoto faculty. Ono Akimasa (Kyushu, mechanical engineering) married the daughter of Miwa Kan'ichirō, professor of mathematics at Kyoto. The brother of Torikata Uichi

(Kyushu, electrical engineering) was Torikata Ryūzō, professor of surgery first at Osaka Medical College, then at Kyoto. At Tōhoku, as we have seen, Inoue Jinkichi (chemistry) married the sister of Araki Torasaburō (physiology). The main Tokyo connections of Kyushu professors were those of Yoshimachi Tarōichi (civil engineering), who married the daughter of Hiroi Isamu, a Tokyo professor in his field, and of Nonaka Sueo (naval architecture), whose father-in-law, Yoshimura Chōsaku, was professor of civil engineering.

Thus, a significant percentage of professors with pre-1921 doctorates had connections in academic society (see table 6.2). But the meaning of these connections is far from self-evident. Critics implied that men with connections not only advanced professionally, but did so undeservedly. This assumption is open to doubt: academic families were remarkably strict about whom they accepted into their ranks.

A principal mechanism for recruiting both sons-in-law and professors for Tokyo's faculty of medicine was a rigorous, comprehensive examination, administered to all graduates of the four-year M.D. course regardless of family or prior performance. Achievement determined both a student's rank in the graduating class and which sections of the graduate program would be accessible to him. Those who did well were eligible for admission to one of the prestigious clinical laboratories; those who performed less impressively could anticipate acceptance by Ogata in hygiene, Kumagawa in biochemistry, or some other professor

TABLE 6.2
Personal Connections of University Professors (%)

UNIVERSITY	FIELD			
	ENGINEERING		MEDICINE	
Tokyo	19	(N = 85)	25	(N = 51)
Kyoto	22	(N = 36)	24	(N = 71)
Kyushu	17	(N = 35)	32	(N = 41)
Tōhoku	33	(N = 6)	32	(N = 28)
Averages	20	(N = 162)	27	(N = 191)

Source: Iseki Kurō, ed., *Dai Nihon hakushi roku*, 5 vols. (Tokyo: Hattensha, 1921–30).

in basic medicine. Examination performance also determined the select few from whom professors chose their sons-in-law or successors. So far as possible, they confined their choices to men placing first, second, or third in the examinations. The talented young medical man—as defined by the examination—might then marry a professor's daughter and, through that means or another, proceed with a career in academic medicine.[36]

The resulting keen competition among the students presumably assured that any potential recruit to the faculty had attained a standard of excellence. One successful veteran of the examinations, Manabe Kai-ichirō, recalled that when he graduated at the top of his class in 1904, the competition was "unbelievably severe," because the examination "determined a person's fate for the rest of his life."[37] Nor was competition confined to the students, as professors also competed for the most promising sons-in-law and successors. Professors in prestigious fields of clinical medicine had the advantage.[38] Dean Aoyama, for example, was able to get the number two man in the class of 1907, as his Internal Medicine Section was particularly well regarded.[39] Ogata, whose Hygiene Section ranked considerably lower in student estimation, tried but failed to marry his daughter to the top man in the class of 1902.[40]

Family ties undoubtedly helped men get appointments in basic science and agriculture, but we cannot know how far this went. The marriage of Suzuki Umetarō to the daughter of Tatsuno Kingo, professor of architecture at Tokyo, may well have helped him become professor of chemistry in the Tokyo agriculture faculty.[41] Similarly, Shibata Keita and Shibata Yūji, professors respectively of zoology and chemistry in the Tokyo faculty of science, probably benefited from their father's having been professor of pharmacology.[42] At Hokkaido University, founded in 1918, Hemmi Takeo's appointment to the faculty of agriculture was probably helped along by the prior appointment of his brother (Hemmi Fumio) to the faculty. But examination performance didn't hurt: Tanakadate Aikitsu, Nagaoka Hantarō, and Honda Kōtarō became professors of physics at Tokyo and Tōhoku, and each man had held first place in his graduating class.[43] Recruitment procedures in agriculture or basic science probably did not differ significantly from those in other technical fields.

The prevalence of academic inbreeding in all universities and fields of science supports this conclusion. The editor of *Ikai jihō* was wrong in claiming that the 1905 Sudō appointment in biochemistry at Tokyo would set a trend for the future. Except for three professors educated under the shogunate (Hashimoto Tsunatsune, Miyake Shū, and Taguchi Kazuharu), two educated abroad (Ikeda Kensai and Ōzawa Kenji), and one educated at Kyoto (Nakamura Hachitarō in pathology), Sudō was the only Japanese appointed to the Tokyo medical faculty in the entire forty-three-year period between 1877 and 1920 who did not have a Tokyo undergraduate degree—and he was appointed in a poorly funded field and failed to receive tenure.[44]

Kyoto, Kyushu, and Tōhoku were about as faithful as Tokyo in appointing only from among themselves. Between 1897 and 1921 Kyoto hired only two men without imperial university degrees: Shimada Kichisaburō, graduate of Kanazawa Medical College (to an assistant professorship of anatomy in 1908), and Matsushita Teiji from Nagasaki Medical College (to a chair in bacteriology in 1903). During its first decade, Kyushu made only one such appointment, Hikita Naotarō, graduate of Okayama Medical College, who held an assistant professorship in ophthalmology for only two years. Tōhoku chose two non–imperial university men, both in 1915: Suzuki Tatsuo from Niigata Medical College (assistant professor of pathology) and Shikinami Jūjirō, graduate of the Kanazawa Medical College (assistant professor of anatomy).[45]

Medicine was not the most inbred field. Between 1877 and 1921, only four non-Tokyo graduates received academic appointments in Tokyo's faculty of engineering, but three of them had foreign degrees—Yamamoto Nagakata (Glasgow), appointed in naval architecture in 1917, Dan Takuma (MIT), assistant professor of mining engineering, 1881–84, Yamada Yōkichi (Stevens Institute of Technology), professor of mechanical engineering, 1886–90—and only one a degree earned in Japan. Miyahara Jirō, who graduated from the Imperial Naval Academy in 1875 and pursued further studies at the Royal Naval College, Greenwich, became professor of naval engineering in 1888. In the other imperial universities, no outsiders were appointed to positions in engineering.

Basic science was a special case, since so few places taught it. Dōshisha University in Kyoto had offered chemistry and physics at its Harris School of Science (1889–97), but bureaucratic hostility killed the program. Neither Waseda nor Keio managed to establish a basic science program.[46] Since only the imperial universities could produce fully trained basic science graduates, anyone contemplating a career in physics, chemistry, biology, geology, or mathematics had few choices. Of course, the same was true in reverse. Imperial universities obtained all basic science professors from sister institutions, except for those trained abroad. Between 1877 and 1893, seven non–imperial university graduates were appointed: Nagai Nagayoshi and Matsui Naokichi in chemistry, Yamakawa Kenjirō and Kitao Jirō in physics, Harada

Toyokichi in geology, Itō Keisuke and Yatabe Ryōkichi in botany. All but Itō had foreign degrees, and all went to Tokyo when candidates were scarce.[47]

Agriculture, forestry, and veterinary medicine had the largest number of professors who did not fit the pattern. There were nine outside appointments nationwide in these fields between 1877 and 1918: six at Tokyo, two at Hokkaido, and a single nomination at Tōhoku. Two of these men (Katō Yasuharu in veterinary medicine, Miyawaki Atsushi in animal husbandry) had foreign degrees; four had graduated from the Tokyo School of Agriculture and Forestry (Tōkyō Nōrin Gakkō). If one excludes the foreign-educated and those trained under the shogunate, the fields by degree of inbreeding would be basic science (126 appointments, all from an imperial university), engineering (166 appointments, one outside), medicine (217 appointments, five outside), and agriculture (105 appointments, six outside).

"Academic inbreeding" also includes preference for one's own alumni, and by that definition was very widespread. Except for the earliest years, when one could become an assistant professor merely by graduating from Tokyo University or one of its parent institutions, possession of a doctor's degree became essential for those who were seeking full rank. Because 70 percent of all doctorates awarded before January 1921 went to graduates of Tokyo University, reliance on the doctorate as a condition of appointment gave them an edge. Their representation in the professoriat ranged from 52 percent in agriculture to 89 percent in engineering. Nevertheless, each university preferred to employ its own graduates whenever possible (see table 6.3).

Consider the proportions of alumni on the faculties of each institution. Column A indicates the percentage of all doctorates, B that of professorships held by the alumni of each university; preferential hiring is shown when B over A is greater than one. Graduates of Kyushu University accounted for only 2 percent of all doctorate holders in medicine, but 13 percent of its medical faculty had obtained degrees there. Only 6 percent of doctorate holders in basic science had obtained their degrees at Tōhoku University, yet 19 percent of the Tōhoku basic science faculty were alumni. Graduates of Kyoto University accounted for just 5 percent of basic science doctorates, yet 25 percent of the professors in that area at Kyoto held degrees from it. And 82 percent of the Tokyo agriculture faculty had Tokyo degrees even though the percentage of all agriculture degree holders from Tokyo was substantially smaller (52 percent).[48] Nitobe Inazō, D.Sc.Agr., graduate of the Sapporo Agricultural College (later the faculty of agriculture at Tōhoku, then Hokkaido, University) did serve for many years at Tokyo Univer-

TABLE 6.3
Preferential Hiring in the Imperial Universities (1877–1920)[a]

FIELD / UNIVERSITY	MEDICINE		AGRICULTURE FORESTRY VETERINARY MEDICINE		SCIENCE		ENGINEERING	
	A	B	A	B	A	B	A	B
Tokyo	62	N = 72 90	52	N = 44 82	72	N = 70 90	89	N = 89 94
Kyoto	21	N = 72 35	0	N = 2 0	5	N = 24 25	4	N = 39 15
Kyushu	2	N = 40 13	0	N = 4 0	0	N = 5 0	0	N = 33 0
Tōhoku	0	N = 25 0	26	N = 25 76	6	N = 27 19	2	N = 6 17
Total N, A Columns	N = 622		N = 161		N = 177		N = 365	

Sources: Dai jimmei jiten, 10 vols. (1957), Dai Nihon hakushi roku, 5 vols. (1921–30). Jinji kōshin roku, 1st ed. (1903); 2d ed. (1908); 4th ed. (1915); 7th ed. (1925); 8th ed. (1928); 9th ed. (1931); 11th ed. (1937). Who's Who in Japan, 2d ed. (1913); 17th ed. (1936). The Japan Biographical Encyclopedia and Who's Who, 1st ed. (1958).
[a]Figures exclude Hokkaido University.

sity, but he was one of just three Sapporo men to do so—and he had at one time studied at Tokyo.[49]

Once the pattern was established, it never changed. Aspirants to professorships in imperial universities needed first to hold a doctorate or get one fast. They usually must have graduated high in their class from an imperial university, preferably the one where they wanted to work. They ought to have connections with an academic family. Only 8 percent of those in medicine had married a professor's daughter at Kyoto and about 10 percent at Tokyo, compared to about 6 percent of those in engineering at Kyoto and 12 percent in the same field at Tokyo. But the proportions of those with valuable connections ranged from about 17 percent in engineering at Kyushu to a third in medicine or engineering at Tōhoku—and these estimates are probably low.[50] The prominence of such connections at Tōhoku and Kyushu suggests that inbreeding became more important, not less, over time.

More to the point is whether this mattered. Were the principles of scientific universalism really compromised by personal connections? Not, it would seem, if examination scores had the importance that the evidence implies. When a young scientist had to pass an examination to qualify for an academic marriage, it seems that achievement was controlling ascription, not ascription achievement. But caution is warranted in reaching conclusions. It could be argued, and was at the time, that examination scores were dubious indicators. Kitasato, who became world-famous, ranked only eighth in his graduating class. Yamamoto Tatsuo had to leave Japan for the Pasteur Institute because he ranked fiftieth. But the system also helped others advance. Yamagiwa Katsusaburō graduated first in 1889 and nearly got a Nobel Prize (1926), while Nagayo Matarō, who had finished second in his class, did important work on viral diseases.[51]

The Research Atmosphere in Academic Laboratories

Men from the past cannot be observed, much less interviewed, and literary evidence supplies most of what we know about atmosphere in the laboratories. But descriptions are not always numerous, and even when they are available, they probably show bias. Who wants to admit that his mentor was really a tyrant who suppressed creativity? Extant accounts may have been atypical, and the availability of sources may vitiate typicality. If a man had many students and dedicated coworkers, we may learn much about his group. If students were few and colleagues indifferent, we may be able to learn very little. Problems notwithstanding, the existing documentation should not be overlooked.

Bias can be controlled using concrete examples (as opposed to characterizations), and by focusing on Tokyo, which trained most scientists.

Tokyo's Physics Laboratory. With the departure of Mendenhall (1882) and Ewing (1883), physics became a Japanese enterprise. Though there were only one full professor (Yamakawa Kenjirō), one assistant professor (Tanakadate Aikitsu), and two lecturers (Muraoka Han'ichi and Nagaoka Hantarō) for most of the decade, changes began toward its end. In 1888 Tanakadate left for Europe, and Nagaoka assumed his duties.[52] Sekiya Seikei joined the group in 1889, and Tsuruta Kenji in 1894, but Sekiya died young (1896), and Tsuruta was inactive.[53] Yamakawa was senior and at first set the pace in spite of his inadequate training and few publications.[54] His contribution was to stimulate students and give them professional confidence. Yamakawa once asked a student to discover how to use equipment employed by Fresnel in work on the conical refraction of light. He told the man he would be the first in Japan to observe the phenomenon if only he could learn how to use it. The procedure worked well, and the student succeeded. By spending long hours of effort in the laboratory's darkroom, he repeated this classic experiment.[55]

Some questioned Yamakawa's effectiveness as a mentor. One called his loud voice intimidating, like "a general chewing out an army."[56] Takagi Teiji, Japan's leading mathematician of the pre–World War II era, said his lectures were unorganized and his manner distracting.[57] But others thought differently and praised them quite highly, and even those who thought Yamakawa intimidating also said he was kind.[58]

Well before Tanakadate returned from Europe in 1904, Yamakawa had slacked off and resigned his professorship, becoming university president in 1901. Muraoka took a position at Kyoto (1897), and Tanakadate assumed supervision. Partly because of his work under Kelvin, Tanakadate was interested in magnetism. He and Nagaoka had supervised a geomagnetic survey of Japan beginning in 1887, publishing their results in the following decade.[59] The work had continued despite his absence and contributed to seismology. Tanakadate published forty papers in the course of his career, gave many public lectures, made trips abroad, and attended a number of scientific conferences. After 1905 he turned more to research and was a pioneer for Japan in aeronautics (see chapter 7).[60]

Tanakadate was an excellent mentor. Like Mendenhall and Ewing before him, he involved students fully in his own work and tried to teach them whatever he knew. The physicist Nakamura Seiji wrote that students were grateful for Tanakadate's "appreciation of their ideas and their questions." Imamura Akitsune, later professor of physics at Tokyo, was impressed by his poise and control. "He would never lose his composure the way we did if some piece of equipment were missing but would always try to solve the problem with something on hand in the lab." Tomoda Chinzō remembered his patience and tolerance. "He was quite different from many professors in the way he responded to questions. Some would just observe that the answer could be found on such-and-such page of a book, but Tanakadate always gave his own answer."[61] But Tanakadate, like his teacher Lord Kelvin, was hard on advanced students if they made many errors.

His affability, sense of humor, and basic egalitarianism were what made Tanakadate successful as a mentor. He was informal with his coworkers, a characteristic that may have come from research trips or dormitory life with students before he got married. In any event, he continued the pattern as a senior professor. At five o'clock every afternoon, the physics researchers generally gathered by a large fireplace for physics discussions, storytelling, and a general socializing that Nakamura called "thoroughly agreeable." Perhaps Tanakadate's style was summarized best by physicist Tomoda Chinzō. "Dr. Tanakadate," he wrote, "always gave an impression that he was learning right along with us."[62]

Before Tanakadate fully retired (1916), Nagaoka took over and set a new tone. Despite the misgivings he had had as a student (see chapter 3), his stance was one of self-confidence. In 1888 he had ridiculed his teacher, C. G. Knott, in a letter to his friend Tanakadate, and he was known to hold no one in awe.[63] Nagaoka impressed some as cynical, cold, and unfriendly, and was famous for criticizing those he disliked. "Dr. Kinoshita Suekichi [later professor of physics at Tokyo] almost trembled around him," wrote physicist Matsuzawa Takeo.[64] "The students feared his [intellectual] acuteness and strict demeanor," according to Ishikawa Teijirō.[65] Some were annoyed by his management style: "Every half hour," Matsuzawa recalled, "Dr. Nagaoka would come down to the basement [where I was working] from his office on the second floor and yell out, 'What's happened?' I was flabbergasted by this, but my *sempai* [older graduate student] finally yelled back, 'He just started the project!'"[66]

But Nagaoka had another side in his dealings with physicists. "He always tried to draw out the students' ability and enthusiasm," wrote Ishikawa, "and he could explain things to them when Tanakadate could not."[67] Unquestionably Nagaoka favored the more competent, more motivated students. The Nobel laureate Yukawa Hideki was familiar with Nagaoka's reputation as a "rather forbidding individual" and met him with some initial trepidation. "But after I became secure in my work, we often talked physics, and I felt like his grandson."[68] Matsuzawa himself recalled, "On one occasion I had to see Nagaoka with Miyamoto Kyūichirō about the experiments we were doing that term. [When we met him at his house] his expression was totally different from the impression he gave in the laboratory. He acted like an easygoing father and ate peanuts and fresh fruit with us. After disposing of business, he never mentioned work."[69]

Whatever was thought of Nagaoka's style, his professional leadership was clearly effective. He was an excellent physicist, and by 1905 his wide-ranging work in geomagnetism, acoustics, metals, tidal wave action, optics, and atomic structure constituted the fulcrum of physics at Tokyo. Aichi Keiichi (later professor at Tōhoku) took a casual observation by Nagaoka about the diffraction phenomena of the telescope and developed it in work on rainbows. Honda Kōtarō's important work on metals, though assisted by Tammann, actually began during his days with Nagaoka. Terada Torahiko wrote a paper on the acoustics of the Japanese flute (*shakuhachi*) that Nagaoka also inspired. And few dissertations were directed by either of the other full professors.[70]

Nagaoka never ceased being critical about work. August Kundt, professor of physics at Berlin University, had mildly disparaged Japanese physics in 1894; Johannes Stark was harsher twenty years later.[71] The Germans insisted on fundamental research and expected that the Japanese would adopt their standard. This was a viewpoint Nagaoka shared. Like Stark, he thought Japanese physicists must stop doing what he called the "dull, mechanical" work exemplified by the national geomagnetic survey and instead offer findings of broad general interest. "It shows the backward state of our physical sciences that [Kundt and Stark] would think this [geomagnetic stuff] appropriate for us," he wrote in a 1913 essay. "It is very lamentable for the scientific community that information imports from Europe to Japan exceed our exports by several thousand times."[72]

Actually, his view was too harsh. Three recent historians of physics have noted that Japanese physics by 1913 was not all "mechanical" or "dull." Graduate student Kuwaki Ayao, later professor of physics at Kyushu, was aroused by Einstein's 1905 paper on special relativity and began to work on relativity theory. Tamaki Kijurō of Kyoto University (later the mentor of Yukawa Hideki) joined this work in 1909. Ishihara Jun introduced quantum theory about 1913 after working with Einstein and Sommerfeld. Nishikawa Masaharu delivered a famous paper on x-rays at about this same time.[73]

Chemistry in the Tokyo Faculty of Science.   Chemistry lacked a dominant figure, but it had important pioneers. One of these was Sakurai Jōji, who had studied in London with A. W. Williamson from

1876 to 1881. Sakurai was an excellent chemist. Though a nonnative speaker of English, he led his class in chemistry and physics and published two major papers while studying in Britain. Two British historians of science have even called his papers (dealing with iodide derivatives of methane) the "only important research done in Williamson's laboratory after 1855."[74] In 1881 Sakurai returned to Tokyo as the first Japanese chemist to become full professor. The work he did justified his rank. He investigated the molecular weights of substances in solution and developed a new technique for determining their boiling points. Samejima Tsunesaburō, later professor of chemistry at Tokyo, called this the "first truly significant chemical research in Japan."[75] Although Sakurai continued to do research, his administrative duties often interfered. From 1907 to 1918 he served as dean of the faculty of science and in 1914 as acting university president. He was also at that time president of the Imperial Academy and represented Japan at international meetings.

Scanty information complicates our assessment of Sakurai as a director of research. Colleagues and acquaintances considered him the essential English gentleman because he was dignified, well-mannered, and always impeccably dressed. He was also a stickler for form and publicly reprimanded students who came late to class or failed to polish their shoes. He also defended his version of the Williamson legacy by removing a colleague from a chemistry professorship (see chapter 3), but he did not consistently foist his ideas on others. In 1900 he arranged for Majima Toshiyuki to study organic chemistry in Zurich and then to join the Tokyo faculty even though Majima rejected Sakurai's advice about his career.[76]

Sakurai was not the only senior chemist in Tokyo's faculty of science. Edward Divers served as full professor for more than a quarter of a century (1873–99), and Haga Tamemasa for thirty years (1883–1913). There were six assistant professors in the early 1880s, but four transferred to the engineering faculty in 1886, and the other two (Kuhara Mitsuru and Yoshida Hikorokurō) left when Kyoto was opened, creating a place for a new senior man, Ikeda Kikunae. For the next twenty years there were very few changes. Matsubara Kōichi joined the group after Divers went home (1899), and Majima took a post in 1903. Shibata Yūji was appointed in 1913, and Katayama Masao in 1919.[77]

Haga Tamemasa was Sakurai's opposite. Sakurai Jōji was elegant and imposing, Haga Tamemasa rumpled and ordinary. Sakurai was strict and slightly aloof, Haga open and readily accessible. Sakurai worked alone, Haga with others. Sakurai was ever the efficient administrator; Haga played the role of the lovable Mr. Chips. Samejima remembered Haga as "erudite but guileless"; Shibata called him a "very kind man."[78] But how effective was he as a model for students? He neither repressed nor threatened them. He even went so far as to confide in students. Though his work on acids was described as "unrivaled" by Japanese peers,[79] Haga in other ways was not so effective. He stuttered so badly that listeners could scarcely take notes on his lectures. His cooperative research took another kind of toll, for Shibata argued that Haga worked so much with Divers that he never really learned how to do his work alone.[80]

Ikeda Kikunae, one of only two noted scientists to hail from Satsuma, was probably the best research director of the faculty's three senior chemists. He was trained at Tokyo and Berlin universities and joined the department in 1896. Shibata testifies to Ikeda's effectiveness:

> Ikeda had a particular character as an educator. He was not the type of professor who could present lectures adroitly or guide us according to some kind of model . . . Nevertheless, he inculcated the essence of scholarship in us. Using simple scalar containers like burettes and pipettes as equipment, he patiently helped us greenhorn students to trust the results of our experiments while discussing the spirit of observation, explaining the methods and results of our calculations, and making us aware of our errors.[81]

Ikeda's success as a mentor in research might explain his attraction for students, but that attraction also had other causes. Ikeda was a physical chemist who developed an interest in the chemistry of taste. In 1908 he discovered and patented a technique for producing monosodium glutamate by hydrolyzing protein. Production of this flavor-enhancing item became a major Japanese industry (Ajinomoto Ltd. is one of the companies) and made Ikeda Kikunae rather a wealthy man. Students interested in using their research to succeed in the marketplace would naturally have flocked to one who had already done so.[82]

While physics or physical science has usually been considered progressive and open, medicine is perceived as conservative and closed. The physicist John D. Bernal attributed the conservatism of medicine to its preservation of medieval traditions.[83] Bernhard J. Stern thought it derived from the reliance of medical men on authority in the face of conflicting theories and methods.[84] Others, including some sociologists, explain the fields' characteristics as a function of client relations, arguing that physicists or chemists, unlike medical men, escape the particularizing effects of nonprofessional judgment by manufacturing no product for laymen.[85] Of course, medicine is not scientific the

way physics is, but some of its patterns are not very different. Bernard
Barber, in an essay called "Resistance by Scientists to Scientific Discovery," noted that the physicists Helmholtz and Kirchhoff resisted
Planck's ideas on the second law of thermodynamics as strongly as
medical men of that period opposed Lister's theory of antisepsis.[86]
Thomas S. Kuhn showed long ago that scientists in all fields cling to
tradition.[87]

Pathology at Tokyo. The Pathology Laboratory at Tokyo University, however, was a model for innovative research. Its senior and junior
professors were open to students, accepting new ideas, and encouraged
creativity. Several of its publications were praised overseas, and one was
a breakthrough in cancer research. In 1916 Yamagiwa Katsusaburō
achieved one of the most important advances in cancer research by
demonstrating that tumors can be produced in animals by prolonged
application of tar to their skin. This work was important for theory
because it placed Virchow's doctrine of chronic irritation as a cause of
cancer on a sound experimental basis, and for methodology because it
enabled researchers to induce tumors in host animals more easily.[88]
The Lancet declared: "It is impossible to over-estimate the importance
of Yamagiwa's discovery for the study of cancer," and in 1926 he became a leading candidate for the Nobel Prize in medicine.[89]

Actually Yamagiwa's work is worthy of attention for both social and
scientific reasons. Colleagues remembered him as persistent and in-
domitable, and some mention his strong will and straightforward manner.[90] Students considered him a source of fatherly encouragement and
responded with feelings of loyalty. Yamagiwa later said the paper could
not have appeared without their support, and the evidence corroborates
this. As a long-term victim of pulmonary tuberculosis, Yamagiwa suffered from very poor health. Lacking the support of colleagues and
friends, he could scarcely have done research at all.[91]

Yamagiwa was a true pioneer, but he was not the first man to serve at
his rank. Erwin von Baelz was professor for three decades (from 1873 to
1902), and Josef Disse and Miyake Shū taught pathology in the 1880s.
Nagayo Matarō taught the subject beginning in 1907. But the Japanese
pathologist who first built a program was an unassuming man named
Miura Moriharu (full professor from 1887). Miura was neither brilliant
nor energetic, but he was effective with students. His younger colleague Nagayo Matarō quoted him as saying in 1909 that the laboratory
could do without electric lights because scientists "need to work only
during the day and should rest their brains at night."[92] Another colleague told *Ikai jihō* that Miura was capable of filling an hour's lecture

in pathology by reading half a page of a book![93] He is also remembered as a kind, dignified man who appreciated good humor and enjoyed leisure time. On research trips outside Tokyo Miura often patronized geisha establishments, and on Saturday afternoons he took laboratory members on walking trips and to dinner at a Western-style restaurant. Such outings usually concluded with a drinking party at which, in Yamagiwa's words, "reserve between professors and students was completely set aside."[94] Lunch-hour socializing within the laboratory was equally common as a means of easing tensions. "Every day," according to Sata Yoshihiko, "the entire staff and Professor Miura would gather at lunch time for *o-bentō* [box lunches] and pleasant conversation, no matter how busy we were . . . Dr. Miura would discuss his views on everything from scientific matters to world affairs and expected us to express our opinions, too. We all looked forward very much to these gatherings."[95]

Miura encouraged criticism from colleagues and students. Between 1896 and 1899 he published several papers and a book on beriberi, all erroneously calling it a paralysis of the peripheral nervous system caused by a toxin in freshwater fish. On one occasion he asked Sata to read and criticize this work and to collect pertinent material on a research trip to Hokkaido. Both men expected the material to confirm Miura's work, but the results badly damaged it. Miura accepted the verdict quite calmly and continued using Sata as a critic of his research, but Sata's reaction was not nearly so calm—he thought he had betrayed his own teacher.[96]

Since Yamagiwa was sick for much of the time, and Miura was not in good health either, Nagayo directed routine affairs nearly from the day he entered the group. A quiet but imposing man from a prominent family, he provided excellent leadership in all his endeavors. He believed in group solidarity and egalitarianism and sought to instill them in the members of the group. He cultivated the members by drinking tea and eating cakes with them every afternoon, and he tried to prevent the graduate students from deferring to him—especially when they were nearly his age—by levying small fines on the use of honorifics. Mitamura Makujirō, later professor of pathology at Tokyo, wrote that Nagayo hoped in these ways not only to develop solidarity but to inculcate his views about scientific objectivity: "Professor Nagayo was never inhibited in criticizing other scientists' work, including theories identified with his own teacher [Ludwig Aschoff], and was not at all bothered if students opposed *his* ideas . . . He always emphasized the need to respect truth, freedom, and especially impartiality."[97] Because of the patterns he helped establish, Nagayo and his staff became very close and undertook several projects together. In 1908 and 1909 they did work in serology and cytology that sought to relate changes in the bodily constitution to secretions in the intestines, and in 1914 they "pointed scientific investigation in a new direction" by anatomical and pathological studies showing cirrhosis of the liver existed in two forms.[98] But their greatest achievement was the conquest of scrub typhus (*Rickettsia tsutsugamushi*), whose pathogen they found and confirmed.[99]

Nagayo Matarō was both able and self-confident. One acquaintance says he had a "will of iron" and admired historical figures like Martin Luther who never admitted defeat. Another recalled the time he told Dean Aoyama to mind his own business after the dean contradicted one of his explanations while attending his class as a visitor. This self-confidence probably resulted from having a father (Nagayo Sensai) who was a pioneer in modern Japanese medicine and an older brother (Nagayo Shōkichi) who was both a prominent Tokyo internist and a member of the House of Peers. Whatever the source of this quality, Nagayo's career was impressive. In 1933 he became dean of the faculty of medicine and in 1934 president of the university. In 1936 he declined Prime Minister Hirota Kōki's invitation to serve as minister of education.[100]

Aoyama's Laboratory of Internal Medicine.   Aoyama Tanemichi was Tokyo University's senior internist for much of the period discussed here. Joining the faculty in 1887 after his studies at Berlin University, he became dean of medicine in 1901 and held the position for about sixteen years. He was an enigmatic figure at best, an out-and-out tyrant at worst. Contemporaries remember the mature Aoyama as a proud, even arrogant man, self-confident and paternalistic; but Aoyama as a youth was exactly the opposite. His father had considered him an economic burden. He stuttered badly in his earlier years, and his confidence was low. But appointment to the faculty made his career and changed his personality. Aoyama gained friends and patients who were wealthy and powerful, became the confidant of Ōkuma Shigenobu, moved into a large house, and spent 100 yen a month on Cuban cigars.[101]

Aoyama mixed little with underlings. One acquaintance says he confined socializing with coworkers to an annual dinner at a Chinese restaurant. Another states that alcohol was very rarely served. Given the rarity in Japan of attitudes like this, it is important to consider what their motivations were. Aoyama as a young man was quite fond of drinking, but later in life his opinion changed. Mitamura attributed the change to Aoyama's sympathy for Protestantism, and another associate agreed.[102] Takahashi Akira, a student of Aoyama who later joined the faculty, recalls Aoyama's scolding students who he thought drank too much and telling him to "supervise them closely" once *he* became a professor.[103]

Disagreements complicate any assessment of the climate in his laboratory. Some sources depict Aoyama as a paragon of professional virtue, but others imply that he was a tyrant. Imamura Yoshio wrote that Aoyama "disliked absolutist ways of thinking" and "respected the rights of the student."[104] Fujita Shūichi stated that Aoyama's skill in diagnosis won the respect of all internists, and added that he was "meticulous in teaching his students."[105] Other reports say Aoyama "showed as much interest in the professional success of his students as if they were his children" and tried to encourage their labors by eating supper with them on occasion.[106]

An evaluation by Mitamura is especially noteworthy. In 1959 Mitamura praised the "mutual competitiveness" and "flourishing research spirit" he thought pervaded the laboratory, and he assigned most of the credit to Aoyama. By his telling, Aoyama was indeed "arrogant" and "haughty" but was also "resolute," "manly," "dignified," and "fatherly." He says Aoyama never assigned research topics to students, but allowed them to study whatever they wished and seldom interfered once their work was under way. Upon its completion, he would offer a "few criticisms," and he readily supported publication. As a result, talented men "gravitated to Aoyama's laboratory" and produced a "succession of scientific publications."[107]

But Mitamura's assertions are suspect. The laboratory did attract a respectable number of students—156 during the thirty years of Aoyama's professorship—including many of the more capable. But the lucrative nature of internal medicine and the career benefits of the dean's patronage, rather than a particularly favorable research climate, probably accounted for this.[108] Much of the evidence suggests that the atmosphere inhibited creativity. Arai Tsuneo says students "reacted sharply to Aoyama's slightest smile or frown" and would hardly ever venture an opinion that was known to run counter to his.[109] Yamada Jirō wrote that the only way to pass Aoyama's oral examination was to "expound to him nothing but his favorite opinions on any particular disease."[110] Of his leadership in the research laboratory, his biographer wrote:

> Whenever a student wrote a paper and submitted it to Aoyama, he would scrutinize it with great care and criticize it sharply. He seldom accepted a new thesis at first reading. In the event that a student presented a particularly bold idea, Aoyama would scold him, saying, 'Are you certain you want to write something so audacious?' Moreover, if the student had contradicted a leading

authority, Aoyama always warned him he must reconsider that part of the argument.[111]

Significantly, the Aoyama group made few contributions to knowledge. The most important one by Aoyama himself was his anatomical-clinical work on plague at Hong Kong (1894). Other members of the group worked on beriberi, investigating its effects on the kidneys, muscles, and diaphragm; on acute and chronic myelitis; on liver disease; and on diseases caused by the leptothrix and salmonella families of bacteria. But none of this matched the standards of other laboratories, and the situation improved substantially only "after [1918 when] Dr. Inada [Ryūkichi] took over the laboratory."[112]

Tōhoku's Science Faculty and Honda's Physics Laboratory.   The faculty of science at Tōhoku University had a good intellectual climate from the start. Professors did complain at first of cramped quarters and a scarcity of colleagues, but in general they were very well pleased. The equipment they had was new, in fact, "had just been imported from Germany."[113] For several years there was no other on-campus faculty to compete for funds and resources.[114] The university president was unusually supportive. Sawayanagi Masatarō held the job only from 1911 to 1913, but he managed to ingratiate himself with the scientists. He was a great believer in the German proposition that professors should devote themselves to teaching and research—and keep their noses out of everything else. Mentioning teaching and research as the "two main duties of the university professor," Sawayanagi called administrative service by them undesirable and declared that a university professor "who cannot do research is a professor in name only."[115]

Thus a strong esprit de corps, with a powerful commitment to research, appeared. "Students who came to this university acquired a particular outlook," according to one of the early professors. "Producing research was the only thing that mattered . . . Some of the professors practically lived in their laboratories. Faculty and students alike worked late into the night with hardly any other real concern." This spirit took tangible form in journals—*Rika hōkoku/Science Reports of the Tohoku Imperial University*, which appeared when the campus first opened, and *Tōhoku sūgaku zasshi* (Tohoku journal of mathematics), published by the mathematicians privately even *before* it had opened. All the groups—mathematicians, geologists, physicists, and chemists—had seminars that helped to encourage their work by giving opportunities to report on new research, especially work that was still in progress. Teachers from the Second Higher School, the Miyagi Industrial School, and the local medical college as well as the university community attended. Researchers allowed time at the biweekly meetings to reporting on the pertinent literature. The chemists called their seminar the *Zasshi kai* (Journal society) and offered summary reports of papers appearing in the international chemical journals. Not surprisingly, in view of all this, the professors had high aspirations. "We were filled," one of them remarked, "with the idea that we had to impress people at even the most prestigious universities abroad."[116]

Honda Kōtarō's laboratory in physics exemplified these trends. He and Nagaoka had "shed their 'inferiority complex' toward Western counterparts." Honda aspired to create his own school,[117] and members of his group worked exceedingly hard. When a student asked permission to suspend a project because of equipment failure, Honda told him to fix the equipment even if it took all night. On one occasion Nagaoka came to Honda's home in Sendai on New Year's Day in hope of exploring an idea but did not find Honda at home—he had already gone to the laboratory. Honda and the members of his laboratory had a clear sense of purpose. There were no differences of treatment meted out except where Honda himself was concerned. This senior professor was the rare farmer's son to enter basic science and had little, if any, respect for anyone's place in society. Honda treated everyone the same. Wearing old clothes, he once arrived an hour late for a talk to business executives who supported his work and proceeded to lecture without an apology. He was also famous for his placid disposition. "No one ever heard him raise his voice or saw him pound the table," wrote Ishikawa Teijirō. "Only by his features could you tell he was angry. The students used to say his birthmark turned red."[118]

But this senior physicist was not very patient, for like his mentor, Nagaoka, Honda customarily visited each member of the laboratory group at least three or four times a day to discover what the person had accomplished since the last conversation. Kaya Seiji stated that Honda would even ask a student about his research if they happened to be in the men's room. "Once when I was working on iron crystals and the influence of magnetism on them, I happened to be standing in the men's room at the stall next to Honda's, and he insisted on knowing the details." Ishikawa thought this kept the students working hard, but Kaya found it highly annoying.[119]

What was the climate in this laboratory setting? Honda was not the defender of orthodoxy that Aoyama was in medicine. He would tell members of his staff that while the physics literature contained many insights and facts, there were also numerous errors needing the correction of "proper experiments."[120] But he never saw his own work as needing correction. "Honda's leadership in research was so strong," wrote a colleague in physics, "that researchers under him were not allowed to publish results that were incompatible with [his] theory or results in similar experiments."[121] His biographer wrote as follows of those who considered such action:

> If a young assistant professor in Honda's laboratory expressed a view contrary to his, Honda might say: "I do not think that is right. If you were to do more research you would agree with me." And if he thought a personality conflict was present, he might go further and say, "I would like to ask how thoroughly you have investigated this. Over what temperature range did you test the material? Have you published a paper on your findings? I would like to see some of your data. I worked on this problem for two years at Tokyo University under Professor Nagaoka. The names of Nagaoka and Honda have appeared on research reports. Please read these reports. I then continued working on this subject in Germany under Professor Tammann's direction and was able to show that my previous reports were correct. These papers were published in a German journal under Dr. Tammann's sponsorship. And they are recognized all over the world. If you are suggesting that some of what I have said is wrong, you have to prove it with experimental evidence." But by this point the younger scientist's head would be down.[122]

There seems little doubt about Honda's intolerance. After all, his research paradigm had a prestigious history. Identified closely with the pioneering work of the physical chemist Gustav Tammann, it was basically classical physics with none of the new quantum theory.[123] Honda spent three years with Tammann at Göttingen and René Du Bois at Berlin (1907–10), where he compiled a record of distinction in research. He published eight papers on the nature and properties of metals that extended Tammann's findings, and he studied the relationship of temperature changes to magnetic properties of forty-three elements when heated to a very high level (about 1000 degrees centigrade). This study in particular brought Honda recognition. Cambridge University asked if he were interested in a possible appointment to its faculty, and Nagaoka said he had made himself immortal.[124]

The laboratory results he got in Tōhoku continued to be impressive for a good many years. After returning to Japan in 1911, Honda assembled a staff of young scientists with training in chemistry and physics. Many of these men became professors; others took employment in industry. While they were working in the Honda laboratory at Tōhoku, they made important contributions to metallurgy as well as to physics and chemistry. One was the invention of a calorimeter which came to be widely used in mining for estimating the volume of ore in a vein. Another was the invention in 1916 of the so-called K.S. magnetic steel, then considered the best in the world. Other studies the group conducted dealt with changes in the magnetic properties of metals when exposed to temperature extremes.

As for Honda's personality, the mature man was widely recognized as having enormous energy and self-confidence, but the child had been just the opposite. Fifth son of a middling level farmer, he was sickly, shy and by reputation slow-witted. But he entered the First Higher School with his brother's support and later graduated from Tokyo University. At Tokyo, he was the top physics major of the class of 1897. He did research that eventually got published; the 1902 publication of his work on magnetic distortions in cobalt, nickel, and steel led Nagaoka to call him a capable man. He was extremely hardworking. A young physicist once asked Honda what to do when round-the-clock work had exhausted him. Honda's reply was, "You could read a book." "But suppose I'm too tired to even read a book?" "In that case, do your experiment. That is what I did when I was your age."[125]

Unquestionably this climate could be oppressive. The staff constantly complained of overwork. "We have to work too hard." "The director is too pushy." "What is life for if we can't let off steam?"[126] Honda was not inclined to socialize. He assigned people topics rather than letting them choose their own. And the research paradigm that the laboratory followed was gradually losing potential. "A characteristic of Honda's school [of chemical physics]," wrote Miyahara Shōhei, "was the effort to pursue 'how does a substance change?', and not [to ask] 'what is a substance in its essential structure?'" Indeed, Honda "could not understand [the] quantum mechanical theory [of metals and magnetism]," according to Kawamiya Nobuo.[127]

Despite Honda's views, though, researchers played sports. Kaya Seiji (president of Tokyo University after World War II) enjoyed mountain climbing. Hayakawa Kazuma was a hunting enthusiast. Others played baseball and tennis. No one really gave up on his work. "Mostly they just played pachinko while exchanging their discontents." There was a certain solidarity in the group—a "mixture of jewels and stones," Ishikawa called it, "rather like a household sharing a common fate."[128] There were also limits to Honda's intransigence. By the mid-1930s, his theory of metals had been exposed as inadequate and had attracted many critics. But in many respects Honda himself had helped produce this result. "The scientists and engineers who developed the science of metals beyond Honda," wrote Kawamiya, "were, more often than not, those who had studied [with him] . . . He . . . made the most important . . . contribution to the science of metals in Japan by producing the driving force for it, a mass of ambitious researchers."[129]

One other feature of the Honda group serves to mitigate a harsh judgment. Despite its affiliation with Tōhoku University, his was not a purely academic laboratory. The business interests that came to support him thought his work theoretical, but academics considered it applied.[130] For applied science his style of direction was appropriate. Industrial laboratories often stress directed research, not "pure" contributions to knowledge. Honda's approach to his students may have been suited to his fundamental goals.

Despite Honda's authoritarian behavior, his staff revered him and were strongly united. Critics of factionalism in Japanese science have usually stressed the role of the professor, but staff solidarity merits scrutiny, too. Solidarity probably impeded creativity at Aoyama's laboratory. If a student dissented too sharply from Aoyama's views, the others would reprimand him.[131] On one occasion, Aoyama's students disrupted a student protest movement against the medical administration so that their own professor, who happened to be dean, would not lose face in the struggle.[132]

Criticism and solidarity could, of course, coexist. The Honda group ate meals together, held informal discussions, took part (minus Honda) in sports, invented a new calorimeter, developed a new type of steel, and did other kinds of valuable research. The Tokyo physics laboratory, which socialized every afternoon, did useful studies in geomagnetism, spectroscopy, acoustics, relativity theory, and other areas. The pathology section of Miura, Yamagiwa, and Nagayo made basic contributions to international medicine and developed a "spirit of harmonious cooperation and mutuality" by regularly eating, talking, and drinking together.[133] Solidarity was only one factor. What most seemed to matter was the management of tension—to which some use of alcohol could make a contribution.

Indulgence in alcohol is popular everywhere, but not in perhaps the same way. Societies may use it to dull sensation or to create certain moods. The Japanese use it to restore solidarity.[134] In an inebriated state, real or feigned, one can speak freely without retribution. Aoyama's attitude is a most revealing case, especially because of his well-known aversion to alcohol. On one occasion he attended a banquet where one of his section members became very drunk. Boasting loudly and cavorting around, he ridiculed Aoyama and called him a horse. The next day, of course, he regretted his actions and tried to avoid his professor. But Aoyama approached him, expressed his forgiveness, and told him he knew what had happened.[135]

No consistent pattern of authoritarian behavior existed among the Japanese scientists of this period. Aoyama and Honda were frequently autocratic, but many of their colleagues were not. Yamakawa Kenjirō, Tanakadate Aikitsu, Nagaoka Hantarō, Sakurai Jōji, Haga Tamemasa, Ikeda Kikunae, Yamagiwa Katsusaburō, Miura Moriharu, and Nagayo Matarō were generally tolerant and open. The authoritarianism we do find has no obvious source—certainly not "feudalism," "tradition," or the prominence of medicine in the research community. Honda, a physicist, was at least as hostile to criticism of his work as anyone in medicine. Miura, a pathologist, sought out criticism even when it went against him. Many of the senior professors were arguably more "traditional" than either Aoyama or Honda. All were former samurai and active patrons of students, trying to instill the traditional value of group solidarity by socializing with them.

Honda and Aoyama were atypical. Each was viewed with indifference by his father. Aoyama's father wanted no more children, and Honda's father thought his youngest son was stupid. Both scientists suffered disabilities as children: stuttering in one case, adenoids in the other. Both were considered unpromising by teachers, and both suffered for a time from low self-esteem. Honda, the farmer's son, ignored differences in status. Aoyama rejected drinking with students because of his Protestant ideals. In short, when Japanese scientists acted like autocrats, it was probably a function of individual psychology. Japanese culture and the prominence of medicine should not be made the scapegoats.[136]

Competition and Cooperation in Japanese Science

Given the prominence of group solidarity, a kind of "roping off" process was probably inevitable. One would expect this result from Tokugawa patterns and from their continuation in Meiji society. Students in the faculty of science at Tokyo did not dare consult or study pharmacological chemistry with Nagai Nagayoshi while Sakurai Jōji was serving as dean because it was "not regarded favorably and was apt to be dangerous."[137] Men belonging to the internal medicine laboratories of Miura Kinnosuke and Irisawa Tatsukichi would not use an institute for x-ray treatment and hydrotherapy established jointly by the three Tokyo internists because the third internist, Aoyama, had made a student of his its director.[138] During World War I, researchers from the Tokyo laboratories in pathology and hygiene simultaneously worked on tsutsugamushi disease yet did not share information, personnel, or facilities.[139] At Tokyo, information was sometimes not exchanged even between the laboratories of physics and chemistry.[140] If this kind of group solidarity characteristic of feudalism did indeed prevent general cooperation, the critics would clearly be right in accusing Japanese science of rejecting scientific values.

In the more complicated situation that existed, scientific cooperation could occur. In 1888 two Tokyo internists admitted a pathology student of Miura Moriharu to their beriberi clinic as a way of enabling Miura to collect the material he needed for research. In 1889 Miura allowed Iijima Isao, from the faculty of science, to use a lecture hall belonging to pathology.[141] In 1894 Kitasato Shibasaburō established *Pasteurella pestis* as the cause of plague through a major cooperative study at Hong Kong with Aoyama Tanemichi even though the two came from hostile institutions.[142] In 1896 Ogata, from hygiene, and Yamagiwa, from pathology, worked together on plague in Taiwan.[143]

Later the patterns changed. After 1900 the physical sciences continued to cooperate. In 1913 Jimbo Kotora of geology and Shibata Yūji of chemistry at Tokyo shared lectures and laboratory time because of their common interest in mineralogy. In the same year Shibata taught Honda Kōtarō and Ogawa Masataka of Tōhoku the use of the spectroscope.[144] In 1916 Tawara Kuniichi, a metallurgist at Tokyo, lent Honda his own microphotographs.[145] But cooperation in medicine became very rare, as the behavior of the internists shows. In 1910 Aoyama got his Tokyo colleagues to work on tsutsugamushi disease just because other schools' researchers had shown interest in it. "We must not allow Kyoto University and Okayama Medical College to surpass our achievements," was justification enough for the dean.[146] Lively competition between the Kitasato and Tokyo groups developed over the cause of the 1918 influenza pandemic.[147]

Consideration of professional societies sheds additional light on competition and cooperation. Professional societies had members from all institutions and offered possibilities for close interaction. One could freely criticize the work of one's colleagues while receiving the critical reactions of others. Medicine led other fields in developing these patterns of criticism. In 1885 the Great Japan Hygiene Society and the Tokyo Medical Society sponsored contradictory lectures on beriberi. Takagi Kanehiro, at the hygiene society, related beriberi to diet. Ogata Masanori, speaking to the medical society, attributed it to a bacterium. This exchange led to a flurry of research, claims, and counterclaims. One development deserves attention. Besides exchanges in letters and journals, the debate was pursued face-to-face. When Ogata presented his widely heralded yet spurious demonstration of the "beriberi bacillus," Takagi not only attended the lecture, but following its conclusion strode to the podium and refuted Ogata's claims in detail.[148]

Open discussion of technical issues was relatively common, particularly in medicine. In the latter 1890s Ogata, Yamagiwa, and Kitasato carried on a lively debate over the details of Kitasato's report on plague in *The Lancet*.[149] In 1902 another debate unfolded over the question of cholera's etiology. The scientific issue was quite modest: whether the incriminating bacteria was or was not the komma bacillus of Koch. But the professional issue was potentially momentous for the future of Japanese medicine. Should exposure in the dailies or exposition in professional journals serve as the vehicle for proper debate? Ultimately the journals won out, but by no means quickly or easily.[150] Meanwhile, professional societies played a crucial role in developing the mores of science. Not only Kitasato but others as well sought to use their potential for stimulating debate. At academic meetings, Tokyo pathologists Yamagiwa and Miura had sharp exchanges on a regular basis, but they set bounds to their argument. "One of them would say after leaving the meeting, 'Forgive my rudeness,' while the other replied, 'Not at all. In science things must be this way.'"[151]

The physical sciences, especially physics, were slower to develop professional patterns of disagreement. In December 1903, at a meeting of the Tokyo Mathematical-Physical Society, Nagaoka Hantarō presented an important model of atomic structure that arranged electrons outside a central positive charge. The model was purely mechanical, not chemical, in nature, and it assumed the adequacy of classical electrodynamics for describing the behavior of atomic-sized systems.[152] But it reflected some cogent analysis and was taken rather seriously in Europe. Henri Poincaré called it a "very interesting attempt."[153] Ernest Rutherford, who received greater credit for modeling work, conceded that Nagaoka had partly anticipated the atomic structure assumed in his model.[154] In Japan, however, reaction to this work was muted. Tomoda Chinzō called it "new" and "credible" in 1905,[155] but very few reacted at all, and Nagaoka accused Japanese physicists of excessive timidity in public.[156] However, physicists became more openly critical in the years after World War I. In the mid-1920s several meetings of the Physical Society were enlivened by a dispute over hydrodynamics.[157]

Chemistry was somewhere between physics and medicine: criticism flourished at the Chemical Society, but not in so forceful a manner. The professional integration of Japanese chemists was one of the aims of the group, whose membership came from all pertinent specialties. Some represented basic science, but more were recruited from agriculture, engineering, or medicine.[158] An effort was made to diffuse information. Beginning in 1890, the Chemical Society held conferences on foreign journal literature. The place and time of the meetings changed often, but by 1913 they were fixed. Once a week on Thursday afternoons they convened in Tokyo's chemistry department. Reports were given on major foreign papers, and socializing followed the meetings.[159]

The Chemical Society also tried to influence how things were published in chemistry. Papers by university scientists had often been published in European languages, but the society dedicated itself to the use of Japanese for this purpose. In the early years (1878–99) publication in the society's own journal (*Tōkyō kagaku kaishi*) was determined by a vote of the members,[160] but by the turn of the century the society had set up an editorial board.[161] All this becomes important when we consider that as a "colonial" endeavor, science in areas outside the "center" has often lacked firm local moorings. Scientists at work in developing societies would concentrate their efforts on pleasing foreign peers and neglect to build ties of their own.[162] This was not the case in Japan, and the Chemical Society is one of the reasons.

The Chemical Society held monthly meetings, and attendance was invariably small. About twenty people would discuss three or four papers given by members and attend the dinner that followed. The atmosphere was usually polite; one source calls it "pleasant." But a plenary session was held once a year, and here things were different. Chemists attended from all over Japan and delivered a wide range of papers. Few holds were barred in discussion, and the sessions were always quite "lively." In fact, the growth of chemistry outside the capital eventually changed the society, as in 1921 the Tokyo Chemical Society became the Chemical Society of Japan.[163]

It is actually not surprising that the physical scientists lagged behind colleagues in medicine. Medical men had debated major issues even in the Tokugawa period, when students of physical science had to struggle just to obtain information. Physicians had worked more or less independently, but physical scientists had been dependent on the government.[164] Moreover, physical scientists were few, their tasks daunting. For example, they had to spend a great deal of time simply reading retrospective and current literature. At Tokyo University special committees of chemists read and reported on materials in English, while others read German, and still others French.[165] Similar arrangements existed in all fields, including medicine.[166] But the pattern of competition was different because medicine had the most money.

By 1914 medicine had substantially more researchers than any other field, with 156 doctorate holders in research positions, compared to 86 D.Sc. holders for all of basic science.[167] It had more facilities for research in upper and lower rank schools, enjoyed leadership with prestige and power, and had major discoveries to its credit. In other ways, however, medicine was beginning to lose its clout. The number of its facilities ceased to expand, and whereas the number of chairs for medicine had steadily increased in the earlier years, growth greatly slowed down later on. Between 1908 and 1917 the number of chairs in medical specialties grew from 71 to 99, a 28 percent increase, but all of this increase came on regional campuses. Tokyo added no chairs. The number of students at the graduate level, however, did consistently rise in medicine. In 1897 there had been eight graduate students in pathology at Tokyo University, three in hygiene, and five in Aoyama's section of internal medicine. By 1908 these figures had risen to twenty-four for pathology, five for hygiene, and ten for the Aoyama section. And in 1917 there were forty-six pathology graduate students, along with fifteen in hygiene and twenty-one in the Aoyama section. Between 1908 and 1917 graduate enrollment increases ranged from 100 to 200 percent.

The employment situation was undoubtedly worsened for would-be researchers when they considered the true dimensions of the candidate pool for university chairs. Professional roles were still inchoate at this time. A man did not have to pass through the graduate school to aspire to a chair. He needed only a degree. From that point of view, the increases in the numbers of men with degrees must have been truly alarming (see table 6.4). Back in 1893 there had been nearly as many chairs as candidates to fill them, that is, thirty degree holders and twenty-three chairs. In 1900 the situation was still not too bad: thirty-three chairs and fifty-six candidates. But by the time of the war, conditions were changing. In 1915 there were four potential candidates for every chair in medicine, and the ratio of candidates to chairs was about 5 : 1 in 1919 and 6 : 1 by 1920.

If small-group research in social psychology gives any indication, strong uncooperative ingroup-outgroup sentiments are a likely result of these patterns. Hare and Bales argue that group solidarity is significantly affected by size.[168] Other things being equal, a large group is more apt to avoid cooperation with other groups because increased numbers produce greater conformity by individuals and because the internal availability of diverse talents reduces the need for contributions from others.[169] Similarly, Collins, Raven, and Dion suggest that cooperation is apt to be undermined by a "perception of opposed fate" such as may arise from the threat of external attack, the sharing of common attitudes, or the realization that the demand for resources exceeds the supply. In either case, group cohesion increases, and greater suspicion of others results.[170] Still a third effect of increased numbers is an obstruction of the group's ability to reach the difficult decisions that may be required in cooperation by scientists. James alludes to this problem of reaching decisions; Hare stresses the diminished ability of even a strong leader to speed up the process.[171]

TABLE 6.4

The Changing Academic Marketplace in Japanese Medicine

YEAR	NUMBER OF CHAIRS	NUMBER OF LIVING DEGREE HOLDERS	RATIO
1893	23	30	1 : 1
1900	33	56	1 : 2
1905	61	114	1 : 2
1910	74	198	1 : 3
1913	74	287	1 : 4
1915	84	357	1 : 4
1917	100	445	1 : 4
1919	104	510	1 : 5
1920	105	578	1 : 6

Sources: For numbers of chairs see *Tōkyō Teikoku Daigaku gojū nen shi*, 2 vols., 1932; *Kyōto Teikoku Daigaku shi*, 1943; *Kyōto Daigaku nanajū nen shi*, 1967; *Tōhoku Daigaku gojū nen shi*, 2 vols., 1960; and *Kyūshū Daigaku gojū nen shi*, 3 vols., 1967. The numbers of living degree holders were calculated from information contained in the following: *Dai jimmei jiten*, 10 vols., 1957; *Dai Nihon hakushi roku*, 5 vols., 1921–30; *Jinji kōshin roku*, 1st ed. (1903); 2d ed. (1908); 4th ed. (1915); 7th ed. (1925); 8th ed. (1928); 9th ed. (1931); 11th ed. (1937); *Who's Who in Japan*, 2d ed. (1913); 17th ed. (1936); and *The Japan Biographical Encyclopedia and Who's Who*, 1st ed. (1958).

Competition for chairs did not exist elsewhere to anything like this extent. Tokyo University had six graduate students in physics in 1897, the same number in 1908, and nine in 1917. The situation in chemistry was similar, except that the numbers were even smaller. In 1897 there were four graduate students in chemistry at Tokyo University. There were still four in 1908 and just six in 1917. Honda's laboratory at Tōhoku University had nine at the end of this period.[172] And employment prospects for academic scientists remained good in both physics and chemistry (see table 6.5).

In 1893 Japan had two chairs in basic chemistry, both at Tokyo, and five living holders of the doctorate in that field. In 1900 there were five chairs and six degree holders. In 1913 there were eleven chairs and

TABLE 6.5
The Academic Marketplace in Physical Science

	CHEMISTRY			PHYSICS		
	NUMBER OF CHAIRS	NUMBER LIVING DEGREE HOLDERS	RATIO	NUMBER OF CHAIRS	NUMBER LIVING DEGREE HOLDERS	RATIO
1893	2	5	1 : 2	2	8	1 : 4
1900	5	6	1 : 1	5	11	1 : 2
1905	6	9	1 : 2	5	16	1 : 3
1910	7	13	1 : 2	7	22	1 : 3
1913	11	16	1 : 1	11	28	1 : 3
1915	12	17	1 : 1	11	29	1 : 3
1917	12	20	1 : 2	11	33	1 : 3
1919	13	23	1 : 2	14	38	1 : 3
1920	13	22	1 : 2	14	46	1 : 3

Sources: For number of chairs see *Tōkyō Teikoku Daigaku gojū nen shi*, 2 vols., 1932; *Kyōto Teikoku Daigaku shi*, 1943; *Kyōto Daigaku nanajū nen shi*, 1967; *Tōhoku Daigaku gojū nen shi*, 2 vols., 1960; and *Kyūshū Daigaku gojū nen shi*, 3 vols., 1967. The numbers of living degree holders were calculated from information contained in: *Dai jimmei jiten*, 10 vols., (1957); *Dai Nihon hakushi roku*, 5 vols. (1921–30); *Jinji kōshin roku*, 1st ed. (1903); 2d ed. (1908); 4th ed. (1915); 7th ed. (1925); 8th ed. (1928); 9th ed. (1931); 11th ed. (1937); *Who's Who in Japan*, 2d ed. (1913); 17th ed. (1936); and *The Japan Biographical Encyclopedia and Who's Who*, 1st ed. (1958).

sixteen doctors of chemistry, and by 1920 these numbers had risen only to thirteen and twenty-two. About the same was true of physics. In 1893 there were two chairs for eight degree holders, but in 1900 chairs in physics had increased to five, while only eleven men held a doctor's degree. In 1913 the system had eleven chairs compared to twenty-eight holders of the doctorate, and in 1920 fourteen chairs and forty-six degree holders. For more than a quarter of a century, the ratio of university research and teaching positions to people qualified to hold them remained almost stable (1 : 2 in chemistry and 1 : 3 in physics). Younger physicists and chemists were much less affected by the state of the market. They had considerable freedom and were reasonably assured of positions in their field. Young medical researchers had to conform and depend on senior professors. Moreover, the medical community was well endowed with talent and resources, while the physical and chemical communities had to stretch theirs. All things considered, it is hardly surprising that medical men were less cooperative and more restrained than physicists and chemists.

CHAPTER SEVEN

SCIENCE AND THE CRISIS
OF WORLD WAR I

World War I posed a major challenge to Japanese science, as it did to science worldwide. "The war differed from previous wars in that it involved whole nations and not only armies," wrote the British physicist John D. Bernal. "Agriculture and industry were pressed into . . . service and so was science."[1] In Japan the war heightened interest in the physical sciences. Indeed, one chemist called it a "blessing from heaven."[2] Nonacademic research flourished there as never before. A significant shift of research activity into private firms and institutions took place. Both public and private sectors showed more inclination to spend money on science at home. Businessmen and officials who had earlier disdained research now became its promoters. Costly projects like the Research Institute for Physics and Chemistry, which could not have gained a foothold before 1914, now moved to the top of the country's agenda.

The blockade of Germany by Britain and France helped to produce these results. Before the summer of 1914, Japan had depended heavily on Germany for industrial chemicals, pharmaceuticals, and precision instruments. All of the Salvarsan 606 used to treat syphilis came from Germany,[3] and most of the thirty-four million yen spent on imported pharmaceuticals also went to that country.[4] Much of the information used in producing aniline dyes was obtained from German-held patents.[5] About 150 Japanese traveled to Germany each year for medical studies.[6] Two years of every three spent abroad by Japanese scientists were spent in Germany.[7] And Germany was the site favored by most Japanese for exhibitions and academic conferences.[8] The blockade created a crisis. Prices of German-made products soared—when one could obtain the products at all. In a matter of weeks, aniline dyes jumped to twenty times their previous price.[9] Serious shortages developed. By late September Tokyo reportedly had a six months' supply of most basic medicines, but Osaka had nearly run out.[10]

Panic and fear were the first responses. As early as August 29, before Japan had activated its alliance with Britain, *Ikai jihō* worried: "Some [German] universities have adopted an anti-Japanese attitude."[11] In mid-September, it wrote: "The shortages are causing great consternation."[12] In May 1915, the vice minister of agriculture and commerce declared, "This blockade has caused major difficulties for many of our Japanese industries."[13] Fear rather quickly gave way to anger—and to a search for appropriate scapegoats. *Asahi Shimbun* ran an exposé series on Tokyo University's faculty of medicine, charging neglect of research by professors.[14] *Ikai jihō* published articles with the same theme. A prominent member of the Japanese Diet expressed himself on the subject as follows: "Now that our ties with Germany are broken, we must establish our own independence . . . But how can we do that with professors who pursue their own profit and insist on holding down various side jobs? . . . Not only does this hinder research, it destroys [academic] discipline all over the country and leads to a loss of professional authority!"[15] Demands were made for basic change. Three scientists who were university presidents saw the prospects for it as great.[16] The aforementioned speaker in the House of Representatives wanted resignations from lazy professors. Some thought other reforms were in order. "For [Tokyo University] to be a place of research, the remnants of factionalism [*gakubatsu*] must be swept out the door."[17]

Foreign study was greatly affected and generated lively debate. Over two-thirds of the 155 men studying abroad when the war broke out were in Germany, and there was no possibility of their staying. Most were able to leave through Sweden, with Britain or the U.S. as their destinations.[18] Some commentators called the cessation in the flow of students to Germany a golden opportunity to stop being an "importer of [technical] knowledge" and become its "creator."[19] "We shall have to discontinue our copying of Germany, however distasteful that is."[20] But others thought the estrangement was temporary. After all, the war resulted from the "Kaiser's ambitions, and not from hostility between the two peoples."[21] Moreover, other destinations were not satisfactory. The U.S. in particular was thought lacking in scientists.[22] Despite the wide range of views on the subject, the context of foreign study had changed fundamentally. By the time the war ended in 1918, the number of Japanese who studied abroad had sharply declined.

Japan, of course, was not alone in facing this challenge. Britain and other countries were also affected, as was Germany, with its strength in research.[23] Like Japan, Britain faced serious shortages—in dyestuffs (90 percent previously imported), pharmaceuticals, tungsten, and zinc.[24] Technical manpower was also at a premium. Chemical engineers were few in Britain.[25] And even in basic science, talent was scarce. But these shortages were relative. England and Wales in 1914 had three hundred graduate students in all basic sciences. In Japan's case, sixty would be a generous estimate.[26] Major concerns were also aroused in all three countries about optimum procedures for using resources. In 1916 German engineers demanded admission to the higher civil service, and their colleagues in Britain and Japan followed suit.[27]

In due time, of course, Japan regrouped and responded to most of the challenges. By December 1914 the government had launched a major survey of research facilities.[28] In 1915 Honda's facilities at Tōhoku were upgraded. A special program of chemical research was inaugurated at Kyoto University. The Industrial Experiment Laboratory expanded. In 1916 company engineers produced giant turbines, which had earlier been imported. In 1917 the Research Institute for Physics and Chemistry opened its doors, and it was followed in 1918 by the Institute for Aeronautics. A new university (Hokkaido) was founded that year, and so was a government program of grants for research. Private universities were finally authorized. A project for fixation of nitrogen received support. Nor were these efforts the limit of progress: private firms also built research facilities, and private foundations for research appeared.

But the progress had limits. University funding increased only slowly. The distribution of benefits brought by the war caused ripples of controversy. The position of technical men in the Japanese bureaucracy was not upgraded at all. High-handed government interference was a problem in medicine that had especially wide implications. When the Ōkuma government gave Kitasato's institute to the Ministry of Education in October 1914, it had little understanding of the events which would follow. Yet by the time they had run their course, the context of scientific research in Japan had changed in major ways.

The Administrative Transfer of Kitasato's Institute

The transfer of the Institute of Infectious Diseases marked the end of an era. Over twenty years Kitasato had built a famous and effective research program with total control over Japan's public health. But he had also antagonized the Ministry of Education by resisting its blandishments and overshadowing its client. Tokyo University had long competed with Kitasato's institute and came to control it completely. But the government's victory over the "Kitasato faction" proved to be pyrrhic. The university did not do well with serum production and attracted much criticism. Its political victory had unfavorable consequences for the Ministry of Education, further antagonizing a hostile Diet, exposing the ministry to attacks in the press, materially affecting educational policy, damaging serum production for the duration of the war.

Political reasons were behind the transfer, but few would say so directly. Leading defenders went so far as to claim that it would actually strengthen research. The minister of education, Ichiki Kitokurō, told the Dōshikai's Government Affairs Study Committee on November 28 that the transfer would save money, rationalize administration, and further the aim of research independence. "Because of the present war in Europe," he said, "it has become impossible for us to send students to France or Germany. We are drawing up plans for greater autonomy and hope the transfer will further them."[29] Prime Minister Ōkuma had earlier expressed such views. "Kitasato and his coworkers," Ōkuma claimed, "should be grateful for the association with Tokyo University, because it sets the standards for Japanese research."[30]

Kitasato's reaction, though tardy, was hostile in every respect. He gave Ōkuma a noncommittal answer on October 6, when the prime minister first informed him of the transfer and asked that he stay as director.[31] A few days later he told Ichiki he was "incapable of understanding the way a scientist thinks," as he prepared to resign from the Ministry of Home Affairs.[32] In a speech to his institute colleagues, he gave his reasons for quitting. First, the transfer decision was wrong because it assumed the institute to have a nonexistent connection with formal scientific education. Then again, it was wrong because it ran counter to worldwide trends in health administration. Third, it was wrong because it threatened to "destroy comprehensive research [sōgō kenkyū] at the institute."[33] To his mind, the Institute of Infectious Diseases was concerned only with combating infectious diseases and advising the government about them. Affiliation of the institute with Tokyo University would contradict the foreign practice of housing bacteriology in separate institutions, while the university's separation of basic and clinical medicine would damage vital aspects of the laboratory's mission.[34]

Kitasato's resignation (October 19) and those of his colleagues posed a serious dilemma for Ōkuma's cabinet. Ōkuma was openly anxious: "Scientists and academics who engage in this kind of [research] work are apt to misunderstand simple facts and cling to ridiculous ideas. We must pay no attention to them . . . It is perfectly apparent to anyone with the slightest scientific knowledge that this transfer has been carried out in a reasonable manner."[35] Ichiki also admitted that the resignations were "causing certain difficulties," and told a Diet committee he did "not care what ministry or bureau qualified successors might belong to."[36] Both officials were troubled by the shortage of serum technicians. After 1905 Kitasato's staff trained various technicians, but none wished to work for the Ministry of Education, and few held positions that could force them to. One, Saizawa Kōzō, opposed the assignment, but his position in the military made him vulnerable. Under direct orders from Mori Rintarō, he ignored charges of betrayal from Kitasato's pupils and offered his services to the Ministry of Education.[37]

Home ministry officials resented the decision to transfer the laboratory. For one thing, they had not been consulted. Ōkuma had personally assumed the home minister's portfolio when he organized his cabinet, and he excluded ministry officials from the transfer planning process out of concern for Kitasato's influence.[38] Such maneuverings naturally raised anxieties about the ministry's role in the government. Vice Minister Shimo'oka Chūji told Ōkuma the university might destroy the organizational arrangements of the institute after acquiring control and raised questions about public health administration.[39] Ōkuma rejected the first point while conceding the second. He added provisions to the transfer documents stating that the Ministry of Education accepted a continuing relationship between the Ministry of Home Affairs and the university-controlled institute. Education guaranteed the laboratory's rights to continue consultations in epidemiology.[40]

Members of the Diet criticized the transfer and the political motivations of its sponsors. Two members of the House of Representatives said the institute's affiliation with Tokyo University would damage its research program. Another said it would increase the cost of public health. Two more lamented Kitasato's possible subjection to a hostile section of the bureaucracy. Wakasugi Kisaburō, a physician who had also graduated from Tokyo University, blamed the entire affair (erroneously) on political machinations by Dean Aoyama. Yagi Itsurō from Nara, also a physician, said Ōkuma and Ichiki were completely ignorant of the "peculiarities of scientific research" and had gravely insulted all Japanese scientists by excluding Kitasato from prior consultation. He and Representative Yoshiue Shōichirō of Hokkaido further charged the cabinet with a lack of political honor. One said the Ministry of Education showed no clear logic in its annexation of research facilities; the other contended that the transfer was "simply a political act."[41]

A Seiyūkai party manifesto denounced the transfer in the *Asahi Shimbun*, arguing that Tokyo University and the Institute of Infectious Diseases were incompatible institutions, since the one was interested in teaching while the other was dedicated to research. The institute would suffer from this association because the university was filled with cliques, rigidly organized by chairs and deficient in research output. The Ministry of Education's annexations of research laboratories were illogical, inconsistent, and uninformed by the measure of foreign experience, and new procedures imposed on the institute by the transfer would cost more than the old and would probably endanger the production of serums and vaccine.[42] At the instigation of Seiyūkai leaders, the

House of Representatives voted to condemn the transfer (187 to 171).[43] Nor were hostile reactions confined to those holding office. Senior statesman Yamagata Aritomo expressed grave reservations about the transfer a week after the government's announcement.[44]

Professional reactions were surprisingly compliant. Several prefectural medical societies passed condemnatory resolutions, but most medical and scientific colleagues either supported it, stifled misgivings in private, or publicly feigned indifference.[45] Koganei Yoshikiyo, professor of anatomy at Tokyo University, came out in favor of the transfer, probably because Mori Rintarō was his brother-in-law. He was belatedly joined by Hirota Tsukasa, professor of pediatrics.[46] Ishiguro Tadanori tried to mediate the conflict from his chairmanship of the Central Hygiene Commission, but he backed off completely when Ōkuma rebuked him.[47] Nagayo Matarō, professor of pathology, was also opposed to the transfer but decided his university position demanded a public show of compliance.[48] The most revealing response was that of the president of the Great Japan Hygiene Society, Kitasato's sponsor in the 1890s. Kanasugi Eigorō began by calling the transfer—in private—the "result of an insidious plot." He decided to protest to Ōkuma and organized a group for that purpose. But once in Ōkuma's office, his demeanor changed markedly. As he told a meeting of Hygiene Society members, "It was an extraordinary thing for a mere group of physicians to visit His Excellency the prime minister and take up his time discussing this matter. The members should understand that we did this only to save appearances . . . If you are all dissatisfied and want us to visit him again, we will. But we felt overwhelmed to have said as much as we did to His Excellency on this subject."[49]

Of course, the transfer was not wholly political; it did have some logic behind it. The Ministry of Agriculture and Commerce administered several research programs with industrial applications. The Ministry of Home Affairs controlled some research in medicine. And the Ministry of Communications had a foothold in the field of electrical engineering. But Imperial Ordinance 279 gave the Ministry of Education an unusually broad mandate by authorizing it to "supervise and encourage *all* [my emphasis] the sciences and the arts."[50] This meant in practice that Home Affairs, Agriculture and Commerce, and Communications concentrated on research with known applications, while Education had the political upper hand in the area of basic research. Thus Home Affairs controlled such facilities as the Tokyo Hygiene Laboratory, the Osaka Hygiene Laboratory, and the Institute of Infectious Diseases. The Ministry of Agriculture and Commerce supervised the Industrial Experiment Laboratory, the Agricultural Experiment Station, and the

Sericulture Research Institute. Communications had jurisdiction over the Electrotechnical Laboratory and the Railways Research Institute. Education had charge of the Seismological Research Commission and the Mizusawa Latitudinal Observatory. Education had used Imperial Ordinance 279 to good advantage while enlarging its role in administering science.

But anomalies remained and were frequently criticized. Yagi Itsurō demanded to know why the Fermentation Laboratory was located in the Ministry of Finance rather than the Ministry of Education—if administrative uniformity were really so important.[51] *Kyōiku jiron* suggested that the government ought to transfer the Industrial Experiment Laboratory to the Ministry of Education, "if it is really so concerned about money."[52] Yagi also thought that the ministry's commitment to medical research should have given it control of the Beriberi Commission.[53] But policy decisions were not based solely on reason. In 1903 the ministry had denied Hasegawa Tai permission to call his Zaisei Gakusha medical academy a "higher professional school," as permitted by law, because of his association with and support for Kitasato.[54] Throughout the Meiji period, the Ministry of Education declined jurisdiction over the Fermentation Laboratory on the grounds that its undertakings were "not academic," yet in 1914 it took control of the Fisheries Institute, which had even fewer pretensions to research activity.[55]

Political motivations *were* behind the transfer of Kitasato's laboratory. Ichiki despised Kitasato and finally admitted this openly.[56] He made three bizarre statements in his remarks to the House of Representatives Budget Committee. He first observed that "private researchers" were incapable of improving the "unsatisfactory state of bacteriological research and vaccine manufacturing in Japan." Then he remarked that a government laboratory had to manufacture serum and vaccine, because no private agencies were doing so. Finally he said changes had taken place at the institute in 1899, when Kitasato became director of this newly established "national laboratory."[57] These remarks as a whole are logically incoherent because the institute *was* a government facility; Kitasato *was* its director; and *only* the institute produced serums and vaccine at the time. But if one imputes a political motivation, the statements begin to make sense. Kitasato was supposedly employed by the government, but his attitude suggested the contrary; the institute was a government laboratory in name but a private laboratory in fact; and Kitasato was obnoxious because he wielded an inordinate amount of informal power, not because he had broken the law.

Ichiki never conceded the transfer's true purpose, but one of his colleagues did. In his memoirs, Izawa Takio, the inspector general of the Metropolitan Police in the Ministry of Home Affairs, openly admitted that the real objective behind the affair was the destruction of the scientist's power:

> [Before its transfer to the Ministry of Education], the Institute of Infectious Diseases was a real barrel of rotten apples. It was supposed to be a state institution, but Dr. Kitasato had made it completely his own property. The chief of the Bureau of Public Health, who was supposed to supervise it, could not do anything without consulting him. Everything at the institute was under Kitasato's control. Since things had been this way for over a decade, one would have to say that the bureaucratic system had been disrupted. The government decided to transfer it to the Ministry of Education because its aims were not being realized where it was, under the Ministry of Home Affairs.[58]

The Ministry of Education got control of the institute, but the price it paid was high. Kitasato managed to establish himself in a situation of even greater autonomy. The ministry lost prestige because of the institute's problems after the transfer, and failed to gain control of several new laboratories which precedent should have accorded it. Fear of cooptation by ministry officials was a factor in each of these results. It manifested itself in the founding of laboratories as an issue of bureaucratic jurisdiction. In the problems of the institute after the transfer, it took the form of a heated debate over the quality of serums and smallpox vaccine. And in Kitasato's activities, one sees this concern reflected in three different ways—his singular establishment of a new private laboratory, his acquisition of a government license to manufacture serums and vaccine, and his attempts to influence government policy by materially aiding candidates for office.

Results and Implications of the Institute Transfer

Kitasato's reestablishment in a new private laboratory was the first major setback for the Ministry of Education. He began planning the Kitasato Institute even before he resigned and almost immediately began research on a temporary basis at facilities he owned. The new institute was somewhat smaller than its well-known precursor, but it set itself much the same mission: research, clinical treatment, and production of vaccine and serums. It also incorporated two major changes, representing simultaneously a broadening of mission and a narrowing of focus. The Kitasato Institute directed its research not only to bacterial diseases but to human and animal diseases in general, giving special attention to tuberculosis.[59] Kitasato's interest in tuberculosis was a major reason for his vigorous opposition to the laboratory's transfer and his establishment of the Kitasato Institute. Professors in the faculty of medicine at Tokyo University had unequivocally stated their lack of faith in the efficacy of Koch's tuberculin and their lack of interest in the prophylactic approach to the disease that Kitasato had tried to advance.[60] Establishment of his own laboratory was motivated by his desire for both intellectual autonomy and institutional freedom.

Money was naturally one source of his strength. From 1893 onward, he had operated a private sanatorium for wealthy tubercular patients. This facility, known as the Yōjō'en, was built on Fukuzawa Yukichi's land with additional funding from a wealthy industrialist, and it proved so lucrative that Kitasato bought out these two in a year. Charges by critics that the Yōjō'en's treatment of former institute patients constituted a "mixing of public and private interests" prompted secrecy about its finances, but word filtered out, and its reputation grew.[61] No figures are available on its profits, but they must have been large. Construction of the new Kitasato Institute in 1915 cost 400,000 yen—about 30 percent of Tokyo University's annual budget.[62] Of this amount, 48,000 yen came from "alumni" and colleagues, another 48,182 yen from the Great Japan Hygiene Society, and 4,500 yen from other donations. The rest of the costs Kitasato bore personally.[63]

The Ministry of Education suffered a second major setback when Kitasato and his institute got a license to make serums. He was able to do this in defiance of the government because he had friends who were still sympathetic and powerful. Two days after his meeting with Ōkuma (October 6), he sent Kitajima Ta'ichi, his loyal deputy director, to see a certain official of the Metropolitan Police, which belonged to the home ministry and had jurisdiction over public health matters in Tokyo. Kitajima requested and obtained this official's seal on the request for a license and forwarded it to himself as chief of the Bureau of Public Health's Section for Preventing Epidemics. He presented the request to the chief of the bureau, who promptly agreed to support it. The bureau chief returned the documents to the Department of Police, which proceeded to issue the license.[64] This set the stage for a bitter public fight over the quality of serums and vaccine.

Battle was joined once the Kitasato group reorganized. The Institute of Infectious Diseases had an inexperienced staff, and their products were soon questioned. Some medical authorities charged that the immunizing capability of the serums had declined, causing a rise in the death rate. Others said the Ministry of Education was trying to conceal the problem by lowering the price of the Japanese serums and making up poor quality by American-made imports. Still others said the institute's serum production was operating at a loss because the public had no confidence and would not buy the products.[65] The Ministry of Education tried to blunt these charges by developing a plausible defense. Although the immunization count of the new serums had indeed dropped, the cure rates had gone up. Prices had been lowered, but only for the purpose of promoting distribution. The amount of American serum imported was small and only for "experimental purposes," and the loss of income resulted from price-cutting, not the refusal of the public to buy.[66]

Self-interest played a role in each of these arguments. The judgment of education ministry critics, for example, might have been affected by ties to Kitasato. Hida Otoichi, who raised the issue of immunization capability, was a bacteriologist on the staff of the Kitasato Institute. Tsuchiya Seizaburō, who leveled the charges of higher death rates, had studied epidemiology with Kitasato.[67] The Kitasato Institute had a conflict of interest. Government subsidies were not available to it, and the Yōjō'en income was not sufficient. Continued operation required other income, and most of this came from serum and vaccine production.[68] But the government's claims were just as dubious. A 1915 study asserting the efficacy of the serums is suspect because it was carried out under the auspices of the Ministry of Education by a professor of pediatrics at Kyushu University.[69] Assertions of improved cure rates were supported by only a single hospital study at a Tokyo University affiliate.[70] The Ministry of Education tried to defend its share of the vaccine and serum market by too-strict inspection of the Kitasato Institute's production.[71]

The ministry's critics were almost certainly right. Vice Minister Fukuhara Ryōjirō denied all allegations of inept performance in serum and vaccine manufacturing on the floor of the Diet, but he admitted in the privacy of the Budget Committee chamber that the "limited ability" of the new serum technicians—including Saizawa Kōzō—might very well lead to inferior products.[72] Others who had also favored the transfer were concerned on this point. In the winter of 1914 Tokyo University's president, Yamakawa Kenjirō, told Ichiki's predecessor, Okuda Yoshindo, that there was "some concern whether serum manufacturing could be carried on at the university."[73] Mori Rintarō wrote in his diary of "anxiety" over the professors' total ignorance of the serum manufacturing process.[74] The chief of the Bureau of Professional Education, Matsuura Chinjirō, told the Budget Committee that the pretransfer diphtheria serum had a higher immunization level than the serum produced by the posttransfer staff.[75] Serum production chief Saizawa admitted in 1928 that it had been "very difficult" to obtain the required minimal level of five hundred immunization units in the first years after the transfer.[76] In view of such facts, it is scarcely surprising that Vice Minister Fukuhara had pleaded with the Diet in 1914 for a cessation of criticism about the laboratory transfer issue, arguing that rumors about incompetent performance and higher death rates from diseases were "not good for the [reputation of the] Ministry of Education."[77]

Another result of the transfer decision was an increase in factional strife. Aoyama got off the first shot even before the transfer's announcement. According to him, the Kitasato group had "not accomplished much for a number of years," despite a large budget and top-flight facilities.[78] About the same time, a long-time Kitasato friend and one-time business partner observed that "jealousy of Dr. Kitasato has increased greatly of late."[79] Relations worsened after the transfer. "The university and Kitasato groups became [real] enemies as the crisis developed," Nagayo Mataro wrote. "Aoyama asked me if he should attend the wedding of Kitasato's daughter, and I told him he'd best stay away."[80] In early 1915 Kitasato's associate, Shiga Kiyoshi—discoverer of the Shiga bacillus—published an essay in which he said, "Those university professors are so lazy they cannot do simple arithmetic!" As a retort, Aoyama called Shiga "a petty little man" in his hearing.[81] The Kitasato camp responded in mid-December 1914, when dedicating the Kitasato Institute. Viscount Kiyoura Keigo, who became prime minister in the next decade, contrasted the honor shown in Britain toward the deceased German scientist Paul Ehrlich with the treatment accorded his friend. "In this country, the only world-famous scientist we have, Dr. Kitasato, has been driven from his lifelong headquarters, the Institute of Infectious Diseases."[82] Not surprisingly, by 1917 the Japanese medical community was more deeply divided than ever.[83]

Even at the time, much of the problem was linked to factions in medicine. The minister of education, Kikuchi Dairoku, spoke plaintively of it even while in office,[84] and with good reason, since factionalism was very widespread. "Each of the genrō [senior professionals] had his own faction," wrote Sakai Tanihei many years later.[85] The press often chimed in by exposing the pattern at Tokyo. "This evil," wrote one publication in 1915, "exists throughout the entire university."[86] University officials, as the war dragged on, showed growing concern about the problem, and President Yamakawa decided to respond after several newspapers had featured the subject and linked it to poor research output. "These so-called gakubatsu [factions] are alleged to exist, but it is hard for us to accept this." The university had contributed to society, and its record was wholly praiseworthy. Of course, it was bad if such patterns existed, but one should not take them too seriously. After all, talk about factions was just a result of some peoples' "feelings of jealousy."[87]

It is especially significant that in 1914 the issue got hooked up with politics, that is, the politics of the larger society. Dean Aoyama and Tokyo University were linked to Prime Minister Ōkuma's ruling Dō-shikai party, while the rival Seiyūkai was favorable to Kitasato.[88] Aoyama had been a friend of Ōkuma, and many saw his influence as the cause of the transfer. The Seiyūkai had published a manifesto opposing the transfer that Kitasato may even have written. Kitasato had ties of long standing with Hara Kei and other Seiyūkai stalwarts, and one of his major colleagues in research called the opening ceremonies of the Kitasato Institute "an attack on the Ōkuma cabinet."[89] With the passing of time, these relations, if anything, polarized more. During the Diet elections of 1917, Kitasato campaigned for Seiyūkai politicians and contributed to their coffers.[90]

For the twenty years previous to the transfer, the Ministry of Education had been increasing its role in administering science, but in the half-dozen years following it, this position was seriously damaged. Since the apparent decline in its share was quite small, one would not know this from the figures. The ministry's share of research laboratories declined only from 13 of 46 laboratories (28 percent) in 1914 to 18 of 67 (27 percent) in 1920. But this indication is misleading, since the numbers are somewhat inflated. The Japanese government built five new specialized laboratories during the war, and the Ministry of Education got control over the three located at imperial universities by default. The ministry's control was minimal at one of these laboratories—the Institute for Aeronautics—and some opposed it. Education had to share control with another agency, and the professors in charge made no little effort to minimize its voice in the project. Finally, the two other laboratories, to which the Ministry of Education could have laid claim, were assigned elsewhere. In all of these cases suspicions aroused by the transfer affair were a major part of the reason.[91]

There remains the question—considering the consequences—of how such an event could have happened. Kitasato had offended many people, and several were determined to punish him. His government base of support had diminished as the power of the home ministry waned. The triumph of administrative legalism (hōka bannō) worked to challenge his reliance on politics. And the growth in the number of bacteriologists made his replacement seem at least formally possible. The minister of education, Ichiki Kitokurō, represented these forces and actively promoted the transfer, but Prime Minister Ōkuma's support of the transfer was what actually allowed it to happen.

This was highly ironic on the face of it. Ōkuma's life experiences and interests gave him every reason to admire Kitasato, or at least to leave him alone. He was a long-time associate and admirer of Kitasato's patron, Fukuzawa Yukichi, and had materially aided Fukuzawa in the founding of Keio University. He had himself founded a major private institution of learning, Waseda University. He had a deep commitment to personal independence and freedom of inquiry, which he expressed in Waseda's motto (*Gakumon no dokuritsu* [independence of learning]). He was actively interested in scholarly matters, most especially engineering and science, working for many years to establish such a program at Waseda. Ōkuma's interests in technical studies went far beyond those of most politicians. He frequently proclaimed that physics was the "base of all knowledge." He relished attendance at lectures by scientists whom the Imperial Academy favored with prizes. And he went so far as to state in an essay that scientists—especially medical scientists—should be active in secular politics.[92]

Ōkuma admired Kitasato and at first resisted the transfer. "He was strongly opposed to Ichiki's plan," according to one source, "because of his high idealism."[93] He even sent a formal directive on September 3 to the Ministry of Home Affairs, in which he called attention to the drug production program and stressed its importance for the nation's public health.[94] Ōkuma was not one to ignore Kitasato's achievements in his Institute of Infectious Diseases. National prestige, after all, did not depend solely on military power but also on the power of science. Kitasato's scientific contributions had enhanced this prestige and deserved greater support.[95]

But Ōkuma finally approved of the transfer. Why did his views change? We cannot be certain of the reason, but a number of factors are worth considering. Ōkuma was deeply committed to enhancing national prestige. For many years he had criticized Japan for reliance on others and stressed the need in matters of science for greater research creativity.[96] He was also a devout believer in the university model of how to organize science. "I [approved the transfer]," he told a visitor, "because medicine is commonly an academic matter and because of the convenience for research."[97] The war affected his assessment of national needs. "We send too many students to Germany each year," he told Kanasugi Eigorō, implying that this must be changed.[98] Moreover, "He was deeply impressed by Germany's ability to contend with several enemies at once," wrote Yanagita Izumi. "Upon considering the matter, he decided this was due to the strength of German [science and] culture."[99]

One should also take account of the man's personality. Ōkuma was intellectually curious, convivial, and known for his wide range of contacts. He had an optimistic outlook on life and believed strongly in the future. But he was also exceedingly sure of himself and could be downright pigheaded. "Once he decided his course, he was even willing to make serums and vaccine if he had to," wrote Kitajima in his memoirs.[100] Moreover, Ōkuma was never attentive to details and was prone to miscalculation,[101] and in some ways, this fault explains why the transfer took place as it did.

Founding of the Research Institute for Physics and Chemistry

While the transfer of Kitasato's laboratory did not reflect credit on Ōkuma, the founding of the Institute for Physics and Chemistry owed much to his intervention. More than any single figure, Ōkuma brought together the disparate coalition of forces needed to plan and construct this facility. Ōkuma prodded the Diet into approving the necessary subsidies, and Ōkuma, more than anyone else, helped to organize the private fund-raising effort. Most of this was done in a quiet, almost clandestine manner and attracted little notice, but this in no way obscures the importance of what the prime minister did. Without the efforts of Ōkuma Shigenobu, the institute would have been greatly delayed and might not have materialized at all.

Ōkuma had not been its original proponent. Physicist Nakamura Seiji had suggested such a laboratory in 1908, and Baron Mitsui, of the *zaibatsu* family, endorsed the idea in 1909. In 1913 the émigré chemist Takamine Jōkichi had attracted attention by a major proposal—creation of a large-scale national laboratory for all fields of science, with a price tag of twenty million yen—the cost, as he put it, of "just one battleship." This was considered too great a sum by the business community, and his proposal withered on the vine, to be brought back to life in the winter of 1914. Eight university scientists found several allies in the business community, drafted a proposal asking for five million yen, and approached certain members of the Diet. Nothing was done on this occasion, but the first major step had been taken.[102]

Japanese proponents of physics and chemistry were in part responding to trends overseas. In 1887 the Germans, after many difficulties, had built the Physicalische Technische Reichsanstalt (PTR). The French by century's end had the Institut Centrale des Arts et Manufactures. The British had the National Laboratory. The Americans established the National Bureau of Standards. The Germans then upped the ante in 1911 with the Kaiser Wilhelm Gesellschaft (KWG) network of laboratories. Nor were all the pertinent initiatives taken by public authorities. A major new trend in Germany and the U.S. was for industry to carry on research. By the turn of the century, facilities for research were rapidly appearing in chemistry, photography, transportation, and especially the electrical fields.[103]

Nevertheless, domestic stimuli were important to Japanese efforts. Japan was simply not well equipped for chemical and physical research. Facilities in these fields were limited in 1914 to the four imperial universities, the Imperial Academy of Sciences, the Industrial Experiment Laboratory, and the Electrotechnical Laboratory belonging to the Ministry of Communications. Even they had limitations. "There was no special provision for research in university budgets," wrote Sakurai Jōji. "Professors simply diverted to research money from the budget for student instruction."[104] And Nagaoka Hantarō recalled in 1933: "I turned to theoretical physics for a time because it was so difficult to get money for equipment. The research facilities we have now were unimaginable then."[105]

With the coming of the war, all of this began to change. In October, the Association for the Chemical Industry (Kōgyō Kagaku Kai) formally asked the Ministry of Agriculture and Commerce to establish a larger facility for chemical research, and the ministry appointed a committee. The committee, known as the Chemical Industry Study Commission (CISC or Kagaku Kōgyō Chōsa Kai), was chaired by the vice minister and included a number of academic chemists. They promptly took up, among other topics, the matter of whether to deal with the problem by enlarging the Industrial Experiment Laboratory or to build a new laboratory—and what to do about physics. Significantly, they opted for an entirely new facility, with physics an integral part. Agricultural chemist Kozai Yoshinao and the chemical engineer Takamatsu Toyokichi were especially influential in debate. They argued that chemistry would suffer if separated from physics, and that both must receive greater stress.[106] Takamatsu's views were decisive. He insisted that the proposed institution undertake research in chemistry "as a scientific discipline," not primarily in chemistry as an industrial enterprise. Simply enlarging the Industrial Experiment Laboratory would not solve the problem because of its aim.[107] Considering his position as the laboratory's director, his views could be seen as objective.

In March and April 1915, details were addressed more directly. The CISC designated five chemists to approach colleagues in physics and solicit their views about the project. Nine physicists, including especially Yamakawa Kenjirō and Kikuchi Dairoku, contributed ideas. After the main commission received the reports it decided to seek not less than 10,000,000 yen for the institute, of which 4,500,000 would cover construction, the remainder to be invested in research. About 160,000 yen was expected to sustain annual operating costs. These recommendations were drafted as a bill and went to the Diet in May.[108]

Reactions in the Diet were in many ways positive. "The present war in Europe is . . . making us keenly aware of the need for scientific research," a member of the House of Peers noted. "Yet our country lacks these [large-scale] facilities."[109] A colleague in the House of Representatives exclaimed, "We cannot continue to copy foreign countries as we have been doing. All the advanced Western countries have established high-level research institutions for physics and chemistry."[110] Almost everyone present endorsed the idea and conceded the need for the institute, but the real issue was cost. The minister of communications, Taketomi Tokitoshi, called the proposed ten million yen absurd and implied he could never support it. Representative Aijima Kanjirō, of the nongovernment Kokumintō party, thought this might be a fatal defect, since the cabinet was divided.[111] For the moment the issue was shelved by changes in the text of the bill. Instead of requiring that the government "adopt an appropriate plan to catch up with advanced countries at this time," the Diet added a proviso calling for the plan to be developed "in accordance with the present financial situation." This was passed by a voice vote.[112]

At this point Ōkuma became more assertive. Probably because Yamakawa Kenjirō, Sakurai Jōji, and Watanabe Wataru had lobbied him twice in April, he began to hold meetings of academic scientists, industrialists, bankers, and officials at his Waseda home. A small meeting was held on June 3, and a bigger one convened two weeks later. Ōkuma referred to the Anglo-French blockade of Germany as a "major problem" and insisted that action be taken. Everyone agreed on the need for the institute, but not on the proper procedure. They finally decided to appoint a committee in the hope of resolving the matter.[113]

Lengthy delays in reaching agreement showed that the subject was far from routine. The attempt had been made—and had failed—to establish the institute solely with government funds. Yet proponents insisted on five million yen as a minimum, and raising such a sum was not easy. Private businessmen would have to come forward. Iwasaki Koyata of Mitsubishi showed considerable enthusiasm when Sakurai asked him for money and at once pledged 500,000 yen,[114] but not all businessmen were so forthcoming, and the fund-raising effort was slow. "Outside the academic community," Sakurai wrote, "few saw the need for scientific research. And funds for research were still scarce."[115] It was eight months after the June meetings before the groundwork was complete. Letters were sent in January 1916 to the prime minister, the minister of agriculture and commerce, and the minister of finance requesting ten years' subsidy totaling 2,000,000 yen, with 250,000 yen to be paid the first year. Ōkuma held two more meetings with potential private donors, and a small committee chaired by Shibusawa Eiichi of the Dai-Ichi Bank and physicist Yamakawa

Kenjirō tried to line up more private contributions.[116] These efforts had succeeded by February 21; the rest was up to the Diet.

Responses in the Diet were mixed. Members praised the project as such and considered the money affordable. "The first thing to learn from the present war in Europe is the need for independent research."[117] "I am delighted it has become government policy." "If only the Japanese Empire had established this kind of laboratory five years ago, or better yet, ten." But questions lurked behind the enthusiasm, revealing a range of concerns. Had the government truly done its best on the issue? A number of members thought not. "Last year Mr. Taketomi called this proposal absurd." "The proposal is late, and the scale [of the plan] is too small."[118] "Does the government really have the fortitude to carry it out?" Would scientists be available once the institute was built? One member claimed that the shortage of research personnel exceeded the shortage of money. Another called the situation "pitiful." "In [Tokyo University's] faculty of science there are about thirty students in chemical research and twenty in physics with various professors supervising them. But the money they have is just 4,000 yen, which would never be true in a foreign university."[119]

Members of the Diet raised several other issues more divisive, if anything, than these. What precisely was the institute's mission? "The main purpose of the laboratory will be applied research," said the chairman of the subcommittee with control of the bill.[120] "This institute is to be essentially a place for pure research," claimed a former education vice minister.[121] Which was it to be? When Representative Suzuki Umeshirō sought clarification from the minister of agriculture and commerce, he was told in essence that it was both.[122] Documents drawn up by the legislative sponsors had stipulated both kinds of work. The question was politically charged. If applied research were the principal aim, then control would be given to the Ministry of Agriculture and Commerce, but if basic research were the objective, then the Ministry of Education could claim it.

Scientists and some of their supporters in business were determined that basic research would come first. "In my laboratory [built in 1916] we do only applied research," Iwasaki Koyata told Sakurai Jōji. "So I am happy that the institute will stress basic research."[123] Nevertheless, the Ministry of Agriculture and Commerce got control of the laboratory. Its minister, Kōno Hironaka, said it was partly because of the industrialists' interests in research applications. The ministry had frequently supported industrial research, said a political councillor in the Ministry of Education, so the industrialists thought this would speed up the process.[124] Moreover, the idea of control by the Ministry of Education alarmed some. Never mind that the ministry had "not done enough" to promote physics or chemistry in the imperial universities, which an education official admitted lacked large-scale facilities.[125] The real issue was its record in science. The Ministry of Education was "behind public thinking in matters of technical research." It had not done enough to promote innovation, and it had grossly interfered with long-established programs.

This was the decisive reason. "The Ministry of Education drove Dr. Kitasato to establish his own independent laboratory," charged Yokota Kōshi, a pharmacist from a district in Hyogo. "This is an instance of [clear-cut] malfeasance."[126] Another representative who cited this case wanted to know how the Ministry of Education envisioned its role in regard to the Institute for Physics and Chemistry.[127] A third member said the ministry's takeover of the Institute of Infectious Diseases showed bureaucratic control, not promotion of research, to be its fundamental long-term concern.[128] These Diet members were not alone in their views. The real reason for the institute's affiliation, according to Minister Kōno Hironaka, was the concern of unnamed people about the Ministry of Education. "It might try to take over the [Institute for Physics and Chemistry] the way it did the Institute of Infectious Diseases."[129]

Education officials were greatly displeased. "Industrial academies are all supervised by the Ministry of Education," noted former vice minister Okada Ryōhei.[130] "Tokyo University's science faculty must be seen as the foundation for the Research Institute for Physics and Chemistry," argued former councillor Egi Kazuyuki.[131] The Ministry of Education certainly did control the faculty of science, conceded the new minister of finance, Taketomi Tokitoshi.[132] Okada Ryōhei—himself named minister on October 9—was especially irate. He noted sarcastically the contradictions in descriptions of the institute's mission and denounced its assignment to a rival government ministry as a "disruption of procedure" and a "violation of our laws."[133] The education minister, Takada Sanae, former Waseda president and a friend of Ōkuma, was not too happy himself. He tried to put the best face on the matter by stressing industrialists' connections with the Ministry of Agriculture and Commerce but with minimal prodding declared that the Ministry of Education "should have had control from the outset."[134]

What, then, was the institute's relationship to the Ministry of Education? "[Agriculture and Commerce] will necessarily proceed in consultation with the Ministry of Education," the minister of finance promised. After all, the university's faculty of science "will serve as the institute's base."[135] In that case, Egi observed, more money would be needed at Tokyo University. But would the funds actually materialize?

The minister of finance responded, "It is our intention to offer the money to assure the [program's] success. In fact, the budget is well on its way."[136] The budget had some way to go. In December 1916, Sakurai Jōji, dean of the faculty of science, noted that just five thousand yen was budgeted for research in physics, while chemistry had even less (four thousand yen). "Members of the faculty can accomplish very little, and promising graduate students are taking other jobs."[137]

The Ministry of Finance was not very generous. In June 1916 President Yamakawa began planning the expansion of physics and chemistry at Tokyo University in connection with the research institute. After seeking the views of Sakurai Jōji, he approached the minister of education, Takada Sanae. Takada was very understanding, but problems arose in the cabinet. The new minister of finance, Shōda Kazue, was not well disposed and demanded postponements in spending.[138] Yamakawa, however, did not waver from his course, and in late 1917 his plans were approved. Even then, they were somewhat restricted. Most of the money (650,000 yen) went for facilities. No new faculty chairs were created, and actual appropriations were delayed twelve months more.[139]

But the cause of establishing the institute continued to gather momentum. The entire Diet approved the subsidies on February 27, 1916, and the corporation to receive them was established in March. Prime Minister Ōkuma began to create a committee of guarantors and in just a few weeks had recruited fifty-five. Thirty of this number proceeded to organize a Founding Commission, with Shibusawa as chair and two chemists, Sakurai and Takamatsu, as members. The industrialists and Ōkuma did most of the fund-raising, and by March 1917 had 2,187,000 yen.[140] Actual operations were planned by the scientists. One basic scientist and one applied scientist had charge of each discipline, and all four were professors at Tokyo University.[141] In April 1917 the imperial family donated 1,000,000 yen, and in September operations commenced.

Tokyo University and the Institute for Aeronautics

Creation of the Institute for Aeronautics at Tokyo University was equally difficult, or more so. Kitasato's supporters in the Diet and elsewhere were intensely opposed to academic ties for it. The military establishment came to view the facility as a trophy to which it had best claim. Not everyone well placed in the central bureaucracy thought such research deserved top priority. But World War I and accompanying developments placed a premium on military research. A small group of parliamentarians (especially in the Peers) was dedicated to the aeronautics project. Prime Minister Ōkuma was supportive, and most of all, two key physicists were determined to make it succeed. Yamakawa Kenjirō, Tokyo University's president, and a retiring professor of physics, Tanakadate Aikitsu, were the forces behind its creation. In mobilizing support for the Institute for Aeronautics they followed Kitasato's strategy.

Japan's earliest interest in aeronautics had a military basis. Several army officers were interested in fixed-balloon reconnaissance and during the 1904–05 war with Russia set out to exploit its potential. None of them, however, had much technical training, and none of their efforts bore fruit. This opened the way for academic scientists. In 1905 Fujisawa Rikitarō was serving as professor of mathematics both at Tokyo University and at the army's School of Artillery and Engineering, and he described the project's failure to his academic colleague in physics. Tanakadate agreed to help out, and the army put him in charge.[142]

An apparent turning point came in 1909. The army and navy were given authority to establish and control a Research Commission on the Military Uses of Balloons, whose chairman was an army lieutenant general. A number of officers were members. But the services' lack of technical expertise once again gave the scientists a role. Tanakadate was still the main figure. Between 1909 and 1912, he attended seminars on aeronautics at Göttingen and Berlin universities, built a small wind tunnel back in Japan, and recruited two students of physics to help him. It was not enough to assure success. The navy withdrew cooperation in 1912 and created its own small program. The army's interests were exclusively practical. Basic research made very little progress.[143]

The outbreak of war gave the program an important, though limited, boost. Tanakadate and an engineering colleague, Yokota Seinen, professor of naval architecture, argued that aeronautics needed a new research format that the university alone could provide. President Yamakawa agreed with this view and presented it to Prime Minister Ōkuma. Tanakadate and Yokota, at about this same time (March 1915), approached three of their friends in the Peers. Furuichi Kōi, Kubota Yuzuru, and Okada Ryōhei each had an interest in aviation and science and promptly agreed to help. Their interest proved valuable. Furuichi had been dean of the engineering faculty, Kubota had served as minister of education, and Okada had twice been vice minister. All belonged to the Aviation Society, as did Ōkuma. As a result of this growing support, the cabinet took up the issue in May.[144]

But 1915 was a year of missed opportunities. Because aviation research was entirely new, its constituency was not very powerful. Some businessmen championed the cause of the Institute for Physics and Chemistry because the blockade cut off the imports they needed, and

government officials were also persuaded by the need to end dependence on Germany. Aeronautical research was quite a different matter.
One might have expected support from the military, for in European
countries caught up in the war, such interest in aviation was strong. But
no such pattern evolved in Japan, since military pressures were few.
With only three hundred casualties for the whole war, there were far
fewer military incentives to innovate.

In 1915 Japan's real interest in aeronautical research was mostly
confined to scientists, and they were attached to Tokyo University,
which was controlled by the Ministry of Education. The new minister of
education, Takada Sanae, was not actually hostile, but neither was he
actively interested. On December 22, he presented his budget to the
House of Representatives and commented on the subject as follows: "I
do believe aeronautical research is needed at this time, and I would like
to ask the Diet to approve the funding for it. After all, you only get
something out if you put something in. But we need a lot of things, and
the financial situation will just not allow it."[145]

Forces were mobilizing, however, to bring about change. On June
13, 1915, Tanakadate met with a group from the Peers. For two and a
half hours he answered questions about the future of aviation, arousing
considerable enthusiasm.[146] In December and January Takada was
attacked in the Diet. Baron Kubota Yuzuru demanded a full explanation
in the Budget Committee of the Peers.[147] Dr. Suzuki Manjirō did the
same in the House. "The Ministry of Education realized that physical
[and chemical] research were needed, so they decided to contribute
some money. But in this case they are very complacent and need to
rethink their views. We need an aeronautics facility now.[148] Okada
Ryōhei told President Yamakawa of the attacks on Takada in parliament, and Yamakawa began to move. On January 21 he summoned two
section chiefs from the Ministry of Education to meet with him and two
other scientists, Tanakadate and Yokota. The five of them drew up a
budget that Yamakawa showed to the vice minister. Bypassing the
minister of education altogether, the two men met in Yamakawa's office
on January 24, and the deal was cut.[149] Education agreed to support a
line-item budget request for land and then for equipment.[150]

It is not clear when Takada converted, but he soon did his best in the
Diet:

As you [members] all know, aeronautics has made extraordinary
progress of late. The war especially has given it a boost. In fact,
aeronautics has shown astonishing growth in all the [belligerent]
countries during the past year. Of course, some design and construction of airplanes has been done in Japan . . . but we lack
facilities for basic research . . . As a response to this need, we

propose to build a laboratory at Tokyo University. I probably do not need to mention this, but [foreign] countries are very competitive in this field, and their military aircraft [research] is secret . . . We cannot wait for what others may do but will have to do our own basic work.[151]

The minister of education then mentioned the efforts of Britain, Germany, and France and announced that 79,640 yen was requested to purchase the site for the laboratory and 103,950 yen for construction. On February 28, just five days later, the Diet approved the request.[152]

For the next two years the major activity focused on Tokyo University. In February President Yamakawa allocated ten thousand yen of the university's money to launch aeronautics research. It was initially housed in the engineering faculty's department of naval architecture. But the faculty of science did the theoretical work, and Tanakadate was the head. In April he took charge of a Study Commission to Develop Aeronautics, and in August this group found temporary facilities to carry out simulated flights.[153] But more support was needed than the program had thus far received. Late in 1916 the government offered fifty thousand yen to build a wind tunnel, and in early 1917 Yamakawa drafted plans for a major staff expansion. The university's full-scale program for aeronautics research required four new chairs in the engineering faculty and one in the faculty of science.[154] At this point a group of supporters raised a troublesome issue. How did basic research on the campus relate to military needs? "I am concerned," said a member of the House on January 29, 1918, "about possible neglect of practical needs, since the university is controlling the program." The minister of education denied any problem. "Liaison is working very well. Many researchers are at work on the problems. Naturally they are working together and helping each other as much as they can."[155]

More difficult problems soon appeared on this otherwise clear horizon. With construction completed and a request for new chairs on the table, the Diet was obliged to reopen the subject. The Budget Committee of the House of Representatives conducted a major review. These sessions were highly contentious. Several of the members had admired Kitasato, and they were not pleased by the ministry's plans. In the discussions, which lasted several days (from January 30 to February 8, 1918), three separate issues were raised. How did the professors at Tokyo University see themselves as professionals? What was the Ministry of Education's conception of the academic's professional role? And what should be the proper foundation for the Institute for Aeronautics?

University professors were said as a group to have at least two major pertinent faults. They were described as mostly concerned about teaching and only sporadically interested in research. "The purpose of universities, after all, is to pass on received information." Moreover, the methods of research they actually use are, for the most part, "very old-fashioned."[156] University professors were also accused of partiality. "Too many chairs in imperial universities," said the scholar of Buddhist studies Higuchi Hideo, "have been established for particular individuals." Tokyo University had improbably gotten an unneeded second chair in pharmacology because the dean of the faculty wanted to make one of his friends a professor.[157] Worst of all, the professors at Tokyo consistently favored their own protégés: "People are very concerned about this constant tendency to form factions inside the campus. The professor is the father at Tokyo University; the lecturers and assistant professors are treated like sons he's adopted . . . Even within the university, some people think this is wrong."[158]

Parliamentary critics claimed that the Ministry of Education had views out of tune with the times. Universities have one function, laboratories another, according to Tsuchiya Seizaburō. "The United States, Britain, and Germany have all found that things work best if some professors focus on teaching, while others do only research." A worldwide trend had developed toward research in specialized laboratories, but the Ministry of Education had insisted on "evil uniformity," always considering Tokyo University both the "supreme institution for higher education" and the principal agency for scientific research. The Ōkuma cabinet had even attached the Institute of Infectious Diseases to the medical faculty, thus confusing an agency for scientific research with one for scientific education. The "evils" of doing so foolish a thing were clearest in exactly this case. Worst of all, according to critics, was the ministry's failure to learn from the war. "Why has Germany shown such military strength?" Tsuchiya challenged his colleagues. "It is because it has succeeded in applying research to the various needs of the war!" The universities of Germany were not the ones to make the greatest inventions. "These inventions have rather come out of laboratories separated from them. This [relative backwardness of the German universities] is why the Kaiser donated large sums for a network of specialized laboratories."[159]

Tsuchiya made yet one more claim that seems pertinent to most—but not all—of the others. This was his apparent conviction that creative research was related to a certain kind of ethos. "Learning in Japan has tended to follow the traditions of [classical] China in its concern for the health of the state. But it is really the scientific endeavors of private individuals which have produced the greatest success. Indeed, this has been a major trend in the history of science worldwide." How, then, should the institute be organized to achieve its greatest potential? First, it should be entirely free of supervision by university professors. He called the idea of establishing the institute at Tokyo University an "example of infantile thinking." Second, it should assemble specialists from the pertinent disciplines with no involvement in teaching. "The Imperial Institute at Munich did not attain its objectives when professors from Munich University were appointed to work there occasionally." Last, it should be intimately affiliated with the Japanese army and navy. "This research is important for national defense. Aeronautical research has made progress undreamed of in the countries now fighting in Europe . . . But our country is lagging behind. To hand over this work to incompetent professors is like fighting a war from an armchair."[160]

Top-ranking officials from the Ministry of Education responded to most of these charges. They were somewhat conciliatory on teaching and research. Vice Minister Tadokoro Yoshiharu conceded the possibility of incompetence among professors but refused to comment at length. "One always expects the replacement of incompetent [academics] by those who can help advance knowledge."[161] Nevertheless, there was no possibility of a laboratory without any teaching. "The [Aeronautics] Institute will have to do teaching," according to Minister Okada, "because of our lack of aeronautics experts. [Teaching] is as urgent as research. Japanese experts must do double duty."[162]

Ministry officials were equally tactful on the issue of academic fairness. "The chair system is unique to Japan," said the chief of the Bureau of Professional Education. "We cannot compare the situation here with that in various other countries."[163] For example, "the German universities have few full professors, but they do have lecturers who offer various courses." "We have always tried to be fair in our faculty appointments and have tried to nominate the person best qualified."[164]

But in regard to the German example and the lessons of the war, the ministry's officials showed some flexibility. Vice Minister Tadokoro did show surprise at Tsuchiya's opposition to the academic link. "Great research has been done in the various universities of Germany." Placing the institute at Tokyo University was "especially convenient" for Japan, although the ministry suspected that particular care was required. Minister Okada stressed that despite the facility's attachment to Tokyo University, it would not belong to any one department. The person who would be named to serve as director might not even be a university professor. Matsuura emphasized this point in the testimony he gave two days later. Aeronautics would probably become a separate department that would in no way exclude those from outside. The ministry would assure that anyone requiring a knowledge of aeronautics could "attend its lectures and take part in its programs."[165]

This defense by the Ministry of Education was sufficient to carry the day. The House of Representatives gave its approval on February 12, and the House of Peers on February 19. By the end of the month the issue was settled. But the ministry's approach did not silence all critics. While not agreeing entirely with Tsuchiya, the House Budget Committee had formally called on the Ministry of Education to "eliminate favoritism from the imperial universities and promote the development of [scientific] research."[166] This caused comment on the floor of the Diet, where a Kitasato ally moved to give it some teeth. "Some members think there are various forms of favoritism in the imperial universities. If these are not eliminated, no aeronautics laboratory must be established at Tokyo University."[167]

Although the Ministry of Education appeared to have won over its opponents—the institute opened on April 1, while the new chairs were funded in July[168]—its victory was less than complete. Yamakawa had originally supported the administrative transfer of the Institute of Infectious Diseases but was later disturbed by its outcome. As a result, he began taking steps to prevent a possible recurrence. Yamakawa decided that a direct attachment of the Institute for Aeronautics to the Ministry of Education would expose the new facility to interference by officials. Even having it under his personal control might not be good enough, so he established a special account for the Institute for Aeronautics, separate from the university's general fund. Yamakawa's biographer called it a "clear example of [the president's] concern."[169]

The Research Infrastructure of Academic Science

Of course, not all new developments in research infrastructure were tied to these specialized laboratories. Even aside from one whole new faculty, Japan's universities got ten new chairs in technical fields during the first three and a half years of the war. In 1915 Kyushu University got a new chair of civil engineering, while Tōhoku received chairs in geology, mathematics, agronomy, parasitology, and agricultural economics. In 1916 a chair in entomology was created at Tokyo University and one in bacteriology at Kyoto, and in 1917 new chairs were added at Tōhoku University in applied chemistry and agronomy. All but two of these chairs had traditional definitions, which seems to show that new understandings of the need for research took time to firm up in Japan. The motivations for most of these chairs is not clear from the sources, but it is almost certain that enrollments were behind them.[170] Their foundation occurred in a period of fiscal austerity. At Kyoto the faculty of science and engineering was divided in 1914 into two faculties, but no new funding went with it. Apart from one small increase in funding at Tokyo, budgets at Kyoto and Tokyo were constant from the beginning until nearly the end of the war.[171]

Tōhoku University was the exception to this pattern of very slow growth. It gained seven of the ten new chairs in technical fields and an entirely new faculty (medicine) in 1915. In 1916 it became the location of a major new laboratory whose mission in part grew out of the war. Some of this growth was predictable. Since Tōhoku had been the smallest and worst funded of the four imperial universities, its expansion potential was greatest. The faculty of medicine was all but inevitable in view of the discipline's status. But the creation in 1916 of the Institute for Metals Research was in many ways qualitatively new, and the procedures by which both it and the faculty of medicine came into existence show the importance of innovative leadership and the prospects for a new kind of funding.

Consider the case of the faculty of medicine. The local prefectural assembly had formally asked Tokyo for a medical program as early as 1881 and actually received it in 1901. But the facilities were modest, and quality was suspect. Even upgrading in 1913 did not by itself lay the basis for a good faculty of medicine. Two interventions were needed. In 1906 the governor of Miyagi prefecture persuaded his assembly to appropriate 400,000 yen for a new prefectural hospital and attached medical college. This impressed the Ministry of Education and led it to think that a faculty was affordable, so that there was little resistance when in 1913 it was proposed to make them a faculty. But these facilities had not been established with the mission of a university in mind. Most of the faculty had no advanced training, and the equipment they had was deficient. Thus, Hōjō Tokitaka, the president of the university, insisted on fundamental changes. In 1915 he dismissed all but four of the twenty-one staff members and won commitments for new medical laboratories.[172]

Hōjō was equally effective in creating the Institute for Metals Research. Before coming to Tōhoku University in 1913, he had taken an undergraduate degree in mathematics, which he taught at the prestigious First Higher School in Tokyo. Following this, he became principal of the Fourth Higher School in Kanazawa and then of the Hiroshima Higher Normal School.[173] Although he lacked a doctorate, this background helped him considerably in mobilizing support for research.

The Institute for Metals Research began with a memo to Hōjō. Early in 1915 the physicist Honda Kōtarō asked the president to represent his needs in discussions with the Ministry of Education. Honda described work he had recently begun on casting procedures for gears and propellers, and he expressed the desire to launch several new projects relating to quality improvements in the casting of iron and steel and the development of various new alloys. Stressing the importance of such work for the Japanese military, and its value for private shipbuilding, Honda formally requested a budget of fifty thousand yen for basic equipment and another fifteen thousand yen for researchers' salaries. To this request Hōjō was favorable, and he readily agreed to mediate.[174]

The Ministry of Education was also sympathetic, but the proposal was not easily realized. Wakatsuki Reijirō, the minister of finance (April 1914–August 1915), insisted on a 50 percent cut in the funding requested. This, Honda said, could not be tolerated, since he had already made verbal commitments. Hōjō accordingly continued his efforts; but the Ministry of Education finally broke off discussions, saying that the Ministry of Finance was not to be moved and no more money could be obtained. At this point Hōjō conceived a new strategy. During his years at the Fourth Higher School he had recommended students for various positions and had saved one man's career. The former student was now an executive with Sumitomo Metals, and Hōjō decided to approach him directly. The executive undertook to advance the proposal, and Sumitomo agreed to pick up the difference—twenty-one thousand yen—with clear indications that more would come later. With the necessary funding now fully in place, the institute was able to open its doors on April 1, 1916.[175]

Institutional developments on the Tōhoku campus served to stimulate activity elsewhere. With the university's acquisition of a faculty of medicine, it now possessed the minimum two faculties required of an imperial university and no longer needed the facilities in Sapporo to justify its legal existence. This encouraged major expansion in the form of a new university. Certain influential people in the city of Sapporo had long sought to obtain an imperial university, and the chances for realizing so ambitious a goal had, nearly overnight, become more realistic, although creation of the new Hokkaido University proved to be very expensive (see chapter 8). But no one could foresee this, and *legal* approval was readily obtained.

Demands for a university in this northernmost region were very long standing, having scarcely ceased from 1876, when the Sapporo Agricultural College first opened.[176] Demands had tended to focus on a program in medicine. Because of the climate and the frontier conditions, certain illnesses were unusually prevalent, and the authorities had sought to address them. An 1871 mission to the region by an American physician had led to the founding of a medical academy, but this solution was not seen as permanent. The facilities were poor, the training deficient, and the location constantly shifting. Permits to practice in Hokkaido were occasionally issued to men who could not qualify elsewhere.[177]

The later campaign to secure a university was not, at first, tied in with medicine. In 1910 a Hokkaido University Establishment Committee was founded by local officials, and their personal views of its constituent parts were vague. An influential statement by a Sapporo newspaper was only slightly more precise. This declaration, made in November 1914, called for adding a technical faculty to the one in existence (agriculture), to be followed by law or humanities. Some thought engineering or basic science should probably come first, but their convictions were not firm. Thus when the prefecture got a major new hospital in 1915, public sentiment shifted toward medicine.[178]

Members of the cabinet in Tokyo were generally well disposed but raised questions about the details. The Hokkaido committee had proposed a budget of 1,460,000 yen, to be expended over eight years, with 90 percent to go to the faculty of medicine. To make their proposal more attractive, they eschewed any claim on the treasury. According to the members of the Hokkaido committee, the sale of certain properties of the faculty of agriculture, together with contributions from the Sapporo government, and, if needed, private individuals, would suffice. This proposition, though superficially plausible, was among the more questionable aspects. Would students enroll in a medical program located in a place like Sapporo? Did not Hokkaido need a faculty of engineering even more than a faculty of medicine? And would the financing scheme actually yield enough revenue for the long term? In the final analysis the plan was approved because the Ministry of Education's three highest officials were solidly behind its key features.[179]

Members of the Diet were equally impressed and raised almost no objections of substance. One member of the Budget Committee in the House of Representatives represented a district on the island of Shikoku, and he called it unfair that Kyushu and Hokkaido would each now have an imperial university when Shikoku lacked even a high school.[180] But no one else protested, and the budget was readily approved. Thus, on March 30, 1918, the fiftieth anniversary of the opening of Hokkaido, the founding of Hokkaido University was announced.[181]

The last major expansion during the war years took place at the two oldest imperial universities. Tokyo University got a chair in genetics in its faculty of science and a chair of serological chemistry in its faculty of medicine. The first was well enough received, but the other was quite controversial. Certain members of the Diet were hostile to the field and with some justification saw the action as political. Similar new developments at Kyoto *and* Tokyo were also intensely discussed. When the Ministry of Education requested major new funding in their faculties of engineering, a lively new debate on a very old subject—*naishoku,* or moonlighting, by university professors—showed simultaneously both how limited and how unbounded were the prospects for change.

Genetics was a field in which Japan took the initiative. Gregor Mendel's epochal studies were rediscovered in 1900, and in 1902 the young cellular biologist Fujii Kenjirō arrived in Europe to conduct research in the field. In 1905 he returned to Tokyo University's faculty of science and began requesting a chair for genetics.[182] Related developments were occurring in the university's faculty of agriculture. In 1906 Toyama Kametarō took his doctorate in agricultural chemistry but promptly switched to the attractive new field. Toyama used silkworm studies to show that Mendel's work applied to insects as well as to plants. His valuable research was praised by foreigners, but Toyama never studied abroad.[183] He paid a high price for not doing so.

Genetics did well in Japanese institutions. Plant breeding research was conducted at the Agricultural Experiment Station from 1907. In 1915 Tōhoku University got a chair of agronomy whose work focused heavily on genetics. From 1911 Toyama began working in the newly founded Sericulture Institute while continuing to teach at Tokyo University. In 1912, his colleague Fujii became full professor in the faculty of science. Since his doctorate was not conferred until a year later, this was clearly unusual. Under ordinary circumstances, a full professorship should have gone first to Toyama, whose degree had been awarded six years earlier. But Fujii had spent four years abroad, while Toyama had never left the country. It is highly probable that this affected the founding of the chair of genetics. On June 12, 1917, the Osaka securities tycoon Nomura Tokushichi gave a partial endowment to Tokyo University specifically for genetics.[184] While it was not entirely the first of its kind, it was the first to be named for genetics, and it went to the faculty of science instead of the faculty of agriculture. Fujii was named to the chair of genetics, undoubtedly because of his background. Toyama, whose work was probably better, soon died an assistant professor. The Diet was probably unaware of these facts since it readily approved supplementary funds when approached by the Ministry of Education.[185]

Serological chemistry was quite a different matter. The Ministry of Education, as we have seen, had badly miscalculated in annexing Kitasato's institute. The quality of its vaccine and serums had plummeted, and the resulting lost sales had led to a deficit. The education minister, Takada, on December 16, 1915, openly conceded a deficit of eighty thousand yen, but he insisted that various "reforms" had cut this figure to thirty thousand yen. The Diet was asked to make up the loss, and after wrenching debate it agreed to cooperate.[186] But money was not the whole issue; there was also the matter of technical skill. The faculty of medicine now running the institute did not have the knowledge to manufacture serums and therefore required a serological chemist.

This request did not have smooth sailing. University authorities had planned for the chair in 1915, but Minister Ichiki Kitokurō was so sensitive to the politics that he refused to endorse it.[187] Meanwhile, problems continued at the institute. By 1917 the issue was critical, and Minister Okada decided to act. The need for caution was soon apparent. Tsuchiya Seizaburō had vigorously attacked the ministry's plan to establish aeronautics at Tokyo University and was equally opposed to this plan. Noting that serological chemistry was usually considered part of toxicology or even bacteriology, he claimed that these subjects were already covered in the university's faculty of medicine,[188] a long-standing argument. Tsuchiya was loyal to his one-time teacher Kitasato and determined to embarrass his opponents. In this case he revived an argument once expounded by Hasegawa Tai, the need for the one-chair rule, which the university had regularly ignored. Tsuchiya claimed that this separate chair was proposed for political reasons.[189] By this point, however, the one-chair idea was fading, and the new chair was easily approved.

Engineering expansion also caused controversy, though everyone agreed that expansion was needed. There were three major issues. Was the rationale for expansion properly presented? Were the solutions proposed equal to the problems? And would the solutions themselves not breed more problems?

The need for expansion was patent. Because of the war and the blockade, companies had begun in-house research in attempts to develop substitute products. Sometimes firms were successful both technically and financially. Marumiya Chemicals built a laboratory in 1915 and successfully developed soaps, while several *zaibatsu* firms made synthetic dyes.[190] But problems remained, and progress was slow. There was an insufficient supply of technical personnel. "Our need is presently greatest in applied chemistry, metallurgy, and mining engineering," according to the education minister, Okada Ryōhei. Much more research was needed in these fields. "In the past we thought it was all right just to copy the discoveries of foreigners."[191] Industries were finding it hard to compete with firms overseas without major assistance from imperial universities. "Fields like applied chemistry are nowadays the basis for industry, and the university professors are really its vanguard."[192]

Recognizing these trends, the imperial universities had developed a plan for expansion. In June 1916 Tokyo's president Yamakawa began discussions with Watanabe Wataru, dean of the Tokyo faculty of engineering. Once they had reached agreement, they approached not the minister of education but the minister of agriculture and commerce. Nakanokoji Kiyoshi fell in with their ideas and promised support in the cabinet. Only three weeks later was the Ministry of Education informed.[193] Certain adjustments were made, but the proposal's essentials remained, and it was presented to the Diet in July 1917. Enrollment was to be sharply increased in applied chemistry, metallurgy, and mining. Faculty positions could be added, but only at the level of assistant professor. Funding would be considered a supplement, to be paid from the general account of the treasury.[194]

Members of the Diet focused attention on the rationale advanced for expansion. No formal mention had been made of research, and some thought this inappropriate. "Surely the Ministry of Education understands the need to expand our efforts in applied chemical research as a function of trends overseas."[195] Far more was needed than simply more graduates. "Factory engineers engaged in the production of aniline dyes are having to cope with problems in which they lack formal instruction. There has been progress, but . . . the companies need help from imperial universities." Representative Kodama Ryōtarō was convinced that more was required even than research. "Do we not need a system whereby professors give lectures outside universities for the particular benefit of Japan's private industries?"[196]

To these views the minister of education was, for the most part, very sympathetic. More research was imperative. BASF in Germany had manufactured synthetic dyes with no contributions from any university, but Japan's situation was different. More off-campus lecturing was definitely needed. "We will all recognize even more of a need for this in the future."[197] Okada candidly admitted that the solutions he proposed were inadequate. The additional students whom the funding could educate would "probably not meet the private demand," and even if Japan could organize better, "The proposals I have made will not be enough" to match the Germans in research. Nevertheless, the minister stressed that he continued to remain optimistic. A professor at Tōhoku University had recently produced nonflammable celluloid. Honda Kōtarō's magnetic steel would now be manufactured by Sumitomo Metals. And Salvarsan 606 had been produced in a special program at Kyoto University and was already being used in its hospital wards. "When [Japanese scientists] carry out research, they are by no means lacking in [technical] originality."[198]

In the view of some members, the solutions proposed were worse than the problems. Market demand for technicians and scientists would be met by fine tuning of major enrollment. Vice Minister Tadokoro Yoshiharu noted that during the first three years of the war, admissions at Tokyo University for applied chemistry, metallurgy, and mining engineering had gone from 35 annually to 105. Things were similar at Kyoto and, on the level below, at the nation's higher schools. The ministry thought this could not be ignored. "We are looking at patterns in the various higher schools," according to Minister Okada, "and trying to match them in the engineering faculties." Indeed, the ministry was trying to meet the expectations of students with as much precision as possible. "Are you not afraid this policy will lead to confusion? asked Representative Takami Hidemichi. "No," replied the bureau chief Matsuura. "Students must often study their second- or third-place subject. One would naturally expect this."[199]

But the greatest concern of the Budget Committee was outside employment. Strong sentiment existed on the one hand for more, not less, consulting (komon) by university professors in various fields. It was not simply a question of lectures. Industry's need for assistance was so great that professors should probably be doing research (kenkyū) at industrial laboratories for two or three months of each year.[200] But even granted the needs of some firms, such a procedure had drawbacks. Representative Takaoka Tadaichirō argued that excessive consulting harmed the instruction of university students by removing their professors from laboratories and classrooms. "Mathematicians are helping insurance companies, and medical professors are treating private patients . . . People in law and all the technical fields are doing [consulting]. There seem to be no restrictions at all." The minister of education could not let this pass. "Most of the consultation is taking place in engineering and medicine. Other professors generally work at private schools." In any case, it could not be avoided. "For the good of the country and the private sector generally, we must allow academic consulting."[201]

After considerable discussion, the plans for expansion were approved. By mid-July 1917 the Diet had authorized the expenditure of 211,740 yen for Tokyo and 122,766 yen for Kyoto. One new assistant professor was immediately hired at Kyoto, and two at Tokyo. In 1918 Kyoto added one chair in applied chemistry, and in 1919 another. Tōhoku University got an applied chemistry chair in 1917 and an engineering faculty in 1919.[202]

Science outside the Academic System

The emphasis on consulting was predictable given the wartime expansion of science in major corporations and the Japanese private sector generally. A host of firms and other private groups had begun new research ventures in many different fields. The Kitasato Institute, founded in 1914, was only the first of its kind. In 1915 Takeda Pharmaceuticals, previously only a marketing firm, began producing its own merchandise by establishing a research division. In 1916 a competitor, Sankyo Pharmaceuticals, followed the same strategy. Nor was the trend unique to medicine. Several firms active in the chemical industry—Marumiya Shoten, Mitsubishi, Mitsui Mining, and Sumitomo Metals—developed research programs. In 1916 Osaka industrialist Shiomi Seiji, who had made a fortune in the chemical industry, gave a million yen for a specialized private laboratory. Known as the Shiomi Institute for Physics and Chemistry, this enterprise affiliated itself with the Osaka prefectural government and was later taken over by the Ministry of Education.[203] Many companies and fields benefited from wartime conditions. The blockade initially caused shortages and created a panic, but confiscation of German patents and market withdrawal of Western competition led to an economic boom.[204] Tokugawa Yoshimi was able to build the Tokugawa Institute for Biological Research in 1917. Asahi Glass could found an applied chemical laboratory in 1918. Tokyo Electric Company established a research laboratory for applied physics the same year, and in 1919, the government-controlled Yawata Steel built an institute for research of interest to it.[205]

Government officials had come to favor this trend. Between 1914 and 1920 various bills were presented to the Diet calling for tax reductions, cheap credit, export subsidies, special research programs, and the like—all proposals for helping the private sector generate new technical knowledge and more effectively utilize knowledge that already existed. Most of this legislation was officially approved and even drafted by government officials whose domains were directly affected. Several different ministries were active, but the Ministry of Agriculture and Commerce was the busiest. With control of everything from the Patent Bureau to the Bureaus of Industry, Agriculture, Forestry, and Fisheries, it was inevitably the center of action. But its strategic position in this major new movement was sometimes unfortunate. Its traditional reliance on direction from outside made it ill-equipped to take risks, and its practice of naming lawyers to all line positions made it slow to recognize trends.

The Bureau of Patents is a case in point. After 1905, all patent bureau chiefs were trained exclusively in law. Two of the seven who held the position before that time had been trained in law. Not one of the bureau chiefs was a man trained in a technical discipline.[206] Japan's modern patent system, as we saw in chapter 4, was heavily based on Spain's. It structured regulations and policies to facilitate acquisition of foreign technology and minimized any individual's rights to protection. Under

Japanese law, for instance, an employee of an imperial university, government laboratory, or publicly supported higher technical school could not obtain patent protection for any invention or discovery on the grounds that research was part of his job. Income obtained from such an invention went entirely to the government employer.[207]

This provision was canceled in 1911, but a number of problems remained. The patent office was understaffed. The bureau chief, Nakamatsu Morio, called attention to this in January 1912, but the problem got steadily worse.[208] In 1912 the number of applications for patents surged as a result of changes in the law, yet in 1913 the Bureau of Patents took a 14 percent cut in staff and had to make do with "assistant examiners." These assistants worked under qualified specialists, but most of them lacked university degrees. No relief was forthcoming until the last year of the war, and even then did not restore all of the cuts.[209]

Shortage of funds compromised the bureau's mission across the boards. Why was the patent office's Exhibit Hall for Inventions combined with the Hall for General Commercial Exhibits? This was indeed unfortunate, according to Vice Minister Oshikawa Norikichi (whose undergraduate degree was in chemistry), but financial shortages "had rendered change difficult."[210] Various other critics thought the laws were deficient. "We have not done very much in our legal system or anywhere else to encourage Japanese invention," said Representative Suzuki Bun'ichi in January 1912. "We must find a means [to promote invention], but the government has not found it yet." Suzuki proposed a system of grants to inventors and a fifty thousand yen pool to launch such a program. When a colleague asked for official reaction, the response was positive. "The government thinks this is urgently needed," said Nakamatsu. "But the Bureau of Patents has no extra money it can use for promoting inventions. Finances have always made such action impossible."[211]

Perceptions changed in part with the war, when the need for reform was more evident. Most people in positions of authority realized that the period of patent protection needed to be lengthened, that violations of patents had to be treated more rigorously, and that the general population had to display more sensitivity to the need for inventive activity. Yet even in these years, change was not rapid. Certain features of the patent laws "have produced stagnation in industrial inventions and gadgets," lamented Representative Oda Ryō in 1916. "This has been harmful to national development." According to Oda, the short period of patent protection was one of the negative features. Since a minimum of three years and a maximum of ten did not afford adequate protection, he favored patents for twenty-five years. (About seventeen is common today.) But the government found this excessive. "We do intend to make changes," the bureau chief, Kawasaki Saijirō, promised. "But they are still being studied, and I cannot explain fully."[212]

One change favoring invention did come in the following year. On October 13, 1917, the Ministry of Agriculture and Commerce issued its "Regulations for Transferring Funds to Encourage Invention."[213] But these regulations authorized loans, not grants, and did not address other needs of inventors. In November 1917 the Japanese Society of Mechanical Engineering sought to spell out those needs in detail, issuing a report written by a long-time patent examiner. Sakata Teiichi, who was also principal of the Tokyo Higher Technical School, proposed a number of reforms: creation of a permanent exhibition hall solely for patented inventions, official regulation of the training of invention consultants, the convening of periodic exhibitions of *Japanese* inventions at which native inventors were honored, improvement of laws for protecting the rights of inventors, more stringent regulation of patent law abuses, and the establishment of an agency for resolving suspected violations of patents. "The present system for protecting inventions," he noted, "still has many deficiencies."[214]

In fairness to the Ministry of Agriculture and Commerce, one should not judge its actions too harshly. Some of its officials did see the need for major reform. Nakamatsu Morio in particular, the bureau chief from December 1907 to June 1913, and also a lawyer, called attention to the role of patent law in stimulating both indigenous technical creativity and economic growth as early as 1889.[215] In 1916 the ministry and the bureau tried for reform but were thwarted by lack of support in the Diet. Substantial revision of patent law posed many complicated problems, and the Ministry of Finance was always ready to deny funding. But the Ministry of Agriculture and Commerce can be faulted on two major grounds. It gave too little attention to its technical staff and was too inclined to accept outside direction. "What kind of reform will encourage invention?" the bureau chief asked in 1918. "Should we give patents to chemical products? To methods of research? We asked the Association for the Chemical Industry (Kōgyō Kagaku Kai) about this, but they could not give us an answer."[216] The bureau chief seemed not to understand that this group was not the best source. Most of its members had made their fortunes exploiting confiscated patents once held by the Germans, and they were not very likely to change their approach.[217]

Taking the case of research on synthetic fibers, we can see that the ministry did not respond quickly to trends. The first known patent for the manufacture of synthetic silk (better known as rayon) had been issued to a British chemist as early as 1855, and by the 1890s a number of companies in Europe were successfully producing it. Progress in synthetic fibers made great strides after the turn of the century. Researchers in France and the U.S. made significant chemical breakthroughs, and German firms in particular improved the means of commercial production.[218] Japanese scientists had taken notice by 1909 and recommended research at that time. But the Ministry of Agriculture and Commerce rejected their views on the grounds that natural silk was superior (chapter 5). In 1913 300,000 yen was spent on imports of the foreign-made textile.[219]

How should Japan respond to this challenge? In January 1914, six months prior to the war, the ministry was relatively confident. When Oka Makoto, chief of the Bureau of Industry, testified before the House Budget Committee at the end of the month, he admitted that a problem existed but saw it as manageable. Japan's market position in natural silk remained very strong, especially by comparison with rivals—France, China, and Italy. Synthetic silk, though cheaper than natural silk, still was not of high quality; color fastness, resistance to fire and moisture, and consistency of weave could not in every case be assured. Everything was under control. The government had made research in the silk industry a continuing budgetary item. In particular, research was taking place at the Kuramae Higher Industrial School, the Ueda Sericultural Technical School, and the Industrial Experiment Laboratory. While the budget for this work was not large (16,000 yen at the Industrial Experiment Laboratory), the ministry was "pleased with the results of the work." Oka expected that importation of synthetic silk would "soon be restricted or prohibited entirely."[220]

But his presentation was seriously deficient, as Oka, a Tokyo law graduate with no technical training, was incompetent to judge. In 1911 he had an acrimonious conversation with the director of the Industrial Experiment Laboratory that showed his lack of understanding (chapter 5). The ministry was later forced to concede that Japan would have to develop a new textile fiber "to withstand competition in the marketplace," according to the agriculture and commerce minister, Kōno Hironaka. In consultation with textile manufacturers, the ministry had agreed to support such an effort. The ministry thought this would take about three years, but the manufacturers thought more time would be needed. Research and development costs were estimated at five million yen, but the companies considered this estimate inadequate. Predictably, the Ministry of Finance felt challenged by the size of the project— but might support funding if the time were extended.[221]

The issue was not whether natural silk was better than rayon, or even whether silk could hold onto foreign markets. The real issue was the future of textiles and the place of research in the textile industry's future. Not everyone found the ministry's report reassuring. Representative Nishitani Kinzō, who was in the silk business, was among the more nervous. "It seems impossible to predict when or how this problem will be solved. And because of the importance [of textiles] in Japan's foreign trade, the search for solutions makes us all very anxious."[222] A colleague's response was even more vigorous. "It seems one cannot get a detailed, satisfactory answer from the minister of agriculture and commerce no matter how many questions one asks," said Representative Horikiri Zenbei, professor of economics at Keio University:

> At this critical time, when many Japanese are trying to do something for agricultural, industrial, or commercial development, the Ministry of Agriculture and Commerce either makes others do everything or acts arbitrarily . . . They have no ideas about the future. They try to evade responsibility by saying that the matter is under study or that . . . they cannot give an answer because it would trouble the Ministry of Finance . . . Would it not be better if we just abolished the Ministry of Agriculture and Commerce? It would be more rational to put [its bureaus] under the Ministry of Finance. We could save the eight thousand yen presently paid in salary to the minister and use it to hire some other officials. This would be excellent for bureaucratic efficiency![223]

These remarks angered Kōno but did Horikiri no harm. After the war he became a councillor in the ministry, and a few years later was appointed ambassador to Italy.[224]

In a third wartime research project, the problems were more subtle. The Ministry of Agriculture and Commerce in 1915 proposed to expand the Industrial Experiment Laboratory, but many were not sure this would work. Some thought the rationale for expansion defective, even if the expansion itself was essential. Others thought an early termination of the war in Europe might prevent a return on investment. There was a suspicion that many private firms might not cooperate fully. One well-placed critic thought ministry interference might make the desired results unobtainable. Nevertheless, the project moved forward to a successful conclusion, since no other alternatives appeared.

The need for expansion was not in doubt. A 1912 report by a Tokyo professor (see chapter 4) had documented the country's trade deficit in chemicals, and the war made the situation worse. The deficit, more than twenty million yen at the time of the study, had reached thirty million yen during the first year of conflict; the Ministry of Agriculture and Commerce became seriously alarmed.[225] Their concern was justified by the response of private business. Private firms, as we have seen, began to take action, but their efforts too often fell short. As of mid-1915,

Asahi Chemicals wanted to manufacture soda. Mitsui was trying to produce synthetic dyes. Several other companies hoped for success in producing synthetic ammonia. But all needed help from the Industrial Experiment Laboratory to achieve any success.[226]

The failure in industrial research at the beginning of the war is not surprising. Few companies employed even as many as ten researchers. Such personnel usually belonged to a company section for product inspection or testing, implying that managers considered their functions practical. Many in the past had had as a primary task the monitoring of foreign technology. Few private firms were equipped to deal with complicated technical problems, for this had been the function of the Industrial Experiment Laboratory and was still more or less its assignment.[227] The Chemical Industry Study Commission (CISC) in May 1915 recommended to the minister of agriculture and commerce that the laboratory be greatly expanded.[228]

When the Budget Committee took up this proposal, members focused on the probable outcome. Could one expect private firms to produce dyes and other chemicals if the capacities of the laboratory grew? For once Oka did not play expert but deferred to a qualified scientist. Takamatsu Toyokichi, the laboratory's director, a CISC member, and a chemical engineer, gave a carefully hedged response. Since the talent required was available, success was "certainly not impossible" *if* the firms could mobilize this talent, and *if* the laboratory were to help them.[229]

Some members of the Diet were not so certain. Representative Yamada Seinen worried that a premature end to the fighting in Europe could preclude any long-term success. Western competitors would immediately return to East Asian markets with much cheaper chemical products than those Japan could produce.[230] Representative Shimizu Ichitarō was greatly concerned by a lack of creative incentives. "We do not have the kind of [patent] legislation that would allow [company employees] to reap the rewards of inventive activity to the extent that inventors in Germany can do. [Japanese] get salaries, but not too much else."[231] The strongest challenge to the ministry's proposal came from Representative Mutō Kinkichi, who was active in textiles and banking, and edited a newspaper called *Industrial News*.[232]

Mutō criticized the plan for two reasons. One was its excessive concern with import reductions. The other was the treatment of technical personnel in the ministry. "Whether the Industrial Experiment Laboratory is well-equipped or not, little research will be done and little enough accomplished unless the engineers are paid better and respected more. But in the past engineers have not been much respected in the Ministry of Agriculture and Commerce."[233] Minister Kōno had to respond, and he made three major points in rebuttal. Japan, he said, had to stop copying the products of others. "Until recently, Japanese manufacturing enterprises rarely operated on a scientific basis. Most of them just copied foreign products." But the same private firms could certainly do better if, as in this case, the government were to help. "These companies in the chemical industry could produce these substances if we gave them certain kinds of assistance." He as minister would have to do more. "I realize that I myself must concentrate attention on the Industrial Experiment Laboratory."[234] But the ministry did not change its ways, and Mutō did not even comment on its treatment of engineers, which would soon become a major issue.

CHAPTER EIGHT

THE RESEARCH SYSTEM IN
AN AGE OF TRANSITION

About a year before the war ended in Europe, Aoyama Tanemichi spoke about changes in the scientific community at his retirement dinner. "Our empire," he said, "has shown [of late] the vitality and energy of a newly emerging country. Our academic community has a new spirit, a growing enthusiasm for research. This has come about because scientists took advantage of the present situation. Truly this spirit of scientific research is the glory of the nation."[1] The retiring dean did not stretch the truth. Significant change was under way, and it did indeed change the climate for research. World War I had inspired a strong inclination toward independence in science and technology, and during the early postwar years, this movement would feature not only greater independence in general but a particular interest in independence of Germany. Primarily because of the war and the attitudes to which it gave rise, Japanese scientists were forced to decide more precisely than before where they stood in the world science community. This scrutiny was painful for some. It was also important for professional growth.

The early postwar years, 1918–20, saw many changes. Public expectations about research by scientists had risen during the war. Now the structure of incentives to carry on research also changed. As before, new facilities were built and old ones upgraded. But a new and potent combination of rewards for those who did research—and penalties for those who did not—was also made part of the system. It included fresh attacks on academic moonlighting, stepped up efforts to stimulate competition, and offered more grants and prizes, earlier retirement for senior professors, and sharply higher salaries for those who remained.

Several university faculties received new facilities, and the concept of the research professorship was born. Private foundations aiming to support research first appeared on the scene. Several new laboratories were created from scratch. Most important, Japan established a competitive system of grants for research and, at the end of this period, a National Research Council. Potent new attitudes favorable to scientific research became characteristic throughout society. Private universities started to become active in technical research, as did the Imperial Army and Navy.

Not surprisingly, a growing feeling that scientists should take part in making the decisions that governed their lives accompanied these sweeping changes. Members of the academic and technical communities demanded that people with scientific educations be elected or appointed to serve in the Diet, and they made cogent proposals to further that end. Within the central bureaucracy there sprang up the so-called engineers' movement, which sought better treatment for government officials with technical backgrounds, including more access to policy-making jobs. The university community did not lag behind. Professors sought and obtained more control over academic appointments and the running of their own institutions. Ultimately, many of these demands would be frustrated, but for a while they seemed to win out.

By 1920 former samurai were no longer a majority in the scientific community. Modern education had made careers in science accessible to the general population, including, for the first time, Japanese women.[2] Research facilities and programs were now in place for scientists in all technical and scientific fields on some kind of regular basis. And criticisms of the scientific community for perpetuating "feudalistic" behavior became ever more widespread and strident. For all of these reasons the early postwar years marked the end of an epoch.

Changes in the Conditions for Scientific Research

There were many indications after World War I that Japanese society took research more seriously. Criticism of professors for neglecting research continued unabated. "The value of the nation's universities is called into question if professors shirk their duty by neglecting research," declared an editorial writer in 1919.[3] "We do not want to turn out ordinary scientists," insisted Representative Yokota Kōshi, a pharmacist, during a 1920 meeting of the Budget Committee of the House of Representatives. "We cannot continue the system now prevailing in the country's imperial universities."[4] Both critics demanded an end to faculty consulting; Yokota wanted more competition and raises in salaries. A physician colleague of Yokota's in the Diet, Kanasugi Eigorō, wanted to go even further. "Some of these professors are too decrepit to do any work, and even some of the younger ones do very little. These people should be fired at once."[5]

Because of such pressures, some changes that improved the climate for research were made. Salaries went up. The Ministry of Education claimed that the average salary for university professors in 1918 was 2,370 yen. Given the realities of wartime inflation, that was probably inadequate.[6] But in 1920, a 30 percent hike took place, making the lives of academics more comfortable.[7] Some measures to increase competition were also put into effect. In February 1920 education's vice minister, Minami Hiroshi, announced that whenever a single professor represented an entire academic subdiscipline, his major lecturing would be shared by colleagues in fields close to his.[8] Later in 1920 a new policy, whereby all professors at imperial universities were obliged to retire upon reaching age sixty, was implemented. It was instigated by Yamakawa Kenjirō, president of Tokyo University, and it reflected broad faculty acquiescence in the view that younger professors would do more research.[9] But on one issue, consulting or outside employment, there was no policy change. Of course, it might be better if professors did not have side jobs, the vice minister of education conceded. "But considering the present state of Japanese culture, [outside employment] may not be so bad."[10]

These policy changes were important for research, but so was the willingness to allocate more money. One could use prior gains to justify asking for more. On March 20, 1918, Count Hayashi Hirotarō delivered a speech to the House of Peers that utilized this strategy effectively. He noted with satisfaction the large sum of money (78,700 yen) now budgeted at Tokyo University for the Institute for Aeronautics. He also pointed out that this level of spending had introduced some major distortions. The two parent faculties, science and engineering, with total authorized spending levels of 58,960 yen and 78,761 yen, respectively, were about to be completely overshadowed. The obvious solution, he pointed out, was to spend more money on both.[11] The government was willing to oblige him, and in 1919 the cabinet recommended, and the Diet approved, substantial new funding for science and engineering at both Tokyo and Kyoto universities. Tokyo got new facilities and equipment. Kyoto got three new chairs in physics, one in biology (its first), and an additional chair in applied chemistry.[12] Even more remarkably, 700,000 yen was approved and allocated for a new astronomical observatory at Tokyo University in 1919, after five years in budgetary limbo.[13]

The government even founded several new laboratories for particular missions. Experiment stations or institutes were established for the tea and silk industries in 1918 and 1919. An Institute for Research on Nitrogen Fixation (IRNF) was built in 1918. Nutrition and fuel research both came to be housed in specialized laboratories (1920), while marine and high-altitude meteorological observatories were built at the end of the decade.[14] The National Institute for Nutrition Research

(NINR) illustrated one important new trend. This was the tendency to draw on American, and not only European, precedents. The NINR was the brainchild of Saiki Nori, a bacteriologist trained at Yale University, where a comparable institution existed. Its chief legislative sponsor in the Diet was Kōno Tetsushi, a physician who had received his M.D. degree from the University of Pennsylvania.[15]

The NINR reflected in part the general enthusiasm for research into vitamins that swept the world at the end of the war,[16] but it also had roots in Japan. "One of its objectives," noted Dr. Yagi Itsurō, a leading supporter in the Budget Committee, "will be to evaluate our rice-based diet with the aim of supplementing or even replacing it." Another root was its relationship to the national bureaucracy. The Ministry of Education did not claim this institution, but the Ministry of Finance did its job for it. The finance vice minister, Shinno Katsunosuke, argued that nutrition studies were a part of physiology and for this reason should be housed on a university campus. Yagi opposed this on the basis that faculties of medicine in Japanese universities did not allow mission research. "[Medical] researchers might investigate the pathological aspects of a topic. If the results interest them, they might investigate its chemical or bacteriological aspects. But each of these sections—pathology, biochemistry, bacteriology—is independent, so the investigators must ask members of each to do the work for them. The latter might say they would do it if they had time [for the project]." Yagi was actually thinking of Kitasato's one-time institute, whose transfer he had opposed in 1914. "Precisely because universities are divided into all of these separate sections . . . Robert Koch left [Berlin] University to establish a separate laboratory."[17] Yagi's objections had their effect. The NINR was assigned to the Ministry of Home Affairs and not to the education ministry.[18]

Postwar stress on scientific research was apparent in other ways, too. Small research funds for biochemistry and physics were established at Tokyo University at the instigation of the retired professor Shibata Keita and in honor of the retired professor Tanakadate Aikitsu, respectively.[19] The Imperial Academy in 1918 created a new prize for research contributions that it named for the former prime minister Katsura Tarō.[20] Several private foundations sprang up with the declared aim of supporting research in all of the natural sciences. The most important of these was the Keimeikai. Created with an endowment of one million yen, the Keimeikai made its intentions unmistakably clear by naming as its president the former minister of education Makino Nobuaki, sponsor of the Imperial Academy and the faculty of science at Tōhoku University.[21]

Other developments on the policy front also exemplified change. In

1920, the Ministry of Education unveiled a plan to spend the extraordinary sum of seventy million yen over a ten-year period on the construction of new research laboratories at all the imperial universities.[22] It did not, in fact, carry out this plan, but it did do three other things: create a system of grants for research, present the concept of the research professorship (initially at the Aeronautics Institute in conjunction with Tokyo University),[23] and complete the establishment of Hokkaido Imperial University. The initial plan for Hokkaido had envisioned an outlay of 1,460,000 yen to be obtained mostly by selling agricultural land that the government had owned for some time. But this strategy did not work, and the actual cost was much higher. In 1919 the land was sold, and in 1920 thirty-one private individuals and local government agencies donated a total of 470,700 yen. Even with that, the two basic programs (agriculture and medicine) were not yet in place. The basic faculties were not complete until 1925, and it cost more than 3.6 million yen, beyond the funds received from private contributors.[24]

Limits to the stress on research included the cost of projects like the establishment of Hokkaido University. Tokyo University's faculty of medicine, which had grown very little for ten years, was authorized to expand in 1918, but construction of facilities did not begin until 1922.[25] The Research Institute for Physics and Chemistry, though formally inaugurated in 1917, had no facilities of its own for another five years. Members of its research team continued to work in laboratories at their home universities.[26] Kyushu University was repeatedly thwarted in its effort to obtain a faculty of science. First proposed in 1919 by President Mano Bunji, a mechanical engineer and former official in the Ministry of Education, the plan was blocked by either that ministry or the Ministry of Finance.[27] The Kyushu science faculty was considered again in 1922–and on a number of other occasions—but was not actually built until 1939.[28]

As for laboratories, the ad hoc Institute for Research on Nitrogen Fixation, formally inaugurated in 1918, reflected wartime concerns about self-sufficiency in fuels and chemicals.[29] But it was geared toward work on the synthesis of ammonia because that work, by chemist Fritz Haber, had been highly influential in Germany's earlier military success.[30] With access to reports on the subject by Haber, scientists at the IRNF duplicated his work in 1920,[31] but they had very little funding. The IRNF was set up with an outlay of just 200,000 yen at a time when, Diet members claimed, the U.S. was spending forty million yen on the problem. The Ministry of Agriculture and Commerce, to which the IRNF was attached, flatly refused in public testimony to authorize more funding, tax exemptions, or any other form of assistance on the grounds that the Japanese chemical industry was making large profits

(March 1918).[32] This situation did not last very long. When hostilities ended in November 1918, the Japanese chemical industry faced serious hardships.[33]

Even with these limits, new attitudes favoring scientific research permeated society. The armed services, for example, established significant new research facilities. In 1919 the army opened both a Technical Headquarters (Rikugun Gijutsu Hombu) and a Laboratory for Scientific Research (Rikugun Kagaku Kenkyū Jo). In 1920 it established a facility called the Aerological Observatory (Rikugunshō Kōkūkyoku).[34] Together with the navy's establishment in 1918 of its Naval Aircraft Experiment Station (Kaigun Kōkūki Shiken Jo), these facilities gave the military limited independence of the professors at Tokyo University. The services continued to rely on Tokyo University for advanced aeronautics training,[35] and they lost their bid for control over the Institute for Aeronautics. In September 1919, President Yamakawa thwarted their effort to name a deputy director whom they could control through the chain of command.[36] They finally had to settle in July 1921 for the appointment to the institute of several researchers who were officers.[37]

Attitudes favoring scientific research were apparent in other ways, too. In 1918, the government granted the forces of private higher education a major victory by authorizing their use of the term *university*. On the surface, this simply meant that private institutions like Keio and Waseda would enjoy the same legal status and privileges as the five imperial universities. But this action by government was also important for scientific research. Because of the high cost of technical education—and even more, of technical research—Keio, Waseda, and Dōshisha in the nineteenth century had all been forced to abandon their efforts to offer programs in technical subjects. In 1908 Tokyo University physicist Yamakawa Kenjirō questioned whether private institutions would ever have the resources for work in medicine, engineering, or science.[38] For a considerable period it seemed that Yamakawa's doubts were justified. Waseda from 1908 made a serious effort to establish a faculty of science and engineering, but limited funds and student demand made its growth slow. Before World War I, in fact, the Waseda faculty had only two engineering programs housed in one small frame building.

The war was responsible for the change, because wartime conditions created a demand for more engineers and technicians. Industrial growth brought far greater profits to industry and higher tax revenues to government. Public pressure on the imperial universities to admit more students overwhelmed their limited resources. Not surprisingly, men like the former education minister Kikuchi Dairoku, who had once opposed rapid expansion of higher education, in 1915 now did a complete about-face and advocated fundamental change.[39] New ventures became possible. In 1916 Waseda was able to add applied chemistry to its program in technical studies, and in October 1918 it began construction of a laboratory for research in this field.[40] Keio University was not to be outdone. Between 1917 and 1920 it built a faculty of medicine with superior equipment costing over 2.7 million yen.[41] The legal change in the status of the private universities was not, as such, the cause of these ventures, but the high costs and risks of technical programs make it difficult to imagine their taking place without it.

It also seemed for a time in the early postwar years that government decisions about scientific research were going to be handled differently. Before the war, men with scientific and technical degrees had sometimes held bureaucratic posts with the right to make policy, while a number of such men had all along served in the House of Representatives. Their participation in the Diet tended to increase, though slowly. Kitasato, for example, campaigned heavily for physician Diet candidates in the 1917 general election and managed to get three or four elected.[42] But by World War I technical men were no longer represented in policy-making posts in the national bureaucracy, though they continued to serve lower down.

The issue of participation in government decisions was troubling to many with technical backgrounds, and they began to address it more fully. In 1916, Shiraishi Naoji, a descendant of a long line of Confucian scholars who was also a civil engineer, was elected to the Diet from Kōchi on a platform of opposition to bureaucratic legalism and support for technical education.[43] The physicist Yamakawa Kenjirō, Tokyo University's president during the war, complained of scientists' lack of influence in high-level policy making in a 1919 letter to the minister of education.[44] A 1919 editorial in *Ikai jihō* offered its analysis of the problem: the bureaucracy had a relative monopoly on scientific and technical information; the Diet was supposed to supervise its actions but lacked the knowledge to do so; but even so, a solution was apparent, namely, to elect more physicians to the Diet. Doctors, after all, belonged to a profession with a "scientific basis" and were able to "think scientifically."[45]

Others shared this point of view and sought to follow through on it. Two scientists, Kitasato Shibasaburō and Kikuchi Dairoku, had already been named to the House of Peers (December 1917). In 1919, President Yamakawa managed to secure appointment to the Peers of chemist Sakurai Jōji as well.[46] In 1920, Matsushita Teiji, professor of bacteriology at Kyoto University, was elected to the House of Representatives. By that time medical men held more than a dozen seats in the

Diet's lower house. Eight of them had formed a caucus to focus on medical, scientific, and technical policies.[47]

While these critics concentrated attention primarily on the Diet, others took on the bureaucracy. In June 1916, the Institute of German Engineers (Verein Deutscher Ingenieuren) had sent an open letter to Chancellor Theobald von Bethmann-Hollweg demanding that top-ranking posts in the German civil service be opened to men with technical training.[48] This action got attention not only in Germany but in Britain and Japan. *The London Times Education Supplement* published a translation in November 1916, and this set off a lively debate. In April 1917, a Japanese translation appeared in *Tōyō gakugei zasshi*. Its author, Matsubara Kōichi, professor of chemistry at Tokyo University, added his own comments to the engineers' text. According to him science was important not only for industrial and commercial development but had a profound relationship to social welfare and the problems of society. It was very important that European countries were debating the exclusion of science graduates from the higher civil service. Britain in particular could well expect to benefit. Finally, the reexamination had evidently come from broad recognition of "this present-day evil."[49]

Matsubara's essay was significant both for what it said and for what it omitted. He made no demand for changes in the substance of Japan's examinations for the higher civil service but only implied that technical men serving in the government should receive better treatment. The chemist's essay attracted wide notice and served to define the terms of debate for what came to be called the "engineers' movement."

This movement began in 1918 with technical experts in the forestry bureau of the Ministry of Agriculture and Commerce. The basic argument of these (mostly young) men was that science and technology be accorded a greater place in postwar public administration. Since better treatment for technical men was part of this scheme, they formed a plan to secure the promotion of Matsunami Yoshimi, a noted forestry expert with many years' experience, to the office of bureau chief. In this effort they enjoyed support not only from technical experts in the rest of the ministry but also from another bureau chief, from the vice minister, and initially from the minister. These officials, however, reckoned without the vigorous intervention of the incumbent chief of the Bureau of Forestry. Okamoto Eitarō, a graduate of the Tokyo law faculty and a career civil servant, complained to the vice minister that making a technical man head of a bureau would "destroy bureaucratic order," and the proposal was dropped.[50]

Matsunami's frustration did not end the movement. It survived the division of the agriculture and commerce ministry in 1925 and spread to the rest of the government. Engineers' caucuses (*gijutsusha konwakai*) formed in many of the ministries. Their members held conventions, gave speeches, and signed and submitted petitions to bureaucratic superiors, but no big changes ever resulted. The reasons even now are somewhat obscure.[51] One can call this, of course, a legacy of feudalism, but the same pattern existed in other countries. Before 1945, only Britain among the European powers made substantive changes in engineers' roles in the national bureaucracy.[52]

In Japan the long-term effort by many professors to win greater autonomy on university campuses promoted narrowness of perspective in some important groups and made communication among them more difficult. For some time before the end of the war, professors had had a major influence over most matters pertinent to the growth of research. In some ways this influence had grown. When Aoyama died late in 1917, President Yamakawa consulted the full professors in Tokyo University's faculty of medicine and accepted their choice for his successor.[53] In December 1917, when Kyoto University was preparing to add a chair of biology, its authorities called in an outside consultant who was himself a professor of biology.[54]

This level of involvement was not enough for some. Following a 1913 confrontation between President Sawayanagi Masatarō (who had moved from Tōhoku University) and his faculty of law at Kyoto, support for the idea that professors should elect the university president grew rapidly. In 1915 the Ministry of Education conceded this right and others as well. In 1919 university senates were given the formal (not, as before, merely informal) right to advise the minister on the creation of chairs. In 1920 the ministry authorized awarding doctorates directly on the basis of faculty decisions.[55] But these changes did not always have the expected result, and by the mid-1920s scientists were complaining that their influence had actually decreased.[56] Academic autonomy tended to enhance the alienating effects of bureaucratic legalism as a negative influence on science.

The postwar era, however, witnessed a powerful push for independence in science, including psychological independence of Germany. The founding of the National Institute for Nutrition Research, based on an American model, was one indicator. There were others as well. From 1917 into the 1920s, the Institute for Metals Research had a lucrative partnership with Westinghouse Corporation through its Japanese patron, Sumitomo Metals.[57] In 1918, the Ministry of Education established a system of grants intended to increase research productivity. In 1920, the country established a National Research Council as a result of political changes in science worldwide. These initiatives unquestionably strengthened the research system. They also forced Japanese scientists to consider their own position in the international community of science. Were they, as some held, clearly second-rate? Were some fields particularly stronger than others? And were some on the verge of even greater contributions?

The Ministry of Education's Science Research Grants Program

Establishment of a system of grants for research was a very important development in Japan's research system. Competitive research grants weakened the near-monopoly professors at imperial universities had on the resources available for research. They served to alleviate the lack of resources in various academic institutions, promoted competition among Japanese scientists in all kinds of professional roles, and helped spread money around in the way that was thought most efficient. Most of all, the Science Research Grants Program established the principle that research would be encouraged and supported in *all* technical fields, not just in those popular at the moment or whose leaders were politically astute.

Such an innovative program did not emerge quickly. The Imperial Academy of Sciences had begun a system of competitive grants in 1913, though its importance was largely symbolic. The total amount of money involved was very small (2,460 yen in 1914, 7,000 yen in 1916, and 20,000 yen in 1918). Funds were divided between humanistic and technical projects and between prizes for prior contributions and for research in progress. Before 1919 only academy members could even apply for the grants.[58] For these reasons, scientists and other observers of the academic scene began demanding an alternative program. Bacteriologist Sata Yoshihiko called for a system of grants for research in a 1914 essay.[59] Sawayanagi Masatarō, former president of Tōhoku and Kyoto universities, added to the pressure in 1915 with a critique of the academy's operations.[60]

Nevertheless, it is hard to determine how the program originated or why it took certain forms. Original records from the Ministry of Education no longer exist, and memoirs rarely mention the subject. From academic journals and Diet records it is possible to shed some light on these questions. One thing we know is that the financial constraints of the war's early months brought academy programs under scrutiny. On June 2, 1915, Wakatsuki Reijirō, the minister of finance, recommended eliminating the special research fund of the Imperial Academy because of financial convenience. Wakatsuki qualified his proposal by saying,

"It will be necessary to find another way to administer funds with which to encourage [scientific] research."[61] His statement later proved to be prescient. In 1921 the academy fund merged with the science research grants system to create a better-funded program.[62]

The Ministry of Education's unwillingness or inability any longer to carry the political burden of apparent favoritism toward government schools was surely another factor in the birth of grants. Ichiki Kitokurō's serious mishandling of the 1914 laboratory transfer had significantly damaged the ministry's credibility. Moreover, Takata Sanae, his successor, had been president of Waseda University, and if anything was thought to favor private-sector schools.[63] The politically astute Okada Ryōhei, who succeeded Takata in October 1916 and remained in office until September 1918, probably saw the need to balance competing public and private demands in the Science Research Grants Program, while spreading the money as far as he could. Such a conclusion seems justified by his defense of the program to the Budget Committee of the House of Representatives.

The committee debated the ministry's budget, including this program, on February 2, 1918. Three committee members raised a number of questions. Hayashi Kiroku, then professor of economics and later president of Keio University, noted that 20,000 yen was now supporting research through the Imperial Academy of Sciences. He called this a "paltry sum of money" and said the academy program had been far too inflexible and its aims too specialized. Implying that the new program should avoid these shortcomings, he declared that much more money should clearly be spent but that "even a coolie" should be able to recognize its purpose. Representatives Matsunaga Yoshizaemon and Kōno Tetsushi spoke more directly to the new program's features. Both expressed concern about availability of funds (150,000 yen for the first year). Matsunaga raised two other issues. According to him, the program did not consider the needs of new recruits to a field. Grants would be so small as to exhaust the funds simply on the purchase of foreign journals and books. Then, the relationship of the program to other means of support for research had not been adequately defined by the ministry. Citing the foundation of the Research Institute for Physics and Chemistry as a major development for Japanese science, he insisted on the need for a unified structure through which to pursue basic scientific research.[64]

Okada's response showed how far the Ministry of Education had now moved away from any compulsion to centralize research. The Science Research Grants Program, he insisted, was not *supposed* to be related to any particular laboratories. Rather, it would try to alleviate the lack of facilities and resources in existing institutions. The money could be used anywhere. "We are talking about helping people to do research even if it is not at their own institution." He also hoped to promote competition. "It is not good if people are doing research at one place, while those at other places are doing none . . . Scientists mostly succeed and obtain best results when they compete with each other." But the government's resources were too limited to expand equipment budgets everywhere, so the ministry had decided to support individual and team research projects. "We hope as much as possible," he concluded, "to encourage research at many different places."[65]

On the whole, the program managed to do this. The first research grants, sixty-five altogether, were announced on July 20, 1918. They were shared by ninety-two investigators at thirty-four academic institutions. All five imperial universities were represented, together with several higher schools, medical colleges, specialized academies, and a few private institutions, including Waseda University. All broadly defined fields were recognized. Grants were awarded for work in physics, chemistry, biology, geology, engineering, medicine, forestry, and agriculture. But it is difficult to say what the distribution meant, since we have only grant titles without descriptions and no information about their budgets. *Kyōiku jiron,* apparently the sole remaining source of information on the subject, reports only that the largest grant was 10,000 yen and the smallest 500. According to it, the research topics selected by the grant recipients "all focused on important problems" and showed the Japanese scientific community's highest [accomplishments] as of this moment."[66]

Not everyone agreed with this fulsome assessment. Miyajima Mikinosuke, now associated with the Kitasato Institute, faulted the program on four counts in an essay published about five weeks after the *Kyōiku jiron* article. First of all, partiality was blatantly evident, with private-sector scientists badly short-changed and Tokyo University researchers too highly favored. In particular, several competent investigators of tsutsugamushi disease—Kawamura Rinya (Niigata Medical College), Ogata Masanori (Tokyo University), and Hayashi Naosuke (Aichi Medical College)—had not received grants for work on this topic. All the funding had gone to Nagayo Matarō's pathology team from Tokyo University's faculty of medicine. This was particularly unfortunate because the Nagayo group had made claims that had not yet been accepted. Second, grant sizes were often inexplicable. The Nagayo group was getting too much, while Yamagiwa Katsusaburō's important cancer project had not nearly enough. Third, some research projects were not operating properly. Among the fifteen team projects that had received the first grants, Miyajima again singled out the Nagayo pathology team because each of the three subtopics—pathogen confirmation, prevention, and treatment—was assigned to one of the three team members. "A professional scientist," according to him, "would surely find this regrettable." Finally, the grant conferrals were apt, however unintentionally, to discredit those projects that did not receive funding. Because the lay public tended to regard official approbation as tantamount to correctness, there was a danger that the work of scientists who did not receive grants would not be widely accepted.[67]

Officials in charge at the Ministry of Education clearly felt obliged to respond. First, Kawamura Rinya and Ogata Masanori were hastily added to the list of recipients.[68] Then these same officials predicted that funding would increase. As of early September, they promised to increase funding by 100,000 yen,[69] but by late October, they scaled this back to 50,000 yen, and they were ultimately able to give no increase at all.[70] The chief of the Bureau of Professional Education, Matsuura Chinjirō, issued a disclaimer with the results of the second year's grant competition.

> This year (1919) we gave out 113 grants . . . And those who requested the grants were about twice the number who actually received them. There should not be any implication that those who did not get grants were unqualified. Some of those [not awarded grants] may be better researchers than those who did get them. But the Ministry of Education's plan was to give the money for one year; and if their work were going to cost too much money, we had to exclude them with regret from funding. Some people are sure to say [we should fund it] if the project is good, no matter how much it costs. But the Ministry of Education's thinking was that we would rather fund two people than one, or two types of research than one.[71]

The bureau chief then added plaintively: "This problem [disbursing the money for grants] caused us a great many difficulties!"[72]

Matsuura's comments raise two issues of major importance. How were the decisions actually made? Were they in any sense reasonable? In dealing analytically with either of these questions, one should recognize the difficulties involved. Matsuura and his colleagues faced a difficult task, and so do present-day historians. The applicant pool for the first round of grants was particularly large, the community of medical researchers heavily factionalized, and the Ministry of Education itself lacked a man who had a technical background and could advise about decisions.

Consider the size of the application pool. According to Matsuura himself, the 1918 requests from scientists at government institutions alone amounted to 3,000,000 yen. But only 145,000 yen was actually available, and that money had also to cover funding requests from researchers in private institutions.[73] This was predictable, since the research community had grown substantially. In 1913, there were only 99 professionally active men with degrees in basic science; but by 1920, there were 165 in this group. The constraints imposed on Japan by the war created both more need for research *and* powerful incentives to do it, yet institutional support for research activities could hardly keep up with either.

Evaluation was also complicated by factions, at least in the medical community. Charges and countercharges between the Kitasato group and Tokyo University's medical faculty had intensified after the laboratory transfer, and they had their effect on research. In July 1915 Nagayo Matarō wrote in his diary of his concern for the reputation of the Institute of Infectious Diseases in the light of its numerous problems. "I do not want the institute to be simply a place for manufacturing serums. We must be more active in scientific research."[74] The topic he selected for reputation enhancement turned out to be tsutsugamushi disease. Because this disease had engaged the attention of numerous researchers over a forty-year period, competition was intense.[75] For example, Nagayo and Kawamura disagreed on the number of insect vector types and on animal transmissibility, while Ogata and Kawamura disagreed completely on effective prophylaxis. On the other hand, Kawamura's ideas about tsutsugamushi disease were much closer to those of Miyajima,[76] so that Kawamura could be linked to the "Kitasato faction" and benefit from the support of its members.[77]

But the Ministry of Education faced one other problem in allocating grants for which it alone was responsible. After Mano Bunji, a mechanical engineer, left the ministry for the presidency of Kyushu University in the fall of 1913, there were no longer any technical people in the top ranks of education bureaucrats. This might not have mattered in some situations, but the ministry was becoming self-contained. Once-intimate ties with Tokyo University were becoming more formal, and growing criticisms from professors in law at Kyoto University had created some longer-term tensions.[78] Whatever the proximate cause of the pattern may have been, the ministry undertook to distribute the grants with very little outside assistance.

Problems caused by ignorance at the ministry were not so clear at the outset. Following the Diet's approval in April 1918 of the Science Research Grants Program, the ministry asked all the institutions under its control to provide it with certain information. Who were the most active researchers? What topics were they investigating? What kind of expenses did they expect to incur during the next twelve-month period?[79] In response to these questions, Kyoto University's faculty senate convened on April 25 to prepare its responses. Professors from the faculties of science, medicine, and engineering decided on a list of twenty-two projects with a total three-year budget of 90,000 yen. Three projects had priority: Kuhara Mitsuru's work in organic chemistry, Tanabe Sakuo's investigation of seismological waves, and Adachi Buntarō's histological studies of human bones.[80] Yet when the awards were announced about nine weeks later, not one of these three was included.[81]

The 113 awards conferred in 1919 also show signs, if not of incompetence, at least of inconsistency. As we have seen, there was considerable interest in Japan in all aspects of chemical research. Accordingly, Matsuura, chief of the Bureau of Professional Education, stated on October 25, 1918, that chemistry would be assigned top priority in the 1919 competition.[82] When the awards were announced, on June 28, 1919, this intention was shown to be unrealized. The list of awards for 1919 gives details about budget.[83] By determining the specialties of the various researchers and knowing the money each was awarded, one can calculate the funding by disciplines. Medicine received the biggest share, with 46,850 yen or 32 percent of all the money allocated (144,580 yen). Chemistry was second with 43,000 yen (30 percent).[84] Physics (also including civil, mechanical, and electrical engineering, as well as naval architecture) at 24,400 yen (17 percent) was a distant third.[85] Biology (botany, zoology, genetics, and entomology) received 15,500 yen (11 percent) in grants. Agriculture (defined here as agronomy, veterinary medicine, forestry, ichthyology, and plant pathology) was awarded 9,830 yen or 7 percent; and most of the remaining 5,000 yen was awarded for projects in dentistry.[86]

Inability to follow its own professed guidelines for 1919, the hasty addition of Kawamura and Ogata to the list of 1918 grant recipients, and the denial of funding to all three of Kyoto University's priority projects as defined by their academic peers is an indication that the Ministry of Education was not following the most rational procedure in administering its program for scientific research. This was argued at the time as well. *Ikai jihō,* in an August 1920 review of the first three grant years, took the ministry to task. The research grants program lacked clear objectives and standards. The ministry was "just giving out little pieces of the pie with no real policy." Distribution of funds was illogical. Recipients had recently been told that their funds would be terminated "until further notice," since different procedures might soon be adopted. Favoritism was evident—unspecified "private elements" had affected selection. Ministry officials were unqualified for their role. "There is a certain amount of talent within the Ministry of Education," the writer of the essay was willing to concede. "But no one there is too well informed about the academic community's [internal] affairs." Worst of all, the ministry opposed a real screening committee, simply asking the opinions of a few Tokyo professors. Such deficiencies, according to the journal, "invite our criticism of irregular actions!"[87]

The program was still a success, however. All grant recipients were formally qualified. About 80 percent already had the doctorate, and all but two held a teaching position. One of the two who was not a professor—Tanaka Keisuke—was a physician on the staff of the Yokote Hospital (Akita Prefecture). But he already had his doctor's degree and had pioneered in the study of tsutsugamushi disease.[88] The other case, that of Takagi Yoshiyuki, shows the ministry's intention to support individuals. Takagi was a clinical physician one year from his doctorate when he received his award (2,500 yen for research on rabies at Kyoto University, where he took his M.D.) in 1919.[89]

Just as its sponsors intended, the Science Research Grants Program aided contributions to knowledge in several different fields. The 4,500 yen awarded to Nagayo Matarō's research team, though controversial, nevertheless aided confirmation of the tsutsugamushi pathogen.[90] Yamagiwa Katsusaburō, who received one of the 1918 grants and won a renewal in 1919, wrote a paper on artificial inducement of tumors that was later recognized as one of the cornerstones of modern-day cancer research.[91] The physical chemist Tawara Kuniichi, who received the largest grant (5,000 yen) in 1919, used his funds for chemical and other scientific studies of classical Japanese swords.[92] This work, for which he received the Imperial Academy of Sciences Prize in 1921, may later have contributed to specialty steels in Japan.[93] Yagi Hidetsugu, professor of electrical engineering at Tōhoku University, received a grant in 1919 that he used in part to develop what is still the world's most widely used antenna for short-wave and television reception.[94] Finally, in 1919 Yasui Kono became the first Japanese woman to win recognition as a contributor to science by receiving a grant in plant cytology.[95] Any one of these projects would have justified creation of the Ministry of Education's Science Research Grants Program. But these five made it a historical landmark.

The problems that cropped up in administering these grants were not unique to Japan, as must be stressed. Competitive research grants were a new phenomenon even in countries that supported science strongly. Italy and the United States began giving grants in the present-day sense only at the end of World War I.[96] In Germany they were also new to the scene. The German experience is particularly illuminating when seen from the Japanese vantage point. Competitive grants for scientific research began in 1914, but the way they were administered left much to be desired by today's standards. During the second decade of this century, they were entirely controlled by individual scientists directing the KWG laboratories (see chapter 4). Albert Einstein, for example, dispensed funds for research in physics by consulting only his assistant director, Max von Laue, and this was a typical pattern.[97] Other small groups were awarding funds, too, but not by rigorous screening.[98] Explicit peer review came only in 1920 with establishment of the Notgemeinschaft der Deutschen Wissenschaften.[99]

Establishment of the National Research Council

Establishment of the National Research Council (Gakujutsu Kenkyū Kaigi) or NRC in 1920 best exemplified the growing independence of Japanese science in a period of major transition. On one level, the NRC gave the scientific community an institutional focus that the Imperial Academy had not managed to provide. Through ninety-four members, representing all fields of study, the council in the interwar period enhanced public awareness of research activities, facilitated the building of several new laboratories and programs, and promoted recognition of Japanese achievements in science worldwide.[100]

On another level, the council's establishment helped liberate Japanese science from its obsession with Germany. The NRC was created as an affiliate of the International Research Council (IRC). Since this agency had been founded as a device for isolating German science, members of the Japanese scientific community were obliged to evaluate carefully their place in the international community of science. Their efforts were painful but also therapeutic, since out of them came both greater self-confidence and greater objectivity in judging themselves and the West.

The NRC and its IRC parent were products of the war. Though designed to enhance cooperation among nations in science, they were also founded with the aim of excluding the former Central Powers. In early April 1918, while the war was still going on in Europe, an invitation to attend the initial organizing meetings reached the Imperial Academy of Sciences in Tokyo. The invitation was accepted at once, and the academy voted to send Sakurai Jōji and Tanakadate Aikitsu, professors respectively of chemistry and physics at Tokyo University, as delegates to the meeting in London.[101] Their selection had much to recommend it. Sakurai at the time was dean of Tokyo's faculty of science and chairman of the academy's division 2 for technical fields, and Tanakadate, with his geophysical research in the late nineteenth century, had done exactly the kind of work the meetings wanted to restore. Because Sakurai had studied with Williamson at London and Tanakadate with Kelvin at Glasgow, both were fluent in English.[102] Two other facts are important. Sakurai was very pro-British and somewhat anti-German. He was also strongly inclined to stress the weaknesses of Japanese science and overlook its accomplishments.

Sakurai's convictions were very deep-seated. Unlike most Japanese scientists, who had studied in Germany, Sakurai was British-educated and admired British culture. He dressed like an English gentleman and was fond of English theater and literature,[103] and he had some dislike for the Germans. In 1885 he had forced a fellow chemist, Nagai Nagayoshi, out of Tokyo's faculty of science partly because Nagai was a pupil of the German chemist August von Hofmann, who had previously been a rival to his own teacher, Williamson.[104] Sakurai's career had given him little satisfaction. He had held a number of administrative posts but published only twenty-eight papers. Several of his papers were important, but their number—in his view, small—distressed him considerably.[105] As a result, he tended in general to view the work of his colleagues through a lens that was highly distorted.

Tanakadate's position was considerably different. His memoirs show that he enjoyed his work. He was not on Nagaoka's level as a physicist, but he did publish fifty-seven papers. He also traveled extensively, taught students effectively, and played important roles in Japanese aviation research on the intellectual and institutional levels. Tanakadate had spent several years in Britain as a young physics student, but he was a genial man with acquaintances on both sides of the European conflict.[106] He was at first opposed to the German exclusion from the IRC and argued with Sakurai about it. "War is war, but science is different. I see no problem in associating with German scientists." Sakurai, however, insisted on the need for Japan to follow British opinion on the issue. According to another Japanese physicist who had traveled with the two to London, their debate continued from the hotel where they stayed to the site of the conference.[107]

The conference was held at the Royal Society and produced the expected results. Germany and its Central Power allies, Austria-Hungary and Bulgaria, were excluded from cooperation in science. To Sakurai and other delegates the reasons were obvious. "The Central Powers," he wrote, "placed no restrictions on their [wartime] atrocities" and had "broken the laws of civilized [nations]." Scientific contacts with such nations as these "would lack any value whatever."[108] But since international cooperation was clearly essential, several additional steps had to be taken. Delegates voted to withdraw from the prewar Association of Science Academies, since the Central Powers belonged to this group. In its place would arise a new central structure called the International Research Council. The IRC would establish "unions" for the various fields of technical research. Each nation's science academy would contribute members to the technical unions, and each delegation would urge its government to create an IRC affiliate in the form of a National Research Council.[109]

None of these motions was particularly surprising. The conference was confined to eight Allied nations and convened at a critical time. An Allied victory was near but not achieved, and feelings of revenge were intense.[110] Delegates from the U.S. and Britain had already worked out many details of the proposed new structures before the meetings began.[111] Even so, not all went smoothly, since opinions varied. French and Belgian delegates, representing the nations that had suffered most, apparently intended to shun their wartime antagonists indefinitely. Other delegates seemed to feel that reconciliation might eventually be possible.[112] The idea of individual NRC's (which the U.S. proposed) was at first a source of contention. By his own telling, Sakurai was himself a leading conciliator. With the aim of achieving at least surface unanimity, he induced Tanakadate to support German exclusion, and then, after securing American understanding, proposed that IRC affiliation for various countries be permitted through either the proposed new NRC or an existing academy of science.[113]

At a meeting in Paris six weeks later (November 26–29), work continued. Delegates, this time from eleven nations, voted unanimously to establish a temporary IRC. A powerful steering committee, with members from France, Britain, Italy, Belgium, and the U.S., was created. Delegates entrusted to it the tasks of evaluating proposals for scientific unions, selecting their members, and convening all subsequent meetings. One issue remained controversial: admission of neutral countries. And the issue of membership for antagonists continued to loom. Britain, the U.S., and Sakurai for Japan wanted offers of membership to be made only with a two-thirds majority in favor, but a harder line prevailed, and a three-quarters vote was required.[114]

This setback in Paris did nothing to lessen the influence of Sakurai at home. While Tanakadate remained in Europe on other academic business, Sakurai returned to Japan in January 1919 and immediately set about organizing a National Research Council. He was so committed to the NRC concept that almost any tactic seemed acceptable.[115] Sakurai willfully misrepresented facts, gave evasive or misleading answers to critical questions from Japanese colleagues, and seems to have stacked the NRC organizing committee to produce the desired result. Ultimately, on December 11, 1920, it all blew up in his face. But by then this mattered very little, since the NRC had become a reality.

Planning the NRC took considerable time. Sakurai gave the Imperial Academy of Sciences a detailed report on the London and Paris meetings on February 25, 1919, but he did not formally propose the NRC for another three months (May 12). His February report was published, so we know what he told the academy. He gave information on the countries and delegates, on the proposed IRC, on the various unions, and on national representation—that is, the NRC. He held nothing back in regard to German exclusion. This was not his first report on the subject. Immediately following the London meeting, he had cabled details to Tokyo and sought approval to represent the academy in Paris.[116] Members of the academy, then, could hardly be surprised when they learned of the German exclusion. Some scientists were clearly unhappy, and Sakurai encountered criticism as soon as he returned to Japan. "Why had I not spoken up for the Central Powers? Why had I not opposed the exclusion?" he wrote some twenty years later. He claims, however, to have paid it no heed, since it came from a "very small part of our scientific community." "I had not anticipated the criticism, and it was totally incomprehensible to me."[117]

These claims were at best disingenuous. His own fellow-delegate, Tanakadate, had already argued against German exclusion, and in July 1919 would support German membership at an IRC meeting in Brussels.[118] Indications that exclusion of Germany was unpopular with the majority of Japanese scientists are strong.[119] What is true, however, is that most scientists—especially those belonging to the Imperial Academy, which had sponsored his trip—were willing to avoid the issue for several reasons. Japan was a prominent member of the Allied Powers, so vigorous support for Germany might offend the Japanese government. Many scientists were undoubtedly flattered by their inclusion in what looked like a major new venture in science. But the strongest reason to keep quiet was their commitment to the NRC concept. Sakurai Jōji had the vision, the control of information, the connections, and the administrative skills to make the NRC a reality. Very few scientists actively opposed him until their opposition was politically innocuous.

Once Sakurai had firm plans, the establishment process accelerated. He submitted his blueprint for the NRC to the Imperial Academy on May 12, 1919, and the members raised quite a few questions. Nagaoka Hantarō was skeptical of Sakurai's proposal to name some corporate executives to the proposed NRC, on the grounds that industry would not benefit from its projects directly. Other members asked about the NRC's relationship to the academy and government bureaucracy, as well as about its mission. To these questions Sakurai replied that industrial-sector representation might promote science applications, that the academy would serve as the NRC's sponsor, and that rapid progress in planning might secure attachment of the NRC to the office of the prime minister. There was also a question about budget.

How much money would the NRC need? To this query Sakurai gave an answer that was either shortsighted or deliberately misleading: money was not a problem, since the NRC would "not need a very large budget."[120] All of these answers later proved wrong. No corporate executives became members of the NRC when the organization was finally constituted.[121] The NRC was attached to the Ministry of Education, not the office of the prime minister.[122] And the budget which Sakurai requested on October 15, 1919, was for a very large sum— 380,000 yen.[123]

The May 12 meeting resulted in formation of an organizing committee. The academy's president, Hozumi Nobushige, a lawyer from Division 1, named a sixteen-man committee, fourteen scientists from Division 2 and two humanists from Division 1. The chairman (mathematician Fujisawa Rikitarō) was from Tokyo University's faculty of science. Despite Hozumi's formal role, it is more than probable that Sakurai influenced the committee's composition. There was no open discussion of who the members should be, Sakurai was named the executive secretary, and the membership was not representative of the larger scientific community. A majority (eight of fourteen) of its scientist members had studied abroad in countries other than Germany.[124] Only one member came from medicine, despite its large role in Japanese research, and his appointment is curious. Ōzawa Kenji had earlier been dean of Tokyo University's faculty of medicine, and in that sense he was quite well qualified. But he was considered an antagonist by Kitasato, the country's foremost researcher and a known admirer of Germany.[125] Ōzawa's training in Europe was unusual for a Japanese medical professor. He had studied at the University of Strasbourg from 1872 to 1875, took his M.D. there in 1875, and later worked at Strasbourg between 1879 and 1883.[126] Ōzawa's exact views on World War I are unknown, but his background arouses suspicion. Quite apart from the war's effect on the Strasbourg region and how he may have seen this, the university was in some respects French in the period when Ōzawa trained there.[127]

Following the committee's deliberations in May, Sakurai in early June began a campaign to sell the NRC concept to a larger public of scientists, intellectuals, and government officials. Publishing articles in intellectual journals was one of his strategies. In a June 5 essay, Sakurai listed a number of Japanese laboratories by name—the Institute of Infectious Diseases was one—and claimed there had been "no unity [or liaison] among them at all." As a result, "They have, in relative terms, wasted both time and effort while failing to produce any major results."[128] In another essay he stressed the need for Japanese industry to support "pure chemistry" more vigorously. World War I, after all, had shown that all the new war-related discoveries or inventions had come from university professors, not applied scientists in industry.[129] Establishment of a Japanese research council would correct such deficiencies by promoting liaison among laboratories and between science and society, besides strengthening the ties of Japanese science with research in the West.[130]

His other strategy was to meet with officials. On June 17 the academy's proposal for the NRC was formally presented to Prime Minister Hara Kei and the minister of education, Nakahashi Tokugorō. This document, though drafted by an academy lawyer, reflected Sakurai's views.[131] Once again he expounded his characteristic themes. The country had built a number of research facilities, but there was little liaison among them, with "few results forthcoming as yet."[132] Thus, creation of an NRC was urgently needed. To sell his argument, Sakurai met several times during June and July with Prime Minister Hara, Education Minister Nakahashi, Vice Minister Minami Hiroshi, and Matsuura Chinjirō, chief of the Bureau of Professional Education. He gave them "detailed explanations and won their support."[133] Following these meetings, Sakurai was confident enough of success to predict on July 15 that the NRC would be established "before the end of the year."[134]

It certainly looked that way for a time. In early October the Ministry of Education approved plans for the NRC. Under the arrangements drawn up, the NRC was to have administrative and professional divisions, between seventy and one hundred members, a total of seven technical unions, formal liaison with the IRC, and a small permanent committee to handle communications with communities of scientists abroad. To assure that its functions could be carried out smoothly, a budget of 380,000 yen was under consideration. Most of the money would go for overseas travel and various forms of professional communication.[135] It is not clear whether the budget request caused consternation or not. Sakurai called attention in the published report to the fact that geographically, Japan was "stuck off in one corner of the Orient" and asserted that this had "caused much inconvenience for [scientific] research."[136]

After this highly auspicious beginning, the cause of the NRC stalled, though not through the Diet's inaction. That institution readily approved the NRC proposal in midautumn with little discussion, leaving all the major provisions intact—including the budget. But even after this, there was no NRC in Japan. Sakurai, in fact, showed some concern for the loss of momentum on December 12 when he reported to the Imperial Academy. "Japan," he said, "has not yet joined the IRC as I had hoped. It is still under discussion in the government. Once our

NRC is established, it can be our affiliating agency. Until then, the academy must fill this role temporarily."[137]

Delay was a product of reactions in Germany and the anxieties this aroused in Japan about the prospects for overseas study. The Versailles Conference had taken place during the first half of 1919, but the German government did not accept the treaty until October 13 of that year.[138] The first reports of hostile reaction in Germany, both to Japan's involvement in the Versailles Conference and to its part in the IRC votes, did not reach Japan until a few weeks after that date. T. Axenfeld, professor of ophthalmology at the University of Freiburg, wrote angrily of both to a former Japanese pupil. "German scientists," he reminded his friend, "gave special help in their laboratories to Japanese in particular. Thus we are awaiting some gesture or explanation for the illegal treatment of Germany, especially the Japanese delegates' acceptance of the decision to boycott science in Germany." In late December Tokyo newspapers were carrying reports that German universities and laboratories were refusing to admit Japanese, with some even suggesting that entering Germany at all was forbidden.[139] And on February 15, 1920, a particularly alarming report was published in an education journal. This report claimed that a conference of German academics had decided to reject all foreign students from Allied countries and forbid the export of German scientific publications. The report specified certain decisions of the U.S. government as the motive behind the new policy but asserted that Japan would become one of the main victims.[140]

Reports of this kind were clearly alarming, but few in the government would admit it. Officials at first pretended nothing was wrong. "Bureaucratic authorities, when asked about the [German reaction], all say the same thing," noted one medical journal in the middle of January, "namely, that they pay no attention to reports in the press."[141] Later in the year they were only somewhat less cautious. In September Vice Minister Minami claimed that only in Munich were Japanese actually barred.[142] Bureau Chief Matsuura insisted that, after all, "*every country*" was creating its own NRC.[143] These less guarded comments reflected new information. In early August 1920 a new German envoy, Wilhelm Solf, arrived in Tokyo and told the Ministry of Foreign Affairs that Germany would accept "large numbers of Japanese foreign students." On August 19 the Japanese chargé d'affaires in Berlin cabled a lengthy and reassuring report on the German situation to superiors in Tokyo.[144] For these reasons, the cabinet finally approved establishment of the NRC on August 17 and allowed its promulgation on August 26.[145]

But not all the action took place in the government. The scientific community had been alarmed for months and in various ways had tried to mollify the Germans. In late December 1919 and early January 1920

Miyashita Sōsuke of the Osaka Medical College wrote to Axenfeld with assurances of goodwill.[146] Tokyo University biologist Ishikawa Chiyomatsu sent laboratory animals to a colleague in Berlin to replace those stolen by Germans needing food.[147] Other Japanese professors sent private messages to colleagues, and at least two made large cash donations to feed the hungry in Munich.[148] It was Kitasato's gesture, however, that attracted the most attention. In June 1920 he wrote Robert Koch's widow a lengthy statement of Japanese goodwill and enclosed a photograph of the Shinto service conducted at his laboratory on May 27 in memory of her husband's career. The letter, written in German, promptly appeared in a German medical journal and elicited favorable comment from all over Germany.[149]

Kitasato's message is worthy of attention as a typical statement of scientists' views. He called the war a mere "political conflict" that in no way reflected any *popular* enmity. For Japanese in general it was "divorced from individuals." Japanese scientists continued to hold the same feelings of esteem for their German teachers that they had before the war. His letter makes no mention of the IRC exclusion or any part that his own colleagues may have had in its making. In fact, the only comment in it with political implications is a criticism of the peace treaty's attempt to "perpetuate enmity," which he contrasted unfavorably with the Confucian moral concepts in which Japanese like him had been reared.[150]

This kind of vague but high-toned apolitical stance was widespread among Japanese scientists. Many commentators in the professional press did link scattered acts of German ill will to the London conference vote and the Japanese scientists' role in it. Tawara Teijirō, for example, criticized Sakurai and Tanakadate for "confusing the role of the scientist with that of the diplomat" and of "deferring to the vulgar opinions of the Powers."[151] But most of the commentary was not for attribution. An unsigned essay in another journal accused the Japanese delegates to the London conference of "ignorance and lack of discernment" and of "licking the boots" of the other scientists present.[152] Most scientists' responses ignored the IRC. Before December 1920 there appears to have been only one public statement by a Japanese scientist seeking to reassure Germans by attacking the IRC, and the circumstances in that case were unusual. The scientist concerned, pharmacological chemist Keimatsu Katsuzaemon, was in Berlin at the time and probably felt that failure to act would cost him access to needed information. As a result, he and about thirty other resident Japanese sent a cable and a letter to the Imperial Academy in Tokyo, protesting Germany's exclusion from the IRC network.[153] The Japanese government acknowledged their action, but the academy ignored it completely.[154]

December 11, 1920, marked the end of such innocence, real or contrived. At the formal inauguration of the new NRC, a heated debate broke out on the issue of German exclusion, when presiding officer Furuichi Kōi called for discussion of any "other business." Inoue Jinkichi, professor of chemical engineering at Tōhoku University, raised the issue first. He called exclusion very unfortunate and insisted that any revival of cooperative work in science would have to include Germany and Austria. Nagayo Matarō, professor of pathology at Tokyo University, attacked not only the policy of exclusion but the motives of those who defended it. Defenders, he suggested, had acted in the belief that opposition was impossible for Japan "because of its present position," and he attributed to them a belief that support for the views of Britain and France was really a moderate position. Calling this view an "insult to the entire scientific community," Nagayo moved that the NRC demand "immediate termination" of the Central Powers boycott and pressure the IRC to this end.[155]

Nagayo's proposal was naturally controversial. Two chemists (Majima Toshiyuki and Katayama Masao) and one physicist (Tamaru Takurō) from Tokyo University rose to support him, and indications were that many felt the same. But not all present would agree to the motion. One senior member of the Imperial Academy conceded that his earlier support of German exclusion was probably wrong, but he said the academy should take up the problem. Sakurai Jōji announced that he was flatly opposed even to discussion of the issue. Debate, however, in no way subsided until Furuichi called an hour's intermission. Following the cooling-off period, the NRC resumed its discussion and finally approved a watered-down version: "The National Research Council of Japan," it said, "expresses to the International Research Council the desire that *all* civilized nations participate freely [in IRC projects]." Even though the council meant "all" to include Germany and the other Central Powers, the force of the statement was considerably diluted.[156]

Several reasons were behind the NRC's hedging. After all, German exclusion, as one scientist put it, was a "limited, conditional thing." The London conference had occurred while the war was still on, and its exclusionary policy could not be permanent. Restoration of peace offered the chance for a revival of the prewar Association of Science Academies, in which Germany was naturally included.[157] Others felt that Japanese scientists could in any case have done little to defend the interests of Germany. "The British, French, and American delegates were acting very self-righteously at the London meeting with no Germans present," another commentator wrote. "It is not difficult to imagine that [Sakurai and Tanakadate] would have been ignored completely [had they spoken up for Germany]."[158] There is some evidence that this cynical view was correct. When Tanakadate attended the July

1919 IRC meeting in Brussels, he did speak up for German involvement and become the target of several snide comments from European delegates.[159]

Sakurai and others lacked confidence in their professional achievements as scientists, and Sakurai's adherence to the exclusion of Germany and willingness to defend it were not just a product of his training in Britain and admiration for British culture and manners. He was both highly deferential to authority and aggressively critical of Japanese science. In 1881 he had reluctantly abandoned his promising research career in London to take a chemistry lectureship at Tokyo University when President Katō insisted he do so. In only two years he advanced to full professor and then was invested with administrative duties. While he clearly regretted this turn of events, deference to authority came naturally to him.[160] In 1913, when Yamakawa Kenjirō was under suspicion in the Ministry of Education and his appointment for a presidential term was held up, Sakurai Jōji was installed in his place precisely because he was considered more pliable.[161]

This combination of deference to authority and low self-image as a research scientist affected his behavior in London. When Nagayo Matarō approached Sakurai during the intermission of the NRC meeting, he asked him to explain his support for German exclusion. Sakurai exploded with a burst of indignation: "Do you people not know where we stand [in science]? Think about it! What have Japanese contributed to science so far? Our accomplishments simply do not permit us to discuss such important matters as this on an equal basis with [scientists from] advanced countries!"[162] Nagayo was a confident man with a different point of view. He told Sakurai he was mistaken and insisted that Japanese achievements had been materially aided by the Germans—however one chose to evaluate them. "Our scientists continued to read German books even while [the countries] were at war," he noted. "The appearance of exclusion will not change this at all." Sakurai was unconvinced but qualified his views the following day when Nagayo came to his home. "I do think that Japan, both in name and in fact, will eventually catch up with the top-ranking countries in politics, diplomacy, and science."[163] This judgment, at least, would be proven correct.

CHAPTER NINE

SCIENCE AND SOCIETY:
A RETROSPECTIVE

Building a tradition of scientific research required Japan to borrow effectively from Western traditions and manage its own simultaneously. There were plausible strategies for solving most problems and numerous pitfalls en route. Rigid adherence to any single model could have been disastrous, or at least prejudicial. European science had arisen much earlier and under much different conditions from those in Japan. Japan lacked Europe's resources, and European activities were closely linked in a synergistic system of enormous vitality. Yet the builders of research made surprisingly few errors. They investigated numerous models, debated every option, and in a great many cases made reasonable decisions. Their achievements were significant. Every major option had well-placed supporters with political influence.

Japanese scientists' greater achievement was to manage the past, a past that was fraught with ambiguities. The Tokugawa government was scarcely dedicated to growth in science, but some functionaries had been interested in it. Tokugawa custom discouraged innovation, even though innovation occasionally took place. The society experienced a rebirth of learning, though none of it led to modern science directly. A mathematical tradition of enormous creativity reached a point of stagnation in the eighteenth century. Medical doctors could carry on freely; most other fields were restricted by government. Tokugawa patterns offered complicated choices, values, and pronounced inclinations to be bent, exploited, or simply set aside if a tradition of research were to arise and flourish.

Consider the formation of the research community, where Western influence was fundamental. The abolition of inherited status in the 1870s made it easier to combine mathematics with a knowledge of physics and was clearly inspired by European precedents. Compulsory schooling allowed more Japanese the choice of careers in the sciences and was also based on European models. Opportunities for Japanese to study in Europe inspired their development of research traditions, stimulated formation of professional roles, encouraged commitment to values and norms, and shaped the establishment of modern research. Role formation was particularly complicated. It showed some clear Western influence: the combination of teaching and academic research to form the role of professor, the norm of publication and rejection of secrecy, and the restrictions imposed on clinical practice by university professors of basic medicine. In other respects it was highly distinctive. Researchers shared membership in professional organizations with colleagues in clinical practice. Ordinary clinicians with the proper connections could carry on research at imperial universities. University professors in all technical fields engaged in consulting or supplementary work.

The scientific community of Meiji Japan was in many respects formed by tendencies inherited from the Tokugawa period. Most early scientists came from the samurai, a small minority (6–7 percent) of total population. Samurai interest in engineering and science developed initially through subtle encouragement from the Tokugawa government and was further stimulated by Western military pressure. But samurai dominance in the Meiji years was particularly due to educational patterns of the Tokugawa period. Samurai were more likely to receive an education than any other members of the Japanese population. Their socialization produced a kind of "need achievement," which drives some men to outdo others. Their attitudes toward schooling were also distinctive. In particular, they had greater endurance of educational hardships, since schooling was the key to reviving family fortunes. The curriculum assisted recruitment to science. Compared to the schooling commoners received, it was philosophical and not closely tied to job performance, and it stressed comprehension of knowledge, not mere mastery of particular specialties.

Tokugawa patterns were helpful in other ways. Most Meiji scientists had fathers with significant connections (at least) to a Tokugawa intellectual—Confucian scholar, *wasan* mathematician, scholar of Dutch studies, or most important, Chinese-style doctor. Meiji scientists came from areas of the country where schools had a long history. The scientists' choices of specialties reflected the past, medicine being most popular. By 1868 medicine in particular was well positioned for an influx of talent because of its substantial earlier development, whereas the physical sciences had ground to make up because of Tokugawa restrictions.

Scholarly conduct was also affected by the Tokugawa legacy. Tending to characterize all technical disciplines in Meiji Japan was an intimacy between mentors and pupils. This included both patronage with respect to employment and also professional nourishment. But the disciplines differed in other ways. The Tokugawa influence was strongest in medicine and, in some respects, botany. Since medical institutions were not deemed a threat to traditional morality, they had operated freely with official approval. Harmful factionalism and entrenched opposition to new ideas had certainly existed in the Tokugawa period, but Tokugawa medicine was more than a chronological precursor to the modern tradition of scientific research. Medical specialists in Tokugawa Japan were already accustomed to open debate and public scrutiny of professional issues. Tokugawa botanists had formed an intellectual society in the Owari region about 1800. Both groups generally publicized their findings. In mathematics, by contrast, the legacy was weak. Tokugawa mathematicians found it difficult to change, so Meiji mathematics was radically reorganized. New kinds of men were recruited to the field, and their role in society was sharply redefined. The physical sciences were institutionally more backward. They were not disciplines at all in the Tokugawa period, having little autonomy, no organizations, a politically high profile, and low self-awareness. There was relatively little factionalism, but neither was there very much open, public criticism. This circumstance substantially accounts for the tardy appearance of such patterns among them.

Institution building, like community formation, showed a sensitive blending of foreign and local influence. Agricultural experiment stations were based on American models. Katō Hiroyuki sold the idea of the comprehensive university almost entirely on the basis of European precedents. Hasegawa Tai, Inoue Kowashi, Toyama Shōichi, and Takayama Jintarō cited institutions in Europe to buttress their proposals. Kitasato constantly invoked the career of Robert Koch as a means of justifying a particular schema for organizing research. Makino Nobuaki, as minister of education, in 1906 used arguments and precedents from European experience to force the creation of a science academy. But particular precedents were also rejected. Government officials and most scientists opposed privatdozenten, the one-chair rule, free migration of students, rapid rotation of university administrators, and second-class housing for engineering and agriculture, despite ceaseless appeals from educators infatuated with practices in Germany and politicians who wished to save money.

Partly this was because Tokugawa institutions were poorly developed, offering no good model to imitate. Scientists and certain educators wanted rapid expansion in research infrastructure, while the politicians and bureaucrats who favored this at all wanted to do it cheaply. The political tug-of-war ensured that there would be neither a one-chair rule nor student migration. General backwardness killed privatdozenten. Few Tokugawa institutions were congenial to modern science. The Bansho Wage Goyō and the Office of Astronomy were supposed to translate documents and restrict their access to government officials, not add to knowledge and publicize it widely. Thus few

Meiji institutions had historical origins in the Tokugawa period. But this does not mean there was *no* continuity. State institutions were prominent in the Meiji period because of their prominence in the Tokugawa period. Such institutions were combined with others to form Tokyo University in 1877, while the Ōsaka Kyūri Jo, Nagasaki Igaku Denshū Jo, Tekitekisaijuku, and Shirandō made important contributions through the early training they offered Meiji scientists.

Institutional continuity was most evident in medicine. Medical academies established by daimyo were the scientific movement's most active leaders in the Tokugawa period, and the later establishment of programs at Tokyo University shows a perceived continuity in this area. Tokyo's modern medical school could use the facilities of its Tokugawa predecessor (the Igakkō), but it was deemed inappropriate for the basic sciences to be housed in the facilities of the Kaisei Gakkō, which was closed down. Continuity was more than just perceived. Medicine's strength enabled Kitasato to mobilize resources for fundamentally new research in a manner and on a scale inconceivable in other disciplines. Agricultural chemist Kozai Yoshinao showed political abilities in a non-medical field, but his institutional accomplishments were considerably less. Medicine was so securely established that its spokesmen could usually prevail in a conflict. Hasegawa Tai managed to cut applied chemistry to the benefit of biochemistry in 1893. He and Kitasato together defeated the Itō cabinet and won public funding for a private medical laboratory. Kyushu University got Ministry of Education support for its faculty of medicine in 1901 despite the cheaper cost and greater need for a faculty of engineering or science at Tōhoku. Kitasato's Institute of Infectious Diseases got brand-new facilities in 1905, when budgets were cut for other scholarly programs because of the war with Russia.

The Tokugawa legacy affected the building of research institutions in its ability to promote competition. Regional competition among daimyo had encouraged school building in the Tokugawa period, while Alternate Attendance diffused innovations. After the Restoration, this legacy affected scientific institutions by constraining attempts to concentrate resources and instead offering precedents for their dispersion nationwide. Providing educational opportunities was attractive politically. Once the commitment was made to build Kyoto University, the door was open to others of its kind. Few regions got them before World War I, but every region wanted an imperial university and could use local subsidies and political maneuvering to make its views felt in the bureaucracy and the Diet. Competition assured momentum. If Tokyo had something, Kyoto had to have it. And if Kyushu were successful, Tōhoku must be, too. It is hardly surprising that Japanese officials in the

Diet and the government strongly supported academic competition. Given a history of daimyo domains that competed in school building for reasons of prestige, they had every reason to build new universities and expand the ones that they had.

The physical sciences, because of their putative links to Catholicism, had been severely restricted and were dependent for support on the government. This is one major reason that so many Meiji physicists were officials' sons. Restoration leadership ended the restrictions, but the pattern of dependence lasted for years. Kyoto University had considerable difficulty starting a program in physical science, and Kyushu University did not have one. The Industrial Experiment Laboratory was poorly supported by government and business. Physicists and chemists in academic life had finally to appeal for outside support because government support was so very inadequate. Such problems derived from the Tokugawa legacy. Vice Minister Makino even cited Tokugawa precedent to explain problems at Kyoto.[1]

Officials' tendency to seek control of successful institutions was well established before 1868 and persisted beyond the Meiji years. Lingering beliefs about state control of scholarship in part lay behind the Ministry of Education's efforts to close Hasegawa Tai's Zaisei Gakusha medical academy, Watanabe Kōki's campaign against Kitasato's laboratory, the 1914 seizure of the same laboratory, the pre-1918 refusal to grant formal equality with the imperial universities to Keio, Waseda, and Dōshisha, and official resentment at these institutions for daring to offer technical programs. The seizure of the Institute of Infectious Diseases is particularly revealing. Here was a scientist of international reputation with epochal achievements in research to his credit. He materially raised the standards of Japan's public health and worked indefatigably on behalf of basic science. Unfortunately his politicking, which was rooted in professional convictions, offended the views of powerful officials and caused his eventual undoing.

Kitasato's fate calls sharply into focus another negative aspect of the Tokugawa legacy, namely, the treatment of scientists by Japanese officials. The Tokugawa state had instituted and the Meiji state continued (after a period of experimentation) strict subordination of technical experts to putative bureaucratic generalists. For this reason Kitasato never held a major official post (his power was de facto, not de jure). But Japan's science management was not so unusual, for Germany, Britain, and France had similar systems. Technical specialists were almost everywhere subordinated to legally trained generalists.[2] Japan's officials were recruited from a broad social base and were competent by the standards of the day.[3] Turning over full authority on pertinent issues exclusively to members of the technical community would have been neither desirable nor politically possible. Agricultural chemist Kozai Yoshinao's advocacy of unproductive spending in animal husbandry shows this too well. The only scientist (Kikuchi Dairoku) who ever had a grip on formal power (as minister of education) could not use it in science's or his country's best interests because of his sometimes archaic and eccentric views.

One might argue that, except for Kitasato, very few scientists had problems with the government. Chemist Nagai Nagayoshi had free access to top officials. So did medical researchers Takagi Kanehiro, Aoyama Tanemichi and even (for about twenty years) Kitasato Shibasaburō; agricultural chemists Sakō Jōmei and Kozai Yoshinao, physicist Yamakawa Kenjirō, mathematician Kikuchi Dairoku, and various other members of the scientific community. Even in the wake of the civil service changes, the Diet offered a channel for certain kinds of access, and consultations with bureaucrats took place regularly. Mori Arinori met with professors in his office at the Ministry of Education, as did his successors and the bureau chiefs under them. Professors were consulted about chairs to be established, and Tokyo University scientists planned the Tōhoku faculty of science.

But there were serious problems with the management of science. Tokugawa traditions, reinforced by German influence, produced an autocratic government slow to sanction autonomy or forthright politicking by scientists and professors. Some technical specialists lost access to the uppermost levels of policy-making men. The most serious problem, however, was the inability of administrators trained exclusively in law to communicate with scientists and technical experts. Physicist Nakamura Yaroku was fired from the Ministry of Agriculture and Commerce because he protested his exclusion from management. Forestry professor and bureau expert Shiga Taizan met with incomprehension from colleagues whose training was only in law. Oka Makoto, chief of the Bureau of Industry, and chemist Takayama Jintarō found it difficult to agree on suitable programs for the Industrial Experiment Laboratory. The physicist Yamakawa Kenjirō rightly attacked the legally trained officials of the Ministry of Finance for their egregious ignorance of science.

Ignorance of science became pervasive in the uppermost strata of the Japanese government. In the early years of the Meiji period, technical experts supervised technical programs. But with civil service reform in the late 1880s—and probably complacency in later years—this flexibility of management gradually disappeared. The Ministry of Agriculture and Commerce and the Ministry of Finance were the worst, but the patterns that made them bad were widespread. It is particularly striking that the Ministry of Home Affairs and the Ministry of Education, which had been more open to the technical community, eventually went the way of the rest of the government, putting "lawyers" in charge of the management of science.

Dominance by "lawyers" with no technical knowledge was a major cause of wrong decisions. The Ministry of Finance rejected the electrical engineers' plan to standardize frequencies of electrical power transmission. Legally trained chiefs of the Bureau of Agriculture cut already modest funding for sericulture research, ignored warnings about foreign research on synthetic fibers, squandered large sums on animal husbandry programs, and wasted scarce talent at the downtown bureau headquarters, which they should have deployed at the (suburban) Nishigahara station. Even medical research was finally disrupted (by the Ministry of Education) when the lawyer-administrator Ichiki Kitokurō managed to seize the Institute of Infectious Diseases. Participation by technical men at the bureau chief level produced better results. Metallurgist Watanabe Wataru, as chief of the Bureau of Mines, helped establish the Industrial Experiment Laboratory, and agricultural chemist Sakō Jōmei, agriculture bureau chief, assigned more technical experts to research functions at the Nishigahara station and fewer to administrative tasks.

Japan's management of science could certainly have been better. Some requirement of probationary service for administrators could have been imposed. Mathematics and science could have been incorporated into the training for higher civil servants; instead their place was diminished. University matriculants for law and humanities did not study mathematics or science after age seventeen, and the classroom time given these subjects was cut in 1900.[4] The government could have followed the practice of some private businesses, which appointed engineers to senior management posts to maximize the effects of scarce technical talent.[5] Failure to do this was particularly ironic in view of the policies of the early Meiji years, when technical men held such posts in areas of the government where their knowledge was needed!

Naturally the system encountered opposition. Educator Fukuzawa Yukichi in 1898 called public attention to officialdom's ignorance of science. Scientists made much the same point.[6] In Germany a group of engineers began to protest their exclusion from management in 1910.[7] In Japan Yamakawa Kenjirō in 1911 attacked the arrogant practices of the Ministry of Finance. Officials like Mori Arinori and Kubota Yuzuru, who made life difficult for scientists, met vigorous opposition from the scientific community. Some technical men abandoned government service, though others shared discontents only with friends.[8]

World War I focused attention on the scientific community. Members were charged with neglecting research, now seen as vital to the national interest. The standard allegation was that the legacy of Tokugawa feudalism had led university professors to compromise research through their neglect of norms of criticism and discussion, their tendency toward favoritism in academic appointments, and their refusal to recognize the public nature of science. Actual behavior in the scientific community was both more subtle and more faithful to the spirit and essence of the researcher role. Japanese scientists could be, and generally were, faithful to the imperatives of scientific criticism even as they tried to be loyal to mentors. Their recruitment procedures in academic life were by no means indifferent to merit. And there was recognition of science's public nature.

Two particular aspects of the Tokugawa legacy were favorable to science at this level. Market demand, as in medicine, had aroused an interest in new techniques and ideas, while the pyramidal structure of the government and society had stimulated competitive pressures. These forces operated freely once feudalism ended, and one obvious result in the scientific community was the emergence of factions. The real issue is how one should see them. If, as alleged, the factions repressed free discussion, made criticism impossible, hoarded all resources, and were totally self-centered, the scientific enterprise in its modern Western form could scarcely have existed in Japanese society at all.

This portrait, however, is largely factitious. For one thing, the system rewarded "merit," though sometimes in frozen forms. One could not obtain a professorship by accident of birth. Strong performance in publications and degrees was essential to success. Family ties, usually of the father-in-law–son-in-law variety, could assist one's appointment, but not if one were without "merit." Such familial ties would not be established if "merit" were absent in the first place. Achievement was a condition of ascription, not ascription a condition of achievement.

Nor were most scientists intolerant of dissent. The typical scientist of the Meiji period showed active concern for younger men under him, striving to elicit their enthusiasm for research by deliberate strategies— storytelling, discussion, eating, and drinking. In these settings, at least, reserve was cast aside and an atmosphere of openness generally maintained.

The impact of factionalism on cooperation and sharing is a more difficult issue. There is little doubt but that Japanese society was prone to factionalism, or that such factions could duplicate effort, waste resources, and generate emotional strife.[9] But to say only this gives an unbalanced view. The extreme self-centeredness that factions could display was not endemic or inherent in the culture; it could be traced to cyclical patterns in the academic market for employment. Factions stimulated intense competition, and competition is essential to development in science. One historian of medicine has argued that the rivalry between the faculty of medicine at Tokyo University and Kitasato's Institute of Infectious Diseases had a beneficial impact on Japanese medicine. "Competition between institute and university contributed greatly to bacteriology in Japan and helped raise its work to international standards."[10] This outcome did not result simply from Tokugawa practices, but their longer term legacy encouraged it.

World War I solved a number of problems that scientists had long had to face. Major new research facilities were built and some old ones improved. The number of positions for scientists increased, though not always in line with supply. Several fields of study that were new to Japan—genetics, aeronautics, some areas of applied chemistry—won greater recognition and financial support. Private business began to fund research directly. A new imperial university was built in Hokkaido. The Ministry of Education's Science Research Grants Program made its appearance in 1918 and the National Research Council in 1920.

Improvements in the treatment of at least some of the scientists also came with the war. Physicists and chemists in academic life could now function politically on something like the level that had historically been possible for their colleagues in medicine. They could play off one agency against another, appeal for support to nongovernmental sources, and hope to contain well-entrenched opposition when the stakes were sufficiently high. These new abilities help explain some important foundations: the Research Institute for Physics and Chemistry, the Institute for Aeronautics, and the Institute for Metals at Tōhoku University.

Wartime conditions had less impact on other important problems. Patent laws were improved, but not as much as they needed to be. Aspiring inventors in the corporate sector were still not protected enough. The patent office staff had inadequate funding, and the laws were too lax. Moreover, some elements of the business community were not wholly willing to change. Exploitation of foreign technology seemed more attractive than research to some, and the suspicion still lingered that patterns of dependence could be reinstated once the war was over. The war had a negative impact in medicine. By stimulating the idea of research independence, it led the Ōkuma cabinet astray. Kitasato's institute was seized by his enemies, and problems quickly followed. Serum and vaccine quality fell along with the income they generated. There was a rise in the death rate from contagious diseases that should have been avoidable. Medicine's most effective champion of basic research was removed from a post of great influence, and the cause of medical research became more politicized and divided than ever. Some of this was due to widespread perceptions of Tokyo University. While officials praised it highly, others attacked it as a bastion of sloth and complacency. Some of the criticism was unfair, but it had its effects nonetheless. Mandatory retirement for university professors at the age of sixty was instituted in 1920 and persists to this day. University funding, especially for Tokyo, did not rise with need, and the university's erstwhile patron, the Ministry of Education, lost much of its political capital. Unfortunately, a ministerial staff (in Agriculture and Commerce) with even less talent and a narrower perspective assumed a more prominent role.

Another result of World War I was to force Japanese scientists to evaluate themselves and their contributions to science. There was the question, for one thing, of overseas study and the directions it should take in the future. By siding with the Allies over the IRC, Japan opened itself up to retaliation from Germany, and even though responses from Germany were muted, scientists and officials in Tokyo worried. As early as January 1920 the Ministry of Education was rethinking foreign study. Trips for "observation" were going to become rare: "study" was to be the principal objective. The ministry might subsidize study in Japan at places other than one's home institution.[11] In midsummer 1920 it was announced that at least some *ryūgaku* students in medicine would spend time in Britain and the U.S. as well as in Germany,[12] and in late September *Ikai jihō* declared that the ministry had made a confidential decision to "abandon the earlier bias toward Germany." The government's view of world trends in science would probably lead to an Anglo-American bias.[13] Whatever the truth of the reports, the *ryūgaku* program definitely changed. The country's leading physicist, Nagaoka Hantarō, who had himself studied in Austria and Germany, began sending physics students to Britain, the U.S., and Denmark.[14] The 130 foreign students dispatched by the ministry in 1921 were reportedly bound for many different countries.[15]

Another basic issue had to do with self-image. Kitasato Shibasaburō, as confident as ever, proposed that Japan try to bring Germans there,[16] and some Japanese scientists shared his views. One took umbrage at the suggestion of some Czech scientists that Japanese abandon Germany in favor of Prague as an appropriate place for overseas study. This implied that Japanese scientists could do no good work without traveling abroad! And why, after all, pay special court to Germany? "Is there something unusual about our situation?"[17] Sakurai Jōji thought that there was. According to him, Japanese scientists had not accomplished much. They duplicated work, hoarded information, and wasted time and resources.[18]

Sakurai was biased and essentially wrong. Kitasato's work on tetanus, which led to the discovery of natural immunity, was a major advance in medicine. Takamine Jōkichi's discovery of adrenalin was an important step in hormone research even though the discoverer misperceived its implications. Of course, Sakurai could discount these projects: the work was done abroad, the first was collaborative (with Emil von Behring), and the second was not elaborated fully. But other research, done on Japanese soil, was also worthy of mention. Shiga Kiyoshi in 1897 discovered the dysentery bacillus that bears his name. Nagaoka Hantarō developed a useful—if ultimately imperfect—model of the atomic nucleus. Sakurai himself developed a new technique for determining the boiling points of substances in solution. Most important, Yamagiwa Katsusaburō showed that tumors could be produced in laboratory animals by applying coal tar to their skins.

Nor was it accurate to charge Japanese scientists with duplicating work and hoarding resources. There was some failure to share information among researchers seeking the cause of tsutsugamushi disease, and in that area efforts were duplicated. Cooperation and sharing seem to have declined in medicine after 1900 because of the tougher academic job market, but several other facts must be taken into account. As in the case of tsutsugamushi research, investigators read each other's work and enjoyed full access to published information,[19] and scientists in a competitive situation are never prone to divulge unpublished material to competitors who might try to "scoop" them for credit.[20]

Sakurai's judgment also ignored the development of scientific societies. These societies discussed major issues and shared information across institutional boundaries. Their membership lists included people from many subspecialties, for example, agricultural chemistry, pharmacological chemistry, and so-called basic chemistry, in the case of the Tokyo Chemical Society. Not all their members were professional academics.[21] Most societies were concentrated in Tokyo, and in that sense their value was localized, but scientists outside the capital city (as in Sendai, the home of Tōhoku University) formed their own local groups before World War I as a way to gain access to new information.

Sakurai was correct in stating that Japanese science faced difficulties. The physical sciences were not well funded before 1914 or even 1920. Manpower, resources, and action were in medicine; other fields got what was left. His emphasis on the country's isolation was well placed. Japan was geographically removed from other centers of science, and this clearly caused problems. Makino Nobuaki noted in 1897 that Japanese scientists who had returned from Europe often fell behind in research because they lacked adequate opportunities for technical discussion. Sakurai in 1919 justified creation of the National Research Council by noting that Japan was "stuck off in one corner of the Orient" and said this had "caused . . . inconvenience for scientific research." A Tokyo professor of physical chemistry, Mizushima San'i-chirō, later wrote that European scientists of Sakurai's era could easily get in touch with colleagues abroad, but that scientists in Japan were handicapped. Travel cost money and time, and chances for discussions with foreign colleagues were rare. Access to foreign journals was absolutely crucial, but delivery of the journals left much to be desired. They were usually well behind the forefront of research by the time they arrived, sometimes by as much as two or three years.[22]

Japan's isolation was both cultural and geographic. Since few if any foreigners—and essentially no scientists—spoke or read Japanese, one had always to consider how best to communicate. Foreign study gave scientists a mastery of languages as well as of technical specialties, but language facility did not solve all problems. To create and maintain a community at home, one had to share findings with colleagues. Most scientific publications and papers by Japanese authors (including papers at meetings) were written or delivered in Japanese, not in German, English, or French.[23] Between the world wars the problem of language attracted more attention from scientists. Sakurai and others spoke and wrote of it often. The National Research Council undertook to address it.[24] No solution was found then, nor has one been found since,[25] underscoring the conviction that the greatest single problem confronting Japanese scientists was their continuing isolation from the world science community.

In view of the difficulties, the scientists of Japan did quite well. Medicine, in particular, was remarkably strong. In 1919 Kyoto University microbiologist Matsushita Teiji wrote, "Japanese medicine at present is not inferior to that of the West and can certainly stand comparison with American medicine."[26] Another observer wrote at this time: "Japanese science is already distinguished. It is not yet on the highest [world] level, but is relatively good and [now] more independent. It continues to require some outside assistance and must diligently collect information abroad."[27] In this respect we can hardly say that Japanese science stands alone.

EPILOGUE

Decades have passed since Japanese science faced up to the challenges of World War I. Years of forward movement have alternated with periods of stagnation or destruction, but in general progress has been striking. Japan's research expenditures as a percentage of GNP now match or exceed those of other major countries. Japanese scientists regularly publish in every major field and are increasingly seen as leading in some.[1] Advanced communications and sophisticated technology have partially reduced isolation in science. Even the elusive Nobel Prize is more frequently awarded to Japanese researchers.[2] Nevertheless, an impression that something is seriously wrong remains. Questions continue to be raised about the fundamental character of the research enterprise, whether basic research is not neglected in favor of a stress on applied research, or whether too much work is done by firms and too little work in Japan's universities. There is still the same tension between the needs of the group and the wishes of individuals that existed in the period discussed in this book and the same fixation with international standards of research creativity and whether, if at all, Japan's system can meet them. One sometimes has the feeling that nothing has changed!

Such perceptions may reflect a limited sense of the past. In the wake of major gains during World War I, expectations rose in the 1920s but were quickly reined in by financial realities. Commitments to the Research Institute for Physics and Chemistry were not in every case honored, and the laboratory was slow in opening.[3] Some private firms built laboratories of their own. Keio and Waseda universities established graduate programs in medicine and engineering. The National Research Council sponsored large group projects in tropical medicine, geophysics, and several other fields. But the first ten years after the war were not very promising in the imperial universities, where only in biology was there much growth.[4] The 1930s were better, as science became the object of several new initiatives. New imperial universities were built at Osaka (1930) and Nagoya (1939), while a faculty of science was added at Kyushu (also in 1939). Major changes were not confined to the campus—the Japan Society for the Advancement of Science (Nihon Gakujutsu Shinkō Kai, or Gakushin) made its appearance in 1932. Though a product of the Depression and Japan's seizure of Manchuria, the enthusiasm for it and the funding it attracted showed several kinds of interests at work.

276

Gakushin began with a report on the state of Japan's research facilities submitted to the cabinet in March 1930. The report documented the relative stagnation of scientific infrastructure and research funding typical of the 1920s and insisted on the need to reverse this direction. Prime Minister Wakatsuki Reijirō favored retrenchment in science because of his background in law and finance and the difficulties of managing a depressed economy. But the vigorous commitment to Manchurian development, his departure from office, and voices critical of academic science eventually produced a more favorable response. The military establishment in Manchuria wanted to promote certain large-scale projects in technical research, and a number of professors had come to the view that universities lacked a strong research environment. The Japan Society for the Advancement of Science addressed these concerns by promoting team research for a number of projects, particularly relating to armaments and energy.[5]

World War II gave the research establishment more opportunities, but a lack of foreign assistance and substantial isolation made pressures much greater and constraints more severe. Two scientific organizations were particularly important in enabling Japan to prosecute the war. The National Research Council was responsible for organizing and coordinating war-related research,[6] and the Research Institute for Physics and Chemistry took on special projects not envisioned by its founders. This case is particularly instructive. The institute could not function solely as a research enterprise because of the lack of funding. By the late 1920s it had already been obliged to develop and sell patented technology and in some cases to manufacture products growing out of its research. In this it had some success, and by 1939 it was a business conglomerate.[7] In such a situation its fate was predictable. Research projects became heavily oriented toward work with expected military applications. Its factories produced such strategic items as piston rings for military aircraft.[8] A basic science program, as in nuclear physics under Nishina Yoshio was, however, retained.

Military defeat in 1945 led to Occupation reforms in the research establishment. The National Research Council was disbanded. The Research Institute for Physics and Chemistry was legally dismembered. An organization called the Science Council of Japan was created in the place of the Imperial Academy. A component of the Occupation called the Economic and Scientific Section, Scientific and Technical Division, was the principal agency in charge. In this context an American physicist named H. C. Kelly played a role far too large for his age (he was born in 1908) or experience (war-related research at MIT).[9]

Some look on Kelly's approach to reform in science as a reflection of New Deal philosophy. He believed, for example, in radical change, without much regard for existing institutions. When Japanese members of a science advisory group—whose formation was partly instigated by Kelly—urged caution in abolishing the Imperial Academy, the American scientist insisted, telling the group they were "going to make history." Kelly also wanted scientists to solve society's problems. In one revealing exchange with the academy's president, Nagaoka Hantarō, he attacked the "individualistic attitude" of basic science researchers and insisted that members of the scientific community consider their responsibilities to all mankind. Another fact that was equally important in the longer run was that Kelly was a proponent of applied research. He wanted the Occupation to "encourage only those research programs which are directed toward improvement of Japan's economy" and went so far as to call basic research a luxury in the light of existing conditions.[10]

Not all scientists agreed with Kelly's outlook, but a good number did, and some were very radical. One scientist named Watanabe Satoshi is known to have influenced Kelly's thinking with his bitter attacks on the Ministry of Education, Tokyo University, and other pillars of the science establishment.[11] In 1946 the Japan Communist Party, with the open support of a number of scientists, published a famous thesis criticizing "feudal remnants" in science.[12] In 1947 the influential physicist Fujioka Yoshio launched a broadside against the prominence of factions in academic life and was publicly applauded by another well known physicist (Sakata Shōichi).[13] The earlier pattern of militarism and the wartime experience, to say nothing of the American Occupation, had radicalized elements of the scientific community and helped to create a self-critical environment.

These same general trends helped intensify a split between academic scientists, the government, and business. Many scientists, embarrassed by their former acquiescence in militarism, supported the leftist League of Democratic Scientists (Minshūshugi Kagakusha Kyōkai, created in 1946), while control of the government remained largely in the hands of conservative politicians sympathetic to business.[14] This pattern of estrangement affected research. Following President Dwight Eisenhower's "Atoms for Peace" address to the United Nations General Assembly in December 1953, business and political circles in Japan became captivated by the notion that atomic power offered *the* solution to Japan's energy problems and decided to import nuclear reactors from Britain. Prominent members of the scientific community—Fujioka Yoshio, Sakata Shōichi, and especially the 1949 Nobel laureate in physics, Yukawa Hideki—cautioned against this excessive optimism and reminded all concerned of the pitfalls. They emphasized that atomic energy was not at that time a proven technology and that to import it successfully would require more research, a point widely accepted in Europe even among groups planning the sale. But political and business leaders had their own point of view. They rejected further research, saying the technology was safe and dismissing the scientists' views as self-interested and alarmist. The results were an inefficient industry and power plant breakdowns through the 1970s.[15]

Apart from the difference in political perspective between scientists, politicians, and the business community, three other factors contributed to this unhappy state. One was the traditional belief in Japan that the most important innovations and technical advances nearly always originated in some other country. There was a "deeply engrained Japanese belief that what had been 'proven' abroad should be imported [directly] rather than developed domestically." Another factor was the basic inability of government officials to understand the limits of reactor technology. "After all, most of them had majored in law in college, not in engineering or physics." The period in which nuclear reactors were imported corresponded to a time of rapid economic growth. "The period of 'massive' importation of power reactors started with the government of Ikeda Hayato (prime minister 1961–64) and continued through the government of Satō Eisaku (prime minister 1964–69) who largely maintained the same [high-growth] policy."[16]

During the past twenty-five years there has been more recognition of basic research, as well as an emphasis on large-scale projects, many (but not all) energy-related. October 1965, when Tomonaga Shin'ichirō won the Nobel Prize in physics, marked one turning point.[17] But the principal event shaping research priorities was the October oil-price hike of 1973. Following the quadrupling of oil prices by the Organization of Petroleum Exporting Countries, Japan responded by dramatically expanding its research budget, in some areas by as much as 400 percent.[18] This expansion showed a feature of the Japanese system strikingly different from the West. While half the research done in Europe and America is funded by government (especially for military projects, in the case of the U.S.), an equal percentage of Japanese research is conducted by firms for private-sector use. Only 8 percent or so is based in universities, with military research getting far less (0.7 percent).[19]

Most recently there has been controversy among scientists in Japan centering less on the structure of research priorities and more on the mechanisms for funding research. Tonegawa Susumu, an MIT biologist and 1987 Nobel laureate in medicine who is also a Japanese citizen, has argued that he might not have been able to carry out his prize-winning research on antibody production had he remained in Japan after 1963. (Most of his work was done in Switzerland.) The reason, he suggests, is that young Japanese scientists in the postwar period have often had difficulty finding money for research because government agencies and academic institutions have usually awarded lump sums to senior scientists, who direct them to favorites. This has too often meant that relatively few resources reach the bottom level of the research community, at least in Japan's universities.[20] In fact, three prominent features of the research funding system could conceivably have caused problems for a talented young scientist: (1) the system tended to allocate funds to particular specialties according to the specialty's prior funding level; (2) a disproportionate amount of research funds went to the more prominent or famous scientists; and (3) there was at times a tendency among principal investigators heading large research teams—particularly in medicine—to allocate funds equally among team members without much regard for differing needs.[21]

But to say this much and look no further gives a distorted perspective. The government (in this case, the Ministry of Education) did stress prior funding levels more than the content of actual proposals, but this was mostly in the period from 1949 to 1966. This priority was set up following extensive consultations with the Japan Society for the Advancement of Science, operated at the highest levels of classification—engineering, say, as compared to basic science—and had relatively little influence on individual grants. Revisions of the basic algorithm for calculating science funding (the "Fujioka Formula") in 1967 and 1981 seem to have decreased the importance of the prior funding record. Charges of preferential funding for the prominent and famous can also be qualified. Such a pattern was more common during the first two decades after the war, when money for research was particularly scarce and peer review panelists were often concerned for young, vulnerable protégés of established researchers. The gradual establishment of two-phase reviewing has allowed some adjustments in the system. With second-phase reviewers representing fields ancillary to the applicant's, funding requests from unpatronized younger scientists have come to enjoy greater success.[22] With Japanese science in a period of youth, greater success will characterize its future, too.

NOTES

Chapter One: The Social Formation of Japanese Science

1. Tamura Masao, ed., *Nihon igaku hyaku nen shi* (Tokyo: Rinshō Igaku Sha, 1957), p. 4.

2. Tetsu Hiroshige, "Social Conditions for the Researches of Nuclear Physics in Pre-War Japan," *Japanese Studies in the History of Science* 2 (1963):84.

3. Ōtsuki Shōichirō, Nojima Tokukichi, and Maki Jirō, "Nihon ni okeru kagaku, gijutsu to kagakusha," in Sakata Shōichi, ed., *Kagaku gijutsu to gendai,* Iwanami kōza, vol. 2 (Tokyo: Iwanami Shoten, 1963):310.

4. Sakata Shōichi, "Kenkyū to soshiki," *Shizen* (September 1947), pp. 10–13.

5. Ōtsuki, Nojima, and Maki (n. 3 above), pp. 292, 287–88.

6. The chemist Sakurai Jōji wrote in his memoirs that scientists were unable to influence government policies, "even when we joined all our forces together." See Sakurai Jōji, *Omoide no kazukazu* (Tokyo: Herald Sha, 1940), p. 113.

7. Yuasa Mitsutomo, *Kagaku shi* (Tokyo: Tōyō Keizai Shimpō Sha, 1961), pp. 228, 282.

8. Sakata (n. 4 above), p. 10.

9. See, for example, Sylvan E. Moolton, "Nihon ni okeru igaku kyōiku kaizen an," *Nihon iji shimpō*, no. 1191 (21 July 1946):3–10; and W. H. Leonard and Harry C. Kelly, "Scientific Research and Technical Competence in Relation to Resource Utilization," in Supreme Commander for the Allied Powers (SCAP), ed., *Japanese Natural Resources* (Tokyo: GHQ, SCAP, 1948).

10. Robert Jastrow, "Science and the American Dream," *Science Digest* 91/3 (March 1983):48.

11. Quoted in "Electronics Research: A Quest for Global Leadership," *Business Week* (December 14, 1981), p. 29.

12. Frederic Golden, "Science: Closing the Gap with the West," *Time* 122/5 (August 1, 1983):56. Reported by Thomas Levenson.

13. Toshio Yukuta et al., "Science Discovery in Japan: Dawn of a New Era," *Science 85* 6/6 (July/August 1985), special advertising section, last page of unpaginated text. This report, prepared by the Stanford Research Institute, is one of the most informative discussions in English of the history and current status of Japanese science.

14. Esaki (Esaki Reona, in Japanese) in 1973 shared the Nobel Prize for Physics (with Brian Josephson) for work on the tunnel diode.

15. Leo Esaki and Hajime Karatsu, "Shortcomings in Japan's R & D Approach," *Japan Echo* 10 (Special Issue) (1983):28.

16. Leo Esaki, "American Individualism vs. Japanese Groupism," *IHJ [International House of Japan] Bulletin* 2/3 (Summer 1982):3.

17. Charles Otis Whitman, *Zoology in the University of Tokio* (Yokohama: Japan Gazette, 1881), pp. 3–4. Whitman taught zoology at Tokyo University in the late 1870s.

18. Sata Yoshihiko, "Byōri kyōshitsu no sōritsu jidai: Miura-sensei no moto ni manabishi koro," in Nagayo Matarō, ed., *Tōkyō Teikoku Daigaku Byōrigaku Kyōshitsu gojū nen shi*, 2 (Tokyo: Tōkyō Teikoku Daigaku Igaku Bu, Byōrigaku Kyōshitsu Gojū Shūnen Kinen Kai, 1939), pp. 22–23.

19. See, for example: "Ibatsu to wa nan da?" *Kōshū iji* 2/3 (1898):154–57; Takebayashi Kō (pseudonym), "Ibatsu to wa nan da to wa nan da?" *Ikai jihō* (hereafter **IJ**), no. 220 (August 20, 1898):574; "Kitasato Shibasaburō hyōron," *Taiyō* 6/3 (March 1902):26–28, (apparently written by Nakahama Tōichirō).

20. Dai Nihon Bummei Kyōkai, ed., *Nihon no kagaku kai* (Tokyo: Dai Nihon Bummei Kyōkai, 1917), p. 18. This publication was partly compiled by Ōkuma Shigenobu, prime minister in 1914–16.

21. See, for instance: Gotō Takeshi, "Urusaki hitobito," pt. 2, *IJ*, no. 1738 (November 26, 1928):2291–92; Morito Tatsuo, *Kagaku kenkyū jo ron* (Tokyo: Kurita Shobō, 1939); and Sakurai (n. 6 above), p. 62. Morito served for a time as minister of education during the late 1940s.

22. There are many examples of this view: Erich Fromm, *Escape from Freedom* (New York: Avon Books, 1965), pp. 57–58; Joseph Needham, *The Grand Titration: Science and Society in East and West* (Toronto: University of Toronto Press, 1969), p. 40; and Thorstein Veblen, "The Opportunity of Japan," in *Essays in Our Changing Order* (New York: Viking, 1934), pp. 248–66.

23. Charles C. Gillispie, "The *Encyclopédie* and the Jacobin Philosophy of Science," in Marshall M. Clagett, ed., *Critical Problems in the History of Science* (Madison: University of Wisconsin Press, 1969), p. 269.

24. Joseph Ben-David, "The Scientific Role: The Conditions of Its Establishment in Europe," *Minerva* 4/1 (Autumn 1965):15–54; idem, "Scientific Growth: A Sociological View," *Minerva* 2/4 (Summer 1964):455–76; Jacques Barzun, *The House of Intellect* (New York: Harper & Brothers, 1959), p. 10; and Gertrude Lenzer, ed., *Auguste Comte and Positivism: The Essential Writings* (New York: Harper Torchbooks, 1970), p. 451.

25. The precise form of these questions was suggested to me by Arthur L. Stinchcombe's review of a book by Robert E. Cole. For the text of the review, see *The American Journal of Sociology* 86/5 (1981):1155–58.

26. Rupert Hall represents the older view of the history of science. See his book, *The Scientific Revolution, 1500–1800: The Formation of the Modern Scientific Attitude*, 2d ed. (Boston: Beacon Press, 1964), pp. 145–59. Robin Horton's work exemplifies the newer perspective. See "African Traditional Thought and Western Science," in Bryan R. Wilson, ed., *Rationality* (New York: Harper & Row, 1970), pp. 131–71; and idem, "Lévy-Bruhl, Durkheim and the Scientific Revolution," in Robin Horton and Ruth Finnegan, eds., *Modes of Thought: Essays on Thinking in Western and Non-Western Societies* (London: Faber & Faber, 1973), pp. 249–305. So far as Japan is concerned, my

own perspective is close to that of Nakayama Shigeru, who believes that the emphasis in Meiji Japan on institution building is a model for historians of the period. For an explanation in English, see his essay, "A History of Universities: An Overview," in Shigeru Nakayama, David L. Swain, and Eri Yagi, eds., *Science and Society in Modern Japan: Selected Historical Sources* (Cambridge: MIT Press, 1974), pp. 72–80.

27. Albert M. Craig, "Science and Confucianism in Tokugawa Japan," in Marius B. Jansen, ed., *Changing Japanese Attitudes toward Modernization* (Princeton: Princeton University Press, 1967), pp. 149–50. See also Tetsuo Najita, "Intellectual Change in Early Eighteenth-Century Tokugawa Confucianism," *Journal of Asian Studies* 34/4 (August 1975):931–44.

28. Craig (pp. 149–50) has made this point. So has the Japanese physicist Kuwaki Ayao. See his essay, "Physical Sciences in Japan," in [Japan's] National Research Council, ed., *Scientific Japan: Past and Present* (Kyoto: Maruzen, 1926), esp. p. 250.

29. See Ōtsuki, Nojima, and Maki (n. 3 above), p. 283. Many Japanese writers claim that Japanese culture and society have refused to adopt a Western-style rationality. Representatives of this view are Yukawa Hideki, Nobel laureate in physics (1949), and the historical linguist Nakamura Hajime. See Yukawa's essay, "Modern Trend of Western Civilization and Cultural Peculiarities in Japan," in Charles A. Moore, ed., *The Japanese Mind* (Honolulu: East-West Center, 1967), pp. 54–55. For Nakamura's views, see *The Ways of Thinking of Eastern Peoples,* trans. Philip P. Wiener (Honolulu: East-West Center, 1964), pp. 531–76. Other observers, however, would say that this is nothing more than a conspicuous example of *Nihonjinron.* On this subject, see Peter Dale, *The Myth of Japanese Uniqueness* (New York: St. Martin's Press, 1986).

30. Yuasa (n. 7 above), p. 282.

31. See Shigeru Nakayama, *Academic and Scientific Traditions in China, Japan, and the West,* trans. Jerry Dusenbury (Tokyo: University of Tokyo Press, 1984), pp. 203, 210–12, 220.

32. Shigeru Nakayama, "Science and Technology in Modern Japanese Development," in William Beranek and Gustav Ranis, eds., *Science, Technology and Economic Growth* (New York: Praeger, 1978), p. 203.

33. Nakayama (n. 31 above), pp. 210–11.

34. Yoshida Mitsukuni, "Meiji no kagakushatachi," *Jimbun gakuhō* 24 (March 1967):230. Similarly, Nakayama wrote: "In giving priority to the construction of an institutional system within which to transplant Western paradigms, Meiji Japan paid more attention to the configuration and format of learning than to its content. Scholars troubled themselves little over how new scholarly paradigms were being born" (Nakayama, pp. 210–11).

35. Shigeru Nakayama, "Japanese Scientific Thought," in Charles C. Gillispie, ed., *Dictionary of Scientific Biography* 15, suppl. 1 (New York: Charles Scribner's Sons, 1978), pp. 737, 741–42.

36. Fukuchi Shigetaka, *Shizoku to samurai ishiki* (Tokyo: Shunjūsha, 1956), p. 249.

37. Nakayama (n. 31 above), p. 208.

38. Nakayama (n. 35 above), p. 728.

39. Kamata Eikichi, president of Keio University in the early part of this century, wrote a remarkable essay on factions in Japanese academic life in which he argued that they have certain positive features—promotion of competition and stimulation of individual effort, in particular. The anthropologist Ishino Iwao has expressed a similar view about factions in Japanese society generally. See Kamata Eikichi, "Gakubatsu ōi ni kangei subeshi," in *Kamata Eikichi zenshū,* 2 (Tokyo: Kamata Eikichi-Sensei Denki Oyobi Zenshū Kankō Kai, 1934):507; and Iwao Ishino, "The Oyabun-Kobun: A Japanese Kinship Institution," *American Anthropologist* 55/1 (1953):705.

40. One commentator described the award to Fibiger as a "goof by the [Nobel] committee," noting that he drew incorrect conclusions from the research that he did on cancer. By contrast, a 1930 obituary essay in *The Lancet,* Britain's leading medical journal, stated that it was "impossible to over-estimate the importance of Yamagiwa's discovery for the study of cancer." See David Wallechinsky and Irving Wallace, eds., *The People's Almanac* (Garden City, N.Y.: Doubleday & Company, 1975), p. 1118, and W. Cramer, "The Late Professor Yamagiwa," *The Lancet* 218 (May 24, 1930):1155.

41. Sakata did his work at the Research Institute for Physics and Chemistry in Tokyo and in the physics department of the University of Nagoya. Esaki did his work at Sony Laboratories in Tokyo.

42. See Joseph Ben-David, *The Scientist's Role in Society* (Englewood Cliffs, N.J.: Prentice-Hall, 1971), p. 21. Nakayama has implicitly argued that a similar bias exists in Thomas Kuhn's approach to the history of science. For Kuhn's view, see Thomas S. Kuhn, *The Structure of Scientific Revolutions* (Chicago: University of Chicago Press, 1962), and for Nakayama's view, "A History of Universities" (n. 26 above), pp. 73–74.

43. In the late 1920s, Nishina Yoshio returned from Niels Bohr's laboratory in Copenhagen and began work in particle physics, which became a distinguished tradition in Japan. For details see Laurie M. Brown, M. Konuma, and Z. Maki, *Particle Physics in Japan, 1930–1950,* 3 vols. (Kyoto: Research Institute for Fundamental Physics of Kyoto University, 1980).

Chapter Two: Science and Society in the Tokugawa Period

1. Shigeru Nakayama (ch. 1, n. 35), "Japanese Scientific Thought," p. 755. See also p. 734: "The Japanese did not believe prior to the twentieth century, that they could contribute to universal systems of knowledge."

2. Kanamaru Yoshio has made the point that the generation of Katō Hiroyuki, a leading Meiji educator, was virtually the first in Japan to "decide on their career specialty according to what they themselves liked." Before this one simply inherited the family occupation. See his article, "Meiji ki ni okeru seiyō kagaku no yunyū ni tsuite, shizoku no hatashita yakuwari o chūshin to shite no shiten settei no tame ni," *Komazawa Shakaigaku Kenkyū,* no. 4 (1972):58.

3. See Nakayama (n. 1 above), pp. 746–47 on the question of professions in the Tokugawa period.

4. Ronald P. Dore, *Education in Tokugawa Japan* (Berkeley and Los Angeles: University of California Press, 1965), pp. 14–15.

5. Donald Keene, *The Japanese Discovery of Europe, 1720–1830*, rev. ed. (Stanford: Stanford University Press, 1969), p. 79.

6. John Whitney Hall, "The Confucian Teacher in Tokugawa Japan," in David S. Nivison and Arthur R. Wright, eds., *Confucianism in Action* (Stanford: Stanford University Press, 1959), p. 287.

7. Maruyama Masao, "Fukuzawa Yukichi no jukyō hihan," in Tōkyō Teikoku Daigaku, ed., *Tōkyō Teikoku Daigaku gakujutsu taikan: Hōgakubu keizai gakubu* (Tokyo: Tōkyō Teikoku Daigaku, 1942), p. 415.

8. On salaries, see Hall (n. 6 above), pp. 277–79.

9. Dore (n. 4 above), p. 115. There was naturally some variation.

10. Shigeru Nakayama, *A History of Japanese Astronomy* (Cambridge: Harvard University Press, 1969), p. 155.

11. Yamasaki Masatada, *Higo iiku shi* (Kumamoto: Chinzei Ikai Jihō Sha, 1929), p. 261. Yamasaki does not say that any physician actually received 5,000 koku, only that it was possible.

12. Cited in Nagai Tamotsu, *Takagi Kanehiro den* (Tokyo: Tōkyō Jikei Kai Ika Daigaku Sōritsu Hachijūgo Nen Kinen Jigyō Iinkai, 1967), p. 54.

13. Nakayama (n. 10 above), p. 155.

14. Dore (n. 4 above), pp. 117–18.

15. Robert N. Bellah, "Intellectual and Society in Japan," paper prepared for the Van Leer Conference on Tradition and Change (Jerusalem, March 1971), pp. 9, 11.

16. Nagai (n. 12 above), p. 38.

17. Grant K. Goodman, *The Dutch Impact on Japan* (Leiden: E.J. Brill, 1967), pp. 109, 99.

18. Dore (n. 4 above), pp. 119–20.

19. Tadashi Yoshida, *The Rangaku of Shizuki Tadao: The Introduction of Western Science in Tokugawa Japan* (Ann Arbor: University Microfilms, 1974), p. 73. See Yoshida's discussion of the Nagasaki interpreters in general.

20. Nakayama (n. 1 above), p. 748.

21. R. H. Knapp and H. B. Goodrich, *Origins of American Scientists* (Chicago: University of Chicago Press, 1952), pp. 16–17.

22. Muramatsu Teijirō, *Industrial Technology in Japan: A Historical Review* (Tokyo: Hitachi Ltd., 1968), pp. 159, 22–26.

23. Ishikawa Matsutarō, "Kinsei buke no kyōiku, shomin no kyōiku," in Umene Satoru, ed., *Nihon kyōiku shi* (Tokyo: Kōdansha, 1976), p. 156.

24. Nakayama (n. 1 above), p. 748.

25. Goodman (n. 17 above), p. 96.

26. John Z. Bowers, *Western Medical Pioneers in Feudal Japan* (Baltimore: Johns Hopkins University Press, 1970), pp. 10–18, 30.

27. Goodman (n. 17 above), pp. 88–89.

28. Ranzaburō Ōtori, "The Acceptance of Western Medicine in Japan," *Monumenta Nipponica* 19/3–4 (Autumn 1964):31.

29. Sawako Ariyoshi, *The Doctor's Wife,* trans. Wakako Hironaka and Ann Siller Kostant (Tokyo: Kōdansha, 1978), pp. v–vi.

30. Terashima Masashi, *Nihon kagaku hattatsu shi* (Tokyo: Keibunsha, 1937), pp. 127–28.

31. Bowers (n. 26 above), pp. 103–30.

32. Goodman (n. 17 above), p. 202, and Terashima (n. 30 above), p. 126.

33. Goodman (n. 17 above), p. 96.

34. Nakayama (n. 10 above), p. 169.

35. Terashima (n. 30 above), pp. 118, 162–63; Goodman (n. 17 above), p. 134.

36. Terashima (n. 30 above), pp. 155–56, and Goodman (n. 17 above), p. 159.

37. Nakayama (n. 10 above), pp. 180–86.

38. Muramatsu (n. 22 above), p. 22.

39. Nakayama (n. 10 above), p. 159.

40. Yoshio Mikami, *The Development of Mathematics in China and Japan* (New York: Chelsea Publishing, 1913), p. 174.

41. See Nakayama (n. 10 above), pp. 88–94, and Itō Shuntarō, "The Introduction of Western Cosmology in Seventeenth Century Japan: The Case of Christovão Ferreira (1580–1652)," *The Japan Foundation Newsletter* 14/1 (May 1986):1–9.

42. Nakayama (n. 10 above), pp. 119, 120, 137–39.

43. Ibid., pp. 166, 194.

44. Ibid., p. 177.

45. Ibid., p. 178.

46. Terashima (n. 30 above), pp. 147–48.

47. Nakayama (n. 10 above), pp. 198–202.

48. Yoshida (n. 19 above), p. 67.

49. See biographical sketches in Dai Jimmei Jiten Henshū Bu, ed., *Dai jimmei jiten,* 10 vols. (Tokyo: Heibonsha, 1957).

50. Mikami (n. 40 above), p. 302.

51. Ōya Shin'ichi, personal communication (November 2, 1976). See James R. Bartholomew, "Why Was There No Scientific Revolution in Tokugawa Japan?" *Japanese Studies in the History of Science,* no. 15 (1976):123.

52. Satō Shōsuke, "Tembō: Yōgaku shi," *Kagaku Shi Kenkyū,* 2d ser., 10, no. 97 (Spring 1971):1–6.

53. Takahashi Shin'ichi, *Yōgaku ron* (Tokyo: Mikasa Shobō, 1939), p. 181.

54. Cited in Kanamaru (n. 2 above), p. 53.

55. Quoted from *Bairi yōkō* in ibid., p. 58.

56. For details, see Yoshida (n. 19 above), pp. 62–75.

57. Terashima (n. 30 above), p. 77.

58. Goodman (n. 17 above), pp. 52, 65.

59. Ibid., p. 41, and Nakayama (n. 10 above), p. 165.

60. See Dore (n. 4 above), p. 71.

61. Ibid., pp. 160–61, 224–26, 322.

62. Quoted in Fukuchi Shigetaka, *Shizoku to samurai ishiki* (Tokyo: Shunjūsha, 1956), pp. 235–36.

63. Ibid., p. 230.

64. Johannes Hirschmeier, *The Origins of Entrepreneurship in Meiji Japan* (Cambridge: Harvard University Press, 1967), p. 61.

65. Dore (n. 4 above), pp. 302–03.

66. Robert N. Bellah, *Tokugawa Religion* (Glencoe, Ill.: Free Press, 1957). See also Dore (n. 4 above), p. 212.

67. Fukuchi (n. 62 above), p. 235.

68. Ibid., pp. 229–30.

69. Dore (n. 4 above), p. 31.

70. Ishikawa (n. 23 above), p. 106.

71. Thomas C. Smith, *The Agrarian Origins of Modern Japan* (Stanford: Stanford University Press, 1959), p. 111.

72. Yoshio Mikami and David Eugene Smith, *A History of Japanese Mathematics* (Chicago: Open Court Publishing, 1914), pp. 207–08.

73. See Dore (n. 4 above), pp. 147, 47.

74. Kozo Yamamura, *A Study of Samurai Income and Entrepreneurship* (Cambridge: Harvard University Press, 1974), p. 46.

75. Cited in Nakayama (n. 10 above), p. 160.

76. Quoted in Nakayama Shigeru, "'Shūshin, seika, chikoku heitenka' to kagaku," *Butsurigaku shi kenkyū* 2/3 (1963):157.

77. Hanami Sakumi, *Danshaku Yamakawa-sensei den* (Tokyo: Ko Danshaku Yamakawa-Sensei Kinen Kai, 1939), pp. 24–25.

78. Nakayama (n. 1 above), p. 752.

79. Ibid., p. 753.

80. Bartholomew (n. 51 above), p. 124.

81. Ogura Kinnosuke, *Sūgaku shi kenkyū* (Tokyo: Iwanami Shoten, 1935), pp. 245, 242, 246.

82. Dore (n. 4 above), pp. 147, 205.

83. Ogura (n. 81 above), p. 235.

84. Nakayama (n. 10 above), p. 160.

85. Mikami (n. 40 above), pp. 301–02.

86. Nakayama Shigeru, *Rekishi to shite no gakumon* (Tokyo: Chūō Kō-ron Sha, 1974), p. 96. See also the English-language version published as *Academic and Scientific Traditions in China, Japan and the West.*

87. Dore (n. 4 above), pp. 17–18.

88. Ibid., p. 71. See also Ishikawa (n. 23 above), pp. 142–43; Dore (n. 4 above), pp. 24–25, 44, 71; and Yamasaki (n. 11 above), p. 8.

89. Ishikawa (n. 23 above), p. 154; Nakayama (n. 10 above), p. 189.

90. Yamasaki (n. 11 above), pp. 35, 33.

91. For a discussion of the Saishunkan's program, see ibid., pp. 11, 35.

92. Yoshio Kanamaru, *The Development of a Scientific Community in Pre-Modern Japan* (Ann Arbor: University Microfilms, 1980) pp. 44–50, 69.

93. Dore (n. 4 above), p. 208.

94. Frederick G. Notehelfer, *American Samurai: Captain L. L. Janes and Japan* (Princeton: Princeton University Press, 1985), p. 134.

95. Yamasaki (n. 11 above), pp. 288–90, 333–34, 295; and Irwin Scheiner, *Christian Converts and Social Protest in Meiji Japan* (Berkeley: University of California Press, 1970), pp. 72, 76–77.

96. Yoshida (n. 19 above), p. 10.

97. Dore (n. 4 above), p. 164.

98. Nakayama (n. 10 above), p. 194.

99. Ibid., pp. 120–21.

100. Kanamaru (n. 92 above), p. 382. See also Ōtani Ryōkichi, *A Brief Account of the Life and Work of Tadataka Inō*. Proceedings of the Imperial Academy of Sciences 1 (Tokyo, 1912):176–80.

101. Masayoshi Sugimoto and David L. Swain, *Science and Culture in Traditional Japan*, A.D. *600–1854* (Cambridge: MIT Press, 1978), pp. 298–300.

102. Yamasaki (n. 11 above), pp. 31, 32; Sugimoto and Swain (n. 101 above), pp. 302–03.

103. See Kanamaru (n. 92 above), pp. 33–36, 148, Sugimoto and Swain (n. 101 above), pp. 396–98, and Yoshida (n. 19 above), p. 7.

104. Yoshida (n. 19 above), p. 7, and Kanamaru (n. 92 above), p. 403. Kanamaru even argues that the linguistic skills of the staff led them away from scientific interests and "perverted" the scientific movement.

105. The Bansho Shirabesho (Institute for investigating barbarian books) was renamed Yōsho Shirabesho (Institute for investigating Western books) in 1862 and Kaiseisho (Institute for cultivation and development) in 1863. Following the Restoration in 1868, there were other name changes before it emerged (with several new components) as Tokyo University in 1877. See Kanamaru (n. 92 above), p. 33. For a summary of post-Restoration developments, see Henry DeWitt Smith II, *Japan's First Student Radicals* (Cambridge: Harvard University Press, 1972), pp. 4–8.

106. Sugimoto and Swain (n. 101 above), pp. 396–98.

107. Kanamaru (n. 92 above), p. 191.

108. Dore (n. 4 above), p. 169.

109. Yagi Eri, Itakura Kiyonobu, and Kimura Tōsaku, *Nagaoka Hantarō den* (Tokyo: Asahi Shimbun Sha, 1973), pp. 51–52.

110. Nakayama (n. 1 above), p. 740. See also Bowers (n. 26 above), p. 143.

111. Sugimoto and Swain (n. 101 above), pp. 377–78, and Bowers (n. 26 above), pp. 25–26.

112. Kanamaru (n. 92 above), pp. 31–32.

113. Bowers (n. 26 above), p. 9. For useful background information on Siebold's education and career, see ibid., pp. 102–09. For his role in the popularization of the Linnaean botanical scheme, see Sugimoto Isao, *Itō Keisuke* (Tokyo: Yoshikawa Kōbunkan, 1960), pp. 43–68.

114. Sugimoto and Swain (n. 101 above), pp. 334, 338–44.

115. John Z. Bowers, *When the Twain Meet: The Rise of Western Medicine in Japan* (Baltimore: The Johns Hopkins University Press, 1980), pp. 10, 30. The school was called the Seitokukan from 1862.

116. Sugawara Kunika, "Meiji shoki no kagaku," *Kagaku kyōiku* 22/4 (1974):247–54.

117. Bowers (n. 115 above), pp. 30–33.

118. Sugawara (n. 116 above), p. 249; Yagi, Itakura, and Kimura (n. 109 above), pp. 26–28, 52–54.

119. Yagi, Itakura, and Kimura (n. 109 above), pp. 52, 26. Regarding Nagaoka, see pp. 26–27. Takamine's association with this school is discussed

by Shiobara Matasaku, *Takamine hakushi* (Tokyo: Shiobara Matasaku, 1926), pp. 9–10.

120. Nagai (n. 12 above), pp. 72–75, 85.

121. Nakayama (n. 10 above), pp. 188–89.

122. Dore (n. 4 above), pp. 265–66. See also Sugimoto and Swain (n. 101 above), p. 334.

123. Of the twenty-three medical academies founded in the Tokugawa period, eleven were established by the shogunate or various daimyo and twelve by private groups. For details, see Bowers (n. 26 above), pp. 93–94.

124. Sugimoto and Swain (n. 101 above), p. 334.

125. Kanamaru (n. 92 above), p. 31.

126. Bowers (n. 26 above), pp. 94, 98.

127. Fukuzawa Yukichi, *The Autobiography of Yukichi Fukuzawa*, trans. Eiichi Kiyooka (New York: Columbia University Press, 1966), pp. 72, 80–81, 334.

128. For information on functions, see Kanamaru (n. 92 above), pp. 291, 400–03.

129. Nagayo Sensai, *Shōkō shishi*, 2 (Tokyo: Nagayo Shōkichi, 1902):178.

130. Yoshida (n. 19 above), p. 5.

131. Yagi, Itakura, and Kimura (n. 109 above), p. 51.

132. Kanamaru (n. 92 above), p. 172. "Only the government could utilize this [translation and research] ability to its maximum extent."

133. Yoshida (n. 19 above), pp. 14–16.

134. Nakayama (n. 86 above), pp. 264–65.

135. The exceptions were primarily (but not exclusively) the shogunate institutions that developed into Tokyo University. See chapter 4 for details.

136. Quoted in Maruyama (n. 7 above), p. 415.

137. Quoted in Dore (n. 4 above), p. 168.

138. Itakura Kiyonobu, "Watanabe Bin to Misawa Katsue," *Kasetsu jikken jugyō kenkyū* 8 (1975):21–48.

139. Itakura Kiyonobu, private communication, December 13, 1976.

140. Mikami (n. 40 above), pp. 303–04.

141. Sugimoto and Swain (n. 101 above), p. 348.

142. Dore (n. 4 above), pp. 164–65.

143. Quoted in Maruyama (n. 7 above), pp. 410–11.

144. Hall (n. 6 above), pp. 287, 291–92.

145. On the subject of bureaucratic generalists and specialists in East Asian political systems, see Nakayama (n. 86 above), p. 70, and Nathan Sivin, "How Does Science Begin?" *Technology Review* 71/3 (January 1969):63.

146. Nakayama (n. 10 above), p. 118.

147. Endō Toshisada, *Zōshū Nihon sūgaku shi* (Tokyo: Kōseisha Kōseikaku, 1960), pp. 64–65.

148. Terashima (n. 30 above), p. 80.

149. In addition to the five domains—Aizu, Satsuma, Sendai, Kyoto, and the shogunal territories—the Mishima and Ise shrines were also authorized to produce calendars. Ōya Shin'ichi, private communication, November 2, 1976.

150. Dore (n. 4 above), pp. 16–17, 5.

151. Goodman (n. 17 above), p. 99.

152. Mikami (n. 40 above), p. 180.

153. Ibid., p. 183.

154. Yamasaki (n. 11 above), pp. 270, 276–77. See also Dore (n. 4 above), p. 44.

155. Goodman (n. 17 above), pp. 94–95.

156. Ibid., pp. 191–92.

157. Nakayama (n. 10 above), pp. 168–69.

158. Goodman (n. 17 above), p. 95.

159. Ibid., p. 65, and Nakayama (n. 10 above), p. 171.

160. Goodman (n. 17 above), pp. 79–85.

161. Ishikawa (n. 23 above), pp. 135–36.

162. Terashima (n. 30 above), pp. 110–11.

163. Nakayama (n. 10 above), p. 178.

164. Dore (n. 4 above), p. 30.

165. Yoshida (n. 19 above), p. 8.

166. Edward Seidensticker described his feelings about Tokugawa Japan this way: "The Tokugawa period is somehow dark and menacing. Too many gifted people were squelched, and whether gifted or not, I always have the feeling about Edo [its capital] that, had I been there, I would have been among the squelched ones." See *Low City, High City* (New York: Alfred A. Knopf, 1983), p. vii.

167. Kanamaru (n. 92 above), p. 382.

168. See in particular Donald Keene's (n. 5 above) excellent account of the "Siebold Affair," pp. 138–55.

169. Ōtsuki Nyoden, *Shisen yōgaku nempyō,* 2d ed. (Tokyo: Hakurinsha Shoten, 1963), entry for 1829.

170. Kanamaru (n. 92 above), p. 388.

171. Satō Shōsuke, "Taigai kankei no kiki to yōgaku," in Sugimoto Isao, ed., *Kagaku shi,* Taikei Nihon shi sōsho 19 (Tokyo: Yamakawa Shuppan Sha, 1967), p. 322.

172. Kanamaru (n. 92 above), p. 390.

173. Watanabe Kazan, "Shoko seiyō jijō sho," and "Saikō seiyō jijō sho," in Satō Shōsuke et al., eds., *Nihon shisō taikei 55: Watanabe Kazan, Takano Chōei, Sakuma Shōzan, Yokoi Shōnan, Hashimoto Sanai* (Tokyo: Iwanami Shoten, 1974), pp. 49, 62.

174. Kanamaru (n. 92 above), p. 393.

175. Nagai (n. 12 above), pp. 8–10.

176. Ogura (n. 81 above), p. 241.

177. Ibid., p. 244, and Meiji Shi Kōza Kankō Kai, ed., *Meiji kagaku shi* (Tokyo: Nihon Bungaku Sha, 1931), p. 10.

178. Minoru Watanabe, "Japanese Students Abroad and the Acquisition of Scientific and Technical Knowledge," *Journal of World History* 9/2 (1965):264–65.

179. Quoted in Yagi, Itakura, and Kimura (n. 109 above), p. 52.

180. Dore (n. 4 above), p. 167.

181. Nakayama Shigeru, private communication, November 2, 1976. For

information on the *Oranda Fūsetsugaki,* see Satō (n. 171 above), pp. 291–92, and Satō Shōsuke, "Rangaku bokkō no sho zentei," in Sugimoto, ed. (n. 171 above), p. 218.

182. Robert A. Nisbet, *The Quest for Community* (New York: Oxford University Press, 1969), pp. 225–47.

183. Watanabe (n. 178 above), pp. 257–59.

184. J. Harris and W. H. Brock, "From Giessen to Gower Street: Towards a Biography of Alexander William Williamson (1824–1904)," *Annals of Science* 31/2 (1974):123. Williamson took charge of these men while they were studying in London.

185. Nakayama (n. 1 above), p. 734.

186. Mikami and Smith (n. 72 above), p. 188.

187. Even during the last years of the Tokugawa era, it is argued that instruction was "hampered by the feudalistic status system" at the Numazu military academy, which taught science and mathematics. See Fujii Shōichirō, "Numazu Heigakkō to sono Nihon kindai sokuchi jigyō e no eikyō ni tsuite," *Kagaku shi kenkyū* 51 (Autumn 1959):3. However, the author presents no direct evidence to prove this.

188. Dore (n. 4 above), p. 52.

189. Ibid., p. 83.

190. Ibid., p. 183.

191. Quoted in Miyajima Mikinosuke, *Kitasato Shibasaburō den* (Tokyo: Iwanami Shoten, 1931), pp. 198–99. Kitasato's remarks were delivered at a memorial lecture for his teacher Robert Koch on December 11, 1917, and were originally printed in "Koch-sensei kinen kōen kai," *IJ,* no. 1225 (December 15, 1917):2184.

192. Dore (n. 4 above), p. 141. Dore also cites the example of one domain school where the instructor arranged in advance for six students to raise questions. No one else was allowed to do so.

193. Ibid., pp. 50–52, 83, 150. The specific reference is to archery. The author also compares mathematics to military arts like archery.

194. Ibid., p. 88. See also Ōtani (n. 100 above), pp. 185–86, 190.

195. Dore (n. 4 above), p. 183.

196. Yoshiharu Scott Matsumoto, "Contemporary Japan: The Individual and the Group," *Transactions of the American Philosophical Society* 50/1 (January 1960):35.

197. Dore (n. 4 above), p. 53. The author's apparent reference is to the absence of anatomical dissections prior to the mid-eighteenth century.

198. Ogura (n. 81 above), p. 238.

199. Yoshida Mitsukuni, "Meiji no kagakushatachi," *Jimbun gakuhō* 24 (March 1967):230.

200. For astronomy, see Sugimoto and Swain (n. 101 above), p. 199. For medicine, see Bowers (n. 26 above), p. 8.

201. Sugimoto and Swain (n. 101 above), p. 289.

202. Dore (n. 4 above), pp. 312–13.

203. Nakayama (n. 10 above), pp. 186–87.

204. Yagi, Itakura, and Kimura (n. 109 above), p. 50.

205. Nakayama (n. 1 above), p. 735.

206. Endō (n. 147 above), p. 65.

207. Sakurai Jōji, "Mathematico-Physical Science in Japan," in Ōkuma Shigenobu, ed., *Fifty Years of New Japan,* 2 (London: Smith, Elder & Co., 1910):247.

208. Sugimoto and Swain (n. 101 above), pp. 374, 380–82.

209. John D. Bernal, *The Social Function of Science* (New York: Macmillan, 1939), p. 80.

210. Nakayama (n. 1 above), pp. 742–43.

211. David Chibbett, *The History of Japanese Printing and Book Illustration* (Tokyo: Kodansha International, 1977), p. 74. I am indebted to Maureen H. Donovan for calling my attention to this book.

212. Sakurai (n. 207 above), p. 243.

213. On *idai,* see Muramatsu (n. 22 above), pp. 22–26.

214. Mikami and Smith (n. 72 above), p. 188.

215. Ogura (n. 81 above), pp. 236–37.

216. Ōtani (n. 99 above), pp. 185–86, 190.

217. Nakayama (n. 1 above), pp. 734–35.

218. Nakayama (n. 86 above), pp. 256–57.

219. Dore (n. 4 above), p. 209. See also Thomas C. Smith, "'Merit' as Ideology in the Tokugawa Period," in R. P. Dore, ed., *Aspects of Social Change in Modern Japan* (Princeton: Princeton University Press, 1967), p. 73.

220. Smith (n. 219 above), pp. 85–88.

221. Nakayama (n. 10 above), p. 194.

222. Michael Yoshino, *Japan's Managerial Ideology* (Cambridge: Harvard University Press, 1968), p. 50.

223. Dore (n. 4 above), p. 156.

224. Kanamaru (n. 92 above), pp. 247–48, 231.

225. Nakayama (n. 1 above), p. 735.

226. Ogura (n. 81 above), pp. 238, 240–41.

Chapter Three: Formation of the Meiji Scientific Community

1. J. M. Cattell and Dean R. Brimhall, eds., *American Men of Science,* 3d ed. (Garrison, N.Y.: Science Press, 1921), p. 787.

2. Marquis de Condorcet, *Outlines of an Historical View of the Progress of the Human Mind,* quoted in Keith Michael Baker, *Condorcet: From Natural Philosophy to Social Mathematics* (Chicago: University of Chicago Press, 1975), p. 176, and Jean Dessau, "Social Factors Affecting Science and Technology in Asia," *Impact of Science on Society* 19/1 (1969):14.

3. C. Ernest Dawn, *From Ottomanism to Arabism: Essays on the Origins of Arab Nationalism* (Urbana: University of Illinois Press, 1973), pp. 197–98, and Joseph Gusfield, "Educational Institutions in the Process of Economic and National Development," *Journal of Asian and African Studies* 1/2 (April 1966):143.

4. Morroe Berger, *The Arab World Today* (New York: Doubleday, 1962), pp.

385–86, and Seymour M. Lipset and Reinhard Bendix, *Social Mobility in Industrial Society* (Berkeley and Los Angeles: University of California Press, 1959), pp. 57–64.

5. Joseph Ben-David, *The Scientist's Role in Society* (Englewood Cliffs, N.J.: Prentice-Hall, 1971), p. 21.

6. Shūgiin Jimukyoku, *Teikoku Gikai Shūgiin Iinkai giroku* (hereafter *TGSIG*), "Dai go-ka dai-ichi gō," House of Representatives Budget Committee, 5th Diet, December 8, 1893, p. 20.

7. Ibid., p. 3.

8. Fukuzawa Yukichi, *The Autobiography of Yukichi Fukuzawa*, p. 92.

9. Masayoshi Sugimoto and David L. Swain, *Science and Culture in Traditional Japan*, A.D. *600–1854*, p. 348.

10. Kenkichirō Koizumi, "The Emergence of Japan's First Physicists, 1868–1900," in Russell McCormmach, ed., *Historical Studies in the Physical Sciences*, 6 (Princeton: Princeton University Press, 1975):17.

11. Shigeru Nakayama, "Japanese Scientific Thought," in Charles C. Gillispie, ed., *Dictionary of Scientific Biography*, 15/1:743.

12. Tominari Kimahei, *Gendai Nihon kagaku shi* (Tokyo: Mikasa Shobō, 1941), pp. 58–59.

13. Mitsutomo Yuasa, "The Scientific Revolution and the Age of Technology," *Journal of World History* 9/2 (1965):187–207.

14. Fukuchi Shigetaka, *Shizoku to samurai ishiki*.

15. Yuasa Mitsutomo, *Kagaku shi*, p. 161.

16. See the discussion of the proposed *hakushi* degree system which took place between Mori Arinori and the members of the Tokyo Academy of Science on October 15, 1885. The text is reprinted in Nihon Gakushiin, ed., *Nihon Gakushiin hachijū nen shi, shiryō 1* (Tokyo: Nihon Gakushiin, 1962):304–08.

17. The debate conducted by the Tokyo academy on October 15, 1885, especially exchanges between Katō Hiroyuki and Mori Arinori, reveals that the degree categories were supposed to correspond closely to the academic programs at Tokyo University. See ibid., p. 308.

18. Mori insisted (more or less correctly) that no other country had a system of degrees quite like the Japanese. See his remarks on this question made on May 7, 1888, when he presided over the first conferrals. Mori Arinori, "Mombushō no gakui juyōshiki ni okeru enzetsu," in *Mori Arinori zenshū*, 1 (Tokyo: Senbundō, 1972):618–19.

19. As a category, *scientist* had the connotation of "eccentric" or "odd," while *hakushi* (doctorate holder) connoted status or prestige. In 1891 Tokutomi Sohō characterized the awarding of new doctorates by the Ministry of Education as a "singularly auspicious event for the nation." Ishikawa Teijirō, biographer of physicist Honda Kōtarō, describes the fuss that residents of Honda's native village made over his reception of the doctorate in 1903, noting that the degree had "tremendous prestige among ordinary people." On August 22, 1914, *Ikai jihō* stated flatly: "An unwritten law holds that if a man has not . . . secured a doctorate, he cannot become a university professor." And consider the following report about the fate of one in academic life who failed to obtain the doctorate. Shortly before World War I, Hashimoto Sessai, assistant professor of internal

medicine at Tokyo University (1899–1914), published a Japanese-language textbook in his field. On being shown a copy by a student, Dean Aoyama Tanemichi angrily grabbed the book and threw it out a second-story window, exclaiming: "There is no need for you to study German if people are going to write trash like this!" Arai Tsuneo, one of three writers reporting on this event, then relates: "Professor Hashimoto was at that time an assistant professor lecturing on diagnostics. But in the end he was unable to obtain his degree [D.Sc.Med.] and was *immediately* obliged to leave the university." See the following sources for details on public attitudes toward the doctorate and its importance in Meiji academic life: Tokutomi Sohō, "Hakushi seizō," *Kokumin no tomo,* no. 127 (August 13, 1891):159; Ishikawa Teijirō, *Honda Kōtarō den* (Tokyo: Nikkan Kōgyō Shimbun Sha, 1964), p. 116; "Kore zekkō no kikai ka?" *IJ,* no. 1052 (August 22, 1914):1481; and Arai Tsuneo, "Tanemichi sumbyō," in Kumagai Kenji, ed., *Omoide no Aoyama Tanemichi-sensei* (Tokyo: Aoyama-Sensei Tanjō Hyakunen Sai Jumbi Iinkai, 1959), p. 142.

20. Mitamura Makujirō, "Tanemichi no sekai dōtoku," in Kumagai (n. 19 above), p. 163. Mitamura, who served as assistant professor and then professor of pathology at Tokyo University between 1920 and 1946, made this remark in the 1950s. Almost certainly he was referring to the interwar period rather than to the half-century which preceded it, the focus of concern here. In the interwar period the truly dramatic increase in the number and percentage of doctorates awarded in medicine, as opposed to doctorates in other fields, took place. For details, see Iseki Kurō, ed., *Dai Nihon hakushi roku,* 3 (Tokyo: Hattensha, 1930). I wish to thank Harry Bang of Ball State University for bringing this issue to my attention.

21. No women received the doctorate in a technical field until after 1920. For details see Nagashima Yuzuru, *Onna hakushi retsu den* (Tokyo: Kagaku Chishiki Fukyū Kai, 1937).

22. Other sources useful in compiling these data were the following official histories of the imperial universities: Tōkyō Teikoku Daigaku, *Tōkyō Teikoku Daigaku gojū nen shi,* 2 vols. (Tokyo: Tōkyō Teikoku Daigaku, 1932 [hereafter **TTDGNS**]); Kyōto Teikoku Daigaku, *Kyōto Teikoku Daigaku shi* (Kyoto: Kyōto Teikoku Daigaku, 1943); Kyōto Daigaku, *Kyōto Daigaku nanajū nen shi* (Kyoto: Kyōto Daigaku, 1967); Tōhoku Daigaku, *Tōhoku Daigaku gojū nen shi,* 2 vols. (Sendai: Tōhoku Daigaku, 1960); Kyūshū Daigaku, *Kyūshū Daigaku gojū nen shi,* 3 vols. (Fukuoka: Kyūshū Daigaku Sōritsu Gojū Shūnen Kinen Kai, 1967); and Hokkaidō Daigaku, *Hokkaidō Daigaku sōki hachijū nen shi* (Sapporo: Hokkaidō Daigaku, 1965). It should be noted, however, that these figures are only close approximations; the figures for Kyoto, in particular, are far from complete.

23. Fukuchi Shigetaka, for example, wrote: "The first field of Japanese science to attain worldwide levels of performance after the Meiji Restoration was medicine. This was because it had a longer tradition than other sciences" Fukuchi (n. 14 above), p. 249. See also Nakayama (n. 11 above), pp. 728–58.

24. For details on the American case, see R. H. Knapp and H. B. Goodrich, *Origins of American Scientists,* pp. 16–17.

25. Population figures are from Ōtsuka Takematsu, ed., *Hansei ichiran,* 2

vols. (Tokyo: Nihon Shiseki Kyōkai, 1928–29), and Irene Taeuber, *The Population of Japan* (Princeton: Princeton University Press, 1954).

26. Motoyama Yukihiko, "The Education Policy of Fukui and William Eliot Griffis," in Ardath W. Burks, ed., *The Modernizers: Overseas Students, Foreign Employees, and Meiji Japan* (Boulder, Colo.: Westview Press, 1985), pp. 265–300.

27. Ivan Hall, *Mori Arinori* (Cambridge: Harvard University Press, 1973), pp. 32–46.

28. Anne Roe, *The Making of a Scientist* (New York: Dodd Mead, 1952), pp. 80–86.

29. Nagai Tamotsu, *Takagi Kanehiro den*, p. 184.

30. Miyajima Mikinosuke, *Kitasato Shibasaburō den*, pp. 5–15.

31. Fukuda Reiju, *Kitasato Shibasaburō hakushi* (Kumamoto: Yūkō Jiron Sha, 1963), pp. 1–7.

32. Ibid., p. 3.

33. Irwin Scheiner, *Christian Converts and Social Protest in Meiji Japan*, pp. 71–72.

34. Yamasaki Masatada, *Higo iiku shi*, pp. 296, 333–34.

35. Nagai (n. 29 above), pp. 38, 17–18.

36. Gustav Eckstein, *Noguchi* (New York: Harper & Brothers, 1931), pp. 27–28. See also Isabel R. Plesset, *Noguchi and His Patrons* (Rutherford, N.J.: Fairleigh Dickinson University Press, 1980), pp. 53–105.

37. Sugimoto Isao, *Itō Keisuke*, pp. 7–10, 42–45.

38. Sugiura Kōtarō, "Ueda Kazutoshi hakushi tsuitō ki," *Kokkan* 52 (October 1938):12.

39. *TGSIG* (n. 6 above), p. 3.

40. Terashima Masashi, *Sekaiteki na Nihon kagakusha* (Tokyo: Izumi Shobō, 1944), pp. 162–63.

41. For information on the status of chemistry in Europe and America at the time, see D. S. L. Cardwell, *The Organisation of Science in England* (London: Wm. Heinemann, 1957).

42. Yoshida Mitsukuni, "Meiji no kagakushatachi," *Jimbun gakuhō* 24 (March 1967):230–61.

43. Shiobara Matasaku, *Takamine hakushi*, pp. 1–10.

44. Majima Toshiyuki-Sensei Ikōshū Kankō Iinkai, ed., *Majima Toshiyuki-sensei, ikō to tsuioku* (Tokyo: Majima Toshiyuki-Sensei Ikōshū Kankō Iinkai, 1970), p. 7.

45. Tanaka Minoru, *Nihon no kagaku to Shibata Yūji* (Tokyo: Dai Nihon Tosho, 1975), pp. 17–24.

46. Nagai's father was interested in materia medica, as was Nagai. In the 1880s the son isolated ephedrine in a pure form from the Chinese herb *ma huang*. It was the "first natural sympathomimetic amine to make its appearance in history" and is used in Western and Oriental medicine alike. See Kanao Seizō, *Nagai Nagayoshi den* (Tokyo: Nihon Yakugakkai, 1960), p. 443.

47. Sakurai Jōji, *Omoide no kazukazu*, p. 2.

48. Quoted in Ishikawa (n. 19 above), p. 56.

49. Hanami Sakumi, *Danshaku Yamakawa-sensei den*, pp. 52–70. Spen-

cer's article was entitled "The Study of Sociology," and it appeared in several successive issues of *Popular Science Monthly,* ed. E. R. Youmans, in 1872 and 1873.

50. Hanami (n. 49 above), pp. 69–70.

51. Nakayama Shigeru (ch. 2, n. 76), "'Shūshin, seika, chikoku heitenka' to kagaku," p. 162.

52. Nakamura Seiji, *Tanakadate Aikitsu-sensei* (Tokyo: Ōbun Shorin, 1943), pp. 1–3, 39–40.

53. Nakayama (n. 51 above), p. 159.

54. Nagaoka was actually best known in Japan as an experimental physicist, despite his well-known work on modeling the atom.

55. Yagi Eri, Itakura Kiyonobu, and Kimura Tōsaku, *Nagaoka Hantarō den,* pp. 13–17.

56. Nagaoka Hantarō, "Butsurigaku senkō o kimeru toki no nayami," reprinted in Nihon Kagaku Shi Gakkai, ed., *Nihon kagaku gijutsu shi taikei* (hereafter *NKGST*), 8/1 (Tokyo: Nihon Kagaku Shi Gakkai, 1964):398–99.

57. Ishikawa (n. 19 above), pp. 17, 29, 56–57.

58. Hazel L. Jones, *Live Machines: Hired Foreigners and Meiji Japan* (Vancouver: University of British Columbia Press, 1980), p. 13.

59. Ogata Hiroyasu, *Seiyō kyōiku inyū no hōto* (Tokyo: Kōdansha, 1961), pp. 79–80, 88–89, 94.

60. Letter of July 2, 1875, reprinted in Kanao (n. 46 above), p. 109.

61. Cited in Jones (n. 58 above), p. 86.

62. *TGSIG.* Cf. "Shūgiin yosan iinkai sokkiroku dai-jūhachi gō," House of Representatives Budget Committee, 3d Diet, March 15, 1892, p. 5.

63. *TGSIG.* Cf. "Dai-ichi ka dai-san gō," House of Representatives Budget Committee, 10th Diet, January 27, 1897, p. 43.

64. Jones (n. 58 above), pp. 74, 75.

65. John Z. Bowers, *When the Twain Meet: The Rise of Western Medicine in Japan,* pp. 89–99, 98.

66. Ibid., p. 64.

67. Noboru Umetani, *The Role of Foreign Employees in the Meiji Era in Japan* (Tokyo: Institute of Developing Economies, 1971), pp. 64–67.

68. Nakamura (n. 52 above), p. 67.

69. J. Harris and W. H. Brock (ch. 2, n. 184), "From Giessen to Gower Street: Towards a Biography of Alexander William Williamson (1824–1904)" pp. 124–25, and Ishikawa (n. 19 above), pp. 61–62.

70. Nakamura (n. 52 above), pp. 47–50.

71. Tōkyō Teikoku Daigaku, *Tōkyō Teikoku Daigaku gakujutsu taikan: Jishin Kenkyū Jo, Tōkyō Temmon Dai, Rigaku Bu* (Tokyo: Tōkyō Teikoku Daigaku, 1942), pp. 139–44.

72. Umetani (n. 67 above), pp. 59–60.

73. Janet Hunter, "The Development of Technical Education in Japan: Foreign Teachers at the Imperial College of Engineering, 1872–1885," unpublished paper, University of Sheffield, 1971, pp. 15–16, 39–41.

74. Jones (n. 58 above), p. 75.

75. Ishikawa (n. 19 above), p. 63.

76. Bowers (n. 65 above), pp. 98, 82, 86–89.

77. Ibid., p. 99.

78. Tōkyō Teikoku Daigaku, *Tōkyō Teikoku Daigaku gakujutsu taikan: Nōgaku Bu, Densembyō Kenkyū Jo, Igaku Bu* (Tokyo: Tōkyō Teikoku Daigaku, 1942), pp. 33–34.

79. Uzaki Kumakichi, *Aoyama Tanemichi* (Tokyo: Aoyama Naika Dōsō Kai, 1930), pp. 42–43, and Nakamura (n. 52 above), p. 71. Ewing did not graduate from Glasgow but did have close ties with Kelvin, who was there.

80. See the discussion in Bowers (n. 65 above), pp. 47–48.

81. Tanaka (n. 45 above), pp. 71–75.

82. Yagi, Itakura, and Kimura (n. 55 above), pp. 114–15.

83. The foreign professors' relative lack of influence on the development of particular lines of research by the Japanese may have been a function of the students' relative youth or of the relatively poor state of research facilities in Japan. There were, however, exceptions. Cargill G. Knott, for example, instigated Nagaoka Hantarō's initial work on magnetostriction, which Nagaoka continued in Europe. See Yagi, Itakura, and Kimura (n. 55 above), pp. 177–78, for details.

84. *NKGST* 8/1 (n. 56 above):352–53.

85. *TGSIG* (n. 63 above), p. 43.

86. *TGSIG*. Cf. "Dai-ichi ka dai-san gō," House of Representatives Budget Committee, 13th Diet, December 13, 1898, p. 30.

87. *TGSIG*. Cf. "Yosan iin dai-ichi bunkakai (Naimushō, Mombushō jokan) kaigiroku (sokki) dai-go kai," House of Representatives Budget Committee, 16th Diet, December 20, 1901, p. 61.

88. Minoru Watanabe (ch. 2, n. 178), "Japanese Students Abroad and the Acquisition of Scientific and Technical Knowledge," pp. 266–68.

89. *TGSIG* (n. 87 above), p. 61. Testimony of Ueda Kazutoshi, chief of the Bureau of Professional Education.

90. Among the ministries involved were Home Affairs, Education, War, Navy, Justice, and Foreign Affairs. Control over all students studying abroad was an enduring goal of the Ministry of Education, toward which the ministry progressed without wholly achieving it.

91. Satō Kenzō, *Kokuritsu daigaku zaisei seido shikō* (Tokyo: Dai-ichi Hōki, 1964), p. 381.

92. *TGSIG*. Cf. "Dai-ichi ka dai-ni gō," House of Representatives Budget Committee, 12th Diet, May 25, 1898, pp. 11–15.

93. *TGSIG* (n. 87 above), p. 61.

94. "Kore zekkō no kikai ka?" *IJ*, no. 1052 (August 22, 1914):1481.

95. "Ryūgaku o haiseyō," *IJ*, no. 925 (March 16, 1912):436.

96. Miura Norihiko, ed., *Ichi igakusha no seikatsu o meguru kaisō: Meiyō Kyōjū Miura Kinnosuke no shōgai* (Tokyo: Ishiyaku Shuppan, 1955), p. 38.

97. Miyajima (n. 30 above), pp. 33–34.

98. Nagayo Hakushi Kinen Kai, ed., *Nagayo Matarō den* (Tokyo: Nagayo Hakushi Kinen Kai, 1944), p. 117. Uzaki Kumakichi states that around 1883 the Ministry of Education was giving each *ryūgakusei* 1,800 yen per year, paid through the Japanese embassy in the particular country. See Uzaki (n. 79 above), p. 54.

99. Yagi, Itakura, and Kimura (n. 55 above), p. 164.

100. Uzaki (n. 79 above), p. 54.

101. Miyajima (n. 30 above), p. 37. Although Miyajima's account suggests that his detachment resulted from dedication to work, Takagi Tomoeda states that his annual stipend from the Ministry of Home Affairs was only 600 yen. See Takagi, "Henrin no ni, san," in Miyajima (n. 30 above), p. 263.

102. Kanao (n. 46 above), pp. 101–02, and Ishikawa (n. 19 above), pp. 144–45.

103. *TGSIG* (n. 63 above), p. 38.

104. *TGSIG* (n. 92 above), p. 11.

105. Ibid., pp. 12–13.

106. One or two spent some time in China. Other countries may have been visited for professional purposes without being noted in biographical sketches.

107. Ben-David (n. 5 above), p. 189. Based on a list of medical discoveries in Fielding H. Garrison, *An Introduction to the History of Medicine,* 4th ed. (Philadelphia: D.B. Saunders, 1929).

108. Ben-David (n. 5 above), p. 189, and Joseph Ben-David and Awraham Zloczower, "Universities and Academic Systems in Modern Societies," *Archives européennes de sociologie* 3/1 (1962):56.

109. Jones (n. 58 above), p. 114.

110. Tanaka (n. 45 above), pp. 83–130.

111. Harris and Brock (n. 69 above), p. 126.

112. Tanaka (n. 45 above), p. 131.

113. Kanao (n. 46 above), pp. 101–02.

114. Hanami (n. 49 above), pp. 77–79.

115. Miyajima (n. 30 above), pp. 39–40.

116. Ibid., pp. 40–41.

117. *TGSIG.* Cf. "Dai-yon kai Teikoku Gikai Shūgiin yosan iinkai sokkiroku," House of Representatives Budget Committee, 4th Diet, December 9, 1892, p. 3.

118. Yagi, Itakura, and Kimura (n. 55 above), pp. 165, 177–78, 170.

119. *TGSIG* (n. 117 above), p. 3.

120. *TGSIG* (n. 92 above), p. 15.

121. Yagi, Itakura, and Kimura (n. 55 above), p. 170.

122. Miyajima (n. 30 above), p. 43.

123. Yagi, Itakura, and Kimura (n. 55 above), p. 160.

124. Kanao (n. 46 above), pp. 113–14, 122–23, 103–06.

125. G. A. Tammann, "Gustav Tammann," in Gillispie, ed. (n. 11 above), 13:242.

126. Terashima (n. 40 above), p. 167.

127. Tetsu Hiroshige, "Ishiwara Jun," in Gillispie, ed. (n. 11 above), 6:26–27.

128. Kanao (n. 46 above), p. 443.

129. Nakamura (n. 52 above), pp. 87–200, and Jed Z. Buchwald, "Sir William Thomson, Baron Kelvin of Largs," in Gillispie, ed. (n. 11 above), 13:374–87.

130. Miyajima (n. 30 above), pp. 61–98.

131. Gloria Robinson, "August Friedrich Leopold Weismann," in Gillispie, ed. (n. 11 above), 14:235.

132. Victor Robinson, *Pathfinders in Medicine* (New York: Medical Life Press, 1929), p. 743. Robinson wrote: "Koch's pupils were not limited to his country or race, and perhaps no disciple gave him sincerer gratification than Kitasato, who brought Koch's technique to Japan."

133. Kitajima Ta'ichi, *Kitajima Ta'ichi jiden* (Tokyo: Kitajima-Sensei Kinen Jigyō Kai, 1955), p. 37.

134. Nagaoka stated that Helmholtz stuttered and would become flustered during his lectures. The Japanese physicist also complained that Helmholtz was never accessible. Planck he criticized for simply reading aloud Gustav Kirchoff's lecture notes, which Nagaoka had already taken down from another course. See Yagi, Itakura, and Kimura (n. 55 above), pp. 171–73. Helmholtz was in the last year of his life and Planck in his first year of teaching at Berlin when Nagaoka knew them. His *overall* evaluation of both men was much more favorable.

135. Ogata Norio, "Ogata Masanori ryaku den," *Igaku shi kenkyū,* no. 8 (1963):40–44.

136. Tanaka (n. 45 above), pp. 93–130.

137. Ibid., pp. 131–377; George B. Kauffman, "Alfred Werner," in Gillispie, ed. (n. 11 above), 14:264–66; Sheldon J. Kopperl, "Georges Urbain," in Gillispie, ed., 13:546.

138. Sakurai (n. 47 above), passim, and W. H. Brock, "Alexander William Williamson," in Gillispie, ed. (n. 11 above), 14:394–95.

139. Nakamura (n. 52 above), passim, and Buchwald (n. 129 above), pp. 374–87.

140. Ishikawa (n. 19 above), passim, and G. A. Tammann (n. 125 above), pp. 242–44.

141. Kanao (n. 46 above), passim, and W. H. Brock, "August Wilhelm von Hofmann," in Gillispie, ed. (n. 11 above), 6:461–63.

142. Miyajima (n. 30 above), passim, and Claude Dolman, "Heinrich Hermann Robert Koch," in Gillispie, ed. (n. 11 above), 7:420–30.

143. Kanao (n. 46 above), front cover. Wilhelm was Hofmann's middle name.

144. Ishihara Jun, *Shisaku no tebukuro* (Tokyo: Ishihara Jun, 1942), pp. 147–48.

145. Ishikawa (n. 19 above), pp. 180–83, and Tammann (n. 125 above), p. 244.

146. Sakurai (n. 47 above), passim, and Brock (n. 138 above), p. 394.

147. Ishikawa (n. 19 above), pp. 83–84.

148. Quoted in Miyajima (n. 30 above), p. 196.

149. Kitasato Zenjirō (son of Kitasato Shibasaburō), personal communication, September 5, 1972.

150. Kitasato Shibasaburō, "Koch-sensei kinen koen kai," *IJ,* no. 1225 (December 15, 1917):2184.

151. Idem, "Ko onshi Robert Koch-sensei o toburau," *Saikingaku zasshi,* no. 176 (June 10, 1910):2.

152. Kitajima (n. 133 above), p. 37.

153. Nagayo Hakushi Kinen Kai (n. 98 above), p. 115.

154. Tanaka (n. 45 above), p. 104.

155. Miyajima (n. 30 above), p. 36.

156. Mitamura (n. 20 above), p. 164.

157. Tanaka (n. 45 above), pp. 119–20.

158. Jacques R. Lévy, "François Félix Tisserand," in Gillispie, ed. (n. 11 above), 13:423.

159. Tanaka (n. 45 above), pp. 119–20.

160. Brock (n. 138 above), p. 394.

161. Ishikawa (n. 19 above), pp. 160–65.

162. Nakamura (n. 52 above), p. 71.

163. John B. Blake, "Scientific Institutions since the Renaissance: Their Role in Medical Research," *Proceedings of the American Philosophical Society* 101/1 (February 1957):51–52.

164. G. Schwarzenbach, "Alfred Werner and His Accomplishments," in *Fasciculus Extraordinarius Alfred Werner, 1866–1919* (Basel: Verlag Helvetica Chimica Acta, 1967), p. 41.

165. Tanaka (n. 45 above), p. 104.

166. Ben-David and Zloczower (n. 108 above), pp. 45–85.

167. John Theodore Merz, *A History of European Thought in the Nineteenth Century,* 1 (London: Wm. Blackwood and Sons, 1923):211–15.

168. Ibid., p. 215.

169. Nagai (n. 29 above), p. 25.

170. Robert R. Williams, *Toward the Conquest of Beriberi* (Cambridge: Harvard University Press, 1961), pp. 20–24, 19, 35.

171. Ibid., p. 20.

172. Gerald L. Geison, *Michael Foster and the Cambridge School of Physiology: The Scientific Enterprise in Late Victorian Society* (Princeton: Princeton University Press, 1978), pp. 24–31, 158–59, 329.

173. Kitasato Shibasaburō, Ogata Masanori, Yamagiwa Katsusaburō, Miura Moriharu, and Shiga Kiyoshi, among others, were all trained in Germany after their graduation from Tokyo University.

174. Tanaka (n. 45 above), pp. 63–64.

175. Kanao (n. 46 above), p. 457.

176. James R. Partington, *A History of Chemistry,* 4 (London: Macmillan, 1964):432. I am indebted to June Z. Fullmer for this reference.

177. Brock (n. 138 above), pp. 394–95, (n. 141 above), pp. 461–62.

178. Partington (n. 176 above), p. 446.

179. Brock (n. 138 above), p. 394.

180. Kanao (n. 46 above), pp. 88–90.

181. Williams (n. 170 above), pp. 14–15.

182. James R. Bartholomew, *The Acculturation of Science in Japan: Kitasato Shibasaburō and the Japanese Bacteriological Community, 1885–1920* (Ann Arbor: University Microfilms, 1972), pp. 163–70.

183. Miyajima (n. 30 above), p. 176, and Mori Rintarō, "Tōkei ni tsuite no bunsō," *Tōkyō iji shinshi,* no. 562 (June 8, 1889):2.

184. Joseph Ben-David, "Roles and Innovations in Medicine," *American Journal of Sociology* 65/6 (1960):561–62.

185. Garrison (n. 107 above), pp. 581–82.

186. Dolman (n. 142 above), p. 426.

187. The two colleagues were Carl Gerhardt and Ernst von Bergmann. For details see Kitasato's letter to Hasegawa Tai, read into the proceedings of the Imperial Japanese Diet: Dai Nihon Teikoku Gikai Shi Kankō Kai, ed., *Dai Nihon Teikoku Gikai shi,* 2 (hereafter **DNTGS**) (Tokyo: Dai Nihon Teikoku Gikai Shi Kankō Kai, 1926–30). Cf. "Yosan sainyū saishutsu sō yosan an Mombushō jokan," House of Representatives, 4th Diet, January 11, 1893, pp. 760–63.

188. Dolman (n. 142 above), p. 426.

189. Sata Yoshihiko, "Kaigai ryūgakusei no zentō," *IJ,* no. 1057 (September 26, 1914):1632; "Tomen no shomondai: Gakujutsu no dokuritsu mondai," ibid., p. 1638.

190. "Ryūgaku o haiseyō" (n. 95 above), p. 436.

191. Ibid., pp. 436–37.

192. "Iwayuru igaku no hattatsu to ryūgaku," *IJ,* no. 1042 (June 13, 1914):1046.

193. Sata (n. 189 above), p. 1632.

194. Mishima Shunken, "Ryūgakusei tozetsu mondai, 2," *IJ,* no. 1060 (October 17, 1914):1748.

195. *DNTGS,* 4. Cf. "Gakusei chōsa kai setchi ni kansuru kengi an," House of Peers, 14th Diet, January 31, 1900, p. 111.

196. Mishima (n. 194 above), p. 1749.

197. *DNTGS,* 9. Cf. "Tōkyō Teikoku Daigaku Ika Daigaku kyōjū no shokuseki ni kansuru shitsumon," House of Representatives, 35th Diet, December 15, 1914, pp. 960–61.

198. *TGSIG.* Cf. "Dai-ichi ka dai-hachi gō," House of Representatives Budget Committee, 10th Diet, March 12, 1897, p. 87.

199. "Kyōjū no naishoku ni tsuite," *IJ,* no. 1001 (August 30, 1913):1615. The report refers to the period in 1898 when Hamao Arata was the university president.

200. See n. 92 above regarding the situation in the faculty of medicine. During the course of this same meeting, the minister of education, Toyama Shōichi, said of the faculty of engineering: "Salaries paid to professors in the imperial universities are very small. Professors in the Faculty of Engineering at Tokyo University returning from study in Europe have great difficulty continuing as professors for very long."

201. Ibid., p. 11.

202. *DNTGS* (n. 195 above), p. 111.

203. Terasaki Masao, "Kōtō kyōiku," in Kaigo Tokiomi, ed., *Inoue Kowashi no kyōiku seisaku* (Tokyo: Tōkyō Daigaku Shuppan, 1968), pp. 370–71, and Iwasaki Jirō, *Bukka no sesō hyakunen* (Tokyo: Yomiuri Shimbun Sha, 1982), pp. 288–89.

204. Terasaki (n. 203 above), pp. 370–71, and *TGSIG* (n. 92 above), p. 12. Ōyama Kenzō, education ministry councillor, stated: "Professors are supposed to live on the salaries they received in the past, but they cannot easily do so . . . Eminent *hakushi* at the university are being paid about 1,600 yen on the average. Yet they are the top-ranking scholars in Japan!"

205. See Terasaki (n. 203 above) regarding the range of payments for research contributions. For the situation in 1907, see "Daigaku kyōjū no zōhō," *IJ*, no. 679 (June 22, 1907):722.

206. For these and various other examples, see "Kyōjū no shūnyū," *IJ*, no. 759 (January 1, 1909):55; no. 760 (January 9, 1909):136.

207. "Kyōjū no shūnyū," *IJ*, no. 762 (January 23, 1909):205; no. 764 (February 6, 1909):262; no. 766 (February 20, 1909):330. The last reports on Yamagiwa's situation.

208. "Kyōjū no naishoku ni tsuite," (n. 199 above), p. 1615.

209. *DNTGS* (n. 195 above), p. 122.

210. *DNTGS* (n. 197 above), p. 969.

211. "Zōhō mondai ni tsuite," *IJ*, no. 792 (August 21, 1909):1179.

212. Kimura Tadashi, ed., *Inoue Kowashi-kun kyōiku jigyō sho shi* (Tokyo: Kimura Tadashi, 1894), pp. 73–74. Quoted in Terasaki (n. 203 above), pp. 380–81.

213. *TTDGNS*, 2 (n. 22 above):1256–57 (fold-out chart).

214. *TGSIG*. Cf. "Daigaku tokubetsu kaikei hōan hoka ikken," House of Representatives Budget Committee, 42d Diet, February 13, 1920, p. 1. The vice minister actually used the phrase "level of culture," but the context indicates that he identified a high level of labor division with a high level of culture.

215. Nihon Butsuri Gakkai, ed., *Nihon no butsurigaku shi*, 1 (Tokyo: Tōkai Daigaku Shuppan Kai, 1978):113, 125–26.

216. Ibid., pp. 124, 130, 126.

217. Ibid., pp. 3, 120.

218. Imoto Minoru, *Nihon no kagaku: Hyakunen no ayumi* (Kyoto: Kagaku Dōjin, 1978), p. 27.

219. See the following sources for the names of the earliest society members: for the Tokyo (later Japan) Chemical Society membership, see Imoto (n. 218 above), pp. 26–33; for the Tokyo Mathematical and Physical Society, see Yagi Eri, "Nihon saishō no butsurigakushatachi, Meiji shoki no butsurigaku no jōtai," *Butsurigaku shi kenkyū* 1/3 (1959):237–62.

220. Yagi (n. 219 above), pp. 239–46.

221. Ibid., pp. 240–52.

222. See n. 217 above.

223. Commission on Medical Education, ed., *Medical Education* (New York: Commission on Medical Education, 1932), p. 344.

224. "Ikai dantai undō shi," *IJ*, no. 1200 (June 23, 1917):1152.

225. Kitajima (n. 133 above), p. 92.

226. On the German situation, see Theodor Billroth, *The Medical Sciences in the German Universities* (New York: Macmillan, 1924), p. 29, and Abraham Flexner, *Medical Education in Europe* (Boston: D.B. Updike, 1912), pp. 145–66.

227. "Ikai dantai undō shi," *IJ*, no. 1201 (June 30, 1917):1191.

228. "Daigaku kyōjū no naishoku," *Tōkyō Asahi Shimbun*, no. 9747 (September 12, 1913):5.

229. Miyajima (n. 30 above), p. 111.

230. Flexner (n. 226 above), p. 148, and idem, *Medical Education* (New York: Macmillan, 1925), p. 40.

231. "Daigaku kyōjū no naishoku" (n. 228 above).

Chapter Four: Laying the Institutional Foundations of Science

1. Chemist Sakurai Jōji attributed this view to many contemporary officials. See his *Omoide no kazukazu*, pp. 19–20.

2. Nakayama Shigeru: "Since the sciences and technology were introduced and developed on the initiative of the Meiji government, the system naturally showed a strong government-managed character from the very beginning. Unlike the situation in Western countries in which individual scientists organized societies for subjects which they preferred, the situation in Japan was one in which colleges and plants were established, and technicians and scientists were produced under government direction." See "A Century's Progress in Japan's Science and Technology," *Technical Japan* 1/1 (1968):78. See also Yuasa Mitsutomo, *Kagaku shi*, pp. 228, 282.

3. The widespread but erroneous notion that German precedents were faithfully followed in the development of Japan's universities and professions was probably as popular in the Meiji and Taishō years as it is today. A 1915 source declared, for example: "The Japanese educational system followed the German pattern in nearly every respect. The manner of teaching, organization, structure, and order were all in the German mold." See "Ika daigaku genjō daha no gi," *IJ*, no. 1076 (February 6, 1915):268–69. Nakayama Shigeru's view is more accurate: "The imperial university . . . turned out not to resemble the German university terribly closely." See his *Teikoku daigaku no tanjō* (Tokyo: Chūō Kōron Sha, 1978), p. 62.

4. Sugawara Kunika (ch. 2, n. 116), "Meiji shoki no kagaku," pp. 249–53.

5. James R. Bartholomew, "Why Was There No Scientific Revolution in Tokugawa Japan?" *Japanese Studies in the History of Science*, no. 15 (1976):111–25.

6. Shigeru Nakayama, "Japanese Scientific Thought," in Gillispie, ed., *Dictionary of Scientific Biography* 15/1:742.

7. Yagi Eri, Itakura Kiyonobu, and Kimura Tōsaku, *Nagaoka Hantarō den*, p. 52.

8. Miyajima Mikinosuke, *Kitasato Shibasaburō den*, p. 115.

9. Nakayama (n. 3 above), pp. 80–90.

10. Miyajima (n. 8 above), pp. 115–16.

11. Janet Hunter (ch. 3, n. 73), "The Development of Technical Education in Japan," p. 12.

12. Shigeru Nakayama, "The Role Played by Universities in Scientific and Technological Development in Japan," *Cahiers d'histoire mondiale* 9/2 (1965):345, and Bernhard J. Stern, "The Role of the Universities and Scientific Societies," in idem, ed., *Historical Materials on Innovations in Higher Educa-*

tion (New York: Planning Project for Advanced Training in Social Research, Columbia University, 1953), p. 122.

13. Two proposals for a comprehensive national university had developed in the last quarter century of Tokugawa rule. One, drafted in 1842 by the astronomer Hoashi Banri, and a second, prepared by Ōki Takatō, who later became minister of education, would have incorporated most standard subjects, including technical ones. For details, see Ishikawa Matsutarō (ch. 2, n. 23), "Kinsei buke no kyōiku, shomin no kyōiku," p. 118.

14. Tōkyō Daigaku Hyakunen Shi Hensan Iinkai, *Tōkyō Daigaku hyakunen shi: Tsūshi* (hereafter **TDHNS**), 1 (Tokyo: Tōkyō Daigaku, 1984):7. See also Michio Nagai, *Higher Education in Japan,* trans. Jerry Dusenbury (Tokyo: University of Tokyo Press, 1971), p. 22.

15. Tōkyō Teikoku Daigaku, *Tōkyō Teikoku Daigaku gojū nen shi* (hereafter **TTDGNS**), 1 (Tokyo: Tōkyō Teikoku Daigaku, 1932):16, 22, 121–26.

16. Ibid., pp. 55–57, 69–113.

17. Quoted in *TDHNS*, 1:394–95, 411–13.

18. *TTDGNS*, 1:257, 233–34, 263, 286.

19. Terasaki Masao, "Teikoku daigaku keisei ki no daigaku kan," in idem, ed., *Gakkō kan no shiteki kenkyū* (Tokyo: Nōma Kyōiku Kenkyū Jo, 1972), p. 204.

20. *TTDGNS,* 1:358, 16.

21. Nakayama (n. 3 above), pp. 79–80, 78.

22. Yuasa (n. 2 above), p. 101.

23. Yuasa Mitsutomo, *Gendai kagaku gijutsu shi nempyō* (Tokyo: San'ichi Shobō, 1961), pp. 24–52.

24. Karasawa Tomitarō, *Kōshinsei: Bakumatsu Ishin ki no erito* (Tokyo: Gyōsei, 1974), pp. 3–10.

25. Nakamura Seiji, *Tanakadate Aikitsu-sensei*, pp. 87–88.

26. Shigeru Nakayama, "Science and Technology in Modern Japanese Development," in William Beranek and Gustav Ranis, eds., *Science, Technology and Economic Growth* (New York: Praeger, 1978), p. 221.

27. Yagi, Itakura, and Kimura (n. 7 above), p. 221.

28. Nakayama (n. 3 above), passim.

29. Nakamura (n. 25 above), p. 44.

30. Ishikawa Teijirō, *Honda Kōtarō den* (Tokyo: Nikkan Kōgyō Shimbun Sha, 1964), p. 60.

31. Hanami Sakumi, *Danshaku Yamakawa-sensei den*, p. 85.

32. John Z. Bowers, *When the Twain Meet*, p. 97.

33. Charles Otis Whitman, *Zoology in the University of Tokio* (Yokohama: Japan Gazette, 1881), p. 29.

34. Sakurai (n. 1 above), pp. 67, 68–69.

35. Nakayama (n. 26 above), p. 208.

36. Sakurai (n. 1 above), p. 70.

37. Katō Hiroyuki, "Tensoku hyakuwa," reprinted in Nihon Gakushiin, ed., *Nihon Gakushiin hachijū nen shi* (hereafter **NGHNS**): *Shiryōhen*, 1 (Tokyo: Nihon Gakushiin, 1962):753.

38. Shūgiin Jimukyoku, *Teikoku Gikai Shūgiin Iinkai Giroku* (hereafter *TGSIG*). Cf. "Dai-go ka dai-ichi gō," House of Representatives Budget Committee, 5th Diet, December 8, 1893, p. 20.

39. Nakayama (n. 3 above), pp. 132–33.

40. Katō (n. 37 above), p. 755.

41. Abraham Flexner, *Medical Education in Europe*, pp. 252–53.

42. Stern (n. 12 above), p. 122; S. Lilley, "Scientific Education and the Ecole Polytechnique," in Stern, p. 125; and Frederic Lilge, "The Break between Science and Philosophy in Germany," in Stern, p. 148.

43. Stern (n. 12 above), p. 70, and Martha Ornstein, "Universities in the Seventeenth Century," in Stern (n. 12 above), pp. 96–101.

44. Alexander Vucinich, *Science in Russian Culture, to 1860* (Stanford: Stanford University Press, 1963), pp. 73–74.

45. A. Hunter Dupree, *Science in the Federal Government* (Cambridge: Harvard University Press, 1957), p. 148.

46. Vucinich (n. 44 above), pp. 35–65.

47. Nakamura (n. 25 above), p. 91.

48. Ōkuma, in fact, was intent on establishing technical education at Waseda from 1882, when he first founded the school under the name Tōkyō Semmon Gakkō. For his views on this subject, see Takagi Jun'ichi, "Rikō Gakubu," in Waseda Hyakunen Hensan Iinkai, ed., *Waseda hyakunen* (Tokyo: Kase Kiyoo, 1979), pp. 456–60.

49. L. F. Haber, *The Chemical Industry during the Nineteenth Century* (London: Oxford University Press, 1958), pp. 198–204.

50. Friedrich Paulsen noted that agriculture *was* incorporated into several of the German universities beginning in 1906, but engineering never was. See Paulsen, *The German Universities and University Study*, trans. Frank Thilly and William H. Elwang (London: Longmans Green, 1906). The introduction of agriculture was opposed by some professors at Tokyo University and by Inoue Kowashi (later education minister) in 1889–90 because it was not represented in German and most other Western universities. Professors Yokoi Tokiyoshi and Satō Shōsuke, however, successfully argued for its incorporation. See Nakayama (n. 12 above), p. 345, and idem (n. 3 above), pp. 142–43.

51. Yuasa Mitsutomo, *Kagaku gojū nen* (Tokyo: Jiji Tsūshin Sha, 1950), p. 53, and Tominari Kimahei, *Gendai Nihon kagaku shi*, p. 79.

52. Hugh Borton, *Japan's Modern Century* (New York: Ronald Press, 1955), pp. 198–202.

53. Dai Nihon Teikoku Gikai Shi Kankō Kai, ed., *Dai Nihon Teikoku Gikai shi* (*DNTGS*), 3. Cf. "Fuken nōji shiken jo kokkō hojō hōan," House of Representatives, 9th Diet, January 18, 1895, p. 441.

54. *DNTGS*, 3. Cf. "Fuken nōji shiken jo kokkō hojō hōan," House of Representatives, 9th Diet, March 18, 1896, p. 1876.

55. Ibid., pp. 1873–74.

56. Ibid., pp. 1873–75.

57. "Densembyō kenkyū jo," *Tōkyō iji shinshi* (hereafter *TIS*), no. 762 (November 3, 1892):47.

58. Ibid.

59. Ibid., and "Densembyō kenkyūshitsu setchi no keikaku," *TIS*, no. 747 (July 23, 1892):39.

60. *DNTGS*, 2. Cf. "Yosan sainyū saishutsu sō yosan an Mombushō jokan," House of Representatives, 4th Diet, January 11, 1893, pp. 760–63.

61. *DNTGS*, 2. Cf. Dai Nihon Shiritsu Eisei Kai setsuritsu densembyō kenkyū jo hojō ni tsuke kengi an," House of Representatives, 4th Diet, February 23, 1893, p. 1021.

62. For Watanabe's remarks, see "Densembyō kenkyū jo ni kansuru Shibaku kai," *Tōkyō nichi nichi shimbun*, no. 6453 (April 29, 1893):4. For details on the antilaboratory movement, see James Bartholomew, *The Acculturation of Science in Japan: Kitasato Shibasaburō and the Japanese Bacteriological Community, 1885–1920*, pp. 61–71.

63. Nakayama (n. 12 above), p. 347.

64. Miyajima (n. 8 above), pp. 99–100; Yanagita Izumi, *Meiji bummei shi ni okeru Ōkuma Shigenobu* (Tokyo: Waseda Daigaku Shuppan Bu, 1962), p. 212; Takagi (n. 48 above), pp. 456–60; and Ueno Naozō, ed., *Dōshisha hyakunen shi* (Kyoto: Dōshisha, 1979), pp. 369–91.

65. Robert M. Spaulding, Jr., *Imperial Japan's Higher Civil Service Examinations* (Princeton: Princeton University Press, 1967), pp. 132–35.

66. Umezawa Hikotarō, ed., *Kindai mei'i ichiyū hanashi* (Tokyo: Nihon Iji Shimpō Sha, 1937), pp. 76, 373–74.

67. Terasaki (n. 19 above), p. 204.

68. Ivan Hall, *Mori Arinori*, pp. 347–48, and Terasaki, (n. 19 above), pp. 194–95.

69. James Bartholomew, "Japanese Modernization and the Imperial Universities, 1876–1920," *Journal of Asian Studies* 37/2 (February 1978):251–52.

70. For a general discussion of Meiji education in English, see Herbert Passin, *Society and Education in Japan* (New York: Teachers College, Columbia University, Bureau of Publications, 1965).

71. *TGSIG*. Cf. "Dai-na kai yosan iinkai sokki giroku dai-sanjūgo (sōkai)," House of Representatives Budget Committee, 2d Diet, December 9, 1891, p. 16. Regarding Kubota's views, see Terasaki (n. 19 above), p. 253.

72. Terasaki Masao, "Meiji chūki no teikoku daigaku hihan," *Daigaku shi kenkyū tsūshin*, no. 5 (January 1972):7–10.

73. *DNTGS*, 1. Cf. "Yosan sainyū saishutsu sō yosan an, Mombushō jokan," House of Representatives, 2d Diet, December 23, 1891, p. 1508.

74. Satō Kenzō, *Kokuritsu daigaku zaisei seido shikō*, p. 181.

75. Terasaki Masao, "Kōtō kyōiku," in Kaigo Tokiomi, ed., *Inoue Kowashi no kyōiku seisaku*, p. 366.

76. Ibid., p. 378.

77. *TGSIG*. Cf. "Dai-go ka Mombushō no bu," House of Representatives Budget Committee, 4th Diet, December 8, 1892, p. 6.

78. Toyama Shōichi, briefly minister of education in 1898, favored the introduction of a privatdozent system in Japan. See Terasaki (n. 19 above), p. 241. Lecture fees were recommended (though never implemented) by Minister

Kikuchi Dairoku in 1901. See "Daigaku kyōju zōho mondai," *IJ,* no. 369 (June 29, 1901):456.

79. *TGSIG.* Cf. "Dai-go ka dai-ichi gō," House of Representatives Budget Committee, 5th Diet, December 8, 1893, p. 23.

80. Ibid., p. 22.

81. *TGSIG.* Cf. "Dai-go ka Mombushō no bu," House of Representatives Budget Committee, 4th Diet, December 9, 1892, p. 7.

82. Quoted in Sugai Oden, "Jitsugyō semmon kyōiku," in Motoyama Yukihiko, ed., *Teikoku Gikai to kyōiku seisaku* (Kyoto: Shibunkaku Shuppan, 1981), p. 300.

83. Based on information reported in W. H. Sharp, *The Educational System of Japan* (Bombay: Government Central Press, 1906), p. 176, and Satō (n. 74 above), p. 183.

84. Nakayama (n. 12 above), p. 349, and Terasaki (n. 19 above), pp. 229–30.

85. *TGSIG.* Cf. "Sōkai Kaigunshō sono ta (sōki Nōshōmushō Mombushō no bu)," House of Representatives Budget Committee, 4th Diet, December 13, 1892, p. 16.

86. *TGSIG.* Cf. "Dai-ichi ka dai-san gō," House of Representatives Budget Committee, 10th Diet, January 27, 1897, p. 44.

87. For detailed information on the career patterns of academic engineers in the pre–World War I era, see vol. 5 of Iseki Kurō, ed., *Dai Nihon hakushi roku.*

88. Sugai (n. 82 above), p. 296.

89. Terasaki (n. 19 above), p. 235.

90. Quoted in Kyōto Teikoku Daigaku, *Kyōto Teikoku Daigaku shi* (hereafter **KTDS**) (Kyoto: Kyōto Teikoku Daigaku, 1943), pp. 9–10.

91. Terasaki (n. 19 above), p. 249.

92. Nakayama (n. 12 above), p. 348.

93. *TGSIG.* Cf. "Dai-ichi ka dai-san gō," House of Representatives Budget Committee, 10th Diet, January 27, 1897, p. 43.

94. *TGSIG.* Cf. "Dai-ni kai yosan iinkai sokki giroku dai-sanjū gō (sōkai)," House of Representatives Budget Committee, 2d Diet, December 9, 1891, p. 13.

95. *TGSIG.* Cf. "Dai-go ka dai-ichi gō," House of Representatives Budget Committee, 5th Diet, December 8, 1893, pp. 21–22.

96. *DNTGS,* 2. Cf. "Yosan sainyū saishutsu sō yosan an, Mombushō jokan," House of Representatives, 4th Diet, January 11, 1893, p. 760.

97. *DNTGS,* 1. Cf. "Yosan sainyū saishutsu sō yosan an, Mombushō jokan," House of Representatives, 2d Diet, December 23, 1891, p. 1509.

98. *TGSIG.* Cf. "Dai-ni kai yosan iinkai sokki giroku dai-sanjū gō (sōkai)," House of Representatives Budget Committee, 2d Diet, November 9, 1891, pp. 18, 19.

99. *TGSIG.* Cf. "Shūgiin Kyūshū Tōhoku Teikoku Daigaku setchi kengi an shinsa tokubetsu iinkai sokkiroku (dai-ichi gō)," House of Representatives Budget Committee, 14th Diet, January 29, 1900, pp. 4, 2; and Sugai (n. 82 above), p. 299. Suzuki Manjirō, a physician and Diet member, in comments to the House of Representatives Budget Committee (December 9, 1893), however, rejected the idea of agriculture and commerce faculties on grounds of alleged un-

popularity. "Our policy should be to establish at leading schools those programs which students want most."

100. *TGSIG*. Cf. "Dai-ichi ka dai-nana gō," House of Representatives Budget Committee, 13th Diet, December 17, 1898, p. 82.

101. *TGSIG*. Cf. "Dai-ichi ka dai-ni gō," House of Representatives Budget Committee, 9th Diet, January 14, 1896, pp. 3–5.

102. Kyōto Daigaku, *Kyōto Daigaku nanajū nen shi* (hereafter **KDNNS**) (Kyoto: Kyōto Daigaku, 1967), p. 16.

103. *KDNNS*, p. 17. See also *TGSIG*. Cf. "Dai-ichi ka dai-ichi gō," House of Representatives Budget Committee, 9th Diet, January 14, 1896, pp. 5–10.

104. *KDNNS*, p. 18.

105. *TGSIG*. Cf. "Dai-ichi ka dai-roku gō," House of Representatives Budget Committee, 13th Diet, December 16, 1898, p. 73.

106. *TGSIG*. Cf. "Dai-ichi ka dai-hachi gō," House of Representatives Budget Committee, 10th Diet, March 12, 1897, p. 87.

107. *TGSIG*. Cf. "Dai-ichi ka dai-roku gō," House of Representatives Budget Committee, 13th Diet, December 16, 1898, pp. 73, 74, 70.

108. Ibid., p. 74.

109. *TGSIG*. Cf. "Dai-ichi ka dai-hachi gō," House of Representatives Budget Committee, 10th Diet, March 12, 1897, p. 88.

110. *TGSIG*. Cf. "Dai-ichi ka dai-roku gō," House of Representatives Budget Committee, 13th Diet, December 16, 1898, p. 73.

111. Ibid., p. 74; cf. "Dai-ichi ka dai-yon gō," House of Representatives Budget Committee, 14th Diet, December 1, 1899, pp. 44, 42; "Dai-ichi ka dai-nana gō," House of Representatives Budget Committee, 13th Diet, December 17, 1898, p. 82; "Dai-ichi ka dai-hachi gō," House of Representatives Budget Committee, 10th Diet, March 12, 1897, p. 87.

112. *TGSIG*. Cf. "Dai-ichi ka dai-san gō," House of Representatives Budget Committee, 13th Diet, December 13, 1898, p. 29; "Dai-go ka dai-ichi gō," House of Representatives Budget Committee, 5th Diet, December 8, 1893, pp. 3, 20, 24. "Dai-go ka Mombushō no bu," House of Representatives Budget Committee, 4th Diet, December 8, 1892, p. 2.

113. Ibid., pp. 20–21.

114. Ibid., pp. 3–4, 19–20.

115. Sugimoto Isao, *Itō Keisuke*, p. 355.

116. Ibid., p. 243.

117. *TGSIG*. Cf. "Dai-go ka dai-ichi gō," House of Representatives Budget Committee, 5th Diet, December 8, 1893, p. 3.

118. *TGSIG*. Cf. "Dai-ichi rui dai-ichi gō yosan iinkai kaigiroku dai-roku kai," House of Representatives Budget Committee, 16th Diet, December 27, 1901, p. 71.

119. Tōhoku Daigaku, *Tōhoku Daigaku gojū nen shi* (hereafter **TDGNS**), 1 (Sendai: Tōhoku Daigaku, 1960):2–4.

120. Quoted in ibid., pp. 10–11.

121. Takane's book, entitled *Daigaku seido kanken,* is described in an essay by Terasaki Masao. See Terasaki (n. 72 above), pp. 10–11.

122. *TGSIG*. Cf. "Yosan iin dai-ichi bunkakai kaigiroku dai-rokkai," House of Representatives Budget Committee, 15th Diet, February 1, 1901, p. 53.

123. Cited in *TDGNS*, 1:64.

124. Ibid., pp. 1–4. Katō Hiroyuki and to a lesser extent Kikuchi Dairoku had favored restrictions on access to university education, but Toyama Shōichi and certain other ministry officials took the opposite view. See Terasaki (n. 19 above), p. 229. I cannot, however, agree with Nakayama Shigeru's view that a preponderance of Education officials opposed university expansion (at least in the 1880s) on the grounds that only one university was needed for what he considers to have been Tokyo University's almost exclusive mission, i.e., to serve as a "window for importing the Western knowledge required for nation building." See Nakayama (n. 3 above), p. 69.

125. *TGSIG*. Cf. "Shūgiin Kyūshū Tōhoku Teikoku Daigaku setchi kengi an shinsa tokubetsu iinkai sokkiroku (dai-ichi gō)," House of Representatives Budget Committee, 14th Diet, January 29, 1900, p. 2.

126. *TGSIG*. Cf. "Dai-ichi ka dai-hachi gō," House of Representatives Budget Committee, 10th Diet, March 2, 1897, p. 87.

127. *TGSIG*. Cf. "Dai-ichi ka dai-ichi gō," House of Representatives Budget Committee, 10th Diet, January 27, 1897, p. 44.

128. Shioda Hiroshige, *Mesu to tate* (Tokyo: Chōgensha, 1963), p. 39, and *TGSIG*. Cf. "Dai-ichi ka dai-yon gō," House of Representatives Budget Committee, 14th Diet, December 1, 1899, p. 42.

129. *TGSIG*. Cf. "Yosan iin dai-ichi bunkakai (Naimushō Mombushō jokan) kaigiroku (sokki) dai-roku kai," House of Representatives Budget Committee, 16th Diet, December 25, 1901, p. 100.

130. *TGSIG*. Cf. "Yosan iin dai-ichi bunkakai (Naimushō, Mombushō jokan) kaigiroku (sokki) dai-go kai," House of Representatives Budget Committee, 16th Diet, December 20, 1901, p. 58.

131. It was claimed that Hasegawa Tai paid "the most attention to the activities of the Ministry of Education of all the three hundred Diet members." See "Hasegawa Tai-shi tai Mombushō," *Kyōiku jiron*, no. 278 (January 5, 1893): 25.

132. *DNTGS*, 2. Cf. "Yosan sainyū saishutsu sō yosan an, Mombushō jokan," House of Representatives, 4th Diet, January 11, 1893, pp. 759–62.

133. Kyūshū Daigaku Gojū Shūnen Kinen Kai, ed., *Kyūshū Daigaku gojū nen shi* (hereafter **KDGNS**), 1 (Fukuoka: Kyūshū Daigaku, 1967):31, and *TDGNS*, 1:16–18.

134. Nakayama Heijirō, ed., *Nijūgo nen shi: Kyūshū Teikoku Daigaku Igaku Bu* (Fukuoka: Kyūshū Teikoku Daigaku Igaku Bu Jimusho, 1927), pp. 1–4.

135. The Kumamoto domain's experience with school establishment in the early 1870s provides an instructive example. The new medical academy used the Japanese-style facilities and some of the equipment of its Tokugawa predecessor, whereas the new academy for Western studies (including mathematics, physics, and chemistry) was deliberately and self-consciously housed in a Western-style building with entirely new equipment from America. See Yamasaki Masatada, *Higo iiku shi*, p. 295, and Irwin Scheiner, *Christian Converts and Social Protest in Meiji Japan* (Berkeley: University of California Press, 1970), pp. 53–54.

136. Regarding Kikuchi's role, see Nakayama (n. 134 above), pp. 3–4. Concerning the consequences for him, see *TGSIG*. Cf. "Yosan iin dai-ichi bunkakai

(Naimushō, Mombushō jokan) kaigiroku (sokki) dai-roku kai," House of Representatives Budget Committee, 16th Diet, December 25, 1901, p. 99.

137. *TDGNS,* 1:16.

138. Ibid., p. 20.

139. "Kiso igaku no fushin o ika sen to suru ka?" *IJ,* no. 678 (June 15, 1907):691.

140. *TGSIG.* Cf. "Yosan iin dai-ichi bunkakai kaigiroku dai-rokkai," House of Representatives Budget Committee, 15th Diet, February 1, 1901, pp. 50–61; "Yosan iin dai-ichi bunkakai (Naimushō, Mombushō jokan) kaigiroku (sokki) dai-go kai," House of Representatives Budget Committee, 16th Diet, December 20, 1901, p. 72.

141. *TDGNS,* 1:33.

142. *KDGNS,* 1:32, 423, 466, 519.

143. *TDGNS,* 1:22, 33, 37.

144. Ibid., pp. 34–35, 65.

145. *KDGNS,* 1:422, 423.

146. Yuasa (n. 51 above), p. 67, and Sakurai (n. 1 above), pp. 70–71.

147. Sakurai (n. 1 above), pp. 70–71.

148. Naikaku Insatsukyoku, *Shokuinroku* (hereafter *Shokuinroku*) (Tokyo: Naikaku Insatsukyoku, 1912), pp. 639–40.

149. *DNTGS,* 8. Cf. "Gakujutsu hatsumei hyōshō ni kansuru kengi an," House of Representatives, 28th Diet, February 25, 1912, p. 1034.

150. *NGHNS,* Shiryōhen: 2:283, 451–54.

151. *NGHNS,* 431–34, Shiryōhen: 2:283, 292. Two project grants were awarded to physicist Nagaoka Hantarō for "research on the Z factor in latitudinal transformations" and for "research on X-rays and their effects." The other grant was awarded to geologist Kotō Bunjirō.

152. Kiyonobu Itakura and Eri Yagi, "The Japanese Research System and the Establishment of the Institute of Physical and Chemical Research," in Shigeru Nakayama, David L. Swain, and Eri Yagi, eds., *Science and Society in Modern Japan,* pp. 167–68.

153. Sakurai (n. 1 above), pp. 113–14.

154. Kikuchi Dairoku, "Teikoku Gakushiin no jushōshiki," *TIS,* no. 1768 (May 18, 1912):39.

155. *DNTGS,* 4. Cf. "Gakusei chōsa kai setchi ni kansuru kengi an," House of Peers, 14th Diet, February 2, 1900, p. 120.

156. *DNTGS,* 4. Cf. "Chūō kōgyō shiken jo setsuritsu ni kansuru kengi an," House of Representatives, 13th Diet, February 20, 1899, pp. 1914–15.

157. *Shokuinroku,* 1902, p. 667, and *DNTGS,* 4. Cf. "Chūō kōgyō shiken jo setsuritsu ni kansuru kengi an," House of Representatives, 13th Diet, February 25, 1899, pp. 1986–87.

158. *DNTGS,* 10. Cf. "Rikagaku o kenkyū suru kōeki hōjin no kokkō hojō ni kansuru hōritsu an," House of Representatives, 37th Diet, February 24, 1916, p. 881.

159. Ōsaka Yūkichi, "Kagaku kōgyō ni tsuite," *Taiyō* 16/11 (1910). Reprinted in Nihon Kagaku Shi Gakkai, ed., *Nihon kagaku gijutsu shi taikei* (hereafter **NKGST**), 2 (Tokyo: Dai-Ichi Hōki, 1961):485.

160. Kamoi Takeshi, "Kōgyō kagaku kenkyū jo setsuritsu ron," *Taiyō* 18/16 (1912). Reprinted in *NKGST*, 2:487–88.

161. Shiobara Matasaku, *Takamine hakushi*, pp. 49–50, 66–67.

162. Ōsaka (n. 159 above), pp. 483–85.

163. *TGSIG*. Cf. "Yosan iin dai-go bunka (Nōshōmushō jokan) kaigiroku (sokki) dai-ikkai," House of Representatives Budget Committee, 28th Diet, January 29, 1912, p. 3.

164. *TGSIG*. Cf. "Yosan iin dai-go bunka (Nōshōmushō jokan) kaigiroku (sokki) dai-ikkai," House of Representatives Budget Committee, 31st Diet, January 29, 1914, p. 1, and "Yosan iin dai-go bunka (Nōshōmushō jokan) kaigiroku (sokki) dai-yon kai," House of Representatives Budget Committee, 31st Diet, February 2, 1914, p. 28.

165. *TGSIG*. Cf. "Yosan iin dai-go ka (Nōshōmushō jokan) kaigiroku (sokki) dai-ikkai," House of Representatives Budget Committee, 30th Diet, March 4, 1913, p. 3.

166. *Shokuinroku*, 1900, p. 617.

167. *DNTGS*, 4. Cf. "Kanritsu Nōji Shiken Jo no shijō o haishi, fukenritsu nōji shiken jo no kokkō hojō hi o zōka suru no kengi," House of Peers, 14th Diet, March 3, 1899, pp. 1533–34.

168. *DNTGS*, 5. Cf. "Naha Konchū Kenkyū Jo kokkō hojō ni kansuru kengi an," House of Representatives, 15th Diet, February 9, 1900, p. 653.

169. *DNTGS*, 4. Cf. "Fuken nōji shiken jo kokkō hojō hōan," House of Representatives, 13th Diet, February 6, 1899, p. 1823.

170. Andō Hirotarō, "Nōji Shiken Jo no setsuritsu zengo," reprinted in *NKGST*, 22:360, and *TGSIG*. Cf. "Dai-ichi rui dai-ni gō yosan iin dai-ichi bunkakai kaigiroku dai-ni kai," House of Representatives Budget Committee, 15th Diet, December 17, 1901, p. 18.

171. *Shokuinroku*, 1909, 1910, pp. 684–85 and 674–75.

172. *DNTGS*, 4. Cf. "Fuken nōji shiken jo kokkō hojō hōan," House of Representatives, 13th Diet, January 18, 1899, p. 1750. My estimate of 250,000 yen takes into account some 39,000 yen spent on the national system of experiment stations, about 86,000 yen spent by the prefectures, and the education ministry's funding of the Tokyo University agriculture faculty and the Sapporo College of Agriculture.

173. These ratios were obtained by dividing each nation's research expenditures by its total income from agriculture and comparing the results. The resulting research investment ratios were .36 for Japan, .60 for France, and 1.02 for Germany.

174. Andō Hirotarō, "Kozai-sensei o tsuioku su," in Ando Enshū, ed., *Kozai Yoshinao hakushi* (Tokyo: Kozai Hakushi Denki Hensan Kai, 1937), p. 60.

175. Ibid.

176. Suzuki Umetarō, *Kenkyū no kaikō* (Tokyo: Kibundō Shobō, 1943), p. 246.

177. *Shokuinroku*, 1906, p. 61.

178. *TGSIG*. Cf. "Dai-ichi rui dai-ni gō yosan iin dai-ichi bunkakai kaigiroku dai-ni kai," House of Representatives Budget Committee, 15th Diet, December 17, 1901, pp. 16–17.

179. Aoyama Tanemichi, "Tokugakusha no shōrai ikaga?" *IJ*, no. 1055 (September 12, 1914):8.

180. See *Shokuinroku* for the appropriate years.

181. John B. Blake (ch. 3, n. 163), "Scientific Institutions since the Renaissance," pp. 31–62.

182. Miyajima (n. 8 above), p. 70.

183. Kitasato Shibasaburō, "Setsuritsu no shushi," *TIS*, no. 1900 (December 12, 1914):2648–49, and *TGSIG*. Cf. "Yosan iin dai-ichi bunkakai (Naimushō, Mombushō jokan) kaigiroku (sokki) dai-rokkai," House of Representatives Budget Committee, 15th Diet, December 25, 1901, pp. 83–88.

184. Hanami (n. 31 above), p. 280.

185. Itakura and Yagi (n. 152 above), p. 169.

186. Yanagita (n. 64 above), p. 434.

187. Cited in Itakura and Yagi (n. 152 above), p. 171. See also Shiobara (n. 161 above), pp. 71–72.

188. Satō (n. 74 above), pp. 183, 293.

189. "Kyōju no naishoku zehi ron," *IJ*, no. 1006 (October 4, 1913):1822.

190. Sakurai (n. 1 above), p. 18.

191. "Tomen no shomondai: Gakujutsu no dokuritsu mondai," *IJ*, no. 1057 (September 26, 1914):1638.

192. This is particularly remarkable considering the Ministry of Education's solicitous attitude toward Itō Keisuke and at least occasional recognition of botanical developments in the Tokugawa period. From the broader perspective of academic disciplines, this fact is a little misleading. In both Tokyo and Tōhoku, chairs in botany and zoology (eight altogether) could be found in both agriculture and science. The difference is made clear by a comparison with chemistry, which had seven chairs in faculties of agriculture and twelve in basic science. But biology was established only at Tokyo, with its comprehensive programs and considerably longer history. The basic science chairs existing in the imperial universities by 1914 are given below in tabular form.

	Tokyo	Kyoto	Tōhoku	Kyushu
Mathematics	6	3	2	1
Physics[a]	6	4	3	1
Chemistry	4	4	3	1
Geology	4	0	2	0
Biology[b]	5	0	0	0
Anthropology[c]	1	0	0	0

Sources: *Tōkyō Teikoku Daigaku gojū nen shi*; *Kyōto Teikoku Daigaku shi*; *Kyōto Daigaku nanajū nen shi*; *Tōhoku Daigaku gojū nen shi*; *Kyūshū Daigaku gojū nen shi*.

[a]Includes astronomy and seismology.
[b]Includes botany and zoology.
[c]Refers to physical anthropology only.

Conditions in Germany help explain the situation, German science and medicine, despite earlier growth, had reached a plateau in the late nineteenth century. The one-chair rule had prevented the creation of new academic posts with prospects for advancement, and the incumbent professors in many fields were quite young. Fields of research lost momentum, some going into decline. While this situation affected most fields, certain of them found other solutions. The best was probably chemistry's, where intervention by business produced a new institution, the pacesetting PTR laboratory. Nothing like this occurred in biology until 1910, when the German government committed itself to a network of laboratories (the Kaiser Wilhelm Gesellschaft or KWG) for scientific research that needed more resources than universities could provide. Biology got a place in this new research system precisely because it was lagging behind. Although the change came too late for prewar research, it did lay the foundation for later advances.

The effects on Japan were significant indeed. Its scientists and officials were not slavishly pro-German—the countries were on opposing sides in the war—but Japanese kept an eye on developments in Germany. Most scientists spent time there. Most officials admired the country. Strong affinities in jurisprudence and public policy existed, and nearly everyone insisted on the importance of German precedents, even when they decided to ignore them. This was the source of the problem for biology. With little or no growth in the academic motherland, its prospects for expansion in Japan were compromised. But as Germany benefited from KWG research, science watchers in Tokyo took note. Thus Kyoto University got a chair in biology in 1919, Tōhoku in 1923. (For details, see: Richard B. Goldschmidt, *The Golden Age of Zoology: Portraits from Memory* [Seattle: University of Washington Press, 1956], pp. 3–4, 8–9, and Awraham Zloczower, "Career Opportunities and the Growth of Scientific Discovery in Nineteenth Century Germany: With Special Reference to Physiology," master's thesis, Hebrew University, 1960; Richard B. Goldschmidt, *In and Out of the Ivory Tower: The Autobiography of Richard B. Goldschmidt* [Seattle: University of Washington Press, 1960], p. 77; Alan Beyerchen, "On the Stimulation of Excellence in Wilhelmian Science," in Jack Dukes and Joachim Remak, eds., *Another Germany: A Reconsideration of the Imperial Era* [Boulder: Westview Press, 1988], pp. 139–68; and *KDNNS*, pp. 92–93, and *TDGNS*, 1:557.)

Chapter Five: Science and the Bureaucracy

1. Jean Dessau, "Social Factors Affecting Science and Technology in Asia," pp. 13–23, and Sir Eric Ashby, "Commentary," in A. C. Crombie, ed., *Scientific Change* (London: Heinemann, 1963), pp. 724–28.

2. Yuasa Mitsutomo, *Kagaku shi*, pp. 228, 282.

3. Sakurai Jōji, *Omoide no kazukazu*, p. 113.

4. Ōtsuki Shōichirō, Nojima Tokukichi, and Maki Jirō, "Nihon ni okeru kagaku, gijutsu, to kagakusha," in Sakata Shōichi, ed., *Kagaku, gijutsu, to gendai*, p. 289.

5. Quoted in Maruyama Masao, "Fukuzawa Yukichi no jukyō hihan," in

Tōkyō Teikoku Daigaku, ed., *Tōkyō Teikoku Daigaku gakujutsu taikan, Keizai Gakubu*, p. 415.

6. W. H. Leonard and Harry C. Kelly (ch. 1, n. 9), "Scientific Research and Technical Competence in Relation to Resource Utilization," p. 514.

7. Bertrand Russell, *The Scientific Outlook* (New York: W.W. Norton, 1962), p. 208. Russell applied this criticism to scientists in Europe as well as Japan.

8. Thorstein Veblen (ch. 1, n. 22), "The Opportunity of Japan," p. 251.

9. Chie Nakane, *Japanese Society* (Berkeley: University of California Press, 1970), p. 102.

10. See Keith Michael Baker, *Condorcet: From Natural Philosophy to Social Mathematics,* p. 79, and Russell (n. 7 above), p. 99.

11. The experience of World War II produced, if anything, the very opposite effect in Japan, *strengthening* the French Enlightenment faith in science as a force in society. See, for example, Nihon Kyōsantō Kagaku Gijutsu Bu, "Nihon no kagaku gijutsu no kekkan to kyōsanshugisha no nimmu," *Zen'ei* 10/11 (November 1946). Reprinted in *NKGST*, 5:112–17.

12. Thomas C. Smith, "'Merit' as Ideology in the Tokugawa Period," in Ronald P. Dore, ed., *Aspects of Social Change in Modern Japan* (Princeton: Princeton University Press, 1967), pp. 71–90.

13. Bernard Silberman, "The Bureaucratic State in Japan: The Problem of Authority and Legitimacy," in Tetsuo Najita and J. Victor Koschmann, eds., *Conflict in Modern Japanese History: The Neglected Tradition* (Princeton: Princeton University Press, 1982), pp. 226–37.

14. Nakayama Shigeru, *Teikoku daigaku no tanjō* (Tokyo: Chūō Kōron Sha, 1978), p. 90.

15. Robert M. Spaulding, Jr., *Imperial Japan's Higher Civil Service Examinations,* pp. 307–08, and Sir Laurence Helsby, "Recruitment to the Civil Service," in William A. Robson, ed., *The Civil Service in Britain and France* (London: Hogarth, 1956), p. 44.

16. Spaulding (n. 15 above), p. 220.

17. On the origins of the Continental system, see C. J. Friedrich, "The Continental Tradition of Training Administrators in Law and Jurisprudence," *Journal of Modern History* 11/2 (June 1939): 129–48. On Japanese intentions, see Nakayama (n. 14 above), pp. 89–91, and Spaulding (n. 15 above), pp. 112–13.

18. Spaulding suggests that Meiji leaders accepted the German emphasis on law uncritically for three reasons: (1) when Japan surveyed the field in the 1880s, the civil service seemed to be most highly developed in Germany and freer there of nepotism, partisanship, and the spoils system they deplored; (2) there was broad agreement between the two states on basic constitutional ideals; and (3) Japan had inherited from the Tokugawa period a tradition of omnicompetent samurai managers who supervised an inferior class of specialists. If this analysis is correct—and it is certainly plausible—it would suggest that the Tokugawa experience was ultimately decisive. See Spaulding, pp. 163–64. Exclusion of the technically trained from higher positions on the basis of authoritarianism is particularly ironic when one realizes that the government made a point of naming scientists and engineers to head imperial universities

during the interwar period and World War II precisely because they could be counted on to avoid confrontation. For background and additional details on this question see Sassa Hiroo, *Zoku jimbutsu shunjū* (Tokyo: Kaizōsha, 1935), pp. 182–87, and James Bartholomew, "Science, Bureaucracy and Freedom in Meiji and Taisho Japan," in Najita and Koschmann (n. 13 above), pp. 295–341. For information on the question of morale and other ill effects, see Spaulding (n. 15 above), pp. 166–67.

19. See, for example, *Shokuinroku*, 1913, pp. 127 (Kitasato) and 622 (the president of Tokyo University).

20. Calculated from information in Iseki Kurō, ed., *Dai Nihon hakushi roku*, 5 vols. (Tokyo: Hattensha, 1930), and Jinji Kōshin Jo, ed., *Jinji kōshin roku*, various editions (Tokyo: Jinji Kōshin Jo).

21. Miyajima Mikinosuke, *Kitasato Shibasaburō den: Nempū*, p. 4. Their marriage took place in April 1883, before Kitasato had even gone to Germany. Baron Matsuo served as governor of the Bank of Japan from 1903 to 1911. See Shunjiro Kurita, ed., *Who's Who in Japan* (Tokyo: Chuseisha, 1913), p. 517.

22. The two were Yamakawa Kenjirō (physicist) and Kikuchi Dairoku (mathematician). Their appointments were owing to their prominence as academic administrators, not as scientists.

23. *TGSIG*. Cf. "Yosan iin dai-gō bunka (Nōshōmushō jokan) kaigiroku (sokki) dai-ikkai," House of Representatives Budget Committee, 31st Diet, January 29, 1914, pp. 6–7.

24. Nagai Tamotsu, *Takagi Kanehiro den*, pp. 93–94.

25. Meiji Shi Kōza Kankō Kai, ed., *Meiji kagaku shi*, p. 17; Nakayama Shigeru, "Kokka kagaku," in Sugimoto Jun, ed., *Kagaku shi*, Taikei Nihon shi sōsho 19 (Tokyo: Yamakawa Shuppan Sha, 1967), pp. 365–66.

26. Kanao Seizō, *Nagai Nagayoshi den* (Tokyo: Nihon Yakugakkai, 1960), p. 103.

27. Kawakami Takeshi, *Gendai Nihon iryō shi* (Tokyo: Keisō Shobō, 1965), p. 108.

28. Taigakai, ed., *Naimushō shi*, 1 (Tokyo: Chihō Zaimu Kyōkai, 1971):1, 139.

29. Ijiri Tsunekichi, ed., *Rekidai kenkan roku* (Tokyo: Hara Shobō, 1967).

30. For the activities of the Tokyo Hygiene Laboratory, see Naimushō Tōkyō Eisei Shiken Jo, ed., *Eisei Shiken Jo enkaku shi* (Tokyo: Fuji Insatsu Sha, 1937). Kitasato worked there in 1883–84, before his work in Berlin.

31. Nagai (n. 24 above), pp. 185, 116, 183.

32. Nakayama (n. 14 above), p. 143.

33. Tominari Kimahei, *Gendai Nihon kagaku shi*, pp. 37–39.

34. Hiroshige Tetsu, "The Role of the Government in the Development of Science," *Journal of World History* 9/2 (1965):322, and *TGSIG*. Cf. "Yosan iin dai-go bunka (Nōshōmushō jokan) kaigiroku (sokki) dai-san kai," House of Representatives Budget Committee, 31st Diet, January 31, 1914, pp. 17–24.

35. *TGSIG*. Cf. "Yosan iin dai-go bunka (Nōshōmushō jokan) kaigiroku (sokki) dai-go kai," House of Representatives Budget Committee, 31st Diet, February 4, 1914, pp. 33–48.

36. Tomita Tetsuo, "The Origin of the Patent System in Japan," *Japanese Studies in the History of Science*, no. 3 (1964):114–26.

37. Tokkyō Chō, *Tokkyō seido nanajū nen shi* (Tokyo: Hatsumei Kyōkai, 1955), pp. 3–4.

38. Tomita (n. 36 above), pp. 114–26.

39. Ōguchi Yoshikatsu, "Nakamura Yaroku-sensei," in Nihon Ringyō Gijutsu Kyōkai, ed., *Ringyō senjin den* (Tokyo: Nihon Ringyō Gijutsu Kyōkai, 1962), pp. 60–61, 38 (hereafter *Ringyō senjin den*).

40. Taigakai (n. 28 above), p. 139.

41. Shiobara Matasaku, *Takamine hakushi*, p. 31.

42. Terasaki Masao, "Teikoku daigaku keisei ki no daigaku kan," in Terasaki Masao, ed., *Gakkō kan no shiteki kenkyū* (Tokyo: Nōma Kyōiku Kenkyū Jo, 1972), pp. 190–92, 202–04.

43. Nakayama (n. 14 above), pp. 56–57.

44. Terasaki (n. 42 above), p. 197.

45. Watanabe Kōki, "Daigaku sotsugyō shōsho juyōshiki," *TIS*, no. 433 (July 17, 1886):970.

46. Watanabe Kōki, "Teikoku Daigaku sotsugyō shōsho juyōshiki," *TIS* no. 538 (July 21, 1888):24.

47. Kikuchi Dairoku, "Rigaku no setsu," *Tōyō gakugei zasshi* (hereafter **TGZ**) 2/33 (1884):75–81. Reprinted in *NKGST*, 2:533–34.

48. Sakurai Jōji, "Rigakusha no kairaku," *TGZ* 5/40 (1888):437–42.

49. Quoted in Ogura Kinnosuke, *Sūgaku shi kenkyū*, 1:252.

50. Katō argued frequently with Mori over the objectives and purpose of university education and academic research in Japan, undoubtedly because Katō adhered fully to the German ideal of "pure" research, while Mori favored an emphasis on "practical" application. See Terasaki (n. 42 above), pp. 185–265, and Tabata Shinobu, "Kyōsha no kenri no kyōshō: Kaidai," in Katō Hiroyuki, *Kyōsha no kenri no kyōshō* (Tokyo: Nihon Hyōronsha, 1942), p. 14. Katō's work was originally published in 1893.

51. *TTDGNS*, 1:934–35.

52. Terasaki (n. 42 above), p. 199.

53. Kurasawa Takashi, *Kyōiku rei no kenkyū* (Tokyo: Kōdansha, 1975), pp. 522–28.

54. Michio Nagai, *Higher Education in Japan: Its Take-off and Crash*, trans. Jerry Dusenbury (Tokyo: University of Tokyo Press, 1971), p. 218. Hamao, in fact, published a history of this institution. See Hamao Arata, *Tōkyō Kōgyō Daigaku rokujū nen shi* (Tokyo: Tōkyō Kōgyō Daigaku, 1940).

55. Terasaki (n. 42 above), pp. 210–14.

56. See Sassa (n. 18 above), pp. 182–87.

57. Terasaki (n. 42 above), p. 212. Thirteen of the young professors were from the college of medicine, with the other technical faculties also well represented. After 1905, however, scientists were rarely at the fore in movements of this sort.

58. Uzaki Kumakichi, *Aoyama Tanemichi*, p. 138.

59. Quoted in Terasaki (n. 42 above), p. 216.

60. R. H. P. Mason, *Japan's First General Election, 1890* (Cambridge: Cambridge University Press, 1969), pp. 131–32.

61. The contributions of Hasegawa and Nakamura in particular are dis-

cussed in Irisawa Tatsukichi, "Hasegawa Tai ron," in Irisawa Naika Dōsō Kai, ed., *Irisawa-sensei no enzetsu to bunshō* (Tokyo: Kokuseidō, 1932), p. 1150, and Irisawa Tatsukichi, "Nakamura Yaroku shi ni atetaru mono," in ibid., pp. 1368–69. Irisawa was professor of internal medicine at Tokyo University for most of the late Meiji and early Taishō eras.

62. Nakamura Seiji, *Tanakadate Aikitsu-sensei* (Tokyo: Ōbun Shorin, 1943), pp. 96–97.

63. Bartholomew (n. 18 above), p. 310.

64. *TGSIG.* Cf. "Dai-san kai Teikoku Gikai Shūgiin Yosan Iinkai sokkiroku dai-nana gō (dai-yon ka)," House of Representatives Budget Committee, 4th Diet, May 13, 1892, pp. 1–5.

65. *TGSIG.* Cf. "Dai-go ka dai-ichi gō," House of Representatives Budget Committee, 5th Diet, December 8, 1893, p. 19.

66. *TGSIG.* Cf. "Yosan iin dai-ichi bunkakai (Naimushō, Mombushō jokan) kaigiroku (sokki) dai-go kai," House of Representatives Budget Committee, 16th Diet, December 20, 1901, pp. 67–68.

67. Matsuura Chinjirō, *Okada Ryōhei-sensei shō den* (Tokyo: Okada Ryōhei-Sensei Denki Hensan Jimusho, 1935), pp. 123–25. This group included Watanabe Kōki, Kamata Eikichi, Takada Sanae—presidents respectively of Tokyo, Keio, and Waseda universities—and the former vice minister of education Tsuji Shinji.

68. Yoshikawa Akimasa, "Sotsugyōsho juyōshiki no enzetsu," *TIS,* no. 643 (July 26, 1890):36.

69. Ōki Takatō, "Ōki Mombu Daijin shukuji," *TIS,* no. 696 (August 1, 1891):36. See also Joseph Pittau, "Inoue Kowashi (1843–1895) and the Meiji Educational System," *Monumenta Nipponica* 20/3–4 (1965):270–82, and Saionji Kimmochi, "Saionji Mombu Daijin shukuji," *TIS,* no. 903 (July 20, 1895):38.

70. Hachisuka Mochiaki, "Kōshaku Hachisuka Mombu Daijin shukuji," *TIS,* no. 1006 (July 17, 1897):33.

71. Among other evidence bearing on this question, see the essay by Yamakawa Kenjirō entitled "Ōkurasho bannōshugi," in Shinjō Shinzō, ed., *Danshaku Yamakawa-sensei ikō* (Kyoto: Ko Yamakawa Danshaku Kinen Kai, 1937), pp. 418–19.

72. Yoshida Mitsukuni, "Meiji no kagakushatachi," *Jimbun gakuhō* 24 (March 1967):230–61.

73. Terasaki Masao, "Meiji chūki no teikoku daigaku hihan," *Daigaku shi kenkyū tsūshin,* no. 5 (January 1972):7–12.

74. Takano Rokurō, *Kitasato Shibasaburō* (Tokyo: Nihon Shobō, 1965), p. 209. Takano does not blame Katō Hiroyuki for the decision directly. However, Katō, who heartily disliked Kitasato, had not only motive but opportunity to involve himself. The motive stemmed from his bitterness over the 1887 beriberi controversy (see chapter 3), and the opportunity from the university president's role in recommending students for overseas study.

75. Bartholomew (n. 18 above), pp. 322–37.

76. *TGSIG.* Cf. "Dai-go ka dai-ichi gō," House of Representatives Budget Committee, 5th Diet, December 8, 1893, p. 1; *DNTGS,* 2. Cf. "Yosan sainyū

saishutsu sō yosan an, Mombushō jokan," House of Representatives, 4th Diet, January 11, 1893, p. 764.

77. "Gakusha to gyōseikan," *Kyōiku jiron,* no. 456 (December 15, 1897): 7–8.

78. *TGSIG.* Cf. "Shūgiin Gakusei Kaikaku Chōsa Kai setchi ni kansuru kengi an shinsa tokubetsu iinkai sokkiroku (dai-ichi gō)," House of Representatives Budget Committee, 14th Diet, December 19, 1899, p. 5.

79. *TGSIG.* Cf. "Dai-ichi ka dai-hachi gō," House of Representatives Budget Committee, 10th Diet, March 12, 1897, p. 86. The original group of scientists who were members included Furuichi Kōi (civil engineering), Yamakawa Kenjirō (physics), Hamada Gentatsu (medicine), and three chemists: Kuhara Mitsuru, Matsui Naokichi, and Nakazawa Iwata. See *Shokuinroku,* 1897, pp. 439–40.

80. Private communication from Uchida Tadashi of the National Institute for Education Research, Tokyo, November 26, 1976.

81. Hanami Sakumi, *Danshaku Yamakawa-sensei den,* p. 322.

82. Kyōguchi Motokichi, *Takada Sanae den* (Tokyo: Waseda Daigaku Shuppan Bu, 1962), p. 171.

83. *TGSIG* (n. 78 above), pp. 1, 6, 5.

84. Matsuura (n. 67 above), pp. 123–25.

85. Official histories of the various imperial universities were used to calculate the number of chairs for division among the administrations of the various presidents. For Tokyo University see *TTDGNS.*

86. Terasaki Masao, "Kōtō kyōiku," in Kaigo Tokiomi, ed., *Inoue Kowashi no kyōiku seisaku,* p. 334.

87. In February 1919 the Imperial Universities Ordinance was revised in a manner which bore on this issue directly. The change in procedure allowed the University Senate (Hyōgikai) consisting of the faculty deans plus two elected professors from each faculty, and chaired by the president, to control the creation of chairs at the campus level. See Sumeragi Shidō, *Daigaku seido no kenkyū* (Tokyo: Yanagihara Shoten, 1955), p. 363.

88. Terasaki (n. 86 above), p. 361. Professors were consulted informally about the creation of new positions even in the 1880s, before there was any chair system as such. See Mano Bunji and Nakamura Tokugorō, *Furuichi Kōi* (Tokyo: Kitabayashi Katsuzō, 1937), pp. 221–22.

89. *TGSIG* (n. 79 above), p. 86. The minister of education, Toyama Shōichi, noted that field priorities in the establishment of chairs were also at this time closely correlated with the selection of officially sponsored candidates for overseas study. See *TGSIG,* cf. "Dai-ichi ka dai-ni gō," House of Representatives Budget Committee, 12th Diet, May 25, 1898, p. 16.

90. Ijiri (n. 29 above), pp. 713–14.

91. Ueda Kazutoshi, professor of linguistics at Tokyo University, held this post from November 1898 through March 1902 and was especially helpful to the scientific community. Significantly, this was precisely the period when Kikuchi Dairoku was also president of the university and managed to establish a record number of new chairs in technical fields. See the analysis of Tadokoro

Yoshiharu, who was himself vice minister of education from 1916 to 1918: "Ueda-sensei no Mombushō jidai o omou," *Kokkan* 45 (March 1938):68.

92. Byron K. Marshall, "Professors and Politics: The Meiji Academic Elite," *Journal of Japanese Studies* 3/1 (Winter 1977):71–97.

93. *Shokuinroku* (n. 79 above), passim.

94. "Densembyō Kenkyū Jo hojōhi kafū no meireisho," *TIS*, no. 789 (April 23, 1893):48.

95. "Eiseikyoku to Kitasato Shi," *IJ*, no. 276 (September 16, 1899):759.

96. Kitasato Kenkyū Jo, ed., *Kitasato Kenkyū Jo gojū nen shi* (Tokyo: Kitasato Kenkyū Jo, 1966), p. 4.

97. Taigakai (n. 28 above), 3:244.

98. Regarding Gotō, see Nakahama Tōichirō, "Kitasato Shibasaburō hyōron," *Taiyō* 6/3 (March 1902), p. 27; Miyajima (n. 21 above), p. 168.

99. See, for example: Nakahama (n. 98 above), pp. 26–27, and "Ibatsu to wa nan da?" pp. 154–57.

100. Takagi Tomoeda, "Henrin no ni, san," in Miyajima (n. 21 above), pp. 266–68.

101. Shibasaburō Kitasato, "The Bacillus of Bubonic Plague," *The Lancet* 11 (1894):428–30. See chapter 6 for additional details on the Hong Kong plague expedition and its scientific consequences.

102. "Kitasato Aoyama Ryō-Hakushi ichigyō kangeikai no gaikyō," *TIS*, no. 868 (November 17, 1894):35–36.

103. *DNTGS*, 3. Cf. "Dai Nihon Shiritsu Eisei Kai setsuritsu Densembyō Kenkyū Jo ni sembatsu kenkyūsei o oku no kengi an," House of Representatives, 8th Diet, March 18, 1895, p. 919.

104. Miyajima (n. 21 above), p. 80.

105. Kitasato was a close friend of Fukuzawa Yukichi during the last ten years of Fukuzawa's life (1892–1902) and was greatly admired by Tanaka Giichi, later prime minister. Since these men published *Jiji shimpō* and *Ikai jihō*, respectively, Kitasato could usually count on a sympathetic press to report his views, though not necessarily to endorse them. See Kitajima Ta'ichi, *Kitajima Ta'ichi jiden*, pp. 99, 107–08.

106. Miyajima, pp. 272–73.

107. See Ijiri (n. 29 above), pp. 790–91, 798.

108. *TGSIG*. Cf. "Shūgiin yosan iinkai sokkiroku (dai-rokka)," House of Representatives Budget Committee, 4th Diet, December 5, 1892, p. 9; "Shūgiin dai-ni kai yosan iinkai sokkiroku dai-yon gō (dai-rokka)," House of Representatives Budget Committee, 2d Diet, December 1, 1891, p. 5; "Shūgiin dai-ni kai yosan iinkai sokkiroku dai-jūyon gō (dai-rokka)," House of Representatives Budget Committee, 2d Diet, December 3, 1891, p. 6; "Shūgiin dai-ni kai yosan iinkai sokkiroku dai-jūhachi gō (dai-rokka)," House of Representatives Budget Committee, 2d Diet, December 4, 1891, p. 1; "Shūgiin dai-ni kai yosan iinkai sokkiroku dai jūyon gō (dai-rokka)," House of Representatives Budget Committee, 2d Diet, December 3, 1891, pp. 1, 3.

109. Ibid., p. 2.

110. Ibid., pp. 2–5.

111. *Shokuinroku,* 1896, pp. 436, 467–68, and 1899, pp. 514, 549.

112. *TGSIG.* Cf. "Shūgiin Yosan Iinkai sokkiroku (dai-yon ka dai-ichi gō)," House of Representatives Budget Committee, 9th Diet, January 13, 1896, pp. 12–13.

113. *DNTGS,* 4. Cf. "Fuken nōji shiken jo kokkō hojō," House of Representatives, 13th Diet, February 6, 1899, pp. 1823–24.

114. Katayama Shigeki, "Shiga Taizan-sensei," in *Ringyō senjin den,* pp. 94–97.

115. Ōta Yūjirō, "Satō Shingorō-sensei," *Ringyō senjin den,* pp. 469–70. See chapter 8 for details.

116. *Shokuinroku,* 1897, pp. 466–68.

117. Hiroshige (n. 34 above), p. 321. Actually the same thing was true in the United States: agricultural interests demanded government assistance, but industrial ones made few such demands. See A. Hunter Dupree, *Science in the Federal Government,* p. 271.

118. Tokyo University's president, Kikuchi Dairoku, called this fact to the attention of the House of Peers in February 1900. See *DNTGS,* 4. Cf. "Gakusei chōsa kai setchi ni kansuru kengi an," House of Peers, 14th Diet, February 2, 1900, p. 120.

119. Asakura Haruhiko, *Meiji kansei jiten* (Tokyo: Tōkyōdō Shuppan, 1969), pp. 203–04; Taigakai (n. 28 above), p. 139; and Kaneseki Yoshinori, private communication, November 20, 1976.

120. Ijiri (n. 29 above), p. 799.

121. Taigakai (n. 28 above), p. 139. It should also be noted that the vice minister of agriculture and commerce was Shinagawa Yajirō, friend and backer of the prominent chemists Nagai Nagayoshi and Takamine Jōkichi. It is a certainty that Shinagawa would have favored this proposal.

122. Kōtarō Mochizuki, *Japan Today: A Souvenir of the Anglo-Japanese Exhibition Held in London, 1910.* (Tokyo: Liberal News Agency, 1910), p. 157.

123. *DNTGS,* 4. Cf. "Chūō kōgyō shiken jo setsuritsu ni kansuru kengi an," House of Representatives, 13th Diet, February 20, 1899, pp. 1914–15.

124. *TGSIG.* Cf. "Shūgiin Gakusei Kaikaku Chōsa Kai setchi ni kansuru kengi an shinsa tokubetsu iinkai sokkiroku (dai-ni gō)," House of Representatives Budget Committee, 14th Diet, January 20, 1900, p. 18.

125. "Mombushō no impishugi o nanzu," *Kyōiku jiron,* no. 551 (August 5, 1900):34–35.

126. *DNTGS* (n. 118 above), p. 124.

127. *DNTGS* (n. 118 above), January 31, 1900, p. 111.

128. Matsuura (n. 67 above), p. 125, and Mishima Shunken, "Ryūgakusei tozetsu mondai II," *IJ,* no. 1060 (October 17, 1914):1748.

129. *TGSIG.* Cf. "Yosan iin dai-ichi bunkakai kaigiroku dai-rokkai," House of Representatives Budget Committee, 15th Diet, February 1, 1901, pp. 52–57. These projects included subsidization of the geological researches of Kotō Bunjirō from Tokyo University, expansion of the laboratory attached to the chair of marine engineering at Tokyo University, construction of laboratories in biochemistry at Tokyo and Kyoto Universities, 680 yen in new funding for the Seismological Research Commission, and salary increases for professors.

130. *DNTGS* (n. 118 above), pp. 109, 112. Toyama was a staunch backer of the privatdozent system and in 1900 published a book entitled *Kyōiku seido ron* expounding his ideas.

131. Hanami (n. 81 above), p. 133.

132. *DNTGS* (n. 118 above), p. 122.

133. This assessment of Katsura Tarō comes from Nagayo Matarō, professor of pathology at Tokyo University and university president at the beginning of World War II. See Umezawa Hikotarō, ed., *Kindai mei'i ichiyū hanashi,* p. 29. An important prize awarded to scientists was named the Katsura Prize.

134. Katsura Tarō, "Dai-ikkai Nihon Rengō Igakkai keikyō," *TIS,* no. 1250 (April 5, 1902):22. The prime minister was not specific on this occasion, but it is nearly certain that he was referring to factionalism among academics. See chapter 6.

135. Mishima (n. 128 above), p. 1748.

136. Dai Jimmei Jiten Henshū Bu, ed., *Dai jimmei jiten* (hereafter **DJJ**) (Tokyo: Heibonsha, 1957), 1–2/2:80–81.

137. "Daigaku kyōju zōho mondai," *IJ,* no. 369 (June 29, 1901):456.

138. Matsuura (n. 67 above), pp. 77–78.

139. "Kikuchi Bunshō no Kyūshū Ika Daigaku dan," *TIS,* no. 1230 (November 9, 1901), p. 39, and **DNTGS** (n. 118 above), pp. 119–25. Then in December Kikuchi further muddied the waters by stating that he and the government *did* recognize the need for *two* new imperial universities—Kyushu and Tōhoku—but simply could not afford to build them (*DNTGS,* 5; cf. "Yosan sainyū saishutsu sō yosan an, Shihō, Mombushō jokan," House of Representatives, 16th Diet, December 28, 1901, pp. 1510–11).

140. *TGSIG* (n. 66 above), pp. 67–68.

141. Matsuura (n. 67 above), pp. 80–81.

142. Kikuchi Dairoku, "Teikoku Gakushiin no jushōshiki," *TIS,* no. 1768 (May 18, 1912):38. In reaching a judgment one must take into account the sum of the policies Kikuchi articulated and followed during the course of his administrative and professional career.

143. "Gakusha to gyōseikan" (n. 77 above), pp. 7–8.

144. Nakayama Shigeru, "Kikuchi Dairoku no Cambridge jidai ni tsuite," *Kagakushi kenkyū,* no. 65 (January–March 1963):36–37. It is worth noting that Kikuchi, when he arrived in Cambridge at the age of seventeen, was far younger than the average Japanese who went overseas to study. Perhaps this made him more impressionable.

145. Although Cambridge University in the 1870s was in the throes of major academic reform, considerable opposition remained to establishing experimental science as part of the regular curriculum. Isaac Todhunter himself was part of this opposition. James Clerk Maxwell, the physicist, once asked Todhunter if he would like to see an experimental demonstration of conical refraction, only to be told: "No. I have been teaching it all my life, and I do not want to have my ideas upset." See J. G. Crowther, *The Cavendish Laboratory, 1874–1974* (New York: Science History Publications, 1975), p. 9. Todhunter made his views on this subject known elsewhere. See Isaac Todhunter, *The Conflict of Studies and Other Essays on Subjects Connected with Education* (London: Macmillan

and Co., 1873), pp. 1–32. Regarding social mobility, see p. 21, where he writes: "We must not expect boys from the humbler classes to excel in the more expensive luxuries of education."

I am indebted to Barbara Reeves for these references to the Cambridge situation and Todhunter's position in it.

146. Matsuura (n. 67 above), pp. 91–92. Representative Fuji Kinsaku in December 1901 contrasted Kikuchi unfavorably with his two predecessors as minister of education "who were only politicians," declaring that he, as an "educator," should have a more positive view. See *TGSIG* (n. 66 above), pp. 76–77.

147. Matsuura (n. 67 above), pp. 91–96.

148. Satō Kenzō, *Kokuritsu daigaku zaisei seido shikō,* pp. 183, 293–94.

149. Marshall (n. 92 above), pp. 71–97.

150. Mitsukuri Kakichi, professor of biology, and Aoyama Tanemichi, professor of internal medicine and dean of the faculty, took the position, "We [professors] ought to end the [boycott] now that the minister of education's resignation has been achieved." See Hanami (n. 81 above), pp. 143–44.

151. Satō (n. 148 above), pp. 183, 293–94.

152. During the six and a half years of Hamao Arata's second presidency at Tokyo University (December 1905–August 1912), fourteen new chairs were established in technical fields, with all four technical faculties represented. This expansion, however, proceeded at a slower pace than the expansion during Kikuchi Dairoku's presidency (April 1898–June 1901), and it was mostly accomplished before 1909.

153. Makino was a believer in what contemporaries referred to as *hōka bannōshugi.* In 1897, as vice minister of education, he told the Budget Committee of the House of Representatives: "Appointments to bureaucratic positions are generally limited to graduates of the law faculty. Graduates in medicine, engineering, and science do not have the qualifications to become officials." See *TGSIG,* cf. "Dai-ichi ka dai-san gō," House of Representatives Budget Committee, 10th Diet, January 27, 1897, pp. 44–45.

154. Tōhoku Daigaku, *TDGNS,* 1:27–28.

155. The members included Tanakadate Aikitsu, Fujisawa Rikitarō, Sakurai Jōji, and Nagaoka Hantarō, all professors at Tokyo University. See Yuasa (n. 2 above), p. 238.

156. *TDGNS* (n. 154 above), 1:27–28, 34–36.

157. See chapter 4 for details.

158. "Kumakawa-hakushi Aoyama-hakushi ni kawaru," *IJ,* no. 1212 (September 15, 1917):1641.

159. Yamakawa Kenjirō, "Yo wa nani o waga kyōiku kai ni okeru saidai kyūmu to shinzuru ka?" in Shinjō (n. 71 above), p. 597.

160. Ōmori Tozan, "Konrai shusshoku no Bunshō," *Chūo kōron* (hereafter **CK**) 28/6 (June 1913):64.

161. *DJJ,* 1–2/2:614; 3–4/1:254; and 5–6/1:161–62.

162. "Okuda Bunshō ni nozomu," *CK* 28/6:70.

163. "Mombushō tōkyokusha no henken," *Kyōiku jiron,* no. 999 (January 15, 1913):45.

164. Hanami (n. 81 above), pp. 206–07. Yamakawa also credits Makino Nobuaki with endeavoring to assure that all the regional imperial universities became equal to Tokyo University in quality. See "Meiji kyōiku shi jo gen Mombushō no zaiaku to shite tokuhitsu taishō subeki jikō," in Shinjō (n. 71 above), p. 599.

165. Satō (n. 148 above), pp. 183, 293–94.

166. Ōmori (n. 160 above), p. 64, and "Aa Densembyō Kenkyū Jo," *Kyōiku jiron*, no. 1063 (October 25, 1914):47.

167. *DNTGS*, (n. 118 above), p. 112.

168. *TGSIG* (n. 64 above), p. 75.

169. Spaulding (n. 15 above), pp. 315–17. Conversely, the Ministry of Education lacked prestige because law graduates were fewer there.

170. Yamakawa Kenjirō, "Gakusei e kunji," in Shinjō (n. 71 above), p. 238.

171. Shibusawa Motoji, *Gojū nen kan no kaikō* (Tokyo: Shibusawa-Sensei Chōshō Shuppan Jigyō Kai, 1953), pp. 205–06.

172. Yamakawa Kenjirō, "Ōkurashō bannōshugi," in Shinjō (n. 71 above), pp. 418–19.

173. "Okuda Bunshō to kataru," *IJ*, no. 990 (June 14, 1913):1098–99.

174. Ibid., and Okada Tomoji, *Aa Okuda-hakushi.* (Tokyo: Impakusha, 1922), p. 141.

175. Uzaki (n. 58 above), p. 83.

176. Ibid., pp. 159–60.

177. Sakai Tanihei, "Genkan ban nikki," in Kumagai Kenji, ed., *Omoide no Aoyama Tanemichi-sensei* (Tokyo: Aoyama-Sensei Tanjō Hyakunen Sai Jumbi Iinkai, 1959), p. 410.

178. The correct delineation of responsibility was first established by Aki Motō. See his article "Taishō sannen no iwayuru 'Denken ikan mondai' ni tsuite," pts. 2 and 3, *Nihon ishigaku zasshi* 13/4 (March 1, 1968):19–40; 14/2 (July 31, 1968):18–67.

179. Uzaki (n. 58 above), pp. 84–85.

180. Kenkichirō Koizumi, "The Emergence of Japan's First Physicists, 1868–1900," in Russell McCormmach, ed., *Historical Studies in the Physical Sciences*, 6:39–41.

181. It is not even clear which scientist outside medicine was the best known to the general public *as a scientist.*

182. Iwazumi Ryōji, "Gijutsukan no kakugi shusseki," in Andō Enshū, ed., *Kozai Yoshinao-hakushi* (Tokyo: Nishigahara Kankō Kai, 1938), pp. 66–68.

183. Yuasa Mitsutomo, *Kagaku gojū nen,* pp. 69–70.

184. The Electrical Engineering Society (Denki Gakkai), for example, was called an "insignificant organization." For a discussion of professional organizations see ibid., pp. 66–70.

185. Quoted in Terashima Masashi, *Sekaiteki na Nihon kagakusha* (Tokyo: Izumi Shobō, 1944), p. 230.

186. Aoyagi Eiji, "Denki kōgaku saikin no shimpō," *Taiyō* 18/15 (1912), reprinted in *NKGST*, 2:485–87.

187. *DNTGS*, 8. Cf. "Kōgyō shiken jo setchi ni kansuru kengi an," House of Representatives, 27th Diet, March 18, 1911, p. 703. Watanabe Wataru, pro-

fessor of metallurgical engineering at Tokyo University and dean of the faculty (1903–19), was very active in the promotion of the mining industry and sought to create more extensive research facilities off-campus as well as on. See Tōkyō Teikoku Daigaku, *Tōkyō Teikoku Daigaku gakujutsu taikan, Kōgaku-bu, Kōkū Kenkyū Jo* (Tokyo: Tōkyō Teikoku Daigaku, 1942), p. 342.

188. "Eiseikyoku to Kitasato shi," *IJ*, no. 276 (September 16, 1899):759.

189. "Gyōsei seiri to Densembyō Kenkyū Jo," *IJ*, no. 473 (July 4, 1903):533; and "Densembyō Kenkyū Jo no dai-kakuchō," *IJ*, no. 915 (January 1, 1912):65.

190. Takano (n. 74 above), pp. 132–38.

191. Miyajima (n. 21 above), p. 78.

192. "Fuji-Tsukuba: Kitajima to Miyamoto," *IJ*, no. 1014 (November 29, 1913):2168, and Izawa Takio Denki Hensan Iinkai, ed., *Izawa Takio* (Tokyo: Haneda Shoten, 1951), p. 109.

193. Kitajima (n. 105 above), pp. 99, 107–08, 58.

194. Takano (n. 74 above), pp. 55–57, and "Dōfudegaoka Yōjōen," *TIS*, no. 819 (December 9, 1893):40–41.

195. Kubota Seitarō, "Kanri Kitasato," in Miyajima, pp. 259–62.

196. "Densembyō Kenkyū Jo no dai-kakuchō" (n. 189 above), p. 65.

197. "Aoba token," *IJ*, no. 988 (May 31, 1913):1032.

198. Ibid. On Uchigasaki's educational background, see Kitajima (n. 105 above), p. 107.

199. Kubota (n. 195 above), p. 261.

200. "Denken ikan no hishi," *IJ*, no. 1095 (June 19, 1915):9–10.

201. *TGSIG*. Cf. "Yosan iin dai-ichi bunkakai (Naimushō, Mombushō jokan) kaigiroku (sokki) dai-ichi kai," House of Representatives Budget Committee, 15th Diet, January 25, 1901, p. 2.

202. A "bacteriologist" for my purposes is defined as a Japanese aged thirty or above who obtained a doctorate of science in medicine with a bacteriological specialty during the period 1888–1920. Numerical estimates invariably rest on a judgmental factor. The primary considerations here were: attainment of skills required to do research (hence the age factor); publication of at least one original piece of research in the field; and peer certification of competence by colleagues at Tokyo or Kyoto. But the argument rests less on the exact number of bacteriologists than on the statistical trend. For details see Iseki (n. 20 above) and James R. Bartholomew, "The Japanese Scientific Community in Formation, 1870–1920," in L. A. Schneider, ed., *Science in Modern East Asia*, 1 (Buffalo: State University of New York, 1980):62–84.

203. For details on the sentiment at Tokyo University, see Kitajima (n. 105 above), pp. 40–41. Hostilities at the Tokyo Hygiene Institute stemmed from the presence of Nakahama Tōichirō, whose animosity is indicated by his article in *Taiyō* (cf. n. 98 above).

204. Tōkyō Daigaku Igaku Bu Hyakunen Shi Henshu Iinkai, ed., *Tōkyō Daigaku Igaku Bu hyakunen shi* (Tokyo: Tōkyō Daigaku Shuppan Bu, 1967), p. 298, and Futaki Kenzō-Sensei Kinen Kai, ed., *Futaki Kenzō-sensei* (Tokyo: Futaki Kenzō-Sensei Kinen Kai, 1969), p. 308. Futaki became deputy director of Komagome Hospital, a Tokyo University–affiliated institution.

205. Iseki (n. 20 above), 2:218–19.

206. Mishima Shunken, "'Aoyama' to 'Kitasato,'" *IJ*, no. 1063 (November 7, 1914):4–7.

207. Katō Fusazō, ed., *Hakushaku Hirata Tōsuke den* (Tokyo: Hirata Haku Denki Hensan Jimusho, 1927), pp. 28–29, 34–35.

208. Ogura Kuraichi, "Meiji nōrin kanryō no tenkei," *Nōrin shunjū* 2/3 (1952):32–37.

209. Spaulding (n. 15 above), pp. 166, 320. Spaulding notes that in 1910, complaints about "duplicative government" referred to the "pairing of legally trained bureau chiefs with technically trained subordinates."

210. Ogura (n. 208 above), p. 35. Unfortunately for him, Sakō declined the appointment in order to become president of the Dai Nippon Sugar Refining Corporation, where he was drawn into a major scandal and ended by taking his own life.

211. Asakura (n. 119 above), pp. 194–95; *DNTGS*, 8. Cf. "Chūō kōgyō shiken jo setsuritsu ni kansuru kengi an," House of Representatives, 27th Diet, March 21, 1911, p. 231; and Yuasa Mitsutomo, *Gendai kagaku gijutsu shi nempyō*, pp. 106–07.

212. Hanami (n. 81 above), p. 412.

213. *TGSIG*. Cf. "Yosan iin dai-go bunka (Nōshōmushō jokan) kaigiroku (sokki) dai-san kai," House of Representatives Budget Committee, 28th Diet, February 2, 1912, p. 14.

214. *TGSIG* (n. 23 above), p. 6.

215. Iwazumi (n. 182 above), pp. 66–68.

216. *TGSIG*. Cf. "Yosan iin dai-go bunka (Nōshōmushō jokan) kaigiroku (sokki) dai-go kai," House of Representatives Budget Committee, 31st Diet, February 4, 1914, p. 47.

217. *TGSIG* (n. 23 above), pp. 1–6.

218. Ibid., pp. 6–7, and *TGSIG* (n. 216 above), pp. 40–41.

219. Kitasato Kenkyū Jo (n. 96 above), pp. 25–27, and Takano (n. 74 above), p. 135.

220. Ōta (n. 115 above), pp. 469–70, advances this argument. "Professional foresters developed the Meiji system of forestry administration based on modern scientific knowledge . . . Subsequently, however, a belief in the superiority of legal studies led to the creation of rigid, inflexible walls in the higher civil service. Doors were closed. Technical specialists were treated as mere auxiliaries."

221. Nohara Tsuneo, "Watakushi no mita Takayama jochō," in Tōkyō Kōgyō Shiken Jo, ed., *Tōkyō Kōgyō Shiken Jo gojū nen shi* (Tokyo: Tōkyō Kōgyō Shiken Jo, 1951), p. 579.

222. Izawa Takio Denki Hensan Iinkai (n. 192 above), p. 109. Izawa was inspector general in the Metropolitan Police Department of the home ministry and assessed the situation as follows: "[Prior to its transfer to the Ministry of Education] the Institute of Infectious Diseases was a real barrel of rotten apples. It was supposed to be a state institution, but Dr. Kitasato had made it completely his own property. The chief of the Bureau of Public Health, who was supposed to supervise it, could not do anything without consulting him. Everything at the institute was under Kitasato's control. Since things had been this way for over a

decade, one would have to say that the bureaucratic system had been disrupted. The government decided to transfer it to the Ministry of Education because its aims were not being realized where it was, under the Ministry of Home Affairs."

223. Silberman (n. 13 above), pp. 226–37.

224. Robert A. Nisbet, in *The Quest for Community* (London: Oxford University Press, 1969), p. 270, argues that in any society autonomy demands a "plurality of authorities."

Chapter Six: Scientific Research in Its Social Setting

1. "Ibatsu to wa nan da?" (ch. 1, n. 21), pp. 154–57.

2. "Ibatsu to wa nan da to wa nan da?" (ch. 1, n. 21), p. 574.

3. "Batsu no Ika Daigaku," pt. 2, *Tōkyō Asahi Shimbun* (hereafter **TAS**), October 29, 1914, p. 5.

4. "Gakubatsu daha no yoi ichirei," *IJ*, no. 554 (January 28, 1905):131.

5. Nakahama Tōichirō, "Kitasato Shibasaburō hyōron," *Taiyō* 6/3 (March 1902):27. Nakahama is not formally listed as the author of the essay in *Taiyō*, but his authorship has been established by Aki Motō.

6. "Daigaku igakka no komponteki kaisei," *IJ*, no. 1047 (July 18, 1914): 1248–49.

7. *TGSIG*. Cf. "Yosan iinkai giroku sokki, dai-nana kai," House of Representatives Budget Committee, 35th Diet, December 16, 1914, p. 82. The emotional struggle over the transfer of Kitasato's institute to the Ministry of Education formed the context of Yagi's remarks. Although Yagi later became an ally of Kitasato, we do not know whether these remarks reflected Kitasato's views. See chapter 7.

8. "Daigaku igakka" (n. 6 above), pp. 1248–49.

9. San'ichirō Mizushima, "A History of Physical Chemistry in Japan," *Annual Review of Physical Chemistry* 23 (1972):7.

10. Tokutomi Sohō, "Shisō jo ni okeru Teikoku Daigaku no kanka," *Kokumin no tomo,* no. 173 (November 23, 1892):753.

11. *DNTGS*, 9. Cf. "Tōkyō Teikoku Daigaku Ika Daigaku kyōju no shokuseki ni kansuru Wakasugi Kisaburō no shitsumon enzetsu," House of Representatives, 35th Diet, December 15, 1914, pp. 960–61. See also ibid., "Tōkyō Teikoku Daigaku oyobi Kyōto Teikoku Daigaku rinji seifu shishutsu kin ni kansuru hōritsuan hoka ikken, dai-yon kai," House of Representatives Budget Committee, 40th Diet, February 8, 1918, p. 32.

12. Kitasato Shibasaburō, "Zai Doitsu-koku Igakushi Kitasato Shibasaburō shi shokan," *Chūgai iji shimpō,* no. 212 (January 25, 1889):105.

13. Kitasato Shibasaburō, "Ogata kyōju zaishoku nijū-go nen kinen shukuga kai, shukuji," *Saikingaku zasshi,* no. 175 (May 10, 1910):553.

14. From a letter to Hasegawa Tai, quoted by him in *DNTGS*, 2, "Yosan sainyū saishutsu sō yosan an, Mombushō jokan," House of Representatives, 4th Diet, January 11, 1893, p. 763.

15. Yuasa Mitsutomo, *Kagaku gojū nen,* p. 234.

16. Compiled from the sources for table 6.1.

17. Yuasa (n. 15 above), p. 234.

18. All the men in the pioneer group of Tōhoku scientists had trained at Tokyo University. One can see what values they brought to the new institution by examining conditions at the old one.

19. Information compiled from Iseki Kurō, ed., *Dai Nihon hakushi roku*, vols. 2 and 3.

20. Hata Sahachirō, "Gakusha to shite no memmoku," in Miyajima Mikinosuke, *Kitasato Shibasaburō den*, p. 278.

21. Miyajima, p. 103.

22. Takahashi Isao, *Shiga Kiyoshi* (Tokyo: Hōsei Daigaku Shuppan Kyoku, 1957), p. 114.

23. Miyajima (n. 20 above), pp. 210, 286–87.

24. Shiga Kiyoshi, *Aru rō kagakusha to segare to no taiwa* (Tokyo: Yomiuri Shimbun Sha, 1953), p. 30; and Takahashi (n. 22 above), p. 116.

25. Fukuda Reiju, *Kitasato Shibasaburō hakushi*, p. 10.

26. Miyajima (n. 20 above), p. 232.

27. Kitajima Ta'ichi, *Kitajima Ta'ichi jiden*, p. 29.

28. Miyajima (n. 20 above), p. 231.

29. Kitasato Kenkyū Jo, ed., *Kitasato Kenkyū Jo nijū-go nen shi* (Tokyo: Kitasato Kenkyū Jo, 1939), pp. 135–64.

30. *TAS* (n. 3 above), p. 5.

31. Iseki (n. 19 above), 2:9, 16, 27, 113, 46.

32. *TAS* (n. 3 above), p. 5.

33. Compiled from Iseki (n. 19 above).

34. Ibid., 2:13, 28, 91, 98.

35. *TAS* (n. 3 above), p. 5.

36. Ibid.

37. Manabe-Sensei Denki Hensan Kai, *Manabe Kaiichirō* (hereafter *Manabe*) (Tokyo: Nihon Onsen Kikō Gakkai, 1950), p. 105.   ·

38. Arima Eiji, "Tamashi ni oeru," in Kumagai Kenji, ed., *Omoide no Aoyama Tanemichi-sensei*, p. 367.

39. Arai Tsuneo, "Mikake ni yoranu shōjikisha," in Kumagai (n. 38 above), p. 141.

40. "Ogata Masanori-sensei tanjō hyakunen kinen zadankai," *Nihon iji shimpō*, no. 1507 (March 14, 1955):1013–14.

41. Iseki (n. 19 above), 5:11.

42. Tanaka Minoru, *Nihon no kagaku to Shibata Yūji*, pp. 17–21.

43. Nakamura Seiji, *Tanakadate Aikitsu-sensei*, p. 52; Yagi Eri, Itakura Kiyonobu, and Kimura Tōsaku, *Nagaoka Hantarō den*, p. 102; and Ishikawa Teiichi, *Honda Kōtarō den*, p. 93. Nakamura and Yagi, Itakura, and Kimura do not state outright that Tanakadate and Nagaoka graduated first in their classes, but they do mention that Tanakadate became a member of the faculty immediately after graduating, while Nagaoka received a full scholarship to graduate school as *tokutaisei* (roughly, "valedictorian").

44. Iseki (n. 19 above), 2:143. On biochemistry's lack of prestige, see Arima (n. 38 above), p. 367, where the author states that Aoyama Tanemichi customarily advised the poorest students in the graduate program to enter the biochemistry section.

45. Compiled from Iseki (n. 19 above), vols. 2 and 3.

46. On the Waseda and Dōshisha cases, see Yanagita Izumi, *Meiji bummei shi ni okeru Ōkuma Shigenobu* (Tokyo, 1962), p. 212, and Ueno Naozō, ed., *Dōshisha hyakunen shi* (Kyoto, 1979), pp. 369–91.

47. Iseki (n. 19 above), vol. 5. Kitao Jirō, though a physicist, received his appointment in the faculty of agriculture.

48. Compiled from Iseki (n. 19 above).

49. Data were compiled from sources used in table 6.1.

50. These figures refer only to relatives in the academic community or the particular disciplinary specialization, not to all relatives who might have aided a career. We have no way of knowing if even all of the academic and disciplinary connections appear in the reference works.

51. For Kitasato, see Iwasaki Katsumi, *Kōmoto Jūjirō den* (Tokyo: Nagasaki Shoten, 1943), p. 50. Yamamoto's case is mentioned in "Batsu no Ika Daigaku," pt. 4, *TAS*, November 2, 1914, p. 5. Yamagiwa is discussed in Tōkyō Teikoku Daigaku, *Tōkyō Teikoku Daigaku byōrigaku kyōshitsu gojū nen shi* (hereafter *Byōrigaku kyōshitsu*), 1 (Tokyo: Tōkyō Teikoku Daigaku, 1939):227, and Nagayo's in Nagayo Hakushi Kinen Kai, ed., *Nagayo Matarō den* (hereafter *Nagayo*) (Tokyo: Nagayo Hakushi Kinen Kai, 1944), p. 96.

52. Tōkyō Teikoku Daigaku, ed., *Tōkyō Teikoku Daigaku gakujutsu taikan: Rigaku Bu, Tōkyō Temmon Dai, Jishin Kenkyū Jo* (Tokyo: Tōkyō Teikoku Daigaku, 1942), pp. 76–77. (Hereafter cited as *Gakujutsu taikan: Rigaku Bu*.)

53. Tsuruta did not publish a single physics paper after becoming full professor and took a leave of absence in 1911. See Yagi, Itakura, and Kimura (n. 43 above), p. 312.

54. Yamakawa published only three scientific papers during his career. See Kenkichiro Koizumi, "The Emergence of Japan's First Physicists, 1868–1900," in Russell McCormmach, ed., *Historical Studies in the Physical Sciences*, 6:67.

55. Hanami Sakumi, *Danshaku Yamakawa-sensei den*, pp. 92–94.

56. Ibid., p. 90.

57. Koizumi (n. 54 above), p. 68.

58. Hanami (n. 55 above), p. 90.

59. Yagi, Itakura, and Kimura (n. 43 above), p. 310.

60. Koizumi (n. 54 above), pp. 79–80.

61. Nakamura (n. 43 above), pp. 227, 228, 225.

62. Ibid., pp. 92–93, 227.

63. Yagi, Itakura, and Kimura (n. 43 above), pp. 114–15.

64. Matsuzawa Takeo, *Waga shi waga tomo* (Tokyo: Misuzu Shobō, 1967), pp. 178–91.

65. Ishikawa (n. 43 above), pp. 78–80.

66. Yagi, Itakura, and Kimura (n. 43 above), p. 518.

67. Ishikawa (n. 43 above), pp. 78–80.

68. Yukawa Hideki, "Yobun," in Yagi, Itakura, and Kimura (n. 43 above), fourth and fifth pages of unpaginated text.

69. Matsuzawa (n. 64 above), pp. 178–91.

70. Yagi, Itakura, and Kimura (n. 43 above), pp. 313, 312, 311.

71. Ibid., pp. 382–83.

72. Originally published under the title "Ōshū butsurigaku jikken jo junran ki," in *Tōkyō Butsuri Gakkō zasshi,* 1912–13; quoted in Yagi, Itakura, and Kimura (n. 43 above), p. 381.

73. Yagi, Itakura, and Kimura (n. 43 above), pp. 384–85, 386. See also Mizushima (n. 9 above), p. 7. For a discussion of Yukawa's relations with Tamaki, see Yukawa Hideki, *Tabibito* (The traveler) (Singapore: World Scientific Publishing Co., 1982), pp. 112, 152, 158, 163–64, 170.

74. J. Harris and W. H. Brock, "From Giessen to Gower Street: Toward a Biography of Alexander William Williamson (1824–1904)," p. 126.

75. Samejima Tsunesaburō, "Kagaku Ka," in *Gakujutsu taikan: Rigaku Bu* (n. 52 above), p. 127. The study was published in 1892.

76. Tanaka (n. 42 above), pp. 37, 65.

77. Samejima (n. 75 above), pp. 122–35.

78. Ibid., p. 128, and Tanaka (n. 42 above), pp. 41–42.

79. Samejima (n. 75 above), p. 128.

80. In Tanaka (n. 42 above), p. 41.

81. Shibata Yūji, "Ikeda Kikunae-sensei," *Kagaku* 16/7 (July 1961):46.

82. Ikeda had enough money to build a chemistry laboratory in his own home after retiring so that he could continue doing research. See Samejima (n. 75 above), pp. 129–31.

83. John D. Bernal, *The Social Function of Science* (New York: Macmillan, 1939), p. 80.

84. Bernhard J. Stern, *Social Factors in Medical Progress* (New York: Columbia University Press, 1927), p. 33.

85. Talcott Parsons, *The Social System* (New York: Free Press of Glencoe, 1951), pp. 335, 340–41, 432–33.

86. Bernard Barber, "Resistance by Scientists to Scientific Discovery," *Science* 134, no. 3479 (September 1, 1961):597.

87. Thomas S. Kuhn, *The Structure of Scientific Revolutions* (Chicago: University of Chicago Press, 1962).

88. W. Cramer, "The Late Professor Yamagiwa," *The Lancet* 218 (May 24, 1930):1155, and Kanematsu Sugiura, "Katsusaburō Yamagiwa," *The Journal of Cancer Research* 14/4 (October 1930):568–69.

89. Cramer (n. 88 above), p. 1155, and H. Schuck et al., eds., *Nobel: The Man and His Prizes* (Amsterdam: Elsevier, 1962), p. 247.

90. Tashiro Yoshinori, "Ko Yamagiwa-kun o kataru," in *Byōrigaku kyōshitsu,* 2:125.

91. *Nagayo* (n. 51 above), p. 261.

92. Ibid., p. 121.

93. "Ika Daigaku genjō daha no gi," *IJ,* no. 1076 (February 6, 1915):268–69.

94. Yamagiwa Katsusaburō, "Ko Nihon Byōri Gakkai meiyō kaichō Miura Moriharu-sensei tsuitō no ji," in *Byōrigaku kyōshitsu,* 1:208.

95. Sata Yoshihiko, "Byōrigaku kyōshitsu no sōritsu jidai, Miura-sensei no shita ni manabishi koro," in *Byōrigaku kyōshitsu,* 2:19–20.

96. Ibid., p. 21.

97. Mitamura Makujirō, quoted in *Nagayo* (n. 51 above), pp. 262–63.

98. Tōkyō Teikoku Daigaku, *Tōkyō Teikoku Daigaku gakujutsu taikan:*

Igaku Bu, Densembyō Kenkyū Jo, Nōgaku Bu (Tokyo: Tōkyō Teikoku Daigaku, 1942), p. 75. (Hereafter cited as *Gakujutsu taikan: Igaku Bu.*)

99. *Nagayo* (n. 51 above), pp. 162–69.

100. Ibid., pp. 261, 101, 279, 288–89.

101. Because of his stutter, the Ministry of Education initially refused to sponsor him for overseas study. See Uzaki Kumakichi, *Aoyama Tanemichi*, pp. 42, 155.

102. Mitamura Makujirō, "Tanemichi no sekai dōtoku," in Kumagai (n. 38 above), pp. 165, 168–70, 397; and Sakai Tanihei, "Genkan ban nikki," in Kumagai, p. 397.

103. Takahashi Akira, "Kanrei no shukuji," in Kumagai (n. 38 above), p. 182.

104. Imamura Yoshio, "Mangekyō," in Kumagai (n. 38 above), p. 182.

105. Fujita Shūichi, "Aoyama Tanemichi," in Umezawa Hikotarō, ed., *Kinsei iretsu den* (Tokyo: Chūgai Igaku Sha, 1954), p. 274.

106. Uzaki (n. 101 above), p. 201, and Hatta Zennoshin, "Kettō sokutei kushin," in Kumagai (n. 38 above), p. 82.

107. Mitamura (n. 102 above), pp. 150–52, 162–63.

108. Arima (n. 38 above), p. 367, states that Aoyama's internal medicine section was the first choice for many first-year graduate students in the faculty of medicine.

109. Arai (n. 39 above), p. 142.

110. Yamada Jirō, "Karuizawa sanso," in Kumagai (n. 38 above), pp. 347–48.

111. Uzaki (n. 101 above), p. 201.

112. This reflects the evaluation of Shiozawa Sōichi, assistant professor of internal medicine at Tokyo University, in the 1930s. See *Gakujutsu taikan: Igaku Bu*, p. 132.

113. Tōhoku Daigaku, *TDGNS*, 1:65.

114. The other faculty, agriculture, continued to be located in Sapporo for a number of years. See ibid.

115. Sawayanagi Masatarō, "Daigaku kyōju no kenshoku," in Sawayanagi Masatarō, *Sawayanagi Masatarō zenshū* (Tokyo: Kokudōsha, 1980) 10:236–37.

116. Quoted in *TDGNS*, 1:65–70.

117. Nobuo Kawamiya, "Kōtarō Honda: Founder of the Science of Metals in Japan," in *Japanese Studies in the History of Science*, no. 15 (1976):147–56.

118. Ishikawa (n. 43 above), pp. 107, 181. New Year's Day is Japan's biggest national holiday.

119. Ibid., p. 180.

120. Ibid., p. 183.

121. Kawamiya (n. 117 above), p. 157.

122. Ishikawa (n. 43 above), p. 182.

123. Kawamiya (n. 117 above), p. 157.

124. Ishikawa (n. 43 above), pp. 157–59.

125. Ibid., pp. 94–95, 215.

126. Ibid., pp. 214–15.

127. Quoted in Kawamiya (n. 117 above), p. 148.

128. Ishikawa (n. 43 above), pp. 214–15.

129. Kawamiya (n. 117 above), p. 158.

130. Ibid., p. 149.

131. Fujita (n. 105 above), p. 274.

132. Arima (n. 38 above), p. 362.

133. *Byōrigaku kyōshitsu*, 1:193.

134. Ezra Vogel, *Japan's New Middle Class* (Berkeley: University of California Press, 1963), pp. 104–06.

135. Uzaki (n. 101 above), p. 204.

136. Japanese cultural patterns, if anything, would have encouraged openness and group discussion, not a closed-minded, autocratic style. See Reinhard Bendix, "Preconditions of Development: A Comparison of Japan and Germany," in R. P. Dore, ed., *Aspects of Social Change in Modern Japan* (Princeton: Princeton University Press, 1967), p. 54.

137. Tanaka (n. 42 above), pp. 63–64.

138. *Manabe,* pp. 141–42. This occurred in 1916.

139. James Bartholomew, "Japanese Culture and the Problem of Modern Science," in Arnold Thackray and E. Mendelsohn, eds., *Science and Values* (New York: Humanities Press, 1974), p. 139.

140. Mizushima (n. 9 above), p. 9. Mizushima was professor of physical chemistry at Tokyo University for many years after World War II.

141. Kubota Fujirō, "Gojū nen mae no Tōkyō Teikoku Daigaku byōrigaku kyōshitsu oyobi tōji no Miura kyōju," in *Byōrigaku kyōshitsu*, 2:10.

142. Murayama Tatsuzō, "Tanemichi sumbyō," in Kumagai (n. 38 above), pp. 215–21. The bacillus is also called *Yersinia pestis.*

143. Ogata Masanori, "Jiden," *Eiseigaku densembyōgaku zasshi* 15/2 (October 13, 1919):132.

144. Tanaka (n. 42 above), pp. 141, 135.

145. Ishikawa (n. 43 above), pp. 192–94.

146. Quoted by Miyagawa Yoneji, "Densembyō Kenkyū Jo," in Kumagai (n. 38 above), p. 322.

147. Ishihara Kikutarō in "Ogata Masanori-sensei tanjō hyakunen kinen zadankai," *Nihon iji shimpō* (hereafter **NIS**), no. 1507 (March 14, 1955):1013.

148. Nagai Tamotsu, *Takagi Kanehiro den,* pp. 117–18, 138.

149. Murayama Tatsuzō in *NIS*, no. 1507:1020.

150. Extensive newspaper coverage of controversies in Japanese medicine began even before Kitasato's return to Japan in 1892, but they intensified after it. Murayama notes that controversies—as in 1902 in a dispute over cholera—could actually begin in the major dailies and then move to the scientific journals and meetings. See "Eiseigaku no reimei o kataru," *NIS*, no. 1956 (October 21, 1961):34. This trend was still visible during the controversy over influenza in 1918, when the somewhat retiring Ogata Masanori, professor of hygiene at Tokyo University, was willing to discuss his scientific views with the popular press as a way of redressing what he considered to have been the biased coverage he received in 1902. See *NIS*, no. 1507:1013.

151. Quoted in *Byōrigaku kyōshitsu*, 1:239.

152. Eri Yagi, "On Nagaoka's Saturnian Atomic Model (1903)," *Japanese Studies in the History of Science,* no. 3 (1964):30, 40–41.

153. Henri Poincaré, *The Value of Science,* trans. G. B. Halsted (New York: Science Press, 1907), p. 109.

154. Yagi (n. 152 above), p. 47. See also the discussion in Koizumi (n. 54 above), p. 91.

155. Tomoda Chinzō, "Sekai no naka no sekai," *Tōyō gakugei zasshi* 22, no. 288 (September 25, 1905):383.

156. Nagaoka Hantarō, *Genshiryoku jidai no akebono* (Tokyo: Asahi Shimbun Sha, 1951), p. 195.

157. Fushimi Kōji, "Nihon ni okeru butsurigaku no seiritsu," in Nihon Butsuri Gakkai, ed., *Nihon no butsurigaku shi* (Tokyo: Tōkai Daigaku Shuppan Kai, 1978), 1:503–04.

158. Uchida Shun'ichi, "Kagaku hyakunen no kaikō to tembō," in Nihon Kagaku Kai, ed., *Nihon no kagaku hyaku nen shi* (Tokyo, 1978), pp. 24–31. Uchida was president of the Japan Chemical Society in 1964.

159. Shibata Yūji, "Nihon Kagaku Kai hyaku nen ni chinamu kaikō to kansō," in *Nihon no kagaku hyaku nen shi* (n. 158 above), pp. 5–6.

160. Samejima (n. 75 above), pp. 122–25.

161. Shibata (n. 159 above), p. 6.

162. George Basalla, "The Spread of Western Science," *Science* 156, no. 3775 (May 5, 1967):611–22. An essay by R. W. Home on the development of physics in Australia provides a useful comparison. See "The Beginnings of an Australian Physics Community," in Nathan Reingold and Marc Rothenberg, eds., *Scientific Colonialism: A Cross-Cultural Comparison* (Washington: Smithsonian Institution Press, 1987), pp. 3–34.

163. Shibat (n. 159 above), pp. 5, 6, 7.

164. Nakayama Shigeru believes this made physical scientists less inclined to take risks. See his essay "Japanese Scientific Thought" in Charles C. Gillispie, ed., *Dictionary of Scientific Biography* 15/1.

165. Tanaka (n. 42 above), p. 62.

166. Sata (n. 95 above), p. 17.

167. The eighty-six include physicists, biologists, mathematicians, geologists, and chemists who had the D.Sc. degree.

168. A. Paul Hare, "A Study of Interaction and Consensus in Different Sized Groups," *American Sociological Review* 17/3 (June 1952):261–67, and Robert Freed Bales, A. Paul Hare, and Edgar Borgatta, eds., *Small Groups: Studies in Social Interaction,* 3d ed. (New York: Knopf, 1966), p. 499.

169. On conformity, see Kishida Motomi, "Iken no henka ni eikyō suru shudan kijun koka no kenkyū," *Shinrigaku kenkyū* 27/2 (August 1956):105–10. On talent, see Marvin E. Shaw, *Group Dynamics: The Psychology of Small Group Behavior,* 2d ed. (New York: McGraw-Hill, 1976), p. 235.

170. Barry E. Collins and Bertram H. Raven, "Group Structure: Attraction, Coalitions, Communication and Power," in Gardner Lindzey and Elliot Aronson, eds., *The Handbook of Social Psychology* (Menlo Park, California: Addison-Wesley, 1969), 4:125, and Kenneth L. Dion, "Cohesiveness as a Determinant of

In-Group Out-Group Bias," *Journal of Personality and Social Psychology* 28/2 (1973):171.

171. John James, "A Preliminary Study of the Size Determinant in Small Group Interaction," *American Sociological Review* 16/4 (August 1951):475, and Hare (n. 168 above), p. 265.

172. Ishikawa (n. 43 above), p. 93.

Chapter Seven: Science and the Crisis of World War I

1. John D. Bernal, *The Social Function of Science,* pp. 29–30.
2. Sakurai Jōji, *Omoide no kazukazu,* p. 20.
3. Miyagawa Yoneji, "Densembyō Kenkyū Jo," in Kumagai Kenji, ed., *Omoide no Aoyama Tanemichi-sensei,* p. 324.
4. "Shikai genrō sempai no kekki," *IJ,* no. 1056 (September 19, 1914):1594.
5. *TGSIG.* Cf. "Yosan iin dai-go bunka (Nōshōmushō jokan) kaigiroku (sokki) dai-ni kai," House of Representatives Budget Committee, 37th Diet, May 28, 1915, p. 14.
6. "Sengo keiei to iiku kikan," *IJ,* no. 1068 (December 12, 1914):2072–73. Not all of these men obtained doctorates. Only those who did so before 1921 are counted in my total of 155.
7. See chapter 3 for details.
8. From statistics presented in Minoru Watanabe (ch. 2, n. 178), "Japanese Students Abroad and the Acquisition of Scientific and Technical Knowledge," pp. 283–85.
9. *TGSIG* (n. 5 above), p. 13.
10. "Shikai genrō sempai no kekki" (n. 4 above), p. 1594.
11. "Ryūgakusei mondai no sokumenkan," *IJ,* no. 1053 (August 29, 1914):1473.
12. "Shikai genrō sempai no kekki" (n. 4 above), p. 1594.
13. *TGSIG.* Cf. "Yosan iin dai-go bunka (Nōshōmushō jokan) kaigiroku (sokki) dai-ikkai," House of Representatives Budget Committee, 37th Diet, May 27, 1915, p. 7.
14. "Batsu no Ika Daigaku," pts. 1–5, *TAS,* October 28, 1914, p. 5; October 29, 1914, p. 5; October 30, 1914, p. 5; November 2, 1914, p. 5; and November 3, 1914, p. 5. For the articles' contents, see chapter 6.
15. *DNTGS,* 9. Cf. "Tōkyō Teikoku Daigaku Ika Daigaku kyōju no shokuseki ni kansuru Wakasugi Kisaburō no shitsumon enzetsu," House of Representatives, 35th Diet, December 15, 1914, pp. 960–61.
16. "Sengo keiei to iiku kikan" (n. 6 above), pp. 2072–73.
17. Mishima Shunken, "Ryūgakusei tozetsu mondai (II)," *IJ,* no. 1060 (October 17, 1914):1749.
18. In 1915 Japanese students tended to relocate in Britain, but from 1916 through 1919, about two-thirds studied in the U.S.
19. Mishima Shunken, "Ryūgakusei tozetsu mondai (I)," *IJ,* no. 1059 (October 10, 1914):1708–09.

20. "Kore zekkō no kikai ka?" *IJ*, no. 1052 (August 22, 1914):1481.

21. Mishima (n. 19 above), p. 1708.

22. "Ryūgaku no hitsuyō nashi," *IJ*, no. 1174 (December 23, 1916):2155.

23. L. F. Haber, "Chemical Innovation in Peace and in War," in C. G. Bernhard, Elisabeth Crawford, and Per Sorbom, eds., *Science, Technology and Society in the Time of Alfred Nobel* (Oxford: Pergamon Press, 1982), pp. 275–78.

24. D. S. L. Cardwell, *The Organisation of Science in England*, pp. 169–70.

25. Haber (n. 23 above), p. 277.

26. Regarding the situation in England and Wales, see Cardwell (n. 24 above), p. 165. So far as Japan is concerned, sixty students may be too high an estimate when we consider that Tokyo University, with the largest programs, had only fifteen graduate students in physics and chemistry (faculty of science) and perhaps another fifteen in geology, zoology, and botany. Kyoto's program was smaller than Tokyo's. Kyushu had no program, and at Tōhoku the numbers could not have exceeded a dozen. See chapters 4 and 6 for additional details.

27. An English translation of the German engineers' letter to Chancellor Theobald von Bethmann Hollweg appeared under the title, "Science and the Civil Service: A German Argument," *The London Times Education Supplement*, no. 84 (November 23, 1916):1. See chapter 8.

28. "Kenkyū hiyō ni tsuite," *IJ*, no. 1062 (October 31, 1914):1837.

29. "Bunshō no ikan mondai benkai," *IJ*, no. 1067 (December 5, 1914):18.

30. "Ōkuma shushō no tenkan iken," *IJ*, no. 1063 (November 7, 1914):10.

31. Kitajima Ta'ichi, *Kitajima Ta'ichi jiden*, p. 42.

32. Miyajima Mikinosuke, *Kitasato Shibasaburō den*, p. 83.

33. Kitasato Kenkyū Jo, *Kitasato Kenkyū Jo nijūgo nen shi*, p. 6.

34. On the institutionalization of bacteriology outside Japan, see Joseph Ben-David, "Roles and Innovations in Medicine," *American Journal of Sociology* 65/6 (1960):561–62; and John B. Blake (ch. 3, n. 163), "Scientific Institutions since the Renaissance," pp. 31–62.

35. "Ōkuma Shushō no tenkan iken" (n. 30 above), p. 10.

36. *TGSIG*. Cf. "Yosan iinkai giroku sokki dai-nana kai," House of Representatives Budget Committee, 35th Diet, December 16, 1914, p. 75.

37. Yamada Hiromichi, "Gun'i to shite no Ōgai-sensei (Tokyo: Ikai Jihō Sha, 1934), p. 386.

38. Fear of Kitasato's political influence in the home ministry as a reason for excluding ministry officials from the transfer planning process is strongly implied, though not explicitly stated, in "Denken ikan no hishi," *IJ*, no. 1095 (June 19, 1915):9–10.

39. "Otemachi yori Hitotsubashi e," *IJ*, no. 1060 (October 17, 1914):11.

40. "Densembyō Kenkyū Jo kangae," *TAS*, October 15, 1914, p. 3.

41. *DNTGS*, 9. Cf. "Densembyō Kenkyū Jo ikan ni kansuru shitsumon," House of Representatives, 35th Diet, December 15, 1914, pp. 961, 957, 962; and *TGSIG* (n. 36 above), p. 66.

42. "Densembyō Kenkyū Jo heigō wa fukanō," *TAS*, October 25, 1914, p. 3.

43. "Shūgiin kaisan: Suisan Kōshū Jo Densembyō Kenkyū Jo," *TAS*, December 27, 1914, p. 2.

44. Hara Kei, *Hara Kei nikki*, 4 (Tokyo: Fukumura Shuppan, 1965):58.

45. Resolutions condemning the laboratory transfer were issued by medical societies in Tokyo and the Kansai region. For details, see "Tōkyō kaigyō igakushi kai no ketsugibun happyō," *Tōkyō iji shinshi* (hereafter *TIS*), no. 1895 (November 7, 1914):40, and "Densembyō Kenkyū Jo ikan no nariyuki," *TIS*, no. 1896 (November 14, 1914):42–43.

46. Sakai Tanihei, "Genkan ban nikki," in Kumagai (n. 3 above), p. 414.

47. Kitajima (n. 31 above), pp. 51–52.

48. Nagayo Hakushi Kinen Kai, ed., *Nagayo Matarō den*, p. 152.

49. Kitasato Kenkyū Jo (n. 33 above), p. 14, and "Dai Nihon Shiritsu Eisei Kai dai-sanjūni-ji teiki sōkai kyōkō gaikyō," *Dai Nihon Shiritsu Eisei Kai zasshi* (hereafter **DNSEKZ**), no. 379, pt. 1 (1914):14.

50. *Shokuinroku*, 1899, p. 482.

51. *TGSIG* (n. 36 above), p. 81.

52. "Aa Densembyō Kenkyū Jo," *Kyōiku jiron* (hereafter **KJ**), no. 1063 (October 25, 1914):47.

53. *TGSIG* (n. 36 above), p. 81.

54. Shioda Hiroshige, *Mesu to tate*, p. 76.

55. *TGSIG* (n. 36 above), p. 81, and "Suisan ikan mondai," *KJ*, no. 1065 (November 15, 1914):36.

56. Ichiki Kitokurō, *Ichiki-sensei kaikō roku* (Tokyo: Ichiki-Sensei Tsuitō Kai, 1954), pp. 65–66. Ichiki in his memoirs calls Kitasato "a kind of a politician" and criticizes him for daring to publicize his opposition in the newspapers.

57. *TGSIG* (n. 36 above), pp. 68–69, 73, 75.

58. Izawa Takio Denki Hensan Iinkai, *Izawa Takio,* p. 109.

59. Kitasato Kenkyū Jo (n. 33 above), pp. 25–27.

60. Takano Rokurō, *Kitasato Shibasaburō,* p. 135.

61. Ibid., pp. 55–57, and "Dōfudegaoka Yōjō'en," *TIS*, no. 819 (December 9, 1893):40–41.

62. Miyajima (n. 32 above), pp. 92–93, 313; and Satō Kenzō, *Kokuritsu daigaku zaisei seido shikō,* p. 293.

63. Miyajima (n. 32 above), pp. 92–93.

64. Kitajima (n. 31 above), pp. 49–50.

65. Kitasato Kenkyū Jo (n. 33 above), pp. 21–24; *DNTGS,* 9. Cf. "Densembyō Kenkyū Jō seizō no diphtheria kessei ni kansuru shitsumon," House of Representatives, 36th Diet, June 2, 1915, pp. 1326–32; and *DNTGS*, 10, cf. "Teikoku daigaku tokubetsu kaikei hō chū kaisei hōritsu an," House of Peers, 37th Diet, February 1, 1916, pp. 67–68. Losses incurred by the production of substandard serum required the Ministry of Education to seek a compensatory special appropriation for Tokyo University.

66. *DNTGS,* 10. Cf. "Teikoku daigaku tokubetsu kaikei hō chū kaisei hōritsu an," House of Peers, 36th Diet, December 16, 1915, pp. 306–10; *DNTGS,* 9 (n. 65 above):1330–31; and *TGSIG*, cf. "Dai-go rui dai-hachi-go yosan iinkai kaigiroku dai-ni kai," House of Representatives Budget Committee, 36th Diet, December 21, 1915, p. 4.

67. Iseki Kurō, ed., *Dai Nihon hakushi roku,* 3:335–36; and Shūgiin Jimu-

kyoku, ed., *Gikai seido nanajūnen shi: Shūgiin giin meikan,* 5 (Tokyo: Ōkurashō Insatsukyoku, 1962):318.

68. Kitajima (n. 31 above), pp. 47–48; Miyajima (n. 32 above), p. 97.

69. Itō Sukehiko, the professor in question, was cited as the author of the report by Fukuhara Ryōjirō, vice minister of education and acting director of the Institute of Infectious Diseases following the transfer. For details, see *DNTGS,* 9 (n. 65 above):1330–31; and Iseki, 2 (n. 67 above):82–83.

70. The study was done at Komagome Hospital, and its results were announced by Matsuura Chinjirō, chief of the Bureau of Professional Education. See *TGSIG* (n. 66 above), p. 4.

71. On October 12, 1915, the government issued home ministry Ordinance no. 12 governing the manufacturing of medical substances and their inspection by the state authorities. The medical community criticized the inspection order as an "attempt to suppress private enterprise." See Kitasato Kenkyū Jo (n. 33 above), pp. 23–24. The Ministry of Education had already given warning of its intentions when Minister Ichiki testified before the Budget Committee of the House of Representatives on December 16, 1914. He noted that the Kitasato Institute's serum and vaccine sales would very likely produce a loss of income for the Institute of Infectious Diseases and noted that the Ministry of Education would "have to adopt measures to deal with this probable loss of income." For details see *TGSIG* (n. 36 above), p. 83.

72. On the floor of the Diet Fukuhara stated: "We sought the opinions of authorities at ten hospitals regarding the [clinical] results obtained from using both the old and new [diphtheria] serums. They agreed that there was no difference." See *DNTGS,* 9 (n. 65 above):1330–31. Six months earlier, in secret testimony before the Budget Committee, he had said: "We have appointed a new [laboratory] director and technicians since Dr. Kitasato resigned, of course, but they have limited ability and probably will not produce very good serums." For details see *TGSIG* (n. 36 above), p. 83.

73. Hanami Sakumi, *Danshaku Yamakawa-sensei den,* pp. 275–76.

74. Yamada (n. 37 above), p. 383.

75. *TGSIG* (n. 66 above), p. 4.

76. Tōkyō Teikoku Daigaku, *Tōkyō Teikoku Daigaku gakujutsu taikan: Igaku Bu, Densembyō Kenkyū Jo, Nōgaku Bu,* p. 446.

77. *DNTGS,* 9 (n. 65 above):1329.

78. Aoyama Tanemichi, "Tokugakusha no shōrai ikaga?" *IJ,* no. 1055 (September 12, 1914):8.

79. Morimura Ichizaemon, quoted in Kitasato Kenkyū Jo (n. 33 above), p. 15.

80. Nagayo Hakushi Kinen Kai (n. 48 above), p. 158. The wedding took place on November 5, 1914.

81. Mitamura Makujirō, "Tanemichi no sekai dōtoku," in Kumagai (n. 3 above), pp. 155–56.

82. Kiyoura Keigo, quoted in Miyajima (n. 32 above), p. 93.

83. "Sōsenkyō go no Dai Nihon Ishi Kai," *IJ,* no. 1195 (May 19, 1917):922.

84. See Kikuchi's speech to the first annual meeting of the Nihon Rengō Igakkai (Japan federation of medical societies) in "Dai-Ikkai Nihon Rengō Igakkai keikyō," *TIS,* no. 1250 (April 5, 1902):21–22, where he admonishes the

members to "avoid emotional conflicts and diligently pursue research and the exchange of scientific information."

85. Sakai (n. 46 above), p. 411.

86. "Ika daigaku genjō daha no gi," *IJ*, no. 1076 (February 6, 1916):268–69.

87. Yamakawa Kenjirō, "Gakushikai sōkai ni okeru enzetsu," in Shinjō Shinzō, ed., *Danshaku Yamakawa-sensei ikō*, pp. 227–28.

88. Mishima Shunken, "Aoyama to Kitasato," *IJ*, no. 1063 (November 7, 1914):1860–61.

89. Kitasato's biographer, the bacteriologist Miyajima Mikinosuke, was one of many contemporaries who believed that Aoyama was primarily responsible for the laboratory transfer. See Miyajima (n. 32 above), pp. 180, 94.

90. See, for example, Kitasato Shibasaburō, "Shūgiin giin kohōsha to shite ishi no funki o yōkyū suru riyū," *IJ*, no. 1187 (March 24, 1917):514–15, and "Kitasato ontai no shutsuba," *IJ*, no. 1189 (April 7, 1917):661.

91. James R. Bartholomew, "Science, Bureaucracy, and Freedom in Meiji and Taisho Japan," in J. Victor Koschmann and Tetsuo Najita, eds., *Conflict in Modern Japanese History*, p. 334.

92. Yanagita Izumi, *Meiji bummei shi ni okeru Ōkuma Shigenobu*, pp. 176, 218, 382–83, 437; and Ōkuma Shigenobu, "Meiji bummei shi jo ni okeru Fukuzawa Ō," in Waseda Daigaku Henshu Bu, ed., *Ōkuma haku enzetsu shū* (Tokyo: Waseda Daigaku Shuppan Bu, 1907), p. 528; Ōkuma Shigenobu, "Gakumon no dokuritsu to Tōkyō Semmon Gakkō no sōritsu," in *Ōkuma haku enzetsu shū*, p. 486; and Ōkuma Shigenobu, "Igakusha to seijika," *IJ*, no. 811 (January 11, 1910):3.

93. "Denken ikan no hishi," *IJ*, no. 1095 (June 19, 1915):9.

94. "Ikai dantai undō shi," pt. 20, *IJ*, no. 1226 (December 20, 1917):2224.

95. "Denken ikan no hishi" (n. 93 above), pp. 9–10.

96. Yanagita (n. 92 above), pp. 413, 438.

97. Quoted in Uzaki Kumakichi, *Aoyama Tanemichi*, p. 155.

98. Quoted in *DNSEKZ* (n. 49 above), p. 8.

99. Yanagita (n. 92 above), p. 438.

100. Kitajima (n. 31 above), p. 51.

101. Joyce C. Lebra, *Ōkuma Shigenobu, Statesman of Meiji Japan* (Canberra: Australian National University Press, 1973), p. 146.

102. Kiyonobu Itakura and Eri Yagi, "The Japanese Research System and the Establishment of the Institute of Physical and Chemical Research," in Shigeru Nakayama, David L. Swain, and Eri Yagi, eds., *Science and Society in Modern Japan*, pp. 181–82.

103. Ibid., pp. 169–73.

104. Sakurai (n. 2 above), pp. 19–20.

105. Nagaoka Hantarō, "Kenkyūshitsu gaikan: Rikagaku Kenkyū Jo Chō Nagaoka Kenkyūshitsu," *Kagaku*, no. 3 (1933):31.

106. Itakura and Yagi (n. 102 above), p. 183; Hanami (n. 73 above), p. 281.

107. Quoted in Suzuki Yōsei, "Takamatsu hakushi to Rikagaku Kenkyū Jo," in Takamatsu Hakushi Shukuga Denki Kankō Kai, ed., *Kōgaku hakushi Takamatsu Toyokichi den* (Tokyo: Takamatsu Hakushi Shukuga Denki Kankō Kai, 1932), p. 310.

108. Itakura and Yagi (n. 102 above), p. 183; Yuasa Mitsutomo, *Kagaku shi*, pp. 233–34.

109. *DNTGS*, 9. Cf. "Rikagaku Kenkyū Jo setchi ni kansuru kengi an," House of Peers, 36th Diet, June 9, 1915, p. 1192.

110. *DNTGS*, 9. Cf. "Rikagaku Kenkyū Jo setchi ni kansuru kengi an," House of Representatives, 36th Diet, June 5, 1915, p. 1398.

111. Ibid.

112. *DNTGS*, 9 (n. 110 above), June 9, 1915, p. 1485–86.

113. Hanami (n. 73 above), p. 281; Yanagita (n. 92 above), p. 436.

114. Sakurai (n. 2 above), pp. 23–24; Itakura and Yagi (n. 102 above), p. 193.

115. Sakurai (n. 2 above), pp. 19–20.

116. Yuasa Mitsutomo, *Kagaku gojū nen*, p. 181.

117. *DNTGS*, 10. Cf. "Rikagaku o kenkyū suru kōeki hōjin no kokkō hojō ni kansuru hōritsuan," House of Peers, 37th Diet, February 25, 1916, p. 151.

118. *DNTGS*, 10. Cf. "Rikagaku o kenkyū suru kōeki hōjin no kokkō hojō ni kansuru hōritsuan," House of Representatives, 37th Diet, February 24, 1916, pp. 879, 881.

119. *DNTGS*, 10 (n. 117 above):151–52. The negative assessment came from the former education ministry councillor Egi Kazuyuki.

120. *DNTGS*, 10 (n. 118 above):879.

121. *DNTGS*, 10 (n. 117 above):152.

122. *DNTGS*, 10. Cf. "Rikagaku o kenkyū suru kōeki hōjin no kokkō hojō ni kansuru hōritsuan," House of Representatives, 37th Diet, Feb. 18, 1916, p. 775.

123. Quoted in Sakurai (n. 2 above), pp. 23–24.

124. *DNTGS*, 10 (n. 117 above):154, 152.

125. *TGSIG*. Cf. "Rikagaku o kenkyū suru kōeki hōjin no kokkō hojō ni kansuru hōritsuan iinkai giroku (sokki) dai-san kai," House of Representatives Budget Committee, 37th Diet, February 22, 1916, pp. 18, 20. These admissions are from Matsuura Chinjirō, chief of the Bureau of Professional Education, and Ōtsu Jun'ichirō, political councillor to the Ministry of Education.

126. *TGSIG*. Cf. "Rikagaku o kenkyū suru kōeki hōjin o kokkō hojō ni kansuru hōritsuan iinkai giroku (sokki) dai-ni kai," House of Representatives Budget Committee, 37th Diet, February 21, 1916, pp. 7–9.

127. *TGSIG* (n. 125 above), p. 20.

128. *TGSIG* (n. 126 above), p. 7.

129. "Rikagaku kaketsu," *TAS*, February 23, 1916, p. 3.

130. *DNTGS*, 10 (n. 117 above):153.

131. Ibid., p. 152.

132. Ibid.

133. "Dakyōan kaketsu," *TAS*, February 26, 1916, p. 3.

134. *TGSIG* (n. 126 above), p. 8.

135. *DNTGS*, 10 (n. 117 above):152.

136. Ibid.

137. Quoted in Itakura Kiyonobu and Yagi Eri, "Rikagaku Kenkyū Jo to Nihon no kenkyū taisei," *Kagakushi kenkyū* 41 (January–March 1957):8.

138. "Shin naikaku to iji yosan," *IJ*, no. 1164 (October 14, 1916):1708.

139. Hanami (n. 73 above), pp. 231–32.

140. Itakura and Yagi (n. 92 above), p. 191.

141. Nagaoka Hantarō, professor of physics, and Ōkōchi Masatoshi, professor of ordnance engineering, had charge of physics. Chemistry was under the supervision of Ikeda Kikunae, professor of chemistry, and Inoue Jinkichi, professor of chemical engineering.

142. Nakamura Seiji, *Tanakadate Aikitsu-sensei*, p. 175.

143. Ibid., pp. 180–82.

144. Ibid., pp. 192–94; Hanami (n. 73 above), p. 314.

145. *TGSIG*. Cf. "Dai-ichi rui dai-ni gō yosan iin dai-ichi bunka (Gaimushō, Shihōshō oyobi Mombushō jokan) kaigiroku (sokki) dai-yon dai," House of Representatives Budget Committee, 37th Diet, December 22, 1915, p. 64.

146. Nakamura (n. 142 above), pp. 193–94.

147. Hanami (n. 73 above), p. 315.

148. *TGSIG* (n. 145 above), p. 64.

149. Hanami (n. 73 above), p. 315.

150. Ibid.

151. *TGSIG*. Cf. "Dai-ichi rui dai-ichi gō yosan iin kaigiroku dai-nijikkai," House of Representatives Budget Committee, 37th Diet, February 23, 1916, p. 245.

152. Hanami (n. 73 above), p. 315.

153. Nakamura (n. 142 above), p. 182; Hanami (n. 73 above), p. 317.

154. Hanami (n. 73 above), pp. 318–19.

155. *DNTGS*, 11. Cf. "Tōkyō Teikoku Daigaku oyobi Kyōto Teikoku Daigaku rinji seifu shishutsu kin kuriiri ni kansuru hōritsuan," House of Representatives, 40th Diet, January 29, 1918, p. 225.

156. *TGSIG*. Cf. "Tōkyō Teikoku Daigaku oyobi Kyōto Teikoku Daigaku rinji seifu shishutsu kin ni kansuru hōritsuan hoka ikken," House of Representatives Budget Committee, 40th Diet, first session, January 30, 1918, p. 2.

157. *TGSIG* (n. 156 above), fourth session, February 8, 1918, p. 32; first session, January 30, 1918, p. 4.

158. *TGSIG* (n. 156 above), second session, February 1, 1918, p. 8.

159. *TGSIG* (n. 156 above), first session, January 30, 1918, p. 2; fourth session, February 8, 1918, p. 32.

160. *TGSIG* (n. 156 above), fourth session, February 8, 1918, p. 32.

161. Ibid.

162. *TGSIG* (n. 156 above), first session, January 30, 1918, p. 2.

163. Ibid., p. 5.

164. *TGSIG* (n. 156 above), second session, February 1, 1918, pp. 7, 8.

165. *TGSIG* (n. 156 above), fourth session, February 8, 1918, p. 34; first session, January 30, 1918, p. 2; second session, February 1, 1918, p. 15.

166. *TGSIG* (n. 156 above), fourth session, February 8, 1918, p. 35. The resolution was introduced by Hatoyama Ichirō, who became prime minister after World War II.

167. *DNTGS*, 11. Cf. "Tōkyō Teikoku Daigaku oyobi Kyōto Teikoku Daigaku rinji seifu shishutsu kin kuriiri ni kansuru hōritsuan," House of Representatives, 40th Diet, February 12, 1918, p. 268.

168. Yuasa Mitsutomo, *Gendai kagaku gijutsu shi nempyō*, p. 123.

169. Hanami (n. 73 above), pp. 318–19.

170. On July 2, 1917, the minister of education, Okada Ryōhei, told the Budget Committee of the House of Representatives: "Every type of industry has shown considerable development of late. As a result, demands for technical people have surged dramatically. In order to respond to this, we have to expand our engineering programs at each of the [imperial] universities . . . [Among other things] we shall establish a new chair of applied chemistry at Tōhoku Imperial University." See *TGSIG*, cf. "Dai-ichi rui dai-ni gō yosan iin dai-ichi bunka kaigiroku dai-ikkai," House of Representatives Budget Committee, 39th Diet, July 2, 1917, pp. 5–6.

171. Special budget supplements were on occasion approved. In this instance, the Ministry of Education requested 957,060 yen for the purposes cited here. Another 420,000 yen was requested for technical education in the various higher schools. Without these supplementary budgets, there could have been little, if any, expansion. For details see ibid.

172. Tōhoku Daigaku, ed., *TDGNS*, 1:715–23.

173. Ishikawa Teijirō, *Honda Kōtarō den*, p. 187.

174. Ibid., p. 188.

175. Ibid., pp. 189–91.

176. Hokkaidō Daigaku, ed., *Hokkaidō Daigaku sōki hachijū nen shi* (hereafter **HDSHNS**) (Sapporo: Hokkaidō Daigaku, 1965), p. 123.

177. Ibid., p. 125. See also Hokkaidō Daigaku, ed., *Hokudai hyakunen shi* (Tokyo: Gyōsei, 1980), p. 529.

178. *HDSHNS*, pp. 123–24.

179. Ibid., p. 125.

180. *TGSIG* (n. 170 above), p. 6.

181. *HDSHNS*, pp. 124, 126.

182. Yuasa (n. 168 above), p. 121.

183. Richard B. Goldschmidt, *In and Out of the Ivory Tower*. See p. 110, where the author writes: "I learned to my surprise [in early 1914] that the great geneticist Toyama with whom I had corresponded was only an assistant professor and worked most of the time in a distant silkworm laboratory."

184. Yuasa (n. 168 above), p. 121.

185. *TGSIG* (n. 156 above).

186. *DNTGS*, 10 (n. 66 above):307.

187. Hanami (n. 73 above), p. 233. Hanami does not try to explain Ichiki's motives, but he did not need to.

188. *TGSIG* (n. 156 above), first session, January 30, 1918, p. 7.

189. Tsuchiya contended that the serological chemistry chair was being established "because of enmity among the professors." See ibid., p. 5. Matsuura Chinjirō, chief of the Bureau of Professional Education, contended that its establishment was owing to the progress of science. "Of course, serological chemistry can be seen as a division of bacteriology. But as more research is done, it seems appropriate to the development of science that we establish a chair in that field."

190. Yuasa (n. 168 above), pp. 114–17.

191. *TGSIG*. Cf. "Tōkyō Teikoku Daigaku oyobi Kyōto Teikoku Daigaku rinji

seifu shishutsu kin ni kansuru hōritsuan hoka ni ken iin kaigiroku dai-ni kai," House of Representatives Budget Committee, 39th Diet, July 4, 1917, pp. 3, 9.

192. *TGSIG*. Cf. "Tōkyō Teikoku Daigaku oyobi Kyōto Teikoku Daigaku rinji seifu shishutsu kin ni kansuru hōritsuan hoka ni ken iin kaigiroku dai-san kai," House of Representatives Budget Committee, 39th Diet, July 6, 1917, p. 15.

193. Hanami (n. 73 above), pp. 230–31.

194. *TGSIG* (n. 191 above), p. 3.

195. Ibid., p. 7.

196. *TGSIG* (n. 192 above), p. 15.

197. Ibid., p. 16.

198. *TGSIG* (n. 191 above), pp. 5, 9; and *TGSIG* (n. 192 above), p. 15.

199. *TGSIG* (n. 191 above), pp. 4, 5, 13.

200. *TGSIG* (n. 192 above), p. 16.

201. *TGSIG* (n. 191 above), p. 6.

202. See *Shokuinroku*, 1917, pp. 737–39, 746–47; 1918, pp. 370–71, 374–75; Kyōto Daigaku, *Kyōto Daigaku nanajū nen shi*, pp. 714–15; and *DNTGS*, 10, cf. "Tōkyō Teikoku Daigaku oyobi Kyōto Teikoku Daigaku rinji seifu shishutsu kin ni kansuru hōritsuan," House of Representatives, 39th Diet, July 8, 1917, pp. 1219, 1291, and House of Peers, 39th Diet, July 13, 1917, pp. 1141–42, 1163.

203. Yuasa (n. 168 above), p. 116; Ichihara Katashi, ed., *Ōsaka Daigaku nijūgo nen shi* (Osaka: Tengyōsha, 1956), pp. 227–28.

204. Miyataki Tsuneo, "Ishō jōrei, jitsuyō shin'an hō seiritsu no shūhen," in Tokkyō Chō Kōgyō Shoyūken Seido Shi Kenkyū Kai, ed., *Tokkyō seido no hassei to hensen* (Tokyo: Ōkurashō Insatsukyoku, 1982), p. 70.

205. Yuasa (n. 168 above), pp. 118–24.

206. Ijiri Tsunekichi, ed., *Rekidai kenkan roku,* pp. 801–02.

207. *TGSIG* (n. 191 above), p. 11.

208. *TGSIG*. Cf. "Dai-ni rui dai-yon gō seigan iin dai-san bunka kaigiroku (sokki) dai-ikkai," House of Representatives Committee on Petitions, 28th Diet, January 31, 1912, pp. 6–7.

209. *Shokuinroku*, 1911, pp. 652–53; 1913, pp. 693–94; 1915, pp. 680–81; 1917, pp. 810–11; 1919, pp. 462–63.

210. *TGSIG*. Cf. "Yosan iin dai-go bunka (Nōshōmushō jokan) kaigiroku (sokki) dai-ikkai," House of Representatives Budget Committee, 28th Diet, January 29, 1912, p. 2.

211. *TGSIG* (n. 208 above), pp. 5, 6.

212. *TGSIG*. "Tokkyō hō chū kaisei hōritsuan hoka ikken iin kaigiroku dai-ni kai," House of Representatives Budget Committee, 37th Diet, February 21, 1916, p. 3.

213. Yuasa (n. 168 above), p. 118.

214. Sakata Teiichi, "Kikai kōgyō hattatsu jochō an," *Kikai Gakkai shi* 22, no. 55 (December 1918):1–38. Reprinted in *NKGST*, 3:260–61.

215. Nakamatsu Morio, "Jitsuyō ishō hō seitei no hitsuyō," *Taiyō* 9/12 (1889), cited in Miyataki (n. 204 above), p. 119.

216. *TGSIG*. Cf. "Tokkyō hō chū kaisei hōritsuan hoka sanken iin kaigiroku

dai-nana kai," House of Representatives Budget Committee, 40th Diet, March 9, 1918, pp. 28–29.

217. Miyataki (n. 204 above), pp. 70–71. Miyataki writes: "Because so much of the Japanese chemical industry was based on exploitation of confiscated German patents, its later development was fated to proceed along the same lines as the German chemical industry."

218. Stanley B. Hunt and Giles E. Hopkins, "Man-Made Fibres," in *Encyclopaedia Britannica,* 9 (Chicago: William Benton, 1972):230–31.

219. *TGSIG.* Cf. "Dai-ichi rui dai-roku gō yosan iin dai-go bunka (Nōshōmushō jokan) kaigiroku (sokki) dai-san kai," House of Representatives Budget Committee, 31st Diet, January 31, 1914, p. 20.

220. Ibid.

221. *TGSIG.* Cf. "Dai-ichi rui dai-roku gō yosan iin dai-go bunka (Nōshōmushō jokan) kaigiroku (sokki) dai-ikkai," House of Representatives Budget Committee, 36th Diet, May 27, 1915, pp. 3–4.

222. Ibid., p. 3.

223. Ibid., pp. 8–9.

224. Asaka Shobō, ed., *Gekidō no Nihon seiji shi,* 2 (Tokyo: Asaka Shobō, 1979):2182.

225. *TGSIG.* Cf. "Dai-go rui dai-jū gō senryō iyakuhin seizō shōrei hōan iin kaigiroku (sokki) dai-san kai," House of Representatives Budget Committee, 36th Diet, June 2, 1915, p. 14.

226. Chikayoshi Kamatani, "The Role Played by the Industrial World in the Progress of Japanese Science and Technology," *Journal of World History* 9/2 (1965):405.

227. Ibid., pp. 403–05.

228. *TGSIG.* Cf. "Dai-ichi rui dai-roku gō yosan iin dai-go bunka (Nōshōmushō jokan) kaigiroku (sokki) dai-ikkai," House of Representatives Budget Committee, December 20, 1915, p. 6. Testimony of Oka Makoto, chief of the Bureau of Industry.

229. *TGSIG.* Cf. "Dai-go rui dai-jū gō senryō iyakuhin seizō shōrei hōan iin kaigiroku (sokki) dai-ni kai," House of Representatives Budget Committee, 36th Diet, June 1, 1915, p. 6.

230. *TGSIG* (n. 225 above), p. 16.

231. Ibid., p. 15.

232. Asaka Shobō (n. 224 above), p. 2277.

233. *TGSIG* (n. 228 above), pp. 6–7.

234. Ibid., p. 6.

Chapter Eight: The Research System in an Age of Transition

1. Quoted in Murayama Tatsuzō, "Tanemichi sumbyō," in Kumagai Kenji, ed., *Omoide no Aoyama Tanemichi-sensei,* pp. 239–40.

2. The biologist Yasui Kono (1880–1971) became Japan's first woman scientist during the early years of the twentieth century when she received a teaching position at the Tokyo Higher Normal School for Women and began doing re-

search in the botanical laboratory of Miyake Kiichi in Tokyo University's faculty of agriculture. Yasui published several papers and even studied abroad (chiefly at Harvard University, 1914–16) before receiving the D.Sc. degree in 1926. While retaining her post at the normal school, she became a research associate at Tokyo University through the patronage of Fujii Kenjirō, professor of genetics in its faculty of science. Twenty women, including Yasui, had received doctorates in basic science, medicine, pharmacology, or agriculture by 1937. None had received it in any field of engineering. For details, see Nagashima Yuzuru, *Onna hakushi retsu den* (Tokyo: Kagaku Chishiki Fukyū Kai, 1937), pp. 4–19.

3. "Naishoku ka honshoku ka?" *IJ*, no. 1309 (July 26, 1919):1264–65.

4. *TGSIG*. Cf. "Daigaku tokubetsu kaikai hōan hoka ikken," House of Representatives Budget Committee, 42d Diet, February 13, 1920, p. 7.

5. *DNTGS*, 11. Cf. "Teikoku daigaku tokubetsu kaikei hōan hoka ikken," House of Representatives, 42d Diet, February 17, 1920, p. 1782.

6. *TGSIG*. Cf. "Tōkyō Teikoku Daigaku oyobi Kyōto Teikoku Daigaku rinji seifu shishutsu kin ni kansuru hōritsuan hoka ikken," House of Representatives Budget Committee, 40th Diet, February 4, 1918, p. 19. Testimony of Matsuura Chinjirō, chief of the Bureau of Professional Education. With respect to wartime inflation, Vice Minister Tadokoro Yoshiharu reported that prices in Tokyo had risen 50 to 60 percent in the previous twelve months. See p. 22.

7. *TGSIG* (n. 4 above), p. 1. Testimony of Minami Hiroshi, vice minister of education. Regarding professors' level of comfort, see Kuwaki Tsutomu, "Omoidasu mama ni," *Kagaku shi techō*, no. 3 (July 1964):1. Kuwaki was the son of Kuwaki Ayao, professor of mechanics at Kyushu University during the Taishō and early Shōwa periods. During the 1920s, his family enjoyed a "good standard of living" and could afford to buy "more books [in Tokyo] than I can presently imagine . . . Unlike today (the 1960s), university professors were rather favored."

8. *TGSIG* (n. 4 above), p. 9. The chief of the Bureau of Professional Education, Matsuura, elaborated on Minami's remarks: "Professor A may give the course during the first semester, and Professor B may give the same course in the second semester. Students can thus attend whichever of the classes they wish." Matsuura stated further that this arrangement was already in effect in Tokyo University's faculty of engineering.

9. Hanami Sakumi, *Danshaku Yamakawa-sensei den*, pp. 331–32.

10. *TGSIG* (n. 4 above), p. 2.

11. *DNTGS*, 11. Cf. "Kagaku oyobi kōgyō kyōiku ni kansuru kengi an," 40th Diet, House of Peers, March 20, 1918, pp. 134–35.

12. *DNTGS*, 11. Cf. "Tōkyō Teikoku Daigaku oyobi Kyōto Teikoku Daigaku rinji seifu shishutsu kin ni kansuru hōritsu an," House of Representatives, 41st Diet, February 1 and 10, 1919, pp. 990–91, 1017–18; and "Teikoku daigaku tokubetsu kaikei hō chū kaisei hōritsu an," House of Peers, 41st Diet, February 14 and March 1, 1919, pp. 700–01, 751–52. For developments at Kyoto University, see Kyōto Daigaku Nanajū Nen Shi Henshū Iinkai, ed., *Kyōto Daigaku nanajū nen shi*, pp. 92–93.

13. Hanami (n. 9 above), p. 235.

14. Yuasa Mitsutomo, *Gendai kagaku gijutsu shi nempyō,* pp. 120–26.

15. Regarding the development of this laboratory, see Taigakai, ed., *Naimushō shi,* 3:230–31, and *DNTGS,* 11, cf. "Kokuritsu Eiyō Kenkyū Jo setsuritsu ni kansuru kengi an," House of Representatives, 41st Diet, February 20, 1919, pp. 1064–66. For information on Saiki, see Iseki Kurō, ed., *Dai Nihon hakushi roku,* 2:161. Regarding Kōno, see Asaka Shobō, ed., *Gekidō no Nihon seiji shi,* 2:1685.

16. See Suzuki Umetarō, *Kenkyū no kaikō* (Tokyo: Kōbundō Shobō, 1943), p. 1.

17. *TGSIG.* Cf. "Kokuritsu Eiyō Kenkyū Jo setsuritsu ni kansuru kengi an iinkai giroku (sokki) dai-go kai," House of Representatives Budget Committee, 41st Diet, March 7, 1919, p. 17.

18. Vice Minister Shinno said: "The warning that [Dr. Yagi] has given us is very appropriate. We shall certainly take his remarks into account during our deliberations." See ibid., p. 18.

19. Yuasa (n. 14 above), pp. 118, 121, and Nakamura Seiji, *Tanakadate Aikitsu-sensei,* p. 136.

20. Yuasa (n. 14 above), p. 109. See chapter 5 for further details on Katsura.

21. Sakurai Jōji, *Omoide no kazukazu,* p. 78.

22. "Gakujutsu kenkyū jo setchi an," *KJ,* no. 1268 (July 5, 1920):17.

23. On the establishment of the research professorship, see Sumeragi Shidō, *Daigaku seido no kenkyū,* pp. 361–62, and Shigeru Nakayama (ch. 4, n. 12), "The Role Played by Universities in Scientific and Technological Development in Japan," p. 354.

24. Hokkaidō Daigaku, *Hokkaidō Daigaku sōki hachijū nen shi,* pp. 125–26.

25. Hanami (n. 9 above), p. 233.

26. Itakura Kiyonobu, Yagi Eri, and Kimura Tōsaku, *Nagaoka Hantarō den,* pp. 462–65.

27. Kyūshū Daigaku Sōritsu Gojū Shūnen Kinen Kai, ed., *Kyūshū Daigaku gojū nen shi: Tsūshi* (Fukuoka: Kyūshū Daigaku, 1967), pp. 424–25. This official history blames the 1919 failure on the opposition of the Ministry of Education. Kuwaki Tsutomu, whose father was directly concerned, claims that the Ministry of Education supported the plan and that it was the Ministry of Finance that opposed it. See (n. 4 above), p. 2.

28. Kyūshū Daigaku Sōritsu Gojū Shūnen Kinen Kai (n. 27 above), p. 427. The science faculty plan was approved only after another of Kyushu physicist Kuwaki Ayao's sons became minister of finance in 1934.

29. Yuasa (n. 14 above), p. 123.

30. On the importance of Haber's work to the German military effort, see J. G. Crowther, *The Social Relations of Science* (New York, 1941), pp. 496–99.

31. Yuasa (n. 14 above), p. 123.

32. *DNTGS,* 11. Cf. "Kagaku kōgyō seisaku ni kansuru shitsumon," House of Representatives, 40th Diet, March 5, 1918, pp. 433–36. The policy statement was presented by Oka Makoto, chief of the Bureau of Industry. Oka was undoubtedly referring to the fact that the NINR did contract research for the

chemical and nitrogen industries. On the scope of its mission, see *Shokuinroku,* p. 462.

33. Yoshi Tsurumi, *Japanese Business: A Research Guide with Annotated Bibliography* (New York: Praeger, 1978), p. 56.

34. Yuasa (n. 14 above), pp. 120–26.

35. "Teidai to hikōki kōza," *Tōkyō Asahi Shimbun,* June 2, 1915, p. 5, reported on the matriculation at Tokyo University of two young naval officers intent on studying aeronautics and conducting research in that field.

36. Hanami (n. 9 above), p. 320.

37. Nakamura (n. 19 above), p. 199.

38. Yamakawa Kenjirō, "Yo wa nani o waga kyōiku kai ni okeru saidai kyūmu to shinzuru ka?" *Jitsugyō no Nihon* 11/26 (December 1908), reprinted in Shinjō Shinzō, ed., *Danshaku Yamakawa-sensei ikō,* pp. 596–97.

39. Hanami (n. 9 above), pp. 324–25. In July 1915 Kikuchi actually proposed that all higher schools and normal schools be designated universities.

40. Nakanishi Keijirō, *Waseda Daigaku hachijū nen shi* (Tokyo: Waseda Daigaku, 1962), pp. 430–32. Before World War I, Waseda's faculty of engineering and science offered majors only in mechanical and mining engineering. See pp. 122–25, 138–42.

41. For details about Keio's medical program, see Miyajima Mikinosuke, *Kitasato Shibasaburō den,* pp. 99–101, 253–54. Kitasato was the first dean of the Keio Medical School, and it was because of his willingness to accept a deanship that Keio at this time opted for a medical program instead of one in engineering and basic science.

42. See chapter 7, n. 90, for details.

43. Nankai Yōhachirō, *Kōgaku hakushi Shiraishi Naoharu den* (Tokyo: Akeishi Tarō, 1943), pp. 370–72, 377.

44. Hanami (n. 9 above), pp. 415–16.

45. "Seiyūkai shozoku ika giin kesshin ikaga?" *IJ,* no. 1284 (February 1, 1919):222–23.

46. Hanami (n. 9 above), pp. 415–16.

47. "Seiyūkai shozoku ika giin kesshin ikaga?" (n. 45 above), pp. 222–23.

48. See "Science and The Civil Service: A German Argument," *The London Times Education Supplement,* no. 84 (November 23, 1916):1.

49. Matsubara Kōichi, "Kagaku to bunkan," *Tōyō gakugei zasshi* 34, no. 427 (April 5, 1917):55–58.

50. Hayao Ushimaro, "Shirasawa Hakushi no kotodomo," in Nihon Ringyō Gijutsu Kyōkai, ed., *Ringyō senjin den,* pp. 552–53.

51. See the discussion of this question in Robert M. Spaulding, Jr., *Imperial Japan's Higher Civil Service Examinations,* pp. 163–78.

52. See the following essays for information on this issue: Sir Laurence Helsby, "Recruitment to the Civil Service," in William A. Robson, ed., *The Civil Service in Britain and France,* pp. 35–47; Leonard D. White, "The British Civil Service," in L. D. White et al., eds., *Civil Service Abroad: Great Britain, Canada, France, Germany* (New York: McGraw-Hill, 1935), pp. 1–54; André Bertrand, "The Recruitment and Training of Higher Civil Servants in the

United Kingdom and France," in Robson, pp. 170–84; and Fritz Morstein Marx, "Civil Service in Germany," in White et al., pp. 161–275.

53. Hanami (n. 9 above), p. 245.

54. Kyōto Teikoku Daigaku, ed., *Kyōto Teikoku Daigaku shi* (Kyoto: Kyōto Teikoku Daigaku, 1943), p. 910. The consultant was Kōriba Hiroshi, professor of botany at Tōhoku University. Kōriba later took the position himself.

55. Sumeragi (n. 23 above), pp. 362–68.

56. See, for example, Manabe Kaiichirō, "Kōza meimoku benbō," *IJ*, no. 1618 (August 8, 1925):1584–85. Manabe wrote: "It must be made possible for people like myself inside the university to influence the authorities when we feel that the progress of science in the university requires it. The present system, under which a creative and progressive proposal can be rejected by nothing more than the desire of government bureaucrats, is killing the university. It is making its development impossible."

57. Ishikawa Teijirō, *Honda Kōtarō den*, p. 209.

58. *NGHNS*, 1:433–34.

59. Sata Yoshihiko, "Kaigai ryūgakusei no zentō," *IJ*, no. 1056 (September 26, 1914):1632.

60. Sawayanagi Masatarō, "Gakumon dokuritsu no shin undō to sono kompon mondai," *Shin Nihon* 5/2 (1915). Reprinted in *NKGST*, 2:562–65.

61. *DNTGS*, 9. Cf. "Teikoku Gakushiin gakujutsu shōrei kin tokubetsu kaikei hō haishi hōritsu an," House of Peers, 36th Diet, June 2, 1915, p. 1125.

62. In 1921 the combined research grants program disbursed a total of 358,443 yen. See *NKGST*, 3:197.

63. See Hanami (n. 9 above), pp. 323, 327.

64. *TGSIG*. Cf. "Dai-ichi rui dai-ni gō yosan iin dai-ichi bunka (Gaimushō, Shihōshō oyobi Mombushō jokan) kaigiroku (sokki) dai-ni kai," House of Representatives Budget Committee, 40th Diet, February 2, 1918, pp. 29, 24–25, 36.

65. Ibid., p. 36.

66. "Kagaku kenkyū shōrei kyūhi," *KJ*, no. 1199 (August 5, 1918):18.

67. Miyajima Mikinosuke, "Mombudaijin Okada Ryōhei kakka ni teisu kagaku kenkyū hojō ni kanshite," *IJ*, no. 1261 (August 24, 1918):1549.

68. See "Kagaku kenkyū hojō happyō," *KJ*, no. 1232 (July 5, 1919):13, 15, where the names of Ogata and Kawamura are shown as having received grants in 1918, even though their names do not appear on the list published by *Kyōiku jiron* on August 5, 1918.

69. "Mombushō no kūshin santan," *IJ*, no. 1263 (September 7, 1918):1634.

70. "Rikagaku shōrei hi zōgaku," *KJ*, no. 1207 (October 25, 1918):15. Comparison of the sums awarded in 1918 and 1919 shows that no increase in funding was allowed. It is virtually certain that the Ministry of Finance blocked any increase.

71. Quoted in "Kagaku kenkyū hojō happyō" (n. 68 above), p. 16.

72. Ibid.

73. Noted in "Kagaku kenkyū shōrei kyūhi" (n. 66 above), p. 18.

74. Nagayo Hakushi Kinen Kai, ed., *Nagayo Matarō den* (hereafter *Nagayo*), pp. 160–61.

75. For details, see Kawakami Hajime, *Gendai Nihon iryō shi* (Tokyo: Keisō

Shobō, 1965), pp. 219–22; Joseph M. Smadel, "Scrub Typhus," in Thomas M. Rivers, *Viral and Rickettsial Infections of Man* (Philadelphia: J.B. Lippincott, 1948), pp. 520–28.

76. Rinya Kawamura, *Studies on Tsutsugamushi Disease* (Cincinnati: College of Medicine, University of Cincinnati, 1926), pp. 133, 156, 178–79, 208. I am indebted to my father-in-law, Dr. Alfred M. Donovan, for calling my attention to Kawamura's book.

77. Miyajima and Kawamura had both worked extensively on various aspects of tsutsugamushi disease. Given the areas of agreement between them— and the areas of disagreement between Kawamura and Nagayo—it is hardly surprising that Miyajima made an issue of Kawamura's initial exclusion from the list of 1918 grant recipients. For details, see Miyajima (n. 67 above), p. 1549, and Kawamura (n. 76 above), pp. 133, 156, 178–79.

78. Michio Nagai, *Higher Education in Japan: Its Take-Off and Crash*, p. 43.

79. *TGSIG* (n. 64 above), p. 36.

80. "Kyōdai shizen kagaku kenkyū," *KJ*, no. 1190 (May 5, 1918):20.

81. "Kagaku kenkyū shōrei kyūhi" (n. 66 above), pp. 17–18.

82. "Rikagaku shōrei hi zōgaku" (n. 70 above), p. 15.

83. "Kagaku kenkyū hojō happyō" (n. 68 above), pp. 13–15. Grants were generally smaller than they had been in 1918, ranging from 300 to 5,000 yen.

84. "Chemistry" here includes biochemistry, soil chemistry, chemical engineering, metallurgical engineering (Tawara Kuniichi's grant), and pharmacology, as well as chemical research done in faculties of science. That Tawara's research was heavily chemical in nature is confirmed by Mishima Tokushichi, professor of chemical engineering at Tokyo University. See his essay "Tawara Kuniichi-sensei no o-shogai," in Tawara-Sensei Kinen Shuppan Iinkai, ed., *Tawara Kuniichi-sensei o shinobu* (Tokyo: Tawara-Sensei Kinen Shuppan Iinkai, 1959), p. 2.

85. In Japan, naval architecture and architecture in general developed strictly within the confines of engineering and physical science, not in the fine arts, as in the United States, and it is therefore regarded as part of physics here.

86. Dentistry projects received 4,000 yen. I was unable to determine the nature of some other projects to which 1,000 yen were awarded. If funding for dentistry is added to that for medicine, medicine accounts for 33 percent of money allocated.

87. "Kagaku kenkyū shōgeki hojō shin hōshin," *IJ*, no. 1365 (August 21, 1920):1281.

88. Kawakami (n. 75 above), p. 220.

89. Iseki (n. 15 above), 3:341.

90. Kawamura (n. 76 above), pp. 178–79; M. Nagayo, T. Tamiya, T. Mitamura, and K. Sato, "On the Virus of Tsutsugamushi Disease and Its Demonstration by a New Method," *Japanese Journal of Experimental Medicine* 8 (1930):309–18.

91. Yamagiwa published on this subject between 1916 and 1923. Probably best known to American researchers is his 1918 paper written in collaboration with S. Ohno, "Über das Resultat des Experimentes zur künstlichen Erzeugung der Epithelialgeschwülste," *Gann: Zeitschrift für Krebsforschung* 12

(1918–19):3–9. Yamagiwa's work continues to be cited. See C. E. Easterley, "Cancer Link to Magnetic Field Exposure," *American Journal of Epidemiology* 114/2 (1981):169–74.

92. See "Kagaku kenkyū shōrei kyūhi" (n. 66 above), p. 17; Mishima (n. 84 above), p. 2.

93. Kaya Seiji, "Chōji," in Tawara-Sensei Kinen Shuppan Iinkai (n. 84 above), p. 463; Fuwa Tasuku, personal communication, 1986. Dr. Fuwa is director of Nippon Steel's research and development laboratory.

94. Hidetsugu Yagi, "Beam Transmission of Ultra Short Waves," *Proceedings of the Institute of Radio Engineers* 16/6 (June 1928):715–41. Reprinted in *Proceedings of the Institute of Electrical and Electronic Engineers* 72/5 (May 1984):635–45.

95. Nagashima (n. 2 above), pp. 4–19.

96. Information about Italy was received from Barbara Reeves, personal communication, January 10, 1986. For the U.S., see John C. Burnham, John E. Sauer, and Ronald D. Gibbs, "Peer-Reviewed Grants in U.S. Trade Association Research," *Science, Technology and Human Values* 12/2 (Spring 1987):42–43.

97. Alan Beyerchen, personal communication, January 10, 1986. On the powers of KWG laboratory directors in general, see Jeffrey A. Johnson, "Academic Chemistry in Imperial Germany," *ISIS* 76, no. 284 (December 1985):521–22.

98. Such organizations would include the Helmholtz Society and the Emil Fischer Society, both of which received funds from industry and government.

99. Beyerchen (n. 97 above).

100. Mano Bunji and Nakamura Tokugorō, *Furuichi Kōi* (Tokyo: Kitabayashi Katsuzō, 1937), pp. 305–13; Sakurai (n. 21 above), pp. 37–39. Both sources give detailed (and complementary) reports on the work of the NRC during the interwar period.

101. *NGHNS*, 1:359.

102. See chapter 3 for further details.

103. Nakamura (n. 19 above), pp. 146–47, and San'ichirō Mizushima, "A History of Physical Chemistry in Japan," *Annual Review of Physical Chemistry* 23 (1972):5–6. See also the account by Sakurai (n. 21 above), pp. 10–17.

104. See chapter 3 for details.

105. Sakurai (n. 21 above), pp. 18–19.

106. Ishikawa (n. 57 above), pp. 65–66.

107. Nakamura (n. 19 above), pp. 146, 147. Nakamura Seiji was the colleague.

108. Sakurai Jōji, "Rengō shokoku gakushiin daihyōsha gikai tenmatsu," *KJ*, no. 1231 (June 25, 1919):23.

109. Ibid., pp. 22–24.

110. A. G. Cock, "Chauvinism and Internationalism in Science: The International Research Council, 1919–1926," *Notes and Records of the Royal Society of London* 37 (1982–83):255. I am indebted to Barbara Reeves for help in locating this essay and the one cited in n. 111.

111. *NGHNS*, 1:344, notes that the Royal Society had been "planning to organize an International Research Council from early in 1918." H. Spencer

Jones credits the initiative jointly to Sir Arthur Schuster of the Royal Society and George Ellery Hale of the U.S. National Academy of Sciences. See his essay, "The Early History of ICSU, 1919–1946," *ICSU Review of World Science* 2 (1960):169–70. The ICSU is the International Council of Scientific Unions, the name by which the International Research Council was known from 1931.

112. Cock (n. 110 above), shows in some detail how ambivalent attitudes toward the Central Powers' exclusion were in Britain, even in 1919. See p. 255 for attitudes in France and Belgium.

113. Sakurai (n. 21 above), p. 23.

114. Sakurai (n. 108 above), p. 24. See also Jones (n. 111 above), p. 171.

115. Sakurai's devotion to the NRC and the IRC is apparent not only from his own writings but from his positions in the two organizations. He succeeded Furuichi Kōi as president of the NRC in 1922 and Guglielmo Marconi as vice president of the IRC in 1937. In evaluating his motives and views, one should keep a number of facts in mind: (1) His 1919 and 1939 reports on the London and Paris meetings are filled with contradictions, and it strains credibility to attribute them all to lapses of memory. Attendance at the London meeting he describes variously as thirty delegates from ten countries (1939) and thirty-three delegates from eight countries (1919). Countries attending reportedly included Sweden, Norway, Denmark, and the Netherlands (1939), as opposed to the correct listings of Brazil and Serbia (1919). (He correctly noted the presence of Japan, Britain, France, Italy, Belgium, and the U.S. in both accounts). The 1939 report could not possibly have been accurate because the conference organizers deliberately left neutral countries out of the early IRC planning. (2) Sakurai tells us in his 1939 account that the atmosphere in London was relatively harmonious, whereas Nakamura Seiji (reporting for the other Japanese delegate, Tanakadate) correctly notes that the "discussions did not go at all smoothly." (3) Sakurai claims that "only a small element within our scientific community" opposed German exclusion, which in fact was patently untrue. (4) He says that criticism of his actions in Japan was "unanticipated," even though the other delegate, Tanakadate, had already argued with him. (5) Sakurai told his fellow academicians in Tokyo on May 12, 1919, that the NRC would not need a very large budget, but then turned around and asked the government for a budget of 380,000 yen—enough to pay the salaries of about a hundred full professors. See text and other notes for additional documentation.

116. Sakurai (n. 108 above), pp. 23, 24.

117. Sakurai (n. 21 above), pp. 36–37.

118. Nakamura (n. 19 above), p. 150. The division of opinion over the exclusion of Germany between Sakurai and Tanakadate was noted even at the time. See Tawara Teijirō, "Zai Berlin Nihonjin no giketsu," *KJ*, no. 1279 (October 25, 1920):23. "One [of the delegates at London (Tanakadate)] did not agree with [German exclusion] deep down. The other [Sakurai] seems to have been an enthusiastic supporter, to the point of making a speech in favor of it."

119. Tawara (n. 118 above), p. 24, cites the Imperial Academy's president, Hozumi Nobushige, as saying in 1920 that exclusion of Germany "did not represent the thinking of [most] Japanese academics." See text for other evidence.

120. *NGHNS*, 1:374.

121. See the NRC membership roster in "Gakujutsu Kenkyū Kaiin kettei," *KJ*, no. 1283 (December 5, 1920):33–34.

122. Yuasa (n. 14 above), p. 127.

123. "Gakujutsu Kenkyū Kai iyō jitsugen," *KJ*, no. 1242 (October 15, 1919):14–15.

124. *NGHNS*, 1:373–76. Of those eight, three had also spent some time in Germany. See p. 376 for the members of the planning committee.

125. Kitasato's attitude toward Ōzawa is indicated clearly in a letter he wrote to Hasegawa Tai on December 11, 1892. The letter was read into the official Diet record by Hasegawa, and its text can be found in *DNTGS*, 2. Cf. "Yosan sainyū saishutsu sō yosan an Mombushō jokan," House of Representatives, 4th Diet, January 11, 1893, p. 763. In the letter Kitasato states that Ōzawa accused him of insincerity during their negotiations about a possible Tokyo University appointment for himself and insisted that he withdraw his conditions for accepting the job.

126. Iseki (n. 15 above), 2:4–5.

127. On the cultural milieu of the University of Strasbourg, see John E. Craig, *Scholarship and Nation Building: The University of Strasbourg and Alsatian Society* (Chicago: University of Chicago Press, 1984), pp. 52, 73–76, 103, 110–11.

128. Sakurai Jōji, "Bankoku Gakujutsu Kenkyū Kaigi ni tsuite," *KJ*, no. 1229 (June 5, 1919):3–4.

129. Sakurai Jōji, "Ichi ki hyaku yū no kan ari," *KJ*, no. 1232 (July 5, 1919):27. In making this claim, Sakurai appears to have had strictly the British experience in mind. His assertions certainly did not describe German developments accurately. The main German figure in war-related research, Fritz Haber, was never a professor.

130. Sakurai (n. 128 above), pp. 3–4.

131. *NGHNS*, 1:377, and Sakurai (n. 21 above), p. 35.

132. Quoted in "Gakujutsu renmei kan'yū kengi," *KJ*, no. 1232 (July 5, 1919):17.

133. Sakurai (n. 21 above), p. 34.

134. Sakurai Jōji, "Gakujutsu kenkyū no renmei," *KJ*, no. 1233 (July 15, 1919):28.

135. "Gakujutsu Kenkyū Kai iyō jitsugen (n. 123 above), pp. 14–15.

136. Ibid., p. 15.

137. *NGHNS*, 1:378–79.

138. For details on the Versailles Conference and the timing of Germany's acceptance of the treaty, see Wayne Andrews, ed., *Concise Dictionary of American History* (New York: Scribners, 1962), pp. 979–80, and William Langer, ed., *Encyclopedia of World History* (Boston: Houghton Mifflin, 1972), p. 978.

139. Quoted in "Ryūgakusei kyozetsu mondai no shingi," *IJ*, no. 1334 (January 17, 1920):118–19.

140. "Gakujutsu fūsa to enjo uchikiri," *KJ*, no. 1254 (February 15, 1920):44–45.

141. "Ryūgakusei kyozetsu mondai no shingi" (n. 139 above), p. 118.

142. Quoted in "Doitsu ryūgaku to Gakushiin," *KJ*, no. 1275 (September 15, 1920):27.

143. Quoted in "Gakujutsu Kenkyū Kaigi kansei," *KJ*, no. 1274 (September 5, 1920):22.

144. "Shutsuen zai-Doku dairi taishi no koden," *IJ*, no. 1370 (September 25, 1920):1454–55. This article quotes nearly the entire text of the cable.

145. *NGHNS*, 1:379.

146. "Ryūgakusei kyozetsu mondai no shingi" (n. 139 above), pp. 118–19.

147. Richard B. Goldschmidt, *In and Out of the Ivory Tower*, p. 189. Goldschmidt was the recipient of Ishikawa's assistance.

148. "Shutsuen zai-Doku dairi taishi no koden" (n. 144 above), p. 1455. The two named here were professors Ōzawa Gakutarō (Tokyo University) and Nishi Seiho (Kyushu University).

149. For the German text of Kitasato's letter, see "Kleine Mitteilungen," *Deutsche medizinische Wochenschrift* 46/29 (15 July 1920):809–10. The Japanese text is reprinted in Tawara (n. 118 above), pp. 23–24. A sampling of reactions in Germany can be found in "Koch-sensei matsuri no hankyū," *IJ*, no. 1368 (September 11, 1920):1383.

150. *Deutsche medizinische Wochenschrift* (n. 149 above), p. 810. In view of Kitasato's evident distaste for Confucianism, this comment must be seen as political! See Miyajima (n. 41 above), pp. 5–7, on his exposure to Confucianism as a child.

151. Tawara (n. 118 above), p. 23.

152. "Shutsuen zai-Doku dairi taishi no koden" (n. 144 above), p. 1455.

153. See Tawara (n. 118 above), p. 25, for details.

154. The vice minister of education, Minami Hiroshi, acknowledged receipt of the cable. See "Doitsu ryūgaku to Gakushiin" (n. 142 above), p. 27. However, there is no record in *NGHNS* of any comment on or response to it.

155. Quoted in *Nagayo*, p. 193. The account of the December 1920 NRC meetings presented here is based on this text, which in turn is based on Nagayo Matarō's diary.

156. Ibid., pp. 194–97.

157. "Shutsuen zai-Doku dairi taishi no koden" (n. 144 above), pp. 1454–55.

158. *Nagayo* (n. 74 above), p. 198.

159. Nakamura (n. 19 above), p. 151.

160. Sakurai (n. 21 above), pp. 10–19.

161. Yamakawa had gotten into political difficulty for defending a man accused of lèse majesté. His biographer, Hanami Sakumi, wrote: "Yamakawa always stood up vigorously for his principles and did not knuckle under to pressure. So it is not surprising that some perceived him as a man likely to keep authority at arm's length. At any rate, Haseba [Sumitaka], as minister of education, began to have second thoughts about Yamakawa and on August 12, 1912, named Dr. Sakurai Jōji, dean of the faculty of science, acting president of Tokyo Imperial University" (Hanami [n. 9 above]), pp. 223–24. The issue continued into 1913 and was finally resolved with the reappointment of Yamakawa, recommended strongly by Sakurai. In trying to understand the way Yamakawa and Sakurai were viewed by the ministry, it is worth recalling that Yamakawa in

1876 had angered the Japanese minister to the U.S. by refusing to return home from foreign study when requested, whereas Sakurai had complied in 1881.

162. *Nagayo* (n. 74 above), p. 196.

163. Ibid., pp. 196, 198.

Chapter Nine: Science and Society: A Retrospective

1. *TGSIG.* Cf. "Dai-ichi ka dai-hachi gō," House of Representatives Budget Committee, 10th Diet, March 12, 1897, p. 87.

2. L. F. Haber, in reference to England, writes: "In England the professional chemist usually played a subordinate role [before World War II] and, as far as policy-making was concerned, he was ignored." See "Chemical Innovation in Peace and in War," in C. G. Bernhard, Elisabeth Crawford, and Per Sorbom, eds., *Science, Technology and Society in the Time of Alfred Nobel*, p. 272. Regarding China, see Nathan Sivin, "How Does Science Begin?" *Technology Review* 71/3 (January 1969):63, where the author writes: "The distinction between the generalist, the gentleman civil servant, qualified by his Confucian indoctrination to speak on questions of purpose and value, and the staff expert, who remained in the background and supplied techniques as they were asked for, was basic in imperial China for over a millennium . . ." On Asia in general, see Jean Dessau, "Social Factors Affecting Science and Technology in Asia," *Impact of Science on Society* 19/1 (1969):19: "Social structures . . . represent the historical product of interaction between structures of pre-industrial societies and the structures imposed by industrialization . . . The main aspect of their influence seems to be the precedence, in the greater part of [Asia], accorded to administrative over technical and scientific personnel."

3. Nakayama Shigeru, *Teikoku daigaku no tanjō*, pp. 120–21.

4. Robert M. Spaulding, Jr., *Imperial Japan's Higher Civil Service Examinations*, p. 191. Classroom time given to instruction in the sciences was reduced because of the perceived need to make more time for foreign-language instruction. See the testimony of Okada Ryōhei, from the Ministry of Education, to the Budget Committee (*TGSIG,* cf. "Shūgiin Gakusei Kaikaku Chōsa Kai setchi ni kansuru kengi an shinsa tokubetsu iinkai sokkiroku [dai-ni gō]," House of Representatives Budget Committee, 14th Diet, January 20, 1900, p. 7).

5. Morikawa Hidemasa, *Gijutsusha: Nihon kindaika no ninaite* (Tokyo: Nihon Keizai Shimbun Sha, 1975), pp. 123–42.

6. Fukuzawa Yukichi, "Nagayo Sensai-sensei kanreki shukuenkai no keikyō," *TIS,* no. 1069 (October 1, 1898):39.

7. Spaulding (n. 4 above), p. 165. See chapter 8 for additional details on the conflict over this issue in Germany.

8. A professor of chemistry at Tokyo University wrote during World War I that the exclusion of scientists and engineers from the higher civil service was one of the "present-day evils." See Matsubara Kōichi, *Tekichokko zappan* (Tokyo: Kawade Shobō, 1941), pp. 578–82.

9. This was the point of Yagi Itsurō's comments to the Diet in December 1914. See *TGSIG.* Cf. "Yosan iinkai giroku sokki, dai-nanakai," House of Representatives Budget Committee, 35th Diet, December 16, 1914, p. 82.

10. Ogata Norio, "Kitasato Shibasaburō ryaku den," *Igaku shi kenkyū*, no. 4 (1962):43.

11. "Ryūgakusei kyozetsu mondai no shingi," *IJ*, no. 1334 (January 17, 1920):119.

12. "Mombushō ryūgakusei nimmei," *KJ*, no. 1270 (July 25, 1920):19.

13. "Shutsuen zai-Doku dairi taishi no koden," *IJ*, no. 1370 (September 25, 1920):1454.

14. Itakura Kiyonobu, Yagi Eri, and Kimura Tōsaku, *Nagaoka Hantarō den*, pp. 440–41. The authors imply that the matriculation of Japanese physics students between 1918 and 1922 at Chicago, Harvard, Cornell, London, Oxford, and Copenhagen was largely owing to the impossibility of foreign study in "defeated Germany." Since it *was* possible to study in Germany during most of this period, however, a more likely explanation is that Nagaoka felt these institutions offered his students the best educational and research prospects.

15. "Mombushō ryūgakusei jūnana mei," *KJ*, no. 1275 (September 15, 1920):23–24.

16. Kitasato's views are cited in "Ryūgakusei kyozetsu mondai no shingi" (n. 11 above), p. 119.

17. "Gakujutsu fūsa mondai," *IJ*, no. 1368 (September 11, 1920):1385.

18. Sakurai's claims to this effect were in part motivated by his desire to justify the NRC politically. They also reflected a deep-seated conviction. See in particular the comments he makes about his career in his memoirs (Sakurai Jōji, *Omoide no kazukazu*, pp. 10–15).

19. This is particularly apparent from an examination of the bibliography in Kawamura's book, *Studies on Tsutsugamushi Disease*, pp. 217–25.

20. See James D. Watson, *The Double Helix* (New York: Signet, 1969), for detailed confirmation of this point.

21. Uchida Shun'ichi, "Kagaku hyakunen no kaikō to tembō," in Nihon Kagaku Kai, ed., *Nihon no kagaku hyaku nen shi*, pp. 24–31.

22. San'ichirō Mizushima (ch. 6, n. 9), "A History of Physical Chemistry in Japan," p. 9.

23. Sakurai (n. 18 above), pp. 278–79.

24. Ibid., pp. 37–38.

25. This problem presents itself to Western scientists today as it has historically for Japanese scientists. For details see U.S. Government, 98th Congress, 2d Session, *The Availability of Japanese Scientific and Technical Information in the United States* (House of Representatives Committee on Science, Research and Technology, March 6–7, 1984 [Washington: U.S. Government Printing Office, 1984]).

26. Matsushita Teiji, "Gakumon no chūshin wa nani tokoro e," *IJ*, no. 1280 (January 1, 1919):4–6.

27. Tawara Teijirō, "Zai Berlin Nihonjin no giketsu," *KJ*, no. 1279 (October 25, 1920):24.

Epilogue

1. Japan has been ranked among the top three nations for fundamental contributions to mathematics for some time. It is now reported to have taken the

leading position in magnetics. See testimony by C. E. Johnson, Jr., on behalf of the Magnetics Society of America, in U.S. Government, 98th Congress, 2d Session, *The Availability of Japanese Scientific and Technical Information in the United States*, pp. 324–35.

2. Nobel prizes in science were awarded to Japanese nationals in 1949, 1965, 1973, 1981, and 1987.

3. Kiyonobu Itakura and Eri Yagi, "The Japanese Research System and the Establishment of the Institute of Physical and Chemical Research," in Shigeru Nakayama, David L. Swain, and Eri Yagi, eds., *Science and Society in Modern Japan*, pp. 193–94.

4. Kyoto University got its first chair in biology in 1919, Tōhoku University in 1923.

5. Hiroshige Tetsu, *Kindai kagaku saikō* (Tokyo, 1979), p. 201, and idem, "Social Conditions for the Researches of Nuclear Physics in Pre-War Japan," *Japanese Studies in the History of Science*, no. 2 (1963):83–85.

6. Idem (ch. 5, n. 36), "The Role of the Government in the Development of Science," pp. 320–39.

7. Itakura and Yagi (n. 3 above), pp. 195–97.

8. Michael A. Cusumano, "'Scientific Industry': Strategy, Technology, and Management in the Riken Industrial Group, 1917 to 1945," in William Wray, ed., *Managing Industrial Enterprise: Cases from Japan's Prewar Experience* (Cambridge: Harvard Council on East Asian Studies/Harvard University Press, forthcoming).

9. Samuel Coleman, "The Reorganization of Japan's Physical and Chemical Research Institute under the Allied Occupation," unpublished paper (1987), p. 8.

10. Shigeru Nakayama, "The American Occupation and the Science Council of Japan," in Everett Mendelsohn, ed., *Transformation and Tradition in the Sciences* (Cambridge: Cambridge University Press, 1984), pp. 357–58.

11. Ibid., p. 368.

12. Nihon Kyōsantō Kagaku Gijutsu Bu, "Nihon no kagaku gijutsu no kekkan to kyōsanshugisha no nimmu," *Zen'ei* 10/11 (November 1946), reprinted in Nihon Kagaku Shi Gakkai, ed., *Nihon kagaku gijutsu shi taikei*, 5 (Tokyo: Nihon Kagaku Shi Gakkai, 1964):112–17.

13. Fujioka Yoshio, *Kagaku kyōiku ron* (Tokyo: Kawade Shobō, 1947), p. 89, and Sakata Shōichi, "Kenkyū to soshiki," *Shizen* (September 1947), pp. 10–13.

14. On the founding of the league, see Hiroshige Tetsu, *Sengo Nihon no kagaku undō* (Tokyo: Chūō Kōron Sha, 1960), pp. 134–35.

15. Details can be found in Hideo Satō's seminal paper "The Politics of Technology Importation in Japan: The Case of Atomic Power Reactors," pp. 7, 16, 22, 25, 48–49. Prepared for the Conference on Technological Innovation and Diffusion in Japan (sponsored by the Social Sciences Research Council), Kona, Hawaii, February 7–11, 1978.

16. Ibid., pp. 64, 49.

17. Tomonaga made an appeal for increased public spending on science

almost immediately after his Nobel Prize was announced. See "Kagaku ni motto kokuhi o," *Asahi Shimbun,* October 22, 1965, p. 9.

18. Estimates based on data from the National Science Foundation and the Japanese prime minister's office are reported in "Japan's High-Tech Challenge," *Newsweek,* August 9, 1982, p. 53. Spending, for instance, on the space development program in Japan tripled between 1973 and 1981. See Alun M. Anderson, *Science and Technology in Japan* (London: Longman, 1984), fig. 10.2, p. 198.

19. Anderson (n. 18 above), pp. 14–16.

20. For a description of Tonegawa's views, see Stephen Kreider Yoder, "Native Son's Nobel Award Is Japan's Loss: Scientist's Prize Points Up Research System's Failings," *The Wall Street Journal,* October 14, 1987, p. 26.

21. Hara Genkichi, *Kagaku kenkyū hi: Sono naritachi to henken* (Tokyo: Kagaku Shimbun Sha, 1982), pp. 106–07, 110, 113–14. A chemist by training, Hara between 1949 and 1974 had charge of all research funds for medicine awarded under the Science Research Grants Program of the Ministry of Education, the program first established in 1918.

22. Ibid., pp. 105–07, 116, 117.

INDEX

Photo Credits